Drug Trafficking in Mexico and the United States

Drug Trafficking in Mexico and the United States

Gabriel Ferreyra

LEXINGTON BOOKS
Lanham • Boulder • New York • London

Published by Lexington Books
An imprint of The Rowman & Littlefield Publishing Group, Inc.
4501 Forbes Boulevard, Suite 200, Lanham, Maryland 20706
www.rowman.com

6 Tinworth Street, London SE11 5AL, United Kingdom

British Library Cataloguing in Publication Information Available

Library of Congress Control Number: 2020930646

ISBN 978-1-4985-2361-5 (cloth : alk. paper)
ISBN 978-1-4985-2362-2 (electronic)

∞™ The paper used in this publication meets the minimum requirements of American National Standard for Information Sciences—Permanence of Paper for Printed Library Materials, ANSI/NISO Z39.48-1992.

"In searching out the truth be ready for the unexpected, for it is difficult to find and puzzling when you find it."

—Heraclitus

"I believe that drugs have destroyed many lives, but wrong government policies have destroyed many more."

—Kofi Annan

Contents

Preface

Drug trafficking is difficult to investigate for obvious reasons. Besides the fact that this activity occurs clandestinely, there is the danger of being targeted by drug trafficking organizations (DTOs) for those who dare to shed light on their criminal enterprises. It is well known that organized crime does not like the spotlight and it would do anything to protect its secret and illegal operations. Despite these obstacles it is possible to conduct research using a triangulation of methods and secondary data (information collected from indirect sources) and this book presents a combination of methodologies with information collected first-hand through participant observation, interviews, and personal experience complemented with data and knowledge collected by public institutions, federal agencies, nongovernmental organizations (NGOs), and other sources.

One particular issue while investigating drug trafficking is to find contradictory or sometimes opposite accounts of the same event. This should not be a surprise given that those involved in drug trafficking activities would be unwilling to tell the truth about their illegal activities and instead tell lies. Thus, sorting out facts and information on drug trafficking activities to corroborate accounts can be time consuming and frustrating. As Andreas (2013) correctly points out, "Information on illicit trade is necessarily imprecise, to say the least . . . the very success of smuggling operations typically depends on not being seen or counted. Documentation therefore tends to be fragmentary and uneven, and it represents rough estimates at best" (Andreas 2013, xxi). Regardless of these obstacles it is always possible to reconstruct incidents and facts on drug trafficking activities to reveal the truth about this phenomenon using information from different sources and accounts, on the understanding that sometimes it will be difficult to know with accuracy all the details of a particular event or situation of the topic.

I was born in Central West Mexico in a state known for drug trafficking activities where marijuana and poppy fields have provided a source of income for peasants and farmers in the mountains of Tierra Caliente for decades. Drug trafficking has also been an opportunity for some people to earn quick money, become wealthy, and earn social and economic status where otherwise there are no options to do so. In those regions more often than not drug traffickers are defined as businessmen rather than lawbreakers and trafficking drugs has been a business opportunity rather than a criminal behavior. While growing up it was the time of consolidation of Mexican DTOs and I remember family members' conversations discussing the economic boom brought by the harvest season of marijuana and poppy plants and how many small businesses would benefit from it. I even met some small-scale *narcos* (drug traffickers) who were business partners of friends. My friends, I, and everyone familiar with these people knew they were wealthy *narcos* involved in the illicit drug trade but this fact was never discussed or mentioned openly and this situation was treated more as a rumor than as a fact.

During those years drug trafficking and drug traffickers were always part of the conversation, gossip, and social interaction with colleagues, friends, and loved ones because their presence was ubiquitous in my hometown and other regions in Mexico. Almost every day people would read headlines in newspapers and watch TV news with information about drug seizures, law enforcement operations against traffickers, or drug-related violence and murders. This persistent exposure to drug trafficking activities and the fact that they took place in nearby locations known to all of us made most people immune to them and we eventually got used to the problem of drug trafficking and its inherent effects in our community. At some point the illegal drug trade was seen and understood as an ordinary event as opposed to an unusual occurrence and nothing about drug trafficking would surprise those living within its proximity.

Drug trafficking is a problem that occurs worldwide but its presence in Mexico and the United States makes it a unique phenomenon that has no comparison in any other place or country in the world. It is not just the size, nature, profit, demand, and incentives to smuggle drugs from Mexico to the United States that underscores its singularity. What makes drug trafficking an unparalleled phenomenon in North America and the United States in particular has been first and foremost government policies and the official response to the problem. In the past century, U.S. drug policy made drug trafficking one of a kind phenomenon, in a legal, economic, political, and social sense. Government decisions such as launching the War on Drugs by the Nixon administration or labeling it a national security problem by President Reagan politicized this phenomenon and transformed it into a mainstream American issue in the last fifty years. Another powerful factor on the prominence of drug trafficking has been the persistent demand for drug in the United States that obviously promoted and justified drug policies and legislation to tackle the problem.

Against this background, drug trafficking in Mexico and the United States has been the focus of significant attention from researchers, journalists, and authors in recent years, as well as mass media reports. There are dozens of books on the topic, as well as hundreds of academic manuscripts, newspaper and magazines articles, government reports, and other sources that have discussed, analyzed, and dissected drug trafficking and its consequences in society and potential answers to solve it. In the United States this pattern of publications has been characterized (with few exceptions) by having experts from a particular discipline, such as political science, economics, or criminal justice, present an interpretation of drug trafficking from their own field of study. This interpretation is generally done through the principles, theories, and knowledge that each discipline possesses to shed light on a particular section or component of the problem. Clearly, these interpretations are welcomed and necessary because they complement the body of literature already available to grasp better the nature of drug trafficking. However, there are some limitations with them such as emphasizing a tunnel vision explanation of drug trafficking while marginalizing the multidimensional character of the problem. Furthermore, these renditions have a tendency to highlight an American perspective of drug trafficking that neglects the point of view of different cultures and nations where drugs are manufactured or transported. Within the American narrative of drug trafficking there is a general emphasis on blaming outsiders or foreign countries for drug trafficking in the United States and focusing on cutting the supply of drugs while punishing offenders and drug users. However, little has been done to meaningfully address drug demand in the United States and take responsibility for the growing problem of drug trafficking and drug addiction epidemics that have permanently impacted American society.

Not all of these publications omit the demand-aspect of the drug trade but certainly they defined drug trafficking in narrow terms by drawing attention to illegal, criminal, economic, or political aspects of it. I argue that drug trafficking is not a criminal, legal, or economic problem only. It is all of the above, as well as a social, cultural, and political phenomenon that is multidimensional in nature. Unlike what many scholars, pundits, and politicians assume, drug trafficking is not a problem to be solved but to be understood first. Because without a comprehensive knowledge of the many variables that create and reproduce drug trafficking, it would be remarkably difficult to address it accordingly. And this is exactly what has happened in the past century given most government actions and policies to combat drug trafficking have failed because they were designed and implemented without knowing the multifaceted nature of drug trafficking. Thus, a central thesis of this book is the argument that drug trafficking should be understood and dealt with as a multidimensional issue that requires a comprehensive approach that includes social, cultural, and public health policies rather than just law enforcement government actions.

This book presents a comprehensive examination of drug trafficking based on sources, references, and qualitative research from both Mexico and the United States while emphasizing the multiplicity of factors that contribute, shape, and determine the issue. To begin with, there is a priority to formulate and define drug trafficking as a complex problem by identifying the numerous connections it has with different social, cultural, economic, and public health phenomena, instead of just focusing on the criminal or legal aspects of the issue. One premise of the book is to reveal the most prominent components of drug trafficking that foster its continuity, from the most obvious such as drug demand and corruption in drug-producing jurisdictions to poverty, unemployment, survival strategy, and drug interdiction policies. There is also a clear effort to challenge the traditional narrative on drug trafficking and present instead a richer, more complicated, and nuanced insight of this phenomenon.

Since drug trafficking has been a lasting phenomenon for nearly a century there is an in-depth analysis of the culture that has evolved among drug traffickers and in communities where this problem is prevalent. This narcoculture (as it is known) has become a global event through mass media, movies, TV shows, music, and literature to the point that it has transformed drug trafficking and *narcos* into a popular phenomenon. In another chapter, I identify and name the most nefarious outcomes of drug trafficking in Mexico (e.g., extreme violence, high murder rates, disappearances, mass graves) in the interest of exposing its most visible and damaging effects in that country. The book also offers a reassessment of the War on Drugs with an update on its unintended results while including a critical examination of the role played by the Drug Enforcement Administration (DEA) in this drug policy. The final chapter provides suggestions such as decriminalization and legalization of drugs to change course on how drug trafficking is dealt with as well as an analysis on how some segments of American society and the world are adopting forward-thinking policies to move beyond drug prohibition. Among other changes, more than ever before there is a clear understanding that a drug-free world is impossible to achieve and that drug trafficking cannot be eliminated because drug use will always be part of human civilization.

The information presented in this book is based on a combination of methodological approaches including participant observation, archival research, content analysis, and my personal experience as a lawyer in Mexico and almost two decades of traveling back and forth between Mexico and the United States. Additionally, I have lived in the Southwest of the United States for more than fifteen years close to the border and have frequently visited both sides of most points of entry in the four states bordering Mexico. From an academic perspective, I conducted qualitative research in the summer of 2011 in Mexico where I interviewed forty-five public officials and experts in the Mexican federal judiciary. This project focused on studying federal courts to understand the judicial branch and how this institution deals with corruption related to drug trafficking. I visited six different jurisdictions including two large cities along the Mexico-U.S. border and talked to federal judges, prosecutors, and court personnel. Based on this fieldwork I wrote my dissertation to graduate from a doctorate program at Arizona State University. This book is informed by that research and the continuous academic interaction I have kept with some of the people I met and interviewed back then.

More recently, I began a research project to study the Mexico-U.S. border to conduct a visual interpretation of trafficking activities in that region. Along with one of my colleagues, Dr. Susan Garza, I visited different points of entry in California and Arizona and interviewed more than thirty people on both sides of the border during field research conducted in January 2018 and January 2019, respectively. Our study is still in progress and we will carry out more interviews and participant observations in New Mexico and Texas in 2020. Although the data collected during the first and second season of that fieldwork is under analysis and pending further completion, this book is informed from that research experience too. The knowledge and facts shared by interviewees and key informants during the collection of data in California and Arizona have been crucial to grasp the essence and dynamics of drug trafficking along the Southwest border.

Government data on drug trafficking is completely different in Mexico and the United States. In the former, at least until recently, official information has been limited, sketchy, and questionable (Mexican officials have a soft spot for embellishing official figures to disguise poor performance and malfeasance). In the latter, data tends to be more reliable, consistent, and updated but prone to reinforce a narrative defending the American perspective on drug trafficking (e.g., strict drug control, the War on Drugs, harsh punishment, and cutting supply but not drug demand). I studied and used official information from government data in Mexico and the United States but triangulated with other sources the information I found to have a more accurate and impartial understanding of drug trafficking patterns and trends. NGOs and other nonpartisan institutions in both countries regularly publish information that offers reliable facts and statistics on drug trafficking and related problems. I have resorted to these sources too to support some of my assertions throughout the book giving credit to these references. Sometimes, internal government agencies (such as the Office of the Inspector General) work as supervisory organs with specialized function to prevent and address wrongdoing, and as a result they publish reports and investigations of their findings. I utilized these documents to support my interpretation of drug trafficking always using evidence-based information and facts.

Considering how dynamic and versatile drug trafficking is, it is difficult to keep pace with the changes and adjustments of this activity. It usually takes time to investigate new drug trafficking patterns, readjustments after kingpins are killed or arrested, and in general any change that occurs in this illegal business. From an academic perspective this situation is frustrating, to say the least, because it creates a context where scholars risk releasing research that it may have changed or be different after publication. An irreplaceable source of information on drug trafficking comes from investigative journalism. Magazine and newspaper articles are a rich source of knowledge and information (many times the only ones) about drug trafficking in Mexico and the United States. Journalists have been able to document the world of drug traffickers and their illegal activities that otherwise would be inaccessible for most people. In Mexico, however, this activity has become extremely risky for them and currently Mexico is one of the most dangerous countries worldwide to be a journalist.

This book relies on investigative journalism to document and support facts and events depicted throughout this manuscript and they come from a vast range of sources in both English and Spanish. This material complements academic references such as books and peer-reviewed articles in English and Spanish that are the main scholarly sources of information utilized to strengthen the comprehensive examination of drug trafficking rendered here. This assortment of reference material represents the holistic process behind this book meant to examine and study drug trafficking from an interdisciplinary and comprehensive approach. Unlike other books, this one is not based on a single field of study but multiple ones such as criminal justice, law, sociology, anthropology, and justice studies. At its foundation this book is the product of social sciences, and through their lenses drug trafficking has been dissected and problematized to reveal its primary features. This way the solutions to the problem will have a higher likelihood of being more successful than previous attempts applying the formula suggested by Maya Angelou: *Know better to do better*. I sincerely hope that this work contributes to a greater comprehension of drug trafficking and the assurance that in the near future this problem will be defined and addressed as public health and social issues where empirical evidence and experts decide the most appropriate policies to mitigate it.

Although I am solely responsible for the content of this book, it would have not been possible to finish it without the help of colleagues, friends, and institutional support. I want to thank Texas A&M University—Corpus Christi and the dean of the College of Liberal Arts Dr Mark Hartlaub, for his support in culmination of the book. A one-course teaching-load reduction in the final stages of the draft was crucial to accomplish an important section of the book. I also want to thank my colleague and friend Wendy Moore who kindly accepted to read and review the entire manuscript to have a more academic final draft of the book. Also, I want to acknowledge the support and patience from Kasey Beduhn, associate acquisitions editor of Lexington Books. Despite the fact that I was unable to meet several deadlines she was gracious enough to believe in me and extend the due date many times so I could submit the final version of the book. Additionally, I want to thank an anonymous reviewer who provided invaluable comments and feedback to make this book a more persuasive and academic work. Finally, I want to thank my family and friends for their support throughout this process, for their encouragement and also for not asking me about the book when academic commitments and other obstacles interrupted my writing. *Carpe noctem* because *Fortuna eruditis favet.*

Gabriel Ferreyra, Los Angeles, California

Chapter 1

What Is Drug Trafficking?

INTRODUCTION

It is routine to define drug trafficking from a legal or law enforcement perspective since these are the domains where drug trafficking is mostly associated with. According to *Black's Law Dictionary*, drug trafficking can be defined as "the act of illegally producing, importing, selling, or supplying significant amounts of a controlled substance" (*Black's Law Dictionary* 2009, 1635). This is a basic definition that provides a general notion of what drug trafficking is, but different laws and jurisdictions define this phenomenon in a broad approach that includes multiple phases of the entire process through which drugs are harvested, manufactured, transported, and trafficked before the final delivery to consumers. In other words, drug trafficking is not just the physical sale of drugs but the entire operation of dealing with them in a farm-to-arm supply chain: cultivating, producing, manufacturing, distributing, selling, financing, and consuming drugs.

Important for the definition of drug trafficking is that this concept has several synonyms that sometimes are used interchangeably such as drug smuggling, illegal drug trade, drug market, narcotics, and others. Overall, these concepts refer to the same activities characterized in the definition of drug trafficking. However, "drug trafficking" is the preferred term because it covers the full spectrum of activities involving drugs (from the raw material to produce them to the user) and this holistic understanding reflects an essential component of this phenomenon that cannot be expressed otherwise. Thus, the term "drug trafficking" will be used throughout this book but occasionally the concepts "drug smuggling," "narcotics," or "the illegal drug trade" will be used alternatively.

Although drug trafficking is a problem that is constantly exposed, discussed, and loathed in the American media due to the ubiquitous presence of drugs and drug addiction in society, the multifaceted implications and complexity of this phenomenon are rarely discussed. When news outlets broadcast reports on the topic, they tend to focus on the most visible components of drug trafficking: profits, smuggling tactics, distribution, violence, and law enforcement operations. As a result, what most people think they know about it is just a partial view of the phenomenon or a distorted idea delivered by news headlines, TV shows, Hollywood movies, and government officials. Even those who will be considered well-versed on the topic, such as public officials in the criminal justice system or those trained to deal with drug trafficking such as Drug Enforcement Administration (DEA) agents, tend to have a tunnel-vision perspective that misses the complex and convoluted nature of this phenomenon.

One unfortunate outcome of such limited point of view is that most of these experts and the general public define drug trafficking just as a criminal issue. The implication being that only with law enforcement, prosecution, and incarceration the problem will be solved. This view has been reinforced by governments and the international community that perceive drug trafficking as a serious threat to public safety and national security mostly (United Nations Office on Drugs and Crime 2019). This assumption is not necessarily incorrect, but it is definitively incomplete because it has contributed to keep drug trafficking as a law and order issue while ignoring other important components of it. Highlighting this shortcoming is important, if only to reveal one of the most crucial aspects of the problem which is that drug trafficking is a multidimensional phenomenon, but it has never been understood as such in the United States.

HOW DOES DRUG TRAFFICKING WORK?

Unlike what most people would think, drug trafficking is a dynamic and versatile activity at every stage of its sophisticated process of bringing drugs to consumers. Similarly to a supply chain system, the entire enterprise of drug trafficking is a complex and labor-intensive process where people, organizations, resources, activities, information, and creativity combine all together to deliver illegal drugs for a price to drug users (Grillo 2011; Wainwright 2016). This elaborated system is in essence motivated by economic interests and profitability but other social, political, and cultural factors play important roles, too. Drug trafficking is truly an international enterprise that affects the global economy, national and international security, public health, community safety, among others outcomes. In addition, drug trafficking influences many areas of public policy: from the most well-known impact on the criminal justice system to foreign policy, border security, health system, and public safety. These effects are not always clear to the public because the official discourse of drug trafficking has been framed within the drug control mentality (emphasis on law enforcement and policies that disrupt the flow of drugs) but ignores the ramifications in society of these actions, certainly for poor people and minorities (Alexander 2012).

Even more evident is the fact that the effects of drug consumption, addiction, and widespread use of drugs are felt worldwide with acute emphasis in societies with a huge appetite for drugs such as the United States, Western Europe, Iran, Russia, and Mexico (United Nations Office on Drugs and Crime 2018). However, the violence and brutality of drug trafficking resulted from organized crime groups fighting each other to maintain the monopoly of the illegal drug trade is mostly felt in countries that harvest, produce, transport, or smuggle drugs. Central America, Colombia, and Mexico to name but a few countries that experience widespread corruption, violence, murder, and organized crime as a result of drug trafficking activities (Boullosa and Wallace 2016; Grillo 2011; López López 2008). Likewise, although a large number of people are involved in the drug business—either producing, smuggling, distributing, selling, or consuming substances—the most negative outcomes usually affect those who are disenfranchised, poor, lower class, and uneducated (Alexander 2012; Grillo 2011; Muehlmann 2014). Finally, despite the overwhelming evidence that the War on Drugs (WOD) and drug prohibition are inefficient, costly, and counterproductive, most countries and international organizations such as the United Nations have supported them unconditionally for decades until recently (Inciardi 2008; Musto 1999).

Drug trafficking operates like a supply chain within a predetermined set of phases that follow one another such as cultivation, harvesting, transportation, distribution, demand, selling, and consumption of drugs (see figure 1.1). This process is far from being the same everywhere. Geography, people, culture, and local context shape how each of those steps occurs. Those differences have rarely been taken into account when explaining or addressing drug trafficking by either the global community or national governments because there is a tendency to homogenize this phenomenon as the same everywhere. Such assumption is inaccurate because there are unmistakable differences from place to place such as how rooted drug trafficking is in the place, local economic and social conditions, culture, and others factors (Inzunza, Pardo, and Ferri 2015).

To further complicate matters, the nature of drugs influences how drug trafficking operates. It is not the same to produce, transport, smuggle, distribute, and sell crystal methamphetamine than cocaine, heroin, or marijuana. Some factors such as access to raw material and its location, characteristics

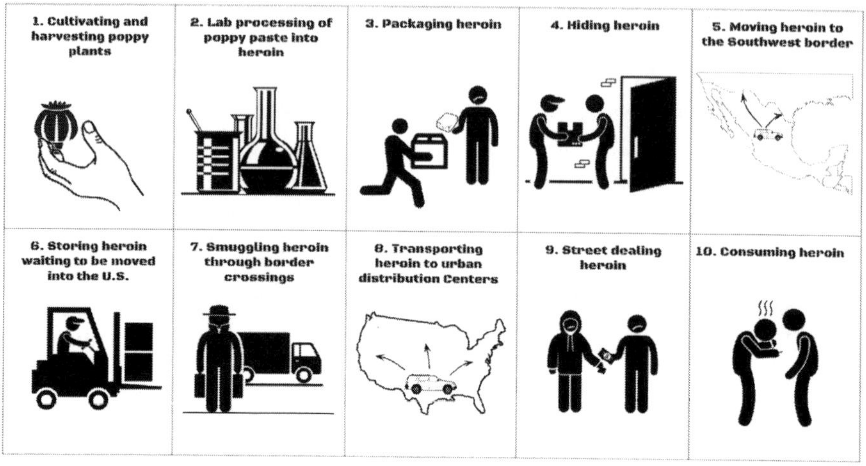

Figure 1.1 Labor-Intensive Heroin Drug Trafficking Process. Concept idea: Dr. Gabriel Ferreyra. Design: Melisa G. Castillo.

of each drug (e.g., addictiveness, easiness to package it, how bulky it is), manufacturing process, drug demand, and black market prices determine strategies in the whole operation of trafficking drugs. Most farmers, peasants, and poor workers involved in the cultivation and harvesting of raw material for illegal drugs are not affiliated to any criminal organization. They simply work the land with the crop that offers them the best chances to make ends meet. Drug traffickers know this and they exploit the poverty and destitution of those farmers by keeping a strong grip on them. This tactic greatly favors traffickers because besides having absolute control of farmer's agricultural ventures, it keeps the cost of drugs down. How? Drug trafficking organizations (DTOs) operate as a monopsony: they are the only buyers of the raw material for drugs and hence monopolize the market. "Just as big retailers protect themselves and their customers from price rises by forcing suppliers to take the hit, cartels keep their own cost down at the expense of coca farmers" (Wainwright 2016, 18).

This practice allows traffickers to send multiple shipments to countries where drugs are consumed and make up for those that are seized during transit between drug hubs or at the border. DTOs know that law enforcement cannot check all vehicles, merchandise, and people that cross national borders or points of entry (e.g., ports, airports, border check points), let alone detect all the drug smuggling attempted by traffickers. As a result, the odds of introducing drugs to America or any other nation favor drug smugglers overwhelmingly (Toro 1998). It should not go unnoticed that drug traffickers are savvy and well aware of similarities, differences, and key properties of the drugs they smuggle. This knowledge is central for managing risk when producing, transporting, storing, and smuggling drugs in order to maximize profits as much as possible (Decker and Chapman 2008).

Unlike what movies, TV shows, and most media outlets assume, today DTOs are not monolithic entities with strong hierarchies, nor they have total control of the entire process of drug trafficking. Instead, drug groups rely in criminal gangs and outside individuals to perform some of the many tasks that drug trafficking requires. In other words, they outsource most of the risks to expendable individuals but keep most of the profits. From independent farmers, drivers, *sicarios* (hitmen) and enforcers to unrelated mules, brokers, and street dealers, DTOs contract with outside people to externalize costs and lower risks. Similar to corporations or legitimate industries worldwide, outsourcing is a major economic, pragmatic, and efficient approach to be successful in drug trafficking (Wainwright 2016). For instance, the raw material of many drugs such as poppy, coca leaves, or pseudoephedrine are never directly produced by DTOs or drug gang members. Instead, they outsource or buy the production of these primary resources from third parties such as poor peasants and farmers without being directly involved in this process. These farmers generate an unlimited amount of raw material for manufacturing drugs in a cheap and relatively easy manner, which in turn influences how drug trafficking operates and keeps the illicit drug trade remarkably profitable. Outsourcing is not the only business strategy that DTOs use to run their illegal enterprise efficiently. Traffickers have also decentralized and fragmented their organizations to protect their operations against law enforcement agencies.

DECENTRALIZATION AND FRAGMENTATION

As a dynamic phenomenon that is constantly innovating and adapting to new practical challenges, drug trafficking has become highly decentralized and compartmentalized in the past decades for different reasons. One of them has been a pragmatic response by DTOs against law enforcement operations meant to dismantle their infrastructure and hierarchies. Traffickers began to compartmentalize drug trafficking activities in their logistics to protect drug shipments and themselves against seizure and arrest while increasing the likelihood of successful trafficking. They did it by dividing into sections every single phase of the drug trafficking process while leaving a small quasi-independent cell in charge of each segment. If a member or the entire cell is arrested, it can be replaced quickly and easily.

For this reason, producers of drug raw materials such as poppy or coca leaves rarely know those who transform these material into heroin and cocaine. Those who manufacture these drugs seldom know those who transport them from where they are harvested to where they are processed and transformed in drugs. Once drugs are packaged, they are transported to a midpoint location (usually a third country) by yet another cell or group of people. Individuals and drug cells that smuggle drugs do not know those who transport them to warehouses and safe locations where drugs are stored. Once drugs have been smuggled in to the country where demand exists, those who distribute and retail the drugs to consumers rarely meet or have any connection with smugglers and so on (Decker and Chapman 2008).

Additionally, the law enforcement strategy of *Leadership Decapitation* based on the assumption that arresting or killing drug lords would eradicate DTOs has been a central principle of anti-drug operations (Phillips 2015). Spearheaded by the DEA and adopted by most Latin American security forces, this strategy has incarcerated or shot to death numerous high-ranking drug leaders, but it has not dismantled or destroyed their organizations. Instead, it just fragmented them. As a result, large DTOs that were prominent in the 1980s and 1990s in Colombia and Mexico began to be fragmented into smaller groups or cells after their leadership was decapitated. Without command, drug cartel members would engage in a turf war to control the remnants of the criminal organization until different splinter groups appeared (Philips 2015).

Some entrepreneurial drug lords (e.g., Miguel Angel Felix Gallardo known as the Godfather) initiated a decentralization process of their organizations even before leadership decapitation became the de-facto law enforcement policy (Boullosa and Wallace 2016; Valdés Castellanos 2013). The implication being that by insulating the entire drug trafficking process, the business will remain operational with minor disruptions. There was an emphasis on protecting what are considered the weakest links of drug trafficking activities such as smuggling operations. And smuggling drugs across the U.S.-Mexican border is one particular part of the drug trafficking business that is extremely insulated to protect drug gangs and the smuggling infrastructure that exist in every point of entry.

As a result, those who transport drugs through the border do not know any of the upper echelons of the DTOs or anyone else besides the immediate cell members who control each operation. Smugglers are usually hired as contractors to deliver the drugs in the United States, a job that involves high risk of long-term imprisonment if they are arrested with Schedule I drugs such as cocaine or heroin. Given the decentralized management of drug trafficking, smugglers are considered expendable mules who can be replaced immediately (Muehlmann 2014). Sometimes undocumented immigrants are used as smugglers by traffickers and forced under threat of violence or death to carry bundles of drugs through the border but these strategies are not very common and successful given how well patrolled and guarded the Mexico-U.S. border is.

THE INGENUITY OF DRUG SMUGGLING

Unlike what many people think, including President Trump, most drugs smuggled into the United States occurs through legal ports of entry, not in isolated places along the Southwest border. Ports of entry include official border crossings, airports, seaports, and the northern border with Canada. Interestingly, to justify building a border wall on the Mexico-U.S. border, the Trump administration has claimed that drugs are smuggled because of the lack of barriers on the Southwest border. Such claim has been debunked by federal agencies and high-ranking officials from his own government who have correctly confirmed the opposite is correct based on facts and data (Bump 2019).

What is true is that smugglers are remarkably entrepreneurial and are always one step ahead of law enforcement agencies when crossing drugs into the United States. To that end, drug gangs sometimes lure people to smuggle drugs from demographics who do not have the stereotypical profile of the "typical" (Hispanic or brown, young, male) trafficker and instead select young or old, well-dressed, educated, pretty, and light-skinned women and men to do so (Grillo 2011, 144). In this regard, the illegal drug trade is notably dynamic and the movement of drugs is handled vigorously and relentlessly. That is why anyone willing to take the risk of earning quick cash would be a smuggler candidate if he or she dares to take a chance (Grillo 2011, 142).

One common tactic used by drug traffickers to smuggle drugs is to hire individuals as mules or burros (those willing to cross the border with drugs for a fee). Traffickers target people who have an American passport or at least permanent residency in the United States who are familiar with border crossing, although this is not necessarily a mandatory prerequisite. Because drug smuggling has been a permanent mark along the Southwest border for decades, everyone living in that region knows smuggling drugs can be an "economic opportunity" if he or she is willing to take the risk. Traffickers know from experience that there is always someone ready to take a chance to smuggle drugs for different reasons: a personal emergency, struggling with unemployment, having a loved one ill, or all of these. Investigative journalist Ioan Grillo put it this way as a young man living in the border explained it to him: "The cartel[s] offered a flat rate: $1,000 to drive sixty pounds of marijuana into the United States; more to take heroin, cocaine, or meth. You could use your own car or they lent you a vehicle. It was about three hours' work, then you got paid right away in cash" (Grillo 2011, 142).

That type of smuggling is just one approach among an endless arsenal of strategies that DTOs use to bring drugs to consumers in the United States, since there is no limit to their ingenuity. From using hidden compartments in cars, trucks, tractor-trailers, boats, and jet skis to flying small airplanes, hiding drugs in commercial flights, drones, tunnels, submersible vessels (narco-submarines), surface mail, express delivery, catapults, and the like. Any imaginable legitimate product or merchandize can be used to hide or disguise drugs: tires, oil painting frames, surfboards, candles, computers, chili peppers, shoes, vegetables (e.g., fake carrots), fruit (e.g., bananas, pineapples) luggage, food (e.g., doughnuts, coconuts, tamales, tortillas, salsa, frozen sharks), statues, console video games, and the like (Decker and Chapman 2008; Grillo 2011; Woody 2017).

The methods of smuggling drugs using the human body are both shocking for their ingeniousness and for the real possibility of dying because of them. There are external and internal concealing strategies. Among the former, the most obvious ones are attaching drugs to the external part of the body by strapping them to the abdomen, chest, legs, and lower back, between the cheeks of the butt, groin area, and the like using packing tape. These tactics do not pose health risks to drug mules besides the possibility of being arrested. Regarding the latter, it implies using human cavities such as the rectum, mouth, and vagina to hide drugs as well as swallowing pellets (or condoms or latex gloves) filled with cocaine, heroin, or even ecstasy. Another method has been concealing drugs under the skin in the buttocks and using breast implants filled with drugs. Depending on the amount of drugs and how long they are kept in the body, any of these internal concealing methods can be deadly to couriers if the device fails and drugs get into the body (Grillo 2011; Museo del Enervante 2018; Woody 2017).

This list is not exhaustive by any means only informative considering how vast drug trafficking tactics are to smuggle drugs. A crucial feature of these trafficking strategies is that they are essential for the illegal drug trade, yet the people in charge of executing them are expendable. This might look like a contradiction, but it is not because it is the result of outsourcing the risks of imprisonment and death to the lowest ranks and file of the long and labor-intensive chain that is drug trafficking. Accordingly, anyone involved in any of these smuggling operations can be arrested or killed without affecting the dynamic of the drug trade and with no consequences for DTOs for the most part. Drug mules and drugs are easily and quickly replaced by others and the illegal drug trade remains untouched. Decentralization, fragmentation, and outsourcing risks have contributed to overcome complex logistics, legal obstacles, and evade law enforcement operations while conducting drug trafficking activities (Decker and Chapman 2008; Grillo 2011).

DRUG TRAFFICKING AND THE LAW

From a criminal justice perspective, drug trafficking is one of the most serious crimes in the United States. A crime that has sent thousands of people to prison for trafficking drugs but mostly for minor possession of them for personal use. The criminalization of drug use and addiction in the United States during the past three decades has led to mass incarceration, a phenomenon defined as the excessive and disproportionate high numbers of people in prisons (mostly minorities) compared to historical levels (Alexander 2012). Both federal and state governments penalize drug trafficking activities and most state laws have similarities in their drug laws because most of them originated from one federal law that consolidated previous anti-drug legislation into a comprehensive and more punitive approach. This statute became known as the Controlled Substances Act (CSA) from 1970, and the law regulates the use, distribution, possession, importation, and manufacture of all substances classified as drugs, legal and illegal. Drugs are classified in five categories or Schedules according to their dangerousness or potential for addiction, medical usage, and the likelihood to produce dependence on people who consume them from.

The classification on the CSA goes from Schedule I, allegedly substances with the most danger for addiction to Schedule V substances with the highest medical potential and less risk for abuse (Marion 2018). Drugs listed as Schedule I have no medical value and high potential for abuse compared to substances listed in the next category. Schedule II drugs have some medical value but still high capacity for abuse. Substances listed in Schedule III still have potential for abuse but much less than those classified in Schedules I and II. Finally, substances listed in Schedule IV and V are defined as having more medical benefits and low chances for addiction.

Based on this classification, drugs that are deemed more addictive and dangerous to people, such as heroin, cocaine or methamphetamine, would have harsher penalties than those classified as less addictive and dangerous, such as hallucinogens, benzene, or mercury. In reality, the classification created by the CSA does not represent an accurate depiction of the nature of drugs. For instance, marijuana is classified as Schedule I similar to heroine with no medicinal value, presumed highly addictive and unable to be prescribed by physicians under any circumstances. This designation is far from reality given that scientific research (Gupta 2015) and anecdotal evidence suggests a potential medical value of marijuana. Hallucinogens, such as peyote and LSD, are also classified in Schedule I as extremely addictive and no medical value, but recent research suggests that these substances could have an untapped potential for medical use (Sample 2017).

Interestingly, peyote is listed as Schedule I, but it is not at all prohibited. The Native American Church (NAC) has a legal exception to use it for legitimate religious purposes. This spineless cactus is considered medicine and a sacred plant by native people who believe that it brings wisdom and sacred knowledge. Other Indigenous groups in Mexico and somewhere else also consider peyote a spiritual substance rather than a drug in the traditional legal definition of the term. This is the reason why peyote consumption is permitted to members of the NAC despite the fact that it is classified as Schedule I by the CSA. Such situation exposes an unmistakable contradiction of this law that has grown larger in the recent years. The CSA represents as legal framework that is obsolete and disconnected from the facts and circumstances of the nature of drugs and drug use in the twenty-first century. This statute requires a serious overhaul to reduce the disparity between the law in the book and the law in action in order to reflect an accurate and scientific understanding of the world of drugs and drug trafficking.

This is a common factor among all drug laws that exist in the United States and that is the severity by which drug use, possession, and trafficking of drugs are prosecuted. Drugs crimes—as they are known in the argot of criminology—refer to violations of any drug law at the federal or state level. Charges for drug trafficking vary according to different variables such as the type of drug being trafficked, the amount of drug being carried, circumstances of the crime (e.g., whether the substances were sold to a minor, in a school), previous criminal record of the offender, among other variables (Belenko and Spohn 2015). Federal and state courts have concurrent jurisdiction to prosecute drug trafficking cases. A noticeable distinction is that the federal government prosecutes mostly large drug trafficking operations targeting drug gangs and interstate drug trafficking. States and local governments, on the other hand, arrest and prosecute minor possession of drugs and small scale drug trafficking. Prosecution of drug offenses in federal courts are usually more severe and include longer periods of incarceration whereas charges for drug possession (without intent of drug distribution) are generally handled through plea bargain agreements, probation, and fines depending on criminal record and other variables (Belenko and Spohn 2015).

One significant drug policy that will be discussed throughout the book is the WOD. This policy is defined as the leading governmental policy in the past fifty years meant to combat drug use and drug trafficking by punishing and incarcerating those who break drug laws. Despite the fact that the WOD has been considered a complete failure by many experts (Andreas 2013; Baum 1996; Bertram et al. 1996; Coyne and Hall 2017; Payan et al. 2013), the U.S. government has insisted on maintaining that approach to no avail. The absurdity of this position could be easily described using the following metaphor.

Imagine that the United States never stopped fighting the Vietnam War after it lost it in the 1970s. Imagine that despite the fact that the North Vietnamese army took over all Vietnam, the U.S. government today is still sending soldiers, warships, and billions of dollars every year to try to change the course of the war. Not only that, imagine that American politicians know with certainty that they cannot reverse the outcome of a lost Vietnam War, yet they persist in fighting it because it has helped them to win elections and it benefits the military-industrial complex. This hypothetical scenario is exactly what has happened with the U.S. drug policy approach on the WOD. Drugs have won the war long ago. Research, data, studies, and reports all have overwhelmingly showed that such drug policy has not worked and will never work (a detailed explanation is presented in chapter 5), yet the American government keeps investing in a strategy that has proven to be a failure (Andreas 2013; Baum 1996; Bertram et al. 1996; Coyne and Hall 2017; Payan et al. 2013).

Drug prohibition did not begin with Nixon and his WOD. It started more than a century ago in 1914 when the Harrison Narcotics Tax Act was passed to regulate—and tax as the name suggests—opiates and derivatives of coca leaves. Even if this law did not intend to prohibit "narcotics" as those substances were labeled, in fact it was the official beginning of prohibition (Musto 1999). A central tenet of the WOD has been the emphasis on defining drug trafficking and drug use as a crime problem solely. Such emphasis on the criminal aspect of the drug trafficking and drug use has led to serious social and criminal justice issues. The WOD dramatically increased the number of people convicted of drug offenses, it contributed to draconian sentencing policies (e.g., mandatory minimum sentences), and affected mostly people of color (Alexander 2012; Belenko and Spohn 2015). All of these effects have been widely discussed by experts and pundits (Alexander 2012; Benavie 2009; Hari 2016; Inciardi 2008). Suffice it to say that the legal aspect of drug trafficking and how it has been addressed in the criminal justice system is inconsistent with the complexity and endurance of the problem.

INTERNATIONAL REGULATION OF DRUG TRAFFICKING

Drug trafficking is a modern concept invented in the twentieth century. According to the United Nations Office on Drugs and Crime (UNODC 2019), drug trafficking refers to the illicit trade—as well as the harvesting, manufacturing, transporting, and selling—of substances that are prohibited by law (UNODC 2019). The legal framework for this definition is provided by a triad of drug control treaties signed in the second half of the twentieth century: the Single Convention on Narcotic Drugs of 1961 (as amended in 1972); the Convention on Psychotropic Substances of 1971; and the United Nations Convention against Illicit Traffic in Narcotic Drugs and Psychotropic Substances of 1988 (UNODC 2019). The first of these treaties laid down the foundations to regulate—prohibit to be more specific—substances that were defined as drugs by the same document. The spirit of the laws was to create international agreement to introduce control measures regarding psychotropic and narcotic substances as well as agreeing on global cooperation to address drug use and drug trafficking in a global scale. Besides the goal to create "international cooperation" among nations, there was a subtle but firm intent of *realpolitik* by Western powers—in particular the United States—to impose a domestic ideology on law enforcement regarding drugs. That ideology presented drug trafficking as a criminal problem only and drugs were defined and classified by their pharmacological components (Transnational Institute 2016).

A major problem with this political ideology was that it ignored the traditional uses that many indigenous people have had with plants such as coca leaves, peyote, magic mushrooms, khat, and marijuana for millennia. According to Western ideology and the legal framework of the Single Convention on Narcotics, active ingredients of these plants were deemed illicit to Western medicine and therefore criminalized. This Convention on Narcotic Use was amended in 1971 where there was an intent to avoid naming plants such as cannabis and coca leaves as drugs and instead a new category of psychotropic substances was created to prohibit active ingredients. However, many social groups' traditions and culture in Latin America, Africa, Asia, and the Middle East were already labeled as dangerous and therefore criminalized by these international legislation (Henman and Metaal 2014).

International laws on drug trafficking in the past half century have emphasized a consensus to handle the problems of drug trafficking nationally when by its nature, it is remarkably dynamic, borderless, and international. Drug trafficking not only crosses borders and involves multiple countries or regions in various degrees and layers, but it also generates a specific context between countries that produce and export drugs and those who consume them. Whether it is production, transportation, smuggling or consumption of drugs, each country has to come up with its own set of decision-making processes, policies, and actions to deal with the issue at the local level. Yet, the illicit drug trade is transnational and deeply embedded and disguised in the legal global economy (Global Commission on Drug Policy 2011).

Even though drug legislation in the international arena became homogenized and fixed with drug control in the 1960s and 1970s, every country has taken different regulatory processes to implement drug legislation. More progressive governments, such as Uruguay and the Netherlands, took a soft stand on non-addictive drugs such as marijuana, but other nations have pursued a more severe position by punishing drug trafficking and drug user with draconian measures and even with capital punishment. There are currently thirty-two countries—including the United States—that have the death penalty written in their laws as punishment for drug offenses. However, only six or seven of these nations (China, Indonesia, Iran, Saudi Arabia, Singapore, and Taiwan) actually impose it, and the rest of them rarely do it (*The Economist* 2015).

One significant issue with international drug laws was that they introduced a "one-size-fits-all" perspective by which all drugs were deemed the same in terms of their addictive and harming effects regardless of the nature of each substance. As a result, plants such as poppy and coca leaves were labeled as equally dangerous as their derivatives such as heroin and cocaine without taking into account scientific evidence showing that they were not the same substances. The decision to label drugs in such terms was based more on ideological arguments than on scientific evidence considering that in those days the United States was able to impose a prohibitionist agenda on the rest of the world (Boullosa and Wallace 2016; Coyne and Hall 2017; Musto 1999). The rationale behind this interdiction was naïve because it would be similar to saying that the world should get rid of nuclear energy just because it can be transformed into nuclear weapons. Even if the latter derives from the former, it is acknowledged that they are two different things. Despite this inherent contradiction, Western world powers supported the Single Convention of 1961 and all the subsequent treaties that endorsed strict drug prohibition, including the criminalization of native sacred plants such as coca leaves. Governments and politicians alike were unable to realize how ethnocentric, parochial, and hegemonic these laws were regarding banned drugs.

Accordingly, the legal framework of drug trafficking assumed a zero-tolerance dogma toward drug consumption: any type of use or abuse of the substances listed on these treaties was defined as problematic, potentially dangerous, and subjected to criminal prosecution. This position disregarded the dynamics of using drugs that differentiates between recreational, moderate, and chronic use with addiction and drug dependence. International treaties also ignored the principles of harm reduction that advocate for strategies to reduce the negative outcomes of drug use. Certainly the concept of harm reduction was not known in those days as it is today, but there was already sufficient scientific evidence about the nature of drugs and their addictive potentials to realize that not all drugs are equal and the same as international legislation suggested (Henman and Metaal 2014).

Science and drug experts played no role in setting up international drug laws because the drive behind them was a political agenda based on drug prohibition. Being a powerful global player for nearly a century, the United States was able to force upon the rest of the world strict drug control policies because of its priority of fighting drug trafficking abroad. Early in the twentieth century, the American government embraced the notion that decreasing the flow of drugs by policing and destroying drugs where they are produced or transported will stop them from reaching America (Andreas 2013). Based on such belief, the United States pushed for international conventions and agreements that reflected that perspective after the First and Second World Wars. As a diplomat, Henry J. Anslinger spent years lobbying and putting pressure in other nations that objected to the American perspective when necessary using a "carrot and stick" approach. In the end, it worked and all countries eventually adopted strict drug control as the only official strategy to deal with drug trafficking and drug use. Interestingly, Anslinger ultimately would become the American's drug czar for nearly four decades and would establish the infrastructure and ideology for the creation of the DEA and the WODs policy in the early 1970s (Boullosa and Wallace 2016; Chasin 2016; McWilliams 1990; Sloman 1998)

THE ECONOMY AND POLITICS OF DRUG TRAFFICKING

Economy

From an economic point of view, drug trafficking is a sophisticated business that resembles any other global business such as oil, tourism, and financial services that commercialize particular commodities within the globalization process. For instance, drug trafficking demands intense labor to produce raw materials which are transformed into marketable merchandise—drugs—at manufacturing premises. Then these goods are shipped to other countries where there is demand. Once drugs arrive in the country of consumption, they are distributed by retailers that bring enormous profits to brokers, middlemen, and drug traffickers (Wainwright 2016). Even though drug trafficking is a complex problem with enduring interconnections with other social and cultural phenomena ultimately "is just an [economic] industry" (Grillo 2011, 135). What this means is that the violence, murders, corruption, incarceration, drug overdoses, health problems, and other significant issues associated with drug trafficking are all subordinated to the fundamental economic principle of making money.

Waingright (2016) makes a persuasive argument that drug cartels operate and are managed like "a global, [and] highly organized business." The more he analyzed the international drug industry from an economist perspective, the more similarities he found between the illegal drug trade and global corporations. Wainwright argues that DTOs behave like Walmart or any other large supermarket by purchasing produce or raw material from poor farmers (e.g. poppy plants, marijuana, or coca leaves), processing and packing products (drugs), then transporting and moving them to markets, and finally selling them to consumers (Wainwright 2016, 17). According to this author, DTOs engage in offshoring (moving drug business operations to third countries to facilitate the trafficking) and outsourcing (hiring an outside group to perform services to lower the cost of labor). These two practices are common among corporations to reduce costs and make the business more efficient.

Similarly, drug trafficking also employs these strategies for the same reasons. For instance, there is evidence that some drug cartels have moved operations to Central America (offshoring) and they have hired hitmen or third-party groups to transport, smuggle, or sell drugs (outsourcing). Both of these economic practices are widely utilized by drug gangs because it contributes to the decentralization of the drug trade (as mentioned earlier) and keeps the industry running efficiently despite law enforcement operations (Wainwright 2016). As a global industry, drug trafficking contributes considerably to the international financial system by providing cash, investments, savings, and other financial benefits to the legal economy through money laundering, under-the-table arrangements, and corruption practices. It is extremely difficult to estimate the amount of money and wealth that circulates globally from the illegal drug trade because of the secretive nature of such operations. The figures and data presented by governments and law enforcement agencies are estimations based on indirect information such as drug seizure at the Mexico-U.S. border, confiscation of assets from traffickers, and testimony from protected witnesses. However, these numbers should be considered more "guesstimations" rather than accurate assessments on the total amount of money that drug trafficking produces.

Being an international organized crime, drug trafficking is considered one of the most lucrative illegal activities worldwide. A 2017 report by the Global Financial Integrity estimated the annual value of drug trafficking between $426 billion and $652 billion, just second behind counterfeiting (Global Financial Integrity 2017; May 2017). This illegal activity represents one-third of the retail value of all other transnational crimes such as arms trafficking and human trafficking. These estimates are conservative since they do not reflect the real profits of drug trafficking for two reasons. First, it only includes four categories of drugs (marijuana, cocaine, opiates, and amphetamine-type stimulants) while omitting synthetic opioids (fentanyl) and others substances labeled as "party drugs" (ecstasy, hallucinogens, LSD) than are profitable and popular among the youth. Second, drug trafficking is a clandestine activity by nature and governments do not know with accuracy how much drugs are successfully smuggled and sold (May 2017). In any case, the estimated value mentioned earlier is a staggering amount that underscores the financial power that drug trafficking has in the global and national markets.

The economic impact of drug trafficking is felt first and foremost in the local communities where drugs are produced. There is an extensive flow of cash from those who work in the drug trade that is earned and spent in the towns and villages where drug traffickers live. Although drug proceeds are not always distributed equally among those involved in the drug trade because the lower end of the production chain (e.g., poor farmers, drivers, mules) barely make ends meet (Muehlmann 2914). Many high-ranking traffickers invest these proceeds in the local economy by buying assets or doing financial investments as money laundering strategies (Santamaría Gómez 2012). Additionally, there are hundreds of small and large businesses on real estate, construction, tourism, banking, car dealers, agricultural equipment, and even churches that benefit from the illegal drug trade, too. This influx of money is reinforced by money laundering operations meant to invest the proceeds from drug trafficking into the legal economy which adds on another route to pour resources into the region. As a result, willingly or unwillingly, portions of the local business community where drug trafficking operates sooner or later ends up doing businesses with drug traffickers. Local businessmen benefit by accepting capital and cash from traffickers while these people are able to invest their dirty money into the mainstream economy and enjoy its dividends (Santamaría Gómez 2012). However, there is not enough scientific data to know with certainty the amount of money that is laundered and invested in some communities where drug trafficking is rampant.

Undeniably, drug trafficking is a market-driven activity, but this characteristic cannot be isolated from the fact that other variables such as drug demand and prohibition policies have contributed to make this phenomenon remarkably profitable. Most notably, since launching the WODs, the politicization of drug trafficking (meaning how politics and politically motivated decisions have influenced government officials' behavior regarding U.S. drug policy) have distorted the problem. Such being the case because in the past fifty years, this politicization has prevented to take a reasonable and objective approach to address drug trafficking in a nonpartisan way. Granted that drug policy is by nature political considering that governments and politicians are behind it, the criticism here is that being political is not the same as being politicized. This means that politicization became a tool to gain personal and partisanship benefits regarding the problems of drug trafficking and drug use with no real interest to solve these issues while advocating exclusively for drug prohibition policies despite the fact that they do nothing to tackle the problem (Bertram et al. 1996).

Politics

Politics is inextricably intertwined with the phenomenon of drug trafficking. The correlation between politics and drug trafficking is deeper than most politicians, pundits, and society would be willing to admit. Drug trafficking would not be the issue that it is today (both nationally and internationally) if not because of the massive impact that American politicians (presidents in particular) have had in shaping drug policy to gain political benefits. For centuries, drugs were not an issue in the United States (they were actually legal) until the early twentieth century when the movement for alcohol prohibition began and eventually became legal. After prohibition was repealed in 1933, for several decades, drugs and drug use were not a national primary concern (Marion 2018). It is true that the Federal Bureau of Narcotics was created in 1930 and that the first drug Czar Henry J. Anslinger took a personal crusade to abolish all drugs, but still the scope and narrative of drug use and drug trafficking did not have the urgency and imminent menace that it would acquire later on. It was not until the second half of the twentieth century in the late 1960s and early 1970s that a radical shift occurred and the politicization of drug policy started with the WODs initiated by President Nixon (Chasin 2016; Marion 2018).

When the media, law enforcement officials, and politicians embrace the WODs to tackle drug trafficking there is a specific set of assumptions that goes along this position. First, the drug problem is usually described in alarming (if not apocalyptic) terms to denounce the dangers of drugs, drug addiction, and traffickers. Second, when considering options to deal with drug trafficking, the media and politicians mostly refer to drug control measures, meaning policies and operations to cut the supply side of drugs. The assumption is that the drug trafficking is a problem caused by outsiders (drug traffickers) who live in Third World countries, but there is little or no emphasis on cutting drug demand (until recently due to the opioid epidemic). Finally, within this political narrative the standard response to deal with drug trafficking and drug offenders has focused on punitive efforts: arrest, prosecution, and incarceration (Alexander 2012; Boullosa and Wallace 2016; Wainwright 2016).

To be fair, some states began to create drug courts in the 1990s to allow treatment and rehabilitation for drug offenders instead of incarceration. Although seems as a positive response, their impact has been modest in the grand scheme of things because not every defendant is eligible for this option and those who are must adhere to strict probation agreements that are difficult to follow. For obvious reasons, drug courts mandate that defendants do not take drugs or otherwise risk going back to prison. But anyone familiar with the nature of drug addiction would acknowledge that relapsing is not uncommon among individuals who have drug dependence. This and other complex issues of drug use are not included in the legal framework of drug courts, and hence, they have not made a significant contribution to deal with drug use (Belenko and Spohn 2015).

Furthermore, the politicization of drug trafficking has led to understanding this phenomenon in simplistic and Manichean terms where government officials and law enforcement agencies see themselves as the "good guys" while traffickers and those who produce or consume drugs are defined as the "bad ones." Such narrative ignores the complicated nature of drug trafficking because it is more than just a legal and criminal problem as this official account implies. Without exception, regions known for harvesting and producing raw material for illegal drugs are afflicted with extreme poverty, lack of economic opportunities, chronic unemployment, poor governance, and widespread government corruption. Whether it is Afghanistan, the Andes, Central America, Colombia, or Mexico, these social and economic dislocations play a crucial role in promoting drug trafficking activities (Grillo 2011; McCoy 2003; United Nations Office on Drugs and Crime 2018; Wainwright 2016). Yet none of this factors have been ever acknowledged in the U.S. political discourse on drug trafficking because of the emphasis on an oversimplified version of the issue.

Part of the politicization of drug trafficking has been driven by ideological and partisanship arguments that do not consider empirical evidence about the drug problem and drug trafficking patterns. It is troubling to see how many politicians and public officials make strong personal statements in favor of the WODs and criminalizing drug users, but do not mention any evidence or data to support that these measures are working. The reason being is there is no scientific evidence available to support those claims. To be clear, it is well-known the damaging effects that abusing drugs has on chronic users. This is not disputed here. Instead, the purpose is to shed light on how and why most public officials and politicians who defend drug prohibition fervently put all illegal drugs in the same category and define them as dangerous and addictive.

These politicians for the most part are also against any alternative path to the WODs such as decriminalization and legalization, even though these options have been implemented successfully in other countries (Ferreira 2017; Hari 2016; Wainwright 2016). This scenario should not surprise anyone given that the topics of drugs, drug use and drug control have been usually approached in America with deep emotions, to obtain political gains, and lacking objective grounds. A dramatic negative outcome of that position has been the reluctance to adopt a comprehensive strategy to deal with drug demand and drug trafficking in a reasonable and scientific manner even when the reality of drug consumption in America shows that drugs and drug use are as routine as apple pie (Grillo 2011; Hari 2016; Wainwright 2016).

Perhaps the most politicized aspect of drug trafficking is how politicians have used the danger of drugs and traffickers as slogans to win elections based on promises to "get tough on crime" by implementing draconian drug laws. This political strategy was successful since Nixon used it for the first time when launching the WODs, but it reached unprecedented levels in the 1980s and 1990s. The overall result was mass incarceration, the increase of female prisoners accused of drug offenses, and the demonization of drug users and minorities (Alexander 2012). Although most politicians do not resort today to this fear-mongering strategy, President Trump has resorted to it in his administration by claiming (without evidence) that a border wall is necessary in the Mexico-U.S. border to stop drug traffickers. Official data and law enforcement agencies have contradicted those allegations persuasively (Bump 2019), but the politicization of drug trafficking remains a common practice in America.

THE AMERICAN DRUG PROBLEM

In his book *Smuggler Nation*, Peter Andreas (2013) makes the compelling argument that smuggling (and the politics of policing it) has played a crucial part in the history of America. From colonial times to the Revolution, the Civil War, and into the Modern Age, smuggling commodities contributed to build up the United States as it is known today. Andreas asks the question "Why do we now have such a massive criminal justice system, including the world's largest prison population?" (Andreas 2013, xi). The answer is in part due to drug trafficking and the law enforcement response to it. The author explains that smuggling is much more than just economics and understanding the inner workings of the illicit drug trade; it covers the political responses by public officials throughout the history of America including its interconnections with capitalism as well as social and cultural phenomena. This is the case because governments make decisions on what commodities are classified as illegal and then conduct law enforcement operations to implement policies and enforce the law. These decisions are by nature political and discretionary (politicians always make exceptions to the rule of law if it is beneficial to their cause) and they are inextricably connected to how smuggling is understood and defined in every epoch. Politics then have shaped and determined the nature and scope of smuggling and the corresponding response to it by each government and administration (Andreas 2013).

It is hard not to concur with Andreas's argument in the sense that smuggling has always been a key component of the U.S. political and economic systems, and smuggling drugs in particular since drug prohibition began in the early twentieth century. For the past hundred years, drug smuggling has been one of the most prominent problems in American public sphere, especially after the WODs was launched. Drug smuggling (and its more contemporary concept drug trafficking) is not an isolated event that occurs spontaneously and erratically. Instead, it responds to clear domestic, economic, social, and political factors that only add more complexity to the smuggling problem. Significant factors that strongly correlate with smuggling are drug demand, drug control, anti-drug law enforcement operations, and profitable gains sought by organized crime groups. All of these factors are mutually interdependent because they influence and reinforce each other. Thus, demand for drugs encourages drug trafficking which in turn causes law enforcement operations to target smuggling. As a result, traffickers react to these operations and adjust by innovating new smuggling strategies to keep up with drug demand. If there is shortage of a popular drug because of interdiction, drug users may switch to another drug that is cheaper or readily available. All in all, drug smuggling/trafficking operates as an important component among other necessary parts of what I call the American drug problem.

I define the *American drug problem* (ADP) as *the relentless demand and consumption of legal and illegal drugs in the United States, its negative outcomes (e.g., opioid epidemic), including drug trafficking, and the official response to it (the WODs)* as these two occurrences promote drug use. According to this definition, the ADP is a comprehensive idea that includes the social, economic, political, and health issues associated with drug use, demand for drugs, drug trafficking, and addiction as well as the policies and government measures taken to address those issues. Drug use, drug trafficking, and addiction are widespread and chronic problems in American society. They are not new by any means given how politicians have used the drug menace and drug smuggling for more than a century to pursue ideological and political gains.

The ADP has reached extraordinary levels of attention by the media, government officials, and society at large in recent decades. This attention has been driven by an aggressive U.S. drug policy approach and how the government has conceptualized the problem of drug trafficking and drug use as a national security issue. At the same time, increase of gruesome violence, murders, and crime in Mexico and other drug-producing countries since the 2000s, along with record-breaking overdoses and deaths in America, has also contributed to position the ADP in the news and political agendas of law enforcement agencies. However, the primary force behind the ADP is the relentless demand for drugs in the United States and it is critical to recognize it to confront the issue.

Drug Demand

Since drug prohibition began in America almost a century ago, the primary approach to deal with the drug problem has been the punishment model, which has been based on the assumption that drug use and addiction can be eliminated once and for all by punishing users and traffickers (Bertram et al. 1996). This model was behind Anslinger's crusade during his long tenure as America's drug czar and it was consolidated by the DEA and the

WODs policy. One major issue with this model is that it ignores the difficult and complex reality of the huge demand for illegal drugs that has existed in America for decades. Ignoring the power of drug demand in the United States has made it easier for politicians, law enforcement agencies, and mass media outlets to blame others for the ADP.

At the same time, the denial of domestic drug demand has made the problem worse over the years because it has disregarded efforts to deal with it in a scientific and evidence-based approach. If there is no open recognition of the problem there will never be serious and accurate measures to address it, let alone devise strategies to tackle it using facts and science. This is a simple inconvenient truth that America must face now: as long as drug demand is not confronted in all of its complexity, drug trafficking and the drug problem will never be a manageable and remediable affair. The negative impact of this lack of public and official acknowledgment of the severity of the problem of drug demand in America is clearly reflected in the distorted understanding of the economics of supply and demand regarding illicit drugs.

The DEA and defenders of the WODs have blatantly ignored that as long as there is demand (drug consumption) for a product (even if it is prohibited), there will always be someone willing to risk freedom or life if it is a profitable enterprise. Also, there has never been a truly national effort to implement treatment and rehabilitation programs to decrease the number of drug users and addiction. Instead, the WODs has primarily attacked the supply side of the issue through interdiction, law enforcement and strict drug control. If drug traffickers like Joaquin *El Chapo* Guzman are arrested or killed, it does not matter because the drug black market and its incentives remain untouched. Therefore, any attempts to cut the supply of drugs are a backward and futile approach because no government effort can ever stop permanently the supply of illegal drugs if there is an insatiable demand for them. Now, let us assume that supply of drugs from Mexico could be interrupted successfully, the supply would only shift to a different location and keep the flow of drugs coming because demand for them is the most powerful motivation to encourage drug trafficking (Wainwright 2016).

The WODs has tried for nearly fifty years to disrupt the supply side of drug smuggling by arresting traffickers and intercepting the flow of drugs into the United States without a permanent successful result. This drug policy has misunderstood the tenets of supply and demand by spending billions of dollars in ineffective work to cease the former while neglecting the latter. Not only that, the DEA has targeted the supply of drugs in other countries but has not invested heavily in drug demand reduction strategies at home even though America is the largest consumer of drugs worldwide (Andreas 2013; Drug Policy Alliance 2019; Wainwright 2016). That being said, of course, the U.S. government has attempted to deal with drug demand for years, except that the response has been overwhelmingly based on a law enforcement mindset and ignoring a harm reduction approach.

Indeed, past government efforts have done nothing to deal with the American demand for drugs except for some timid measures that did not change the dynamics of drug trafficking and illegal drug use. Attempts such as the anti-drug advertising campaign "Just Say No" during the Reagan administration (famously promoted by First Lady Nancy Reagan) were a complete failure. Scientific research conducted years later about whether or not this slogan was an effective tool to deter youths from using illegal drugs shows that the campaign did not work at all (Lilienfeld and Arkowitz 2014). The same can be said of other efforts to reduce drug use such as the "National Red Ribbon Campaign" awareness, prevention drug misuse and addiction strategies, as well as Mandatory Rehabilitation Programs, among others programs.

I am not claiming that these efforts have all been a complete failure; the problem is that they have not been scientifically evaluated to determine whether or not they have accomplished what they meant to achieve. Without a program assessment that scientifically demonstrates these measures work, they will always be anecdotal strategies only. Most of these approaches emphasize scary tactics to discourage the youth and potential users from experiencing drugs in the first place. Rather than informing and teaching them how to make wise choices using evidence-based knowledge, most programs show the worse-case scenarios of drug use to scare people. When young users experiment with drugs and they do not experience any of the negative effects announced by the programs, the information (and adults telling them not to use drugs) loses credibility and drug users have a higher likelihood of making poor decisions regarding drug use.

Sometimes drug demand has been modestly recognized by the government as a serious social, economic, and health problem in America but only to justify the rhetoric and publicity of the WODs and to defend law enforcement operations conducted by the DEA and local and state police agencies. In fact, the amount of resources invested in drug control (arresting, prosecuting, and jailing drug users and street dealers) is directly proportional to the volume of drug demand in the United States. If the United States spends annually nearly $50 billion on the WODs without any success (Drug Policy Alliance 2019), this amount of money provides a good estimate of how immense drug demand is in the United States. For that reason, it difficult to get one's head around the fact that the American government has never provided a full, open, and public admission on how serious demand for illegal drug is and what would be the real cost to deal with it.

Without this admission (and the subsequent mandatory response to it), it seems problematic to find a new model to tackle the ADP and how it could work at all. Why? Because similar to those twelve-step programs, such as

Alcoholics Anonymous, that require anyone beginning the recovery process to acknowledge that the person has an addiction or an alcohol problem, American society and its government have to admit without conditions the nature and seriousness of domestic drug demand. Only after such admission is made public, transparent, and official, there could be hope that a transformative process to deal with the ADP could happen that would change the status quo and launch a new period of effective and reasonable drug policy and management of drug trafficking. Enough about drug demand, now it is time to switch to the opposite side of the problem and examine drug trafficking in Mexico to provide a detailed analysis of its origins and primary characteristics to better understand the issue and why it has become what it is today.

Chapter 2

Drug Trafficking in Mexico

Origins, Development, and Consolidation

CONTEXTUALIZING DRUG TRAFFICKING

It is well known in the criminal justice field that when comparing and contrasting institutions such as the police, the courts, and the corrections between different countries it is assumed that culture, social norms, and history influence and determine the format and content of those institutions. The same rationale can be applied to the problem of drug trafficking: in every country, drug trafficking has a different meaning, definition, understandings, content, and format. True, there are similarities between some nations such as Mexico, Colombia, Peru, or Argentina in the way the problem is approached and dealt with. However, local characteristics such as the domestic nature of the drug trade, geography, poverty levels, and economic and social development, as well as national and international drug demand, make drug trafficking a distinct phenomenon for each country to a certain extent.

Drug trafficking in Mexico is a unique affair because of the crucial geographical characteristic that sets it apart from any other nation. It shares a common border of nearly 2,000 miles with the world's largest consumer of drugs. Sharing a large border is not the only reason that makes drug trafficking in Mexico out of the ordinary but it is one contentious feature that complicates the nature of the problem. There are other border problems between Mexico and the United States that are directly or indirectly connected to drug trafficking such as immigration (legal and illegal), international trade, national security, mutual economic interdependence, and border environmental issues. All of them are part of the political agenda that forces these nations to cooperate and—many times—quarrel between the two and accuse each other of not doing enough to deal with the illegal drug trade.

Besides the War on Drugs, sharing border, and drug demand in America, there are also historical, social, cultural, and legal differences between Mexico and the United States that have shaped how these two countries understand and address drug trafficking. These differences and discrepancies have long been studied and explained by scholars, officials, and experts on both sides of the border—albeit in contrasting and sometimes opposite ways (Astorga 2015; Baum 1996; Bertram et al. 1996; Boullosa and Wallace 2016; Grillo 2011; Inciardi 2008; Valdés Castellanos 2013; Wainwright 2016). There is no need to reformulate in detail all those arguments about the problem, but it is crucial to highlight some important features of drug trafficking to shed light on why it is such a complicated and contentious issue between Mexico and the United States and how the problem can be dealt with more efficiently and effectively.

From a historical perspective, Mexico and the United States have experienced disagreements for different reasons. First, the cession or dispossession (depending on who interprets this event) of half of Mexico's territory by the United States through the Guadalupe-Hidalgo treaty after the 1846–1848 war between the two countries. Second, the two U.S. invasions of Mexico in 1847 first and in 1914 later with the occupation of the port of Veracruz. And finally, the subtle but active meddling of the U.S. government in Mexican politics for decades during most of the twentieth century. These historical events have contributed to shape and determine each country's attitudes, stereotypes, assumptions and how drug trafficking is tackled differently on both sides of the common border (Boullosa and Wallace 2016; Grillo 2011; Valdés Castellanos 2013).

The best description that I have ever read of the differences and tumultuous relationship between Mexico and the United States was described in a memoir by Jeffrey Davidow, former U.S. ambassador in Mexico (1998–2002). In his book *The U.S. and Mexico: The Bear and the Porcupine* (2004) Davidow recounts a fable where a bear and a porcupine have an encounter in a forest. The porcupine is traveling with its nose in the earth searching for seeds and berries when suddenly a bear almost steps on it. The porcupine makes its quills stand up. The bear stops and laughs about it: "Do you think you can kill me with your little arrows?" the bear proclaims. "No. But do you think you can step on me without suffering the pain of my quills?" responds the porcupine (Davidow 2004, xii). The bear represents the United States and the porcupine Mexico. The metaphor being that both animals have little in common but they are condemned to share the forest together and be mindful of one another's presence because if not, they would end up hurting each other. According to Davidow, this fable represents the lack of understanding between Mexico and the United States as well as the negative consequences of ignoring their mutual interdependence and failure to cooperate for the betterment of both nations (Davidow 2004).

It should not be a surprise then that Mexico and the United States look at their shared problems in dramatically different ways: from national security, immigration, economic intendependence, diplomacy, to the War on Drugs (WOD) and drug trafficking. All of these mutual problems are usually defined and interpreted in opposite ways. Of course there are also commonalities and mutual interest to find a united front. But drug trafficking has been a thorn in the relationship of both countries and they have collided in defining what this problem is and the best approach to tackle it. Drug trafficking has challenged the relationship between the two nations for decades and the difficulties were aggravated after the 11 September 2001 attacks in the United States.

More recently, the election of President Donald Trump has increased the animosity between the two nations given the tendency of the American president to blame Mexico for common neighboring issues such as immigration, border security, and drug smuggling. While differences are usually the most highlighted features, there are also close similarities between Mexico and America by virtue of sharing borders, neighborhoods, and cultural integration that have led to mutual influence in societal aspects and border life. Food, language, culture, music, family ties, immigration, mutual tourism, and economic interdependence are all components of this shared proximity between the two countries (Bender 2012). The North American Free Trade Agreement (NAFTA) that took effect in 1994 is a good example of this mutual understanding. Because of this inextricable interdependency between Mexico and the United States, it was unprecedented and aggressive to hear candidate Donald Trump while launching his campaign to accuse Mexicans of being criminals. This and other negative comments by President Trump blaming Mexico for the problems of illegal immigration and drug trafficking only hurt both countries and create mutual animosity that interferes with the need to address common problem in a constructive and effective manner.

For Mexico however, this strained relationship has been experienced in a more profound, significant, and chaotic manner compared to the United States because of the unequal, asymmetrical, and subordinated role that Mexico has played towards the powerful and almighty America. Many Mexicans exemplify this complex relationship with a well-known saying that it has been attributed to former Mexican president and dictator Porfirio Diaz: *Pobrecito de Mexico, tan lejos de Dios y tan cerca de Estados Unidos* (Poor Mexico, so distant from God, and so close to the United States [Fagen 1977]. The assumption being that despite Mexicans having a deep religious faith in God, He is always far from Mexico while America, the most powerful nation in the twentieth century, is so close to Mexico. The corollary being that the relationship between Mexico and the United States is both a blessing and a curse. Regardless of either interpretation, the fact is that such relationship is ambiguous and uncertain and this has had profound implications when dealing with drug trafficking. To explain the complicated layers and complexities of drug trafficking in Mexico as well as the United States it is necessary to contextualize some historical and cultural facts of their mutual association and how it has been understood respectively. The nature of this relationship will inform the critical analysis of drug trafficking throughout this book in order to make clear that the problem is not always as obvious as everyone may assume.

The American drug problem (as described in the previous chapter) is well-documented in the United States. It has been widely examined (Bertram et al. 1996; Coyne and Hall 2017; Drug Policy Alliance 2019; Inciardi and Mcelrath 2015; Musto 1999; Walker 2015) and depicted in the media (newspapers, television, movies) within a particular narrative throughout the twentieth and twenty-first centuries. For the most part this narrative has been built in the belief that others (foreigners and immigrants) are the culprits of drug availability in America while reproducing the idea (at least until the epidemics of opioid addiction began to change the script) that drug users are usually noncitizens, minorities, the lower class, and anyone who is seen as an outsider racially, ethnically, culturally, and socially (Musto 1999; Alexander 2012).

According to this pattern, it is not uncommon in American society that some public officials (e.g., President Trump) and right-wing news media point fingers at Mexico as the culprit of the American drug problem for—allegedly—failing to address serious domestic issues such as corruption, weak government, gruesome violence, and ineffective law enforcement against drug cartels and traffickers. On the opposite side, Mexican society for the most part usually assumes that drug trafficking is an American-made problem because of its enormous appetite for drugs. In Mexico, many politicians, officials, and the general public have believed for decades that if there was no demand for drugs in the United States there would not be drug trafficking in Mexico or the western hemisphere for that matter. This argument is not exclusive of Mexican society because several Latin American governments have also argued a similar position in past decades: demand from drugs in America encourages drug trafficking somewhere else. For Mexico, the proximity to the United States makes this explanation more significant because of the sharing border and the direct burden in terms of law enforcement, violence, and crime imposed on Mexico (Boullosa and Wallace 2016; Grillo 2011).

Because most public officials in Mexico have understood drug trafficking as an American-made issue, it has made it extraordinarily difficult to see the problem with objectivity, let alone assume a proactive approach to deal with it. Blaming the United States for drug trafficking is good politics in Mexico, but it ignores that drug use and abuse has never been an American problem only. Drug use and abuse have existed in Mexico since the late 1800s, albeit in smaller rates compared to the United States. Also, such attitude hides the elephant in the room regarding chronic and systematic corruption in Mexico that aggravates the issue without question. Additionally, domestic drug use and abuse in Mexico have increased dramatically in the past decade—something unheard of in the past—due to drug trafficking organizations' decision to create a domestic drug market to profit from it. As a side note, this internal drug use has transformed the dynamics of drug trafficking in Mexico because drug gangs have now an additional incentive to control and protect strategic drug corridors and plazas that are crucial to their illegal business.

FUNDAMENTALS OF DRUG TRAFFICKING IN MEXICO

The history of drug trafficking in Mexico has been widely documented somewhere else in both Spanish and English (Astorga 2015; Boullosa and Wallace 2016; Grillo 2011; Recio 2002; Valdés Castellanos 2013). Instead of repeating what it has been said on drug trafficking, I want to emphasize seven themes that stand out as essential components of the nature, characteristics, patterns, and evolution of drug trafficking in Mexico. These components provide a context on how and why drug trafficking has become what it is today and they help to understand the multifaceted and complex essence of the issue.

One Problem, Two Approaches

One distinct feature of drug trafficking in North America is the disparity and asymmetrical interpretation of this phenomenon between Mexico and the United States. This should be obvious since both countries have two completely different legal and political systems, not to mention laws that treat the problem according to their own institutional ideologies. But beyond this obvious fact, there have always been countless finger-pointing moments between the two governments about who is responsible for the problem of drug trafficking. Either Mexico for its out-of-control presence of drug trafficking organizations, corruption, and poor rule of law or the United States for its large drug market, ineffective drug policy, and stubborn attitude of strict drug control (Boullosa and Wallace 2016; Riding 1985; Valdés Castellanos 2013).

Having contrasting interpretations on how to deal with drug trafficking has created mutual distrust leading to a permanent state of confusion and misunderstanding. Since the origins of prohibition in the early twentieth century, the United States consistently has had the dominant position to decide drug policy on its own. America has used its hegemonic power to basically force the Mexican government to adhere to U.S. drug policy ideologies and strategies based on drug control. Officially and reluctantly Mexico has agreed to this political dominance, but in reality Mexico never bought the prohibitionist agenda (until recently) and did not enforce drug laws in a consistent manner when drug prohibition began (Astorga 2015; Boullosa and Wallace 2016).

Early on in the twentieth century, the beginning of the Mexican Revolution and the subsequent political unrest prevented the central government from enforcing the rule of law at the national level. This situation allowed local authorities and strong men (caciques) to turn a blind eye to drug trafficking activities or were themselves directly involved in such illegal affairs. In those days the unofficial position of Mexican authorities was that Mexico had nothing to do with drug use in America and its prohibitionist agenda. As a result, there was no interest in joining American efforts toward eliminating drug availability. These attitudes created misunderstandings and distortions in how Mexico would partner up with the United States and respond to drug trafficking in the years to come (Astorga 2016; Boullosa and Wallace 2016; Enciso 2015). Unfortunately, a similar situation prevails today and even if both nations share a mutual interest to tackle drug trafficking and they proactively work together towards that end, their respective domestic agendas dominate over the common good for solving this problem together.

The Bear and the Porcupine

Another important component of drug trafficking in Mexico and a point of contention behind the different interpretations in both countries is the uneven correlation of power. The United States has been the most powerful nation in the twentieth century while Mexico has been a developing country for years, still on the making. America's worldwide dominance has been felt politically, militarily, economically, and culturally everywhere on the planet for the last century. But for Mexico this domination has been perceived deeply and sometimes as a threat to its sovereignty given the 2,000 miles of sharing border and Americans' expansionist ethos. During the nineteenth and twentieth centuries this U.S. attitude was displayed against Mexico through an invasion and an occupation. Nevertheless, American's geopolitical influence on Mexico has been more subtle and using indirect means economically, politically, and culturally (Davidow 2004; Riding 1985).

Mexico has a totally different genesis, culture, and history than the United States and that has added more complexity to their relationship. Think about Canada, which shares similar language, history, and culture to the United States. Over the centuries, the relationship between Canada and the United States has been more proactive, stable, and amicable while the relationship between Mexico and America has been more complex and problematic because these two countries look and interpret the world in contrasting ways. Such antagonism has become fertile soil for all sorts of tense events and misunderstandings that increase and recede in political and economic cycles over time. On the other hand, though, no one could ignore that common ground exists and treaties like NAFTA—and its new version under the Trump presidency, The United States Mexico Canada Agreement (USMCA)—and countless bilateral agreements confirm the mutual cultural and economic interdependence between the two countries. That being said, it should not go unnoticed the fact that the United States always has had a predominant position in this relationship and that in itself generates an unbalanced correlation of power that affects mutual government responses to drug trafficking (Davidow 2004; Riding 1985).

Understandably, then, drug trafficking in Mexico has been subordinated to America's drug policy with little room for Mexico to maneuver. Drug prohibition as it is known today was an American invention and this approach was imposed upon Mexico since its inception. Even today, when Americans' influence in the world begins to decline and its relationship with Mexico has become more equitable and proportionate, the Mexican government cannot ignore the opinion and policies of its northern neighbor regarding domestic decisions on drug trafficking. To that end, drug trafficking has been and still is the thorniest problem for both nations, even more problematic than immigration, the economy, or terrorism because of the dramatic consequences for both Mexico (e.g., extreme violence, crime, high murder rates) and the United States (e.g., drug demand, the opioid epidemics, and endless flow of illegal drugs through the common border).

Corruption: Mexico's Achilles' Heel

For decades the U.S. government has complained against its Mexican counterpart about the systematic problem of corruption in government institutions and at all levels of the administration (Davidow 2004; Morris 1991; Riding 1985). Corruption is a worldwide problem affecting every single country according to International Transparency and no society is immune from it. What stands out in Mexico—and many other Latin American countries—is the widespread levels of corruption and how common the problem is in everyday life (Morris 1991; Riding 1985). Corruption is a complicated phenomenon to understand and control because it is more than just a problem of dishonesty, misconduct, or wrongdoing. Cultural, social, and historical elements are combined to shape and predispose the nature and characteristics of corruption. Therefore, corruption does not mean the same everywhere and this brings in another set of issues. No doubt most countries have common elements of this concept such as its illegality, secrecy, and abuse of public office. However, some practices such as gift-giving, cronyism, graft, and grease payments (money paid to facilitate government action or circumvent red tape) may not be considered bribery in countries such as Mexico, China, or Nigeria while in America or Western Europe they would be (Transparency International 2007). This blurred line creates opportunities for both civil society and public officials to engage in corrupt behavior disguised as common and normalized conventions in the community.

Under the authoritarian regime that ruled Mexico for more than seven decades, the government tolerated all types of corruption in order to maintain political stability. This tolerance generated a social acceptance and normalization of corruption in Mexican society to the extent that it became an undesirable but necessary tool to navigate bureaucracy, make up for poor salaries, and become wealthy out of holding public office. In this context of widespread institutional and social corruption, drug trafficking thrived because of the endless possibilities to break the law and be corrupt without major legal consequences for perpetrators: everyone could be bought. Corruption was a crucial factor (and still is today) in the early development of drug trafficking and that contributed to set up the infrastructure (e.g. cultivation of territories, creating drug corridors, local and international connections, and controlling key smuggling zones to cumulate drug trafficking expertise) to build such profitable, efficient, and entrepreneurial illegal activity. Regrettably, not much has changed in contemporary Mexico and corruption remains one of the most pervasive problems that facilitates drug trafficking activities (Riding 1985; Morris 1991).

Narcocracy: When Politicians Become Narcos and Vice Versa

There is abundant evidence about the close collusion between Mexican politicians and drug traffickers and how widespread it is. Often the label of being a politician and being a drug trafficker are easily interchangeable: some politicians become drug traffickers and sometime traffickers become politicians. This phenomenon can be defined as *Narcocracy*: this is, government led by drug traffickers or drug trafficking groups. Such practice has also been called *Narco-politics* and it is not exclusive of Mexico. Other nations such as Afghanistan, Colombia, and the Philippines have experienced it in different forms and times. I do distinguish between Narcocracy and Narco-politics though. Narcocracy refers to a situation where drug traffickers or members of drug cartels become politicians to reach public office and exercise political power or vice versa when politicians or public officials themselves become drug traffickers to support or expand their political career. Narco-politics on the other hand involves situations where traffickers or members of DTOs actively provide financial support to politicians or public officials in exchange for protection, but these criminals do not seek public office. With that said, many times it is difficult to distinguish between these two phenomena because of the nature of their activities (e.g., clandestine, illegal, and difficult to investigate). For the sake of simplicity, I will use both concepts interchangeably in this book although they are not the same.

Drug trafficking in Mexico could not be understood without the active support from the political system and establishment as a whole at all levels of government: local, state, and federal. This support goes beyond the well-known practice of public officials and politicians supporting traffickers in exchange for bribes (Zavala 2018). Rather, the Mexican political system, in particular the party structure of the ancient regime that ruled Mexico for most of the twentieth century, the Institutional Revolutionary Party—*Partido Revolucionario Institucional* (PRI)—developed a cozy relation of mutual interdependence between itself and drug traffickers for decades. It was convenient for both because the government regulated and controlled (informally of course) the illegal drug trade while maintaining political stability by allowing local officials to engage—directly or indirectly—in this illegal business to claim a sort of taxation via corruption. Drug traffickers on the other hand were able to conduct their businesses unmolested due to official protection. Important for this cozy situation was that the government always had the upper hand and strict control and when a trafficker or group turned into a problem or embarrassment at the eyes of the U.S. government, Mexican officials could easily press charges and arrest those traffickers. This relationship ended up being widely accepted by the Mexican establishment for decades to the point that it became a de facto non-written policy (Boullosa and Wallace 2016; Zavala 2018).

This complicity between officials and traffickers is not new and it can be traced back to the onset of drug trafficking a century ago. This informal arrangement lasted decades but once drug traffickers consolidated their power and the official regime began to decline, traffickers resorted to violence to persuade officials to cooperate with them. In this way, drug gangs instituted the policy *plata or plomo* (literally *silver or lead* meaning a bribe or a bullet) to lure or force public servants to protect them. During the peak of PRI, money would be enough to co-opt politicians, and when that did not work, violence was used. Eventually, the decline of the authoritarian regime at the end of the past century left a vacuum of power throughout Mexico that was filled out by drug groups in the early 2000s that switched the balance of power in favor of drug organizations against the government (Grillo 2011; Valdéz Castellanos 2013).

Institutional Weakness and Disregard for the Rule of Law

Mexico endured a dictatorship by General Porfirio Diaz for more than three decades (1876–1911) that led to the Mexican Revolution (1910–1920), a period of social, political, and economic turmoil. After this civil war, the Mexican state emerged crippled and precarious to implement major social and economic reforms to overcome the damage of the revolution and the political circumstances left by the previous authoritarian regime of General Diaz. Accordingly, in the following decades the government sought the reconstruction of the Mexican state through the implementation of economic, social and political changes but without having the resources necessary for those adjustments. This period overlapped with the implementation of drug control policies in America first, followed by a similar approach by the Mexican government later on. However, given the post-revolutionary context of the country, enforcing drug laws was never a priority. In fact, there were few government policies regarding drug trafficking during those decades because this issue was not a priority (Astorga 2016; Boullosa and Wallace 2016; Riding 1985).

As a result, there was a considerable gap between the law in the books and the law in practice since inaction was the only strategy to deal with drug trafficking by the federal government because there was no strategy at all (Valdés Castellanos 2013). Considering the large damage inflicted by the Mexican Revolution and its social, economic, and political aftermath, it should not be a surprise that the government in those years prioritized these problems to the detriment of less urgent issues such as the illegal drug trade and drug traffickers. These issues did not even appear as problems because consumption of illegal substances was defined as a medical, not a criminal problem and drug use was not prevalent at that time (Enciso 2015).

The post-revolutionary government did not bring democracy to Mexicans and instead it led to another authoritarian regime (not as brutal as the previous one but still autocratic in nature) that took over in 1929 and lasted seventy-one years by the time it ended in 2000. Because of the centralized nature of the country's government, many institutions never had the strength to withstand by themselves as independent and efficient parts of the public administration. During most of the twentieth century, the federal administration maintained political stability and every time a new president took office (every six years) the power was passed on. Yet institutions such as the police, the prosecutor's office, and the courts were kept subordinated and weak intentionally because they were used politically to maintain the status quo and prosecute dissidents if needed. Along with that, ignoring the rule of law became part of the government's strategy to undermine checks and balances that could challenge the control of the one-party rulers. This strategy eventually permeated Mexican society and citizens learned to disregard the law because it was applied selectively according to powerful interests and prone to be influenced by corruption, and not to dispense justice. Consequently, main criminal justice institutions in charge of confronting drug trafficking were—and have been until recently—incapable of confronting drug trafficking in an effective and meaningful way (Enciso 2015; Grillo 2011; Valdés Castellanos 2013).

Poverty, Underdevelopment, and Destitution

Poverty, lack of unemployment, underdevelopment, and isolation of communities where drugs are harvested and manufactured have all played a pivoting role in promoting drug trafficking activities. More often than not, poor farmers in the mountains of Mexico have resorted to the cultivation and harvesting of marijuana and poppy as an alternative option to make ends meet. Traditional crops such as corn, beans, and squash have become unsustainable—besides for self-consumption—to earn a living. Low market prices and cheap imported grains from the United States (where farmers are heavily subsidized by the government) have impacted Mexican farmers' ways of living. This is even more complicated for those farmers who need to transport their produce from isolated communities to urban settings to sell them in the city markets (Muehlmann 2014).

Poor communities where drug manufacture is common tend to be remote, underdeveloped, difficult to access them, and they have been traditionally neglected by the government. As a result, drug traffickers have taken advantage of these conditions by offering impoverished farmers cash through the cultivation of illicit crops. To entice farmers, traffickers facilitate farmers' work by offering them advance cash payments, protection from law enforcement operations, agricultural tools, and even collecting the harvested raw material for drugs where they are produced. This entrepreneurial approach has created a mutual interdependency between farmers and traffickers based on the illegal drug trade that produces an unlimited amount of drugs to be exported to consumer markets while farmers have a reliable source of income to survive poverty and destitution (Grillo 2011; Valdés Castellanos 2013).

The Force of Drug Demand in the United States

Another crucial component of drug trafficking between Mexico and the United States mentioned in chapter 1 has been the constant demand for drugs in the latter. For decades, many Latin American countries such as Mexico and Colombia affected by the illegal drug trade have criticized the hypocrisy of U.S. drug policy for wanting to impose upon their countries a zero-tolerance approach towards drugs while at home, America has done little to nothing to address the huge demand for illegal substances. Although the U.S. government began to address domestic demand for drugs recently, most attempts have been insignificant and without a clear policy to cut the insatiable appetite for drugs domestically.

Having the world's largest drug market, America has been a net consumer of drugs while Mexico was mostly a source and transit country for them. The U.S demand for drugs has created powerful incentives for drug traffickers to smuggle them into America and make enormous profits. This trend has caused a headache for Mexico because no matter what measures the country takes, it will be difficult if not impossible, to stop drug trafficking due to the luring effect of demand. It is a basic principle of economics—demand and supply—and as long as demand exists there will be someone willing to risk anything to supply the demand if it is profitable. Hence, the complicated and disparate interpretation of drug trafficking between the two nations.

Drug consumption exists in any country because drug use has always existed in human civilization. There is abundant evidence that for millennia humans have used substances to alter their minds and reality for different reasons such as religious ceremonies, mystical experiences, recreational purposes, and so on (Escohotado 1999; Walton 2002). Today is no different and according to experts and research (Belenko and Spohn 2015) most people who consume drugs do it in a moderate way without any major health, legal, and personal consequences. Yet, no other industrialized country has struggled in past decades with a steady consumption of illegal drugs and constant epidemics of drug abuse than the United States. This demand for drugs has fluctuated over different periods of time depending on variables such as drug use trends, price of substances, availability of them, social, political, and cultural factors, as well as consumers' demographics. What remains a fact is that drug consumption in America has been relentless, dynamic, and vigorous for decades (Andreas 2013; Inciardi 2008; Musto 1999).

The problem of drug demand in the United States is multifaceted and complex to address and it is interconnected to primary components of American society such as the criminal justice system, the health care system and the political system, as well as religious and national ideologies. Today in America, it is impossible to approach drug use, addiction, and drug trafficking from an objective, moderate, and enlightened viewpoint. Politics, dogma, ignorance, and emotions tromp over logic, science, and facts regarding drugs in our society. This explains in part why drug demand has not been properly understood, let alone tackled with the correct government policies for such as issue to be solved. As a result, drug consumption as a national public health and social problem remains mostly unaddressed because the focus has been on punishing drug users and smugglers while ignoring the primary causes of why there is so much demand for drugs in America. Ignoring drug demand and punishing drug users have been the driving force behind the WOD approach, and it will remain unchallenged for the near future if a new model is not adopted, which means that drug trafficking will continue its unbeaten path as it has in the past century (Bertram et al. 1996; Drug Policy Alliance 2019; Hari 2016).

All in all, the combination of these seven dominant factors created a context by which drug trafficking in Mexico (and by association in the United States) became a mainstream economic, social, and cultural activity that evolved into the problem that it is today. This has not been always the case, though, and drug trafficking in Mexico began as a small-scale business when a set of circumstances overlapped. In order to grasp its complexity and gain a more holistic understanding of this phenomenon, its origins and development are explained next.

THE BEGINNING OF DRUG TRAFFICKING (1900–1949)

Drug trafficking (DT) is a phenomenon that is constantly changing and adapting to the reality of drug use and demand. During a particular time, a generation may be interested in a specific drug or drugs that become trendy and drug traffickers supply that demand. Later on another drug becomes more fashionable and the black market makes it available to satisfy users. This cycle of new illegal drugs substituting old ones or old ones regaining a fresh acceptance is part of the ever-changing nature of drug use and addiction. DT has evolved into a business that meets, adapts, and serves the needs of drug demand. Besides drug demand, DT is organized and managed in numerous ways by traffickers to circumvent or avoid law enforcement practices and operations to manage each drug and its black market according to the geography of production, manufacture, smuggle, and consumption of drugs.

Not surprisingly there is a triangulation of mutual interdependence between drug demand, law enforcement, and DT by which these three activities unintentionally influence and shape each other. A socioeconomic circuit is formed when drug use demands a particular drug and DT satisfies that demand by delivering it. Law enforcement intervenes to destroy that circuit but the most it can do is to disrupt, but never eradicate, the drug flow. Drug demand then adapts to that disruption and so it does DT to the point that it becomes a cat-and-mouse game where none of the main stakeholders can claim victory. These stakeholders (drug traffickers, drug users, and law enforcement agents) overlap in a particular operation, period, or moment. All of them will be gone at some point and will be replaced with new people and strategies, but the core of DT and drug use remain unchanged.

More than a century ago when prohibition of cocaine and opium became effective in the United States, a black market appeared and their supply and demand went underground instead of disappearing. Drug prohibition automatically turned the illegal commercialization of these two drugs highly profitable. Such event created an opportunity for supplying the drugs from somewhere else (since there was already demand for them) and the first traffickers turned to Mexico to provide opium and marijuana (cocaine came from the Andean region because only there coca leaves can be grown). This was a process that took several decades in the making and the consolidation of drug prohibition occurred effectively until the 1930s with the establishment of the Federal Bureau of Narcotics led by Harry J. Anslinger (more on him in chapter 5) and with the passing of the Marijuana Tax Act of 1937 (Musto 1999). In Mexico, drug prohibition came up several years after the United States passed the first drug control laws because drug consumption was not a serious problem considering the country had to deal with a different and more serious existential problem: the Mexican revolution of 1910. Opium in Mexico was prohibited in 1920 and marijuana in 1926. However, the political instability in the aftermath of the revolution and the lack of a powerful central government made it impossible to enforce Mexican prohibition, which allowed the perfect conditions for a thriving illegal drug market (Astorga 2015; Enciso 2015).

Early Drug Traffickers as Entrepreneurs

A distinctive characteristic of the DT in Mexico during the first half of the past century was the absence of drug cartels as they are known today. Instead of criminal organizations, what existed were regional drug lords, families, and independent traffickers who were in charge of the drug business in Mexico. Routinely, they would arrange their own production, transportation, smuggling, and distribution of drugs according to their business size, interests, political connections, and drug production. Along with the absence of drug cartels, there were three distinctive features of early DT: little domestic drug use, minimum violence among traffickers, and the relative ease of getting into the DT business since there were no risks associated with it (Astorga 1995). Local demand for drugs existed but it was minimal and less profitable compared to sending drugs to America. In Mexico, drug use was frowned upon and had a strong stigma attached in conservative Mexican society where the family played a significant role to maintain social control of the youth's behavior. Any attempt or behavior on illicit drug consumption by a curious youngster would be rapidly scolded and shunned by family members. Instead, alcohol was tolerated and seen as a more socially accepted option for drug intoxication compared to marijuana or opium.

Violence between traffickers existed but it was minimal because communities where DT thrived were small and everyone knew each other. Frequently, the drug business was in the hands of the most experienced and elderly members of the family, and when conflicts arose, they settled the disputes with their counterparts cordially rather than fighting or exerting violence. In addition, the drug market created a new economy to benefit the community with no competition at that time. Because anyone could enter the DT business and with a shot of luck make money without infringing any personal interest, violence was marginal (Astorga 2015). Given the post–Mexican Revolution context of the country and the incapacity of the federal government to enforce the laws, drug traffickers enjoyed freedom and impunity to conduct their illegal enterprise. Public officials and politicians were easy to bribe and frequently those officials themselves became actively involved in the illicit drug trade. Corruption during the early development of DT in Mexico was pervasive at all levels of the government bureaucracy—from the low ranks of local and state police departments and customs officers all the way up to army commanders, governors, and federal officials (Astorga 2015; Enciso 2015; Zavala 2018).

Official documents from both Mexico and the United States as well as newspaper reports from Mexican outlets at that time reveal the nature, characteristics, and faces of early drug traffickers in the drug business (Astorga 2015, 2016; Enciso 2015). It is important to keep in mind that in the first half of the twentieth century the U.S.-Mexico border looked completely different than it does today. Crossing drugs through the border back and forth from Mexico to the United States was a relatively easy activity for today's standards. Early drug traffickers were both Mexican and American citizens, although the emphasis was mostly in the former since they were the ones who conducted most of the labor-intensive part of the business.

In Mexico, like in the United States, opium consumption was brought by Chinese immigrants who migrated to the country to labor as workers building the railroad network and mining in Northern Mexico in the 1860s. These immigrants had the seeds and the know-how to cultivate, harvest, and extract the semi-dry gum from poppy plants to have it ready for smoke in designed opium dens. Soon, poppy plants began to be planted and harvested everywhere in the mountains of the Sierra Madre (the Rocky Mountains of Mexico) in Sinaloa state. Chinese immigrants were heavily involved in the trafficking of opium at first, but then Mexican traffickers took over the business and the knowledge and know-how of the poppy industry went to Mexican farmers, peasants, and businessmen. They learned how to cultivate, harvest, and manufacture this drug and the Sinaloa became the epicenter of opium production. Besides Sinaloa, other states such as Sonora and Baja California also turned into DT hubs because of their closeness to the U.S.-Mexico border. The Chinese communities had contacts and connections with their counterparts in the United States and a networking of trafficking developed after opium was prohibited in America in 1914 (Enciso 2015; Grillo 2011; Valdés Castellanos 2013).

Not all opium smuggled into the United States was produced and harvested in Mexico though. A large amount came from Asia which implies that traffickers had to have connections with suppliers in that continent in order to organize the whole process of smuggling it. This fact implies that there were Chinese traffickers in charge of those operations because only they could have built the infrastructure to import opium from Asia in those days. In the early 1930s, however, a wave of anti-Chinese sentiment inundated Mexican cities in Northern Mexico such as Culiacan, Ciudad Juárez, and Mexicali. Apparently, this sentiment was instigated by either drug traffickers or powerful alcohol smugglers who wanted to seize the Chinese's profitable illegal business to confiscate their drug infrastructure and wealth. It is not clear whether the reason behind this attitude against Asians was the result of a deliberated effort from rival traffickers or plain racism from Mexican communities who saw the Chinese as outsiders and a threat to the social cohesion. As a result, the Mexico government conducted a massive expulsion of Chinese-Mexicans in the early 1930s that left the DT business in the hands of Mexican traffickers (Astorga 2015; Enciso 2015; Grillo 2011; Valdés Castellanos 2013).

Alcohol Prohibition Opens the Door for DT

It is impossible to ignore the strong correlation between alcohol Prohibition in America and the dawn of DT in Mexico. The passage of the Volstead Act in 1919 and the subsequent beginning of alcohol interdiction in 1920 forced the U.S. government to direct most of its law enforcement resources and efforts to deal with this problem. The immediate consequence of alcohol Prohibition was a spiral of violence, murder, and criminal activity as well as the establishment and consolidation of the American mafia that has been well documented (Okrent 2011; Recio 2002). For this reason, the smuggling of marijuana and opium from Mexico to the United States had a low priority for the federal government (at least until 1933 when Prohibition was repealed). This lack of effective law enforcement against these two drugs provided the context for DT networks to cement their businesses on both sides of the border and prosper in the illicit drug trade for decades to come (Okrent 2011; Recio 2002).

Before the end of alcohol Prohibition in 1933, there was already a whole binational and profitable business based on the production, distribution, smuggling, and selling of alcohol from Mexico to the United States. When Prohibition ended it automatically rendered useless the business of alcohol smuggling but the infrastructure supporting it remained intact and traffickers scrambled to substitute it with other profitable business. They found it with opium and marijuana. Although Chinese immigrants initiated the business of opium trafficking, they were not the only ones profiteering from these illegal activities. Among the first and more prominent traffickers of the 1910s—when the era of prohibition began in America—were Mexican officials, one of them was the governor of Baja California, Esteban Cantú (1916–1920) a military man known as an opium and arms trafficker (Astorga 2015; Enciso 2015). Despite public remarks that his administration had prohibited selling opium, he never designed any policies or government actions towards that goal. In fact the opposite was true. Diplomatic cables, law enforcement reports, and newspaper articles reveal that this governor was actively involved in DT activities to smuggle opium into the United States (allegedly he was addicted to it). He was never indicted of such crime in either country and Governor Cantú finished his tenure undisturbed (Enciso 2015; Valdés Castellano 2013).

Another famous drug trafficker of this epoch was a woman named Maria Dolores Estevez Zuleta, better known as *Lola la Chata*. She was the most famous female drug trafficker of her time and the police on both sides of the border were aware of her activities. She spent a thirty-year career as a marijuana and heroin trafficker from the early 1920s to the 1950s in both Mexico City and Ciudad Juárez. Despite the fact that women were not considered suitable as drug traffickers during those years, she was a savvy and streetwise peddler who learned the inner workings of DT at an early age from her mother and became an expert on the drug business as a trafficker herself in Mexico City at the famous barrio La Merced (a sort of Harlem in New York City during the 1960s). She excelled in developing connections with the police, government officials, and politicians to run her trafficking and smuggling operations with efficiency and almost total impunity for most of the 1920s (Carey 2009; Enciso 2015).

Lola la Chata businesses remained overlooked by authorities for years but in the late 1930s, both Mexico and the United States had identified her as a prominent drug trafficker due to the prosperity of her illegal businesses. The recently created Federal Bureau of Narcotics, led by Harry J. Anslinger, had a file on her and shared his concerns with J. Edgar Hoover (director of the Federal Bureau of Investigations) about Lola's criminal activities and their impact in the United States. She was arrested multiple times but her imprisonment did not stop her drug activities which proved how powerful and influential she was at that time. She was finally captured in 1957 and sentenced to prison for several years where she died of heart failure in 1959. This female trafficker became a legend on her own due to the gender boundaries she broke and her successful long run in the drug business in the mid-twentieth century (Carey 2009).

Other drug traffickers known from those years such as Ignacia Jasso González (known as "La Nacha"') (Campbell 2009) operated as independent retailers in the manufacture, distribution, smuggling, and sending illegal drugs to the United States. The regulation and eventual prohibition of marijuana and opium in Mexico was not a clear and straightforward process to be carried out, though. That generated a great deal of ambiguity in enforcing the law and people´s attitudes towards these substances in Mexico. Similar to the United States, marijuana and opium were legally available in pharmacies and drugstores in Mexico before prohibition and some people did not see them as harmful substances. Marijuana was popular among Mexican soldiers and the lower class during the Mexican Revolution as drugs are always present in wartimes (Bergen-Cico 2012) while smoking opium was associated with the aristocracy and Chinese immigrants.

The 1930s and 1940s were decades where smuggling drugs into the United States was conducted on a small scale and without much sophistication, and DT was seen as a business activity rather than a criminal behavior in Mexico. The U.S.-Mexico border was essentially broad open except for some official border crossings which facilitated smuggling operations. It is worth remembering that the Border Patrol was officially established in 1924, but it took several decades before it was consolidated as a powerful federal law enforcement agency. For the first ten years of its existence this agency dealt mostly with the unintended effects of alcohol prohibition because alcohol was the major concern for the federal government. Issues such as opium or marijuana trafficking were not a priority because most crime became associated with bootlegging and organized crime associated with alcohol prohibition (Okrent 2011).

During these years, some regions in Mexico became the epicenter of drug production, trafficking, and smuggling of opium and marijuana to America but Sinaloa emerged as the heart of DT. Located in north-western Mexico and with a booming agricultural industry as a result of its fertile soil, great climate, and availability of water and rivers, Sinaloa was the ideal area to plant and grow marijuana and opium. There was one region of the state where production of these drugs thrived in particular: *The Golden Triangle* which is located in the mountain section that connects Sinaloa and its bordering states of Chihuahua and Durango. This territory turned into a drug-producing hub and acquired a reputation of being source of the most pot and opium coming from Sinaloa. In those days traffickers were known either as *gomeros* (gummy producers), *contrabandistas* (smugglers), *cultivadores* (farmers), *hampones* (thugs), or *mafiosos* (mafia men). The term drug trafficker had not been coined yet, but Mexican society began to notice that drug production and trafficking had expanded and flourished enough in Sinaloa to eventually become known as the cradle of DT (Astorga 2016).

In those years, drug demand increased in the United States which was attributed to several factors, among the most prominent was American's involvement in World War II. Since memorial times, rulers have given drugs to soldiers in order to withstand the horrors of war and to deal with pain, fear, and misery (Bergen-Cico 2012). When the United States entered World War II official demand for opium grew in order to produce morphine for wounded soldiers fighting in the front. However, the traditional sources of the raw material (Turkey, China, Afghanistan, and Southeast Asia) were disrupted because of the war. Since the supplier routes were cut or unreliable, legend has it that the American government requested Mexico to increase opium production in order to meet the demand for morphine (Grillo 2011). Mexico's closeness to the United States would guarantee a steady supply of the drug in a timely manner. According to the official account, such situation never occurred but indirect evidence suggests otherwise. There are testimonies from opium producers of those days who recall going from Sinaloa to the U.S.-Mexico border (there are approximately 600 miles between Culiacan, the capital of Sinaloa, and Nogales, Arizona), to cross it and sell the drugs for cash (Grillo 2011). Regardless of whether or not this is true, opium production in Mexico increased considerably after the World War II (Valdés Castellanos 2013).

DT BECOMES CENTRALIZED (1951–1979)

The pulling and pushing factors that encouraged DT to thrive in Mexico during the first half of the past century not only remained intact but they grew almost exponentially, specifically drug demand in America from the 1950s onward. Ironically, the establishment of large DT organizations in Mexico (better known today as drug cartels) is correlated with law enforcement operations against DT activities. At first, DT was only a decentralized activity where pockets of traffickers associated with local corrupt police officers and politicians profited from the drug trade. DT was an independent business in the sense that individuals, rather than organizations, conducted most of the work behind it. Trafficking drugs is a labor-intensive activity that requires many people to cultivate, harvest, manufacture, transport, warehouse, smuggle, and commercialize illegal substances. In the early days of DT most of those activities were done separately. Certainly, many individuals who engaged in any of the different stages of DT knew each other and probably controlled one or two steps of the process. However, the traditional approach was that most of them worked independently, having no bosses above them and collaborating together when it was mutually beneficial (Astorga 2015; Enciso 2015).

During the second half of the twentieth century DT evolved into a more organized and complex activity that reflected another level of sophistication. Individual traffickers began to form small organizations to coordinate and control the entire process of DT. From collecting opium gum from farmers, packing and transporting it, to smuggling it into the United States, everything under one single management. After years of experience, traffickers looked to consolidate their activities to make it more efficient and profitable considering how time-consuming the whole process of trafficking drugs was. The first sign of this expansion was the dramatic increase in the cultivation and harvest of marijuana and opium. Like other successful businessmen, drug traffickers noticed that the economy of scale proved more cost-effective and lucrative than the opposite. Instead of manufacturing and smuggling small amounts of drugs they began trafficking large quantities, which demanded more raw material and a substantial increase in the production chain. Media reports for that time explain that poppy fields had become ubiquitous in Sinaloa state and that local and state governments seemed to ignore them (Enciso 2015).

The U.S. government grew more concerned about the flow of drugs coming from Mexico and put pressure on the southern neighbor to crack down on opium production. In 1948, reluctantly the Mexican government began an eradication campaign targeting the fields in Sinaloa first and other states later on (Boullosa and Wallace 2015; Enciso 2015). The previous year, the federal government had created the Federal Security Directorate(DFS)—*Dirección Federal de Seguridad*—to address political instability and the growing problem of DT. The creation of this new police agency signaled a major transition to confront DT from being a public health issue into a criminal one. The DFS was an intelligence and political police force known for its close connections to the CIA. The DFS centralized law enforcement efforts against DT in the hands of the federal government, unlike previous decades where local and state agents conducted most of the police operations against them. Thus, eradication campaigns and emphasis in law enforcement revealed the inauguration of drug prohibition at a large scale in Mexico never seen before mostly imposed by the United States. Mexico ended up reversing previous emphasis of treating drug use as a health problem rather than a law enforcement one (Enciso 2015).

As DT became more organized and demand for drugs expanded in America, there was an increase in the number of morphine and heroin laboratories for their manufacture. Considering the infrastructure needed to build such facilities (e.g. equipment, chemicals, experienced labor skills, premises, and official protection), only those who possessed the resources or connections would have been able to set them up. This suggests that more experienced drug traffickers integrated capital and assets to expand their businesses into a new level of production and smuggling never seen before. More drugs available meant that they needed to be moved to the north quickly and efficiently. Newspaper articles as well as official documents reveal how airplanes were used for the first time for transporting drugs to the border and sometimes to smuggle them into the United States in those years (Enciso 2015; Valdés Castellanos 2013).

Slowly but steadily the illegal drug trade became a major source of employment, income, and economic expansion for hundreds of communities in the mountains of Sinaloa and other regions of Mexico. For poor farmers it was a way for earning a living, for middle-class families it was a business to make quick cash, and public officials in charge of anti-drug operations a source of extra income by way of bribery. As the phenomenon turned more visible and routine in those communities, it lost its negative stigma as a criminal activity and thus became tolerated, if not publicly and socially accepted. These social, cultural, and economic elements surrounding drug trafficking added more complexity to it because they provide a glimpse to understand the problem beyond the realm of criminal justice system and explain why DT is engrained and normalized in many poor communities throughout Mexico.

All of this could not have been possible without the number one factor that brought about DT in the first place: increasing and endless demand for drugs in America. During the 1960s and 1970s there were some sociocultural events that led to an increase in drug use in the United States. First and foremost, it was the counterculture movement of the hippies in the 1960s that grew as an anti-establishment subculture that experimented and embraced open drug use as one way to challenge the status quo. Although different psychedelic drugs were widely used, marijuana was by far the most consumed substance during those years and its demand skyrocketed. Considering that most of the marijuana came from Mexico, drug traffickers' businesses prospered and the illegal drug trade expanded even more into the United States. There was some domestic production of marijuana in America in those days but not large enough to satisfy its growing domestic demand (Boullosa and Wallace 2016).

Second, most of the heroin and opium consumed in the United States back then came from Turkey, via France. The Nixon administration put pressure on Turkey, whose cultivation and production was legal, to stop opium smuggling. In 1972, Turkey prohibited the commercialization of opium and the trafficking network of heroin in France was dismantled. However, these measures did not disrupt the flow of opium and heroin to America, just shifted it somewhere else. Such phenomenon is known as the *balloon effect*, because when you press one side of the DT distribution network (like a balloon), the air—the drug flow—just moves to bump out another side but the balloon remains the same (Grillo 2011). This effect also forced opium producers in Sinaloa to produce more opium and marijuana and ultimately these traffickers were indirect beneficiaries of drug prohibition in Turkey and law enforcement operations in France because the drug demand did not change in the United States.

By this time violence and shootouts among traffickers and between them and the police were more visible and frequent than ever before as more competition and centralization of DT activities confronted criminals. This is the time when the word *narcotraficantes* (drug traffickers) is used in the Mexican media for the first time, but it will not widely apply to them until a few decades later. In the 1950s there was not a particular demographic or drug trafficker prototype to develop an identifiable trend in society. Those arrested for opium trafficking were farmers, businessmen, students, workers, women, and men, as well as upper-, middle-, and low-class individuals (Astorga 2016).

In the 1960s, however, experienced and professional drug traffickers took the lead to turn the illegal drug trade into a more profitable and efficient business to maximize its infrastructure. The most famous of them was Pedro Avilés Pérez, the first Mexican drug lord who organized massive DT operations in the United States in that decade. He has been acknowledged as the first generation of major drug traffickers and a primary figure regarding DT activities according to the DEA. Since the 1940s this trafficker was able to make connections with American mafia members such as Max Cossman, known as the *King of Opium*. In Mexico, Pedro Avilés Pérez pioneered a large-scale approach to cultivate close relations with politicians and public officials to gain their protection and facilitate his business. Among his lieutenants were two young men, Ernesto Fonseca Carrillo and Miguel Ángel Félix Gallardo, who would eventually become leaders on their own and control the first Mexican drug cartels later on. Pedro Avilés's leadership lasted more than two decades and he was killed in 1978 during a mysterious shootout near Culiacan Sinaloa with the federal police. Rumor has it that he was sold out by one of his lieutenants and ambushed after his whereabouts were leaked to law enforcement agents, a situation somehow ordinary in this type of illegal activity (Astorga 2016; Enciso 2015).

As drug traffickers cemented their businesses, their influence, violence, corruption, and lawlessness grew more powerful. The federal government was forced to take proactive measures to tackle and control the problem due to U.S. political pressure. As a result, in 1977 the Mexican government launched a massive eradication campaign nicknamed *Operación Cóndor* to end the cultivation of both opium and marijuana. According to official documents, 10,000 soldiers stormed the mountains of Sinaloa state along the borders of Chihuahua and Durango states (the famous Golden Triangle of drugs) in the north-central part of Mexico. There is evidence that soldiers engaged in human rights abuses against the local population by looting, raping women, and killing civilians during this operation (Enciso 2015).

As word of these abuses spread out in these communities, people fled to cities and states, sending hundreds of future traffickers throughout northern and central Mexico where they eventually would reorganize and open new DT operations there. With the support and technical assistance of the American government, Mexican authorities allowed the use of the powerful chemicals *Paraquat* and *2,4-D* as herbicides to destroy opium and marijuana fields respectively. The use of theses herbicides was controversial because it destroyed not just drug fields but also other crops that provided an economy of subsistence for farmers while causing health issues in the communities affected by the aerial spray (Enciso 2015; Valdés Castellanos 2013). As a result of this operation, the flow of drugs coming to the United States declined temporally. It truly disrupted business as usual in Sinaloa (the heart of the illegal trade) but it did not stop DT for very long. Senior traffickers moved out from Sinaloa to Guadalajara (the second-largest city in Mexico) to keep conducting their businesses while expanding and passing on the DT business into the hands of a new generation of traffickers. Violence also reached unprecedented levels for those years and 1976, in particular, was a bloody one with a record number of murders in Sinaloa as traffickers fought each other to control a piece of the illegal drug trade (Enciso 2015).

THE GUADALAJARA CARTEL (1980–1989)

In the early 1980s DT in Mexico was in the hands of drug lords from Sinaloa. They have moved in to the city of Guadalajara—the capital of Jalisco state—after the Mexican and U.S. governments had conducted Operation Condor. Guadalajara turned into the epicenter of the drug business in Mexico and traffickers enjoyed absolute impunity in their criminal activities. They had police protection by local and federal members of the security forces as well as state politicians and public officials (Grillo 2011; Valdéz Castellanos 2013). Given the size of the city and its metropolitan area, Guadalajara provided the perfect location for traffickers to launder the illegal proceeds and the opportunity to blend in as "businessmen" to hide their real mob credentials.

Unlike the violent DT syndicates that would flourish decades later with strict hierarchies and under the grip of one strong drug lord, the organization that eventually became known as the Guadalajara cartel was integrated by a clan of families, most of them born in Sinaloa. Among them were the following: the Arellano-Félix brothers (Ramón, Benjamin, Francisco Javier, and Eduardo); the Carrillo Fuentes brothers (Rodolfo and Vicente), the Caro Quintero brothers (Rafael, Miguel, and Emilio), the Beltran-Leyva brothers (Alfredo, Arturo, and Héctor), the Guzman Loera brothers (Joaquin *El Chapo* Guzman and brother Arturo Guzman), the Zambada family (Ismael El Mayo, his brother Jesús and son Vicente), Juan José Esparragoza and Héctor Palma Salazar, among other traffickers (Grillo 2011; Valdéz Castellanos 2013).

It is worth spelling the names of members of these clans since every one of them would eventually form its own DT organization and fight against each other or join other groups. Interestingly, the members of these families knew each other well and even had kindred or friendly relationships. For that reason they did not see each other as rivals in those days but as partners in crime—literally—allied in the same criminal enterprise. Each clan was in control of a particular DT corridor and border crossing with some kind of autonomy in the drug business. Clans, however, were organized by a kingpin named Miguel Ángel Félix Gallardo known as *El Padrino* (the Godfather) who coordinated the most important aspects of the enterprise. Like the rest of the clan members, he was born in Sinaloa and had begun his career as a drug trafficker in the 1970s.

El Padrino had a vast amount of knowledge, connections, and experience in the inner workings of DT to run the organization smoothly and free from conflicts between the clan families. As such, the group of clans under the Godfather's command became known as the Guadalajara cartel because all of them lived in that city and had their main base of operations there. As a seasoned trafficker Félix Gallardo kept an extended network of police and political protection around his illegal activities. He would pose as a philanthropist and businessman while keeping a low profile to avoid unwanted police attention. Also, he lured politicians and high-ranking officials from security forces to receive bribes in exchange for protection for his lieutenants and drug businesses (Boullosa and Wallace 2016; Grillo 2011).

The 1980s was a decade where large-scale DT activities shifted from the Caribbean to the Mexico-U.S. border because of more effective law enforcement in the drug corridor that Colombian cartels had successfully created throughout the Caribbean. Cocaine became a glamourized drug in America during this time and Miami turned into the epicenter of smuggling operations for the Medellin cartel led by the famous Pablo Escobar Gaviria. When shootouts, violence, police corruption, and money laundering became headlines nationwide, the Reagan administration set up a task force led by Vice President George Bush and successfully shot down that smuggling corridor. Demand for cocaine and marijuana, however, remained steady and disrupting the flow of trafficking did not make any difference in the illicit drug market in terms of availability and consumption of these two drugs (Boullosa and Wallace 2016; Grillo 2011).

As the Caribbean corridor for trafficking drugs was closed, smuggling them shifted to the Southwest border. The Guadalajara cartel benefitted greatly from this displacement of the illegal drug trade to the Mexican side of the U.S. border because it gave it advantage over the Colombian organizations that had to rely on Mexican traffickers for smuggling cocaine (the most profitable illicit drug). In the long run, the Colombian gangs lost their dominance in the DT business and the Guadalajara cartel began a cycle of criminal expansion that lasted several years even after this organization collapsed as a result of a turf war (Grillo 2011).

The Enrique Camarena Case

Red Ribbon Week is a drug prevention program nationwide to create awareness among school kids about the risks of drug use and addiction. It was created after the assassination of DEA agent Enrique "Kiki" Camarena in 1985 and to honor him (DEA 2019). He had been assigned to the DEA's office in Guadalajara as an undercover agent and through informants Camarena collected intelligence about a large marijuana farm called *Rancho Búfalo* located in Chihuahua state owned by Rafael Caro Quintero, a member of the Guadalajara cartel clans. Camarena passed on this information to the Mexican army and soon the place was raided and more than 10,000 tons of marijuana were burnt (Grillo 2011; Valdés Castellanos 2013).

Knowing that Camarena had leaked the information of the raid, in early February of 1985, members of the Guadalajara cartel kidnapped, tortured, and viciously killed the DEA agent. Camarena's death enraged the DEA and the U.S. government responded aggressively against the perpetrators and the Mexican government. It became evident that Mexican police officers were involved in Camarena's death and public officials were covering up and delaying the murder's investigation. The DEA launched its own criminal investigation known as *Operation Leyenda* to probe who was behind Camarena's homicide. Eventually the names of Félix Gallardo and two lieutenants Rafael Caro Quintero and Ernesto Fonseca Carrillo came out as the perpetrators who have ordered the assassination of the DEA agent. The two lieutenants were captured a few months later after Camarena had been killed, but *El Padrino* enjoyed a vast network of police and political protection that sheltered him for several years. It was not until April 1989 when he was finally arrested for the murder and sentenced to prison (Grillo 2011). Camarena's assassination was a watershed event that transformed the dynamics of law enforcement against DT in both Mexico and the United States. Besides leading to the debacle of the Guadalajara cartel and ultimately its fragmentation into a handful of new cartels, the DEA emerged as a prominent player in hunting drug lords on Mexican soil to bring them to justice in America (Grillo 2011; Esquivel 2013).

THE HYDRA OF DT: CARTELS CONSOLIDATE (1990–2005)

The capture of the Guadalajara cartel's leadership created a vacuum that was exploited by lieutenants of the organization. There are different versions of what happened when Félix Gallardo was captured, in terms of who would have the control and criminal assets of the cartel (Boullosa and Wallace 2016; Grillo 2011). The most accepted version is that after his capture the main lieutenants met at the famous tourist resort of Acapulco in 1989 to discuss the future of the business. Under a bloodless agreement, they decided to divide among themselves the territories, drug corridors, and border crossings to the United States which were under their control, based on geographical affiliation. According to Blancornelas (2006), the original agreement allocated border-crossing cities such as Nogales, Tecate, and Mexicali to high- and middle-ranking traffickers who were part of the Guadalajara cartel, however, only a few of them were capable of holding their positions and consolidating power.

The alleged mafia agreement did not work out as planned because of rivalries, personal ambitions, and economic interests. After a few years of internal fights, broken alliances, and precarious leadership, a few of those lieutenants prevailed and went to build some of the most powerful DT organizations for the years to come in Mexico. The eastern part of the country along the Gulf of Mexico including the border towns of Matamoros and Nuevo Laredo were given to the Gulf cartel in the hands of Juan Garcia Ábrego. The country's central trafficking route, including the strategic border city of Ciudad Juárez, was given to what became known later on as the Juárez cartel in the hands of the Carrillo Fuentes brothers. The south-western territory that included Sinaloa state and its many commercial interconnections to the United States was left in the hands of Joaquin *El Chapo* Guzman and associates and became the Sinaloa cartel. The north-western part, which included the border city of Tijuana, was given to the Arellano-Félix brothers and became known as the Tijuana cartel (Blancornelas 2006; Boullosa and Wallace 2016; Grillo 2011).

There were other minor associates or groups who had bastions or control over specific drug corridors, but were not powerful enough to form their own organization so they had to take sides and join a larger group. At the time, three organizations were able to control most of the drug trade along the Mexico-U.S. border: The Gulf, Juárez, and Tijuana/Arellano-Félix cartels. The Sinaloa had also a lot of power but only in its native state since Joaquin *El Chapo* Guzman was still doing time in a Mexican prison since his capture in June of 1993. However, after his first prison escape in 2001, the Sinaloa cartel began its growth into the most powerful drug group for several years (Blancornelas 2006; Boullosa and Wallace 2016; Grillo 2011).

These criminal organizations thrived in the following years after they began to conduct business independently. Considering that the leaders knew each other, it was not uncommon for them to cooperate together when there was mutual interest. Sometimes they formed temporary alliances to smuggle drugs into the United States and other times one cartel would pay a tax or fee for using the border crossing of another cartel and vice versa (Grillo 2011). By this time, the once almighty drug cartels of Colombia were on the verge of collapsing after their leadership was either arrested or killed. Accordingly, Mexican cartels cemented their strongholds and power in the drug business in part because the Mexico-U.S. border became the main region to smuggle drugs to America.

To give credit where it is due, the consolidation of Mexican cartels was also the result of drug lords' ingenuity and talent to traffic, smuggle, and sell drugs using pioneering strategies in the early 1990s. The leadership of each new cartel focused on a particular niche of the illicit drug business by exploiting the tight control they had over border crossings and resorting to technology. When that was not enough, like any organized crime group, they used corruption and violence. Such strategy led to a prosperous expansion of these organizations in terms of size, wealth, power, and influence to dominate the illicit drug trade to the point at which they formed truly corporative conglomerates. For instance, the leader of the Juárez cartel, Amado Carrillo Fuentes, began to use small jets to smuggle drugs and its success was such that he became known as the *Lord of the Skies*. He was not the first trafficker who used airplanes to smuggle drugs (the Medellin cartel and Cuban traffickers in the early 1980s resorted to this trick to smuggle drugs into Florida too). However, Carrillo Fuentes did it on a massive scale using a state-of-the-art flotilla of jets that showed his audacity and entrepreneurship to excel in the illegal drug business (Valdés Castellanos 2013).

On the other hand, the Sinaloa cartel specialized in building tunnels along the Tijuana-San Diego border using sophisticated technology to smuggle drugs to the north and weapons and money to the south. The Tijuana/Arellano-Félix cartel recruited members of Central American gangs established in Southern California to become enforcers and hitmen for the organization. Also, this organization began to use extreme violence against rivals and traitors to coin a reputation as a ruthless drug cartel. The Gulf cartel was highly successful in infiltrating law enforcement agencies at the three levels of government and co-opting high-ranking officials that provided protection and crucial information to run the trafficking business prosperously. The Gulf cartel also developed a sophisticated method to transport and smuggle large quantities of drugs into the United States using an efficient distribution network along the border in South Texas. None of these strategies were exclusive to a single organization, though. Instead cartels used, combined, and tested them all together in order to pursue a more entrepreneurial and efficient agenda in drug trade (Valdés Castellanos 2013).

Besides the cunning and cleverness of cartel´s leadership there were other external factors that contributed to the solidification of DT and criminal organizations in these years. One of them was the diversification of the drug market in the United States in terms of demand and drug enforcement. During the 1980s, cocaine became a popular drug that was associated with the middle and upper classes as well as celebrities and trendy lifestyles as a party drug. *Time* magazine and other media outlets ran covers and endless articles about the widespread use of the drug, its allure, and the dangers of it to the point in which America became—and still is—the world's largest consumer of cocaine (Central Intelligence Agency 2017; DEA 2018).

When the federal government finally cracked down on the cocaine smugglers, the Caribbean route was shut down, and cocaine trafficking moved to the U.S.-Mexico border. Colombian traffickers made a deal with Mexican organizations to pay a fee for transporting, storing, smuggling, and delivering cocaine. Basically, the U.S.-Mexican cartels would provide a sort of private package delivery service to the Colombians for a fee. Eventually the Mexican organizations realized that they were in control of the most complicated stage of the business and demanded a bigger share of the profit. The Colombians began to pay with cocaine instead of money which turned out to be more profitable for the Mexican cartels. From each 2 kilograms of cocaine sent from Colombia to Mexico, one would be delivered in the United States to the Colombians and the other would be payment for the Mexican traffickers. Ultimately, Mexican organizations such as the Juárez cartel began to negotiate with other Colombian traffickers to buy cocaine directly from them, ending the parcel delivery deal. This move finally gave Mexican cartels the upper hand and marginalized the Colombians in the cocaine business by taking control of the entire process of DT (except production of the drug) thereafter (Grillo 2011; Valdés Castellanos 2013).

Another decisive event that also contributed to the development of DT and expansion of cartels in the 1990s was the implementation of the NAFTA in 1994 that allowed for more economic interconnection between Mexico and the U.S. As a result, assembly plants (called *Maquiladoras* in Mexico) multiplied along the Mexican side of the border when multinationals flocked there to take advantage of cheap labor and proximity to the United States. Binational trade grew exponentially and so did border crossings into the United States to send back all the commodities manufactured by the maquiladoras. DT organizations took advantage of the new opportunities opened by the legal trade to smuggle drugs hidden in legitimate merchandise. As the two countries fortified their economic, cultural, and social interdependence, communities moving back and forth on the border increased border crossings and got opportunities to traffic drugs. Mexican towns located in border crossings became important locations to the illegal drug trade and cartels in control of them thrived with this new illegal economic boom (Grillo 2011; Muehlmann 2014).

DT Violence as a Strategic Tool

The period of cordiality between Mexican cartels that followed after the partition of the Guadalajara organization was short-lived. As cartels' businesses expanded they began to invade the boundaries of other cartels, leading to fights and violence. Initially, this violence was sporadic and geared towards minor and independent traffickers who did not pay fees to smuggle drugs in certain border crossings. Major traffickers such the Arellano-Félix brothers, Joaquin *El Chapo* Guzman, and Ismael *El Mayo* Zambada were friends during the life of the Guadalajara cartel and they maintained an amicable relationship afterwards. For instance, the border crossing of Tijuana was priceless for traffickers given its proximity to California (a lucrative drug market hub) and the profitable drug corridor along the West Coast. The Tijuana organization kept the control of this plaza and any other organization had to pay a fee to smuggle, store, and move drugs there. The Sinaloa cartel refused to pay and violence exploded between both organizations in what is considered to be the first most visible rivalry among cartels (Grillo 2011).

The battle between these two organizations lasted for nearly two decades and it was fought in different geographies of Mexico, not just Tijuana—although this city was the epicenter. There is almost a soap opera-like story behind this conflict because the main kingpins of both cartels tried to kill each other due to resentment, ambition, and personal vendettas. This bloody tragedy of traffickers has been described at length somewhere else (Boullosa and Wallace 2016; De Mauleón 2010; Valdés Castellanos 2013).

Violence is consistently exercised by DT organizations against rivals, police officers, and citizens to generate fear and command obedience because it facilitates their criminal activities. But violence it is also employed against cartel members as a disciplinary measure and to punish disloyalty, treason, and mistakes. Violence has to be certain, swift, and excessive in nature to maintain control and respect among the rank and file of the criminal syndicate. In addition, when disagreement arises regarding cartel's businesses, its members cannot resort to courts or mediators to solve disputes, therefore violence is the only tool at their hands to handle and settle conflicts. The same principle applies for organizations working together or under alliances to protect mutual interests. If an argument or animosity emerges between cartels, they will turn to violence to settle their accounts. Accordingly, when major cartels lost their leadership, middle-rank lieutenants resorted to violence against former mates to get control of the organizations, and this unleashed bloodshed that ultimately atomized cartels into smaller cells or groups.

Empowered Drug Traffickers Fill the Power Vacuum

Another interesting phenomenon that contributed to the multiplication of DT organizations was a political shift in Mexican society. The authoritarian government that ruled Mexico for seventy-one years began to lose the grip on power at the end of the twentieth century. It was a gradual but steady process that culminated when the regime lost the presidential election in July of 2000. This electoral milestone was viewed as an opportunity to veer Mexico into a democratic process, but expectations disappeared when the new government failed to deliver the desired change. An unusual consequence of this political transformation was that the centralized power and absolute authority held by the President began to evaporate and eventually disappeared. The central government no longer had the influence to control and rule upon governors and local politicians. Now local powers could challenge the authority of the president without fearing political retribution, something unthinkable when the ancient regime ruled (Boullosa and Wallace 2016; Valdés Castellanos 2013).

Most municipal and state police agencies across the country did not have the institutional capacity and resources to enforce the law against drug traffickers, and for that same reason, they were susceptible to be bribed by criminals. Eventually, drug gangs would infiltrate many local polices forces where DT was prevalent to guarantee official protection. In many cities and counties, the police would work directly to whichever drug group was in charge of the region and become its enforcers. As the centralized regime relaxed its grip of influence, cartels began to take over small towns and regions because they had the power and resources to do so. Through a radical version of the traditional carrot-and-stick approach called *plata o plomo* (police officials either joined cartels by receiving bribes or they were killed), criminal organizations were able to co-opt entire police departments and have officers working directly for drug gangs (Finnegan 2010; Grillo 2011; Valdés Castellanos 2013).

Local authorities were incredibly vulnerable to predatory practices from DT organizations and they lacked the infrastructure to fight back against them. As the balance of power was shifting from the central government to the local and state governments, drug cartels realized it was cheaper and easier to control the local police than federal agents or the army. During these years of consolidation, most drug cartels employed a soft approach using mostly corruption. Violence was always a last resort in the event that corruption or other means could not get the desired effect. All in all, drug traffickers benefited from the political vacuum left by the ancient regime which contributed to the greatest expansion ever for DT organizations (Astorga 2015; Finnegan 2010; Grillo 2011).

The Big Four of DT

During the last decade of the past century, four large drug cartels emerged as the most powerful criminal organizations that ever existed in Mexico. Their power and influence fluctuated according to alliances, political support from the federal administration in office, and law enforcement operations from the DEA. If a cartel became too powerful and visible, it would inevitably attract the attention from law enforcement agencies and its leadership would be arrested or murdered. This approach is known as the *leadership decapitation* strategy meant to take out drug lords to bring down drug cartels (Philips 2015).

First, the Juárez and Gulf cartels thrived in the early 1990s exploiting different trafficking strategies, regions, and border crossings. Eventually the Gulf cartel's leader Juan Garcia Ábrego was arrested and the rival Juárez drug organization's boss (Amado Carrillo Fuentes) died after undergoing cosmetic surgery to change his appearance (Boullosa and Wallace 2016; De Mauleón 2010). Then it was the turn of the Tijuana cartel (Arellano-Félix brothers), an organization that once was designated as the most powerful one in the hemisphere. As most of the brothers either were arrested or killed, the organization's influence decline and the group engaged in a turf war that fragmented its infrastructure (Epstein 2016). In a bizarre twist, the demise of the Tijuana cartel created a criminal vacuum of power that was filled out by the Sinaloa cartel. The latter gang flourished after *El Chapo* Guzman escaped from prison and regained control of the gang in 2001. The organization remained supreme for more than a decade until the *El Chapo* was finally arrested again, extradited to the United States and sentenced to life in prison.

The origins, growth, consolidation, and decline of these four cartels—Tijuana, Sinaloa, Juárez, and Gulf cartels—have been widely reported in newspaper articles (Epstein 2016) and books (Boullosa and Wallace 2016; Deibert 2015; De Mauleon 2010; Grillo 2011; Valdés Castellanos 2013) in both English and Spanish. It is not the goal of this book to repeat what somebody has already explained about these drug groups, just to acknowledge the criminal organizations' roles they have had in the history of DT. Thus, the Tijuana, Sinaloa, Juárez, and Gulf cartels became widely known as the leading organizations that, at any moment during those years, thrived and gave rise to other criminal groups that sprung up after the original leaders were either killed or arrested.

The criminal strategy followed by the four pioneer cartels was similar in design to the larger world of organized crime. First, cartels used a widespread network of political and police protection that gave them impunity and total control of their criminal activities without fear of incarceration. The use of corruption went beyond the traditional practice of graft by which public officials received money to ignore DT activities. Instead, it involved a sophisticated strategy to buy off entire local police departments, state law enforcements agencies, and both civilian and military high-ranking members at the federal government in charge of enforcing drug laws (Zavala 2018). Sometimes this structure of institutional protection in favor of cartels went so far as to infiltrate the office of the Mexican presidency (Ravelo 2012).

Second, cartels created an advanced and experienced organizational infrastructure that handled DT business in an efficient and competent manner, which ranged from drug manufacture, smuggling, and distribution to drug consumption despite the complicated nature of trafficking illegal drugs. Third, as cartels grew more powerful so did their emphasis on the use of violence to protect their assets and maintain absolute control of the business. To accomplish this goal, cartels resorted to an army of enforcers and sicarios (hitmen) who executed their duties in a brutal, precise, and vicious manner to instill fear among rivals and society (Grillo 2011; Valdés Castellanos 2013).

Finally, social and economic circumstances created a hidden economy of dependence within communities with heavy DT activities (where production, transportation, smuggling, and distribution of drugs occurred). Such dependency led to social tolerance or plain acceptance of the drug business in those regions as a normalized activity. This social complicity contributed to the success of DT because it eroded the line between legal and illegal businesses and more often than not the local communities sided with the cartels in detriment of law enforcement and the rule of law (Grillo 2011; Valdés Castellanos 2013).

For more than a decade, the aforementioned cartels maintained cohesiveness in their internal structures to be recognized as large DT organizations at work. Sometimes new faces or drug lords would emerge here and there to substitute leaders who were killed or arrested. Nevertheless, main cartels remained unchanged during most of the 1990s while DT prospered and its proceeds created an underground economy to sustain many poor communities but also mid-size businesses and financial institutions that laundered money. The expansion of these DT organizations came to an end when most of them began to break up into smaller organizations or disintegrate due to elimination of leadership, infighting, and the development of a new type of DT organization characterized as smaller, decentralized and more violent.

Compartmentalization and decentralization of cartels contributed to the expansion of DT organizations first. A more autonomous and fragmented division of labor meant that cell members did not know much about the inner workings of the entire organization, nor did they know the identities or whereabouts of the leaders. This change allowed drug cells to perform their duties more efficiently and independently and with little supervision. Having quasi-independent cells and groups carrying out different steps of the DT production chain made it more difficult for law enforcement agencies to disrupt and dismantle these drug gangs. If an entire cell was captured in a drug raid, it could be easily replaced by another one without affecting the cartel's main activities. Later on these cells gained immense self-government in their criminal affairs, and when the leadership was decapitated, they felt empowered to exist separately if needed. Thus after the arrest or murder of a drug lord, cells engaged in a turf war to control the remnants of the organization. This would lead to fragmentation and divisions where at least two new smaller drug cells—sometimes multiple ones—battled each other for the territories and drug corridors that the former cartel used to control.

THE FRAGMENTATION OF DRUG CARTELS (2006–PRESENT)

All of the original four cartels—Tijuana, Sinaloa, Juárez and Gulf—thrived, expanded for years, and eventually began to decline. As they grew bigger, powerful, and more influential, their leaders became more visible and exposed to law enforcement operations. Ultimately, most of the known drug lords and their subsequent replacements were captured or eliminated. The decline of the big four cartels led to a process of fragmentation where a combination of circumstances overlapped.

- A new type of drug trafficker emerged who was more inclined to be aggressive, competitive, and better trained than previous peers.
- The transition from large DT organizations into smaller groups was characterized with significant internal infighting that brought the use of gruesome violence to settle traffickers' disagreements, and
- Law enforcement agencies in both countries failed to predict this fragmentation and did not have a plan to counter the fragmentation of cartels that took place in the mid-2000s.

The strategy based on fragmentation and compartmentalization that benefited the original four cartels in their expansion and growth was possible because they hired armies of hitmen as enforcers to accomplish their illicit activities more efficiently. Some cartels even formed alliances with junior drug traffickers that had split from rival organizations to undermine adversaries. In the end, this strategy backfired because as these enforcers gained independence, experience, and control of the armed wing of the business, they turned against their former bosses and established their own drug cell. Such event usually occurred when the government decapitated an organization that gave drug gangs an opportunity to take partial control of the cartel's business. Sometimes a criminal group would split on its own and embarked in a spiral of violence that would fragment even more the original organization into smaller pieces (Boullosa and Wallace 2016).

When cartels were expanding and growing in size all of them adopted different strategies towards that goal: corruption, innovative smuggling strategies, developing criminal networks, and so on. A crucial tactic was to hire seasoned enforcers to protect their territories and confront rivals by employing brutal violence. The Tijuana cartel recruited gang members from the famous Barrio Logan in San Diego as well as scions from wealthy middle-class families in Tijuana as hitmen (Boullosa and Wallace 2016). The Sinaloa cartel restructured its cells of enforcers with street gangs such as "the Artist Assassins" (Grillo 2011). The most effective recruiter was the Gulf cartel under the command of Osiel Cárdenas Guillen. He managed to change the nature of DT in Mexico forever by recruiting former Mexican Army Special Forces known as GAFES (*Grupo Aeromóvil de Fuerzas Especiales*) soldiers who had deserted the army.

Cárdenas Guillen wanted to have the best hitmen to protect him against rivals and he lured an army lieutenant (Arturo Guzmán Decena, known as Z1) as his first recruit. Soon, the kingpin was able to recruit around fifty more men who deserted an elite group and other branches of the army and turned into enforcers of the Gulf cartel. The deserters became known as Los Zetas because the radio code for its first recruited member—Z1—was the letter Z and the group adopted the plural version of the letter Z in Spanish: Los Zetas. Ultimately, this group would become a powerful DT organization on its own that transformed the meaning of drug cartels in Mexico as explained next (Correa-Cabrera 2017; Grillo 2011; Osorno 2017).

Los Zetas: A Turning Point

By the mid-2000s Los Zetas were a formidable, well-trained and professional paramilitary group with cutting-edge knowledge on unconventional warfare, weapon systems, communication systems, and other military instruction exclusive of Special Forces. They were disciplined, efficient, ruthless, and deadly. Los Zetas became the face of formidable violence from the Gulf cartel directed at rivals, law enforcement agents, and civil society. This paramilitary force developed into a new type of criminal organization in itself that changed the landscape of DT (Correa-Cabrera 2017; Osorno 2017). With unparalleled military training and fearsome logistics to carry out any gruesome criminal activity with total impunity, Los Zetas group transformed into a killing machine like no other cartel had seen before and with no match by law enforcement agencies in Mexico to stop them. They developed a terrifying reputation of being a brutal and cruel group impossible to resist and capable of doing anything. This fearsome reputation became a batch of honor for them because it allowed them to expand and export their area of influence rapidly (Osorno 2017; Valdés Castellanos 2013).

In addition, Los Zetas set up training camps in rural areas to train new recruits in the tactical knowledge of guerrilla warfare that proved effective and gave them the upper hand against their former employer the Gulf cartel, rivals, and the police. Simultaneously, they took neighboring territories held by opponents using fear or violence but also creating alliances with smaller drug gangs. One effective strategy used to expand and control more plazas and drug corridors was their approach to pass on their military instruction training to other allied criminals. Los Zetas also used their fearsome reputation as a bargaining tool to subdue rivals and potential allies without resorting to violence. This tactic was promptly copied and adopted by other cartels and they began to use extreme violence as well. This escalation of violence led to an unprecedented surge of murders, shootouts, disappearances, and civil conflict never seen before in Mexico in the first decade of the twenty-first century (Correa-Cabrera 2017; Osorno 2017; Valdés Castellanos 2013).

Los Zetas is probably the most well-known example of how cartel fragmentation occurred after the big four cartels began to decline. When the paramilitary group Los Zetas branched off from the Gulf cartel, it formed its own criminal organization in 2010. Los Zetas had not only monopolized the violence as enforcers, they also engaged in criminal activities that no other cartel ever conducted such as kidnapping, extortion, racketeering, piracy, and gasoline theft. Los Zetas siphoned gasoline from government pipelines as a way to expand their criminal activities (Correa-Cabrera 2017). Using a very entrepreneurial but vicious approach Los Zetas expanded the area of influence of the Gulf cartel in swift and dramatic ways using a network of local criminals and hitmen.

This drug gang managed to create an impressive organizational structure that coordinated and executed their criminal activities through logistics only compared to successful corporations. In a short period, they expanded to major cities in nearly 16 states where they controlled hundreds of cells specialized in kidnapping, extortion, human trafficking, and drug dealership. Los Zetas built a true criminal corporation and unfortunately other organizations soon learned their tactics and imitated them (Correa-Cabrera 2017; Osorno 2017; Valdés Castellanos 2013).

There are different versions of what exactly motivated the conflict between Los Zetas and their former boss the Gulf cartel organization. One suggests that a lieutenant of the Gulf cartel killed another lieutenant of Los Zetas, then the latter asked the former to hand over the killers. They refused and that triggered the confrontation. Regardless of the reason, it is clear that Los Zetas accumulated substantial power as paramilitary enforcers and began to control territories, which caused the Gulf organization to feel threatened by their former enforcers. As Los Zetas become their own independent cartel in 2010, they started a bloody civil war with the Gulf cartel throughout the territories that used to control both groups along the north-east part of Mexico in the states of Tamaulipas, Nuevo Leon and Veracruz. Cities such as Matamoros, Reynosa, Nuevo Laredo and Monterrey became ground zero for this battle where gruesome murders and violence skyrocketed in early 2010 (Correa-Cabrera 2017; Osorno 2017).

In 2012 Los Zetas underwent its own internal fragmentation when the two main groups in charge of the gang disputed the leadership of Los Zetas and split the organization into several factions between the two well-known leaders of the group Miguel Treviño Morales and Heriberto Lazcano. Reportedly, the power struggle was motivated by several factors such as betrayals, business expansion, low-ranking members discouraged by their leaders' policies, and the inevitable use of violence to settle accounts when disagreement occurs. In any case, infighting eroded the influence of the group and, similar to other cartels' internal conflicts, the factions fought each other and sabotaged their criminal activities causing their leaders to be arrested or killed (Correa-Cabrera 2017; Osorno 2017). The result was that now several smaller cells of Los Zetas known as *La Vieja Escuela* (Old School) and the *Cartel del Noroeste* (Northeast cartel) are currently pitted against each other. They have been fighting a vicious war that includes drive-by shootings, murders, kidnappings, beheadings, and gruesome violence in order to take control of the drug corridors and all the criminal activities that characterized Los Zetas (Correa-Cabrera 2017). A similar process occurred among the big four cartels that ruled during the 1990s and early 2000s.

The Beltran-Leyva Brothers Split from the Sinaloa Cartel

For years it has been argued by the DEA and mass media that Joaquin Guzman Loera (known as *El Chapo*—the shorty) was the main boss of the Sinaloa cartel. However, since the early 1990s, there have been several leaders in charge of this organization besides *El Chapo*. Among them were Ismael Zambada known as *El Mayo*, Héctor Palma Salazar known as *El Guero* (the blondie) and Juan José Esparragoza known as *El Azul* (the blue one). The Sinaloa cartel incorporated other lieutenants such as Ignacio Coronel Villareal known as *Nacho Coronel* and the Beltran-Leyva brothers (Arturo, Alfredo, Héctor, and Carlos) into the structure of the leadership in a sort of federation, rather than a strong hierarchical structure (Grillo 2011; Osorno 2009). When *El Chapo* and *El Guero* were arrested in 1993 and 1995 respectively, the organization continued to run its criminal operations without disruption because some of the leadership remained in charge. It is true that once *El Chapo* escaped from prison in 2001, he relaunched the Sinaloa organization as the most powerful DT group of the first century but he was only the most visible face of it. The other leaders were always there to continue the business except that they kept a low profile to avoid unwanted attention from the DEA and Mexican law enforcement agencies (Grillo 2011; Osorno 2009).

Having a diversified leadership proved to be a smart strategy to maintain cohesion in the Sinaloa cartel, but ultimately it created a context that facilitated a fragmentation of the organization when infighting arose and leaders were killed or captured. The first major fracture of this cartel took place in 2008 when Alfredo Beltran-Leyva, *El Chapo's* right-hand man at the time and one of five brothers working as lieutenants for the cartel was arrested in the city of Culiacan (Valdéz Cárdenas and Méndez 2008). True or false, the brothers concluded that Alfredo's arrest was the result of a betrayal by *El Chapo* Guzman and they broke away to form their own organization that became known as the Beltran-Leyva cartel. Similar to other cartels' splits, this internal fracture led to a bloodbath between the two groups that undermined the Sinaloa cartel by forcing the entire organization to take sides.

Because the Beltran-Leyva brothers were high-ranking members of the Sinaloa cartel for decades, they knew all the infrastructure and people connected with the logistics of DT. Not surprisingly, the brothers used that knowledge to build their own organization while undermining the Sinaloa syndicate. The newly formed Beltran-Leyva cartel even formed an alliance with the remnants of the Juárez organization and Los Zetas who were willing to join the brand new cartel to fight their archenemy Sinaloa group—a graphic example of the ancient proverb "the enemy of my enemy is my friend." The Beltran-Leyva gang became strong enough to dispute and conquer Sinaloa cartel's strongholds as well as take over drug corridors and precious territories going toe-to-toe with its former boss *El Chapo*. In a short period of time it became one of the most powerful DT organizations, equal to Los Zetas, Sinaloa, and any other cartel. The brothers created several groups of enforcers and hitmen to fight rivals and protect their territories. These cells were strategically located in different cities and states throughout Mexico where the cartel had their main strongholds, which in turn created the context for the fragmentation into smaller organizations later on (Pérez Salazar 2014).

The success of the Beltran-Leyva cartel was short-lived, however, and in December of 2009, Arturo Beltran-Leyva (the kingpin in charge of the organization) was killed during a shootout with Mexican marines in Central Mexico. Thereafter, the cartel went on a spiral due to infighting to take control of the organization until it disintegrated into multiple cells. In the long run, the splinter groups formed their own independent organizations and became known as *Los Mazatlecos* (The Mazatlan people), *Los Negros* (The Black ones), *La Barredora* (The Sweeper truck), *Guerreros Unidos* (United Warriors), *Los Rojos* (The Red ones), among others. They ended up fighting a vicious turf war to keep some pieces of the bygone Beltran-Leyva gang.

To compensate the smaller size and the fragmented nature of these cells they developed a crime policy of extraordinary violence against rivals and civilians. It is true that gruesome violence was already a hallmark of Los Zetas when they branched off from the Gulf gang. Yet, the frequency, fury, and target of this new violence by smaller DT cells reached unusual intensity again. Needless to say that the problem of DT became more complicated to address because now a new breed of drug gangs took violence and criminal activities to a whole new level never seen before. This led to an increase of murder rates where thousands of people disappeared, and were buried in mass graves throughout Mexico, as it will be explained in detail in chapter 4 (Boullosa and Wallace 2016; Guillen, Torres Turati 2018; Pérez Salazar 2014).

The Remnants of the Tijuana Cartel

Most of the Arellano-Félix brothers that led the glorious days of the Tijuana cartel ended up in prison or killed during the early 2000s. Eduardo Arellano-Félix, the last brother to lead the organization, was arrested in 2008, and from then on the organization splintered into two major factions when lieutenants disputed the leadership of the cartel. One group was led by Luis Fernando Sánchez Arellano, also known as *El Ingeniero* (the Engineer), nephew of the seven brothers. His group fought a bitter and bloody battle with the rival cell commanded by Teodoro Garcia Simentel, known as *Teo* or *El Tres Letras* (the Three Letter One), who had been a Tijuana cartel enforcer since the mid-1990s under the orders of Ramón Arellano-Félix. Garcia Simentel left the organization and established his own gang, forming an alliance of convenience with the Sinaloa cartel to fight off the remnants of the Tijuana cartel. This split led to a local war in the city of Tijuana, and throughout the Mexican state of Baja California, between the two factions from 2008 to 2010 with a remarkable surge of brutal deaths and vicious attacks that put Tijuana on the spot as one of the most violent cities worldwide (Boullosa and Wallace 2016).

The two factions undermined each other during those years, and in early 2010, *El Teo* was arrested in the capital of Baja California Sur state while *El Ingeniero* was captured in June of 2014. As of 2020, some remnants of the Tijuana cartel have joined forces with the Sinaloa organization to control the city, while others have recently made an alliance with the newest cartel that calls itself Cartel Tijuana New Generation. Tijuana is a crucial border crossing for DT business given its proximity to California and the huge drug market in the West Coast; for this reason it will always be a disputed territory for any criminal organization in the drug business for years to come. Crime and murder rates went down after 2014, and the city seemed to recover from the bloodshed in the following couple of years. From 2017 onwards, however, violence returned to Tijuana and murder rates soared again to the point that it became the most violent city worldwide again (Martell 2019). The main source of violence was a turf war between rival gangs but intensified by the desire to control the city's newest profitable black market of methamphetamines and synthetic opioids (Linthicum 2019).

La Familia Michoacana (The Michoacán Family)

Like any other new splinter group in the DT business in the early years of the twenty-first century, *La Familia Michoacana* (LFM) organization was born out of smaller gangs blended together that coalesced under the leadership of several drug lords. The group's headquarters was the state of Michoacán (in particular the South part of the state known as *Tierra Caliente*—hot lands), located in Central West Mexico. The cartel made its official debut in the national and international news in September of 2006 when five severed human heads were dropped onto the dancing floor of a bar in Uruapan, the second largest city of Michoacán with a message: "La Familia doesn't kill for money, it doesn't kill women, it doesn't kill innocent people—only those who deserve to die. Everyone should know: this is divine justice." (Finnegan 2010, 3). The message represented a hallmark of the new category of organized crime syndicates that penetrated the social base of entire regions to create a context where drug traffickers substituted the sovereign power of the state and set up their own criminal government using support from the community (Boullosa and Wallace 2016; Finnegan 2010; Grayson 2012; Grillo 2011).

Similar to Los Zetas, LFM cartel not only trafficked drugs, it expanded its portfolio to other criminal activities such as kidnapping, extortion, selling protection, and even extracting "taxes" from local governments. Before becoming an independent gang, the LFM had an alliance with Los Zetas during the early 2000s when the later expanded throughout Mexico sharing their criminal skills to local gangs. During this time, the leadership of LFM was in the hands of three major drug lords who were all born in Michoacán state. Eventually, LFM got tired of being subordinated to Los Zetas and declared its independence by expelling or killing its former bosses. By then, LFM had established its own brand as a cartel and launched a strategic criminal approach to take over dozens of municipalities throughout the state of Michoacán. This strategy focused on co-opting local politicians by financing their electoral campaigns and bribing entire police departments in most towns to force the police to work for the organization. Those who accepted LFM's deal were rewarded with money and power. Those who refused were killed, usually in a brutal way to set an example for those who did not abide by the cartel's rules. As a result, tortured, mutilated, and decapitated bodies were frequently displayed in public places during the LFM's reign of terror in Michoacán (Finnegan 2010; Grayson 2012).

Unlike any other drug gang, LFM developed a cult-like ideology to indoctrinate its members through religious, moral, and ethics beliefs that fitted the criminal enterprise of the group. Allegedly, one of the leaders, Nazario Moreno González, known as *El Más Loco* (the Craziest One), wrote and published his own manifesto or "bible" that listed the main principles and beliefs of the gang. Because all members of the syndicate were born in Michoacán state and the group defended "family values and saw themselves as family," the group adopted the name *LFM* (Michoacán Family). As the group became more powerful, it expanded beyond the state borders to neighboring territories and cities in Central Mexico using the same bloody approach of taking over small towns and cities through violence and narco-politics (Finnegan 2010).

The criminal regime of LFM was short-lived and once the federal government began to identify its leaders, it unleashed a crackdown on them. The fact that the organization had local and regional protection from police officers made it difficult for federal authorities to capture or kill the main leaders. Around 2010, the cartel split because of an internal dispute among the leadership. As a result, a new organization called *Los Caballeros Templarios* (the Knights Templars) branched off and both fractions engaged in a brutal fight that left gruesome murders throughout the territories controlled by the two gangs. Similar to other cartel fragmentations, after the split, both bands formed alliances with other cells or drug groups to reinforce their strongholds.

A breakthrough that helped dismantle most of these two splinter syndicates occurred when citizens, tired of being exploited and robbed by the gangs, formed armed vigilante groups or *auto-defensas* (self-defenses) in the lowlands of Michoacán and chased away cartel members (more on this in the following chapter). As of 2020, Michoacán state and the former strongholds that were part of the LFM organization and its split branch the Knight Templars remain under dispute and gruesome violence, shootouts, high murder rates, and public display of decapitated bodies have returned to Michoacán state. Several new DT groups such as *Los Viagras*, the Cartel Jalisco Nueva Generacion, remnants of LFM, and other gangs are now disputing the control of drug corridors and black markets in Central West Mexico given the crucial role that this region plays in the DT business (De Mauleón 2017a; Phillips 2019).

Cartel Jalisco Nueva Generación (CJNG): A New Challenge

Another fragmentation within the Sinaloa cartel occurred with the killing of one of its lieutenants, Ignacio Coronel Villarreal, *Nacho Coronel*, in 2010 during a shootout with Mexican soldiers in Guadalajara city. He was an essential component in the cartel's business regarding methamphetamine and cocaine trafficking to the United States. The DEA offered $5 million reward for his whereabouts. Villarreal was also known as *The King of Ice* for his successful involvement in DT of synthetic drugs. His death generated a power vacuum in the region and yet another splinter occurred because different cells began to fight for control of the territory and DT businesses that belonged to *Nacho Coronel.*

After some drug cells shifted loyalty, they joined small groups of hitmen from remnants of the gang previously known as the Milenio cartel that engaged in DT activities in Central West Mexico during the 1990s. An alliance was forged among all of them and a new organization was born around 2008. It was named *Cartel Jalisco Nueva Generación* (Jalisco New Generation Cartel), also known for its initials CJNG. Similar to the Beltran-Leyva group, this new drug group became powerful and successful in the illicit drug trade in a short period of time. Although the organization was born in Jalisco state and had its epicenter of activities in its capital Guadalajara city, the group expanded rapidly to neighboring states such as Michoacán and Colima. Since the CJNG was not yet known by law enforcement agencies, it was able to capitalize on the vacuum of power left by law enforcement operations against the Sinaloa cartel (Gallegos 2016).

Soon after, the CJNG increased its presence to other states such as Nayarit, Guerrero, Morelos, Veracruz and even Mexico City, and like any other splinter groups it used gruesome violence and subjugation of the local police and politicians to exert absolute control in their drug corridors and conquered territories. The dimension of violence, sophisticated weaponry, and armies of enforcers were shown in Guadalajara city and its metropolitan area on May 1, 2015, when the CJNG unleashed a wave of violence against law enforcement agencies and public places to disrupt a police operation meant to arrest the leaders of the cartel. Using a rocket-propelled grenade, members of the CJNG shot down a military helicopter killing seven soldiers. This was the first time such an action took place in the Mexican WOD. Using a coordinated strategy throughout the region, nearly forty roads and highways were intentionally blocked by cartel members burning stolen vehicles (*narco-bloqueos* in Spanish). Also, multiple bank branches, gas stations, and vehicles were set on fire to distract state security forces and overwhelm first responders, among other criminal actions. The CJNG strategy of public violence expanded to neighboring states such as Colima, Michoacán, and Guanajuato where the organization had a strong presence and similar actions were replicated on that day (Partida 2015).

For some experts, the CJNG has substituted the influence and criminal activities of the Sinaloa cartel along the Pacific drug corridor in Mexico (Gallegos 2016). In fact, the former has become the most dangerous rival of the latter and they began to fight each other in crucial regions for the DT business. Tijuana is one example of this bitter fight. The CJNG actively looked to form alliances with other DT cells that became weak when their leaders were killed or captured. These two strategies—forming convenient alliances and overpowering rivals—turned out beneficial for the organization because it was able to gain control of multiple territories and plazas in a brief period of time that increased its dominance in the illegal drug trade (De Mauleon 2017a).

Previous drug cartels spent ten to fifteen years to reach the size of DT operations and control of key drug corridors that the CJNG built in only five years. As of 2020, the organization has a presence in nearly half of the states throughout Mexico and it continues its expansion into new DT territories at the expense of the Sinaloa cartel and other fragmented drug cells. Interestingly, the CJNG is the only organization with access to the Mexico-U.S. border from both the Gulf of Mexico and the Pacific Ocean, as well as to Mexico's South border with Central America. This access to the northern and southern borders and major maritime ports in both the Caribbean and the Pacific Ocean has given the cartel dominance in handling major DT operations because it can smuggle in and out of the country large quantities of drugs such as methamphetamines and synthetic opioids like fentanyl.

This dominance of ports of entry and borders where imported and exported goods and merchandise pass through every day are used by the CJNG to smuggle chemical precursors from Asia into Mexico to produce its most profitable illicit business: synthetic drugs. In addition, this organization has developed sophisticated money laundering methods using legitimate businesses such as high-end restaurants, advertising companies, vacation residences, and selling Tequila, among others. CJNG's DT networks extend to Europe, Asia, the United States and Canada, controlling most of the logistics of DT operations: production, transportation, smuggling and distribution of drugs. All of this activity falls under the leadership of Nemesio Oseguera Cervantes (also known as *El Mencho*), the main drug lord of the organization.

He went from being a small and low-ranking cartel member in the past to become one of the most powerful kingpins in contemporary Mexico due to his public display of violence against local and federal security forces and rivals. Despite the fact that he remains one of the most wanted men by the DEA and Mexico law enforcement agencies, he remains a fugitive. The U.S. Department of State is offering a record $10 million reward for his arrest and conviction (U.S. Department of State 2019). If he is eventually captured or killed, as he probably will be, another drug lord would probably step up and run the organization or its remnants as it has happened with other cartels, because the infrastructure and components of DT will remain the same, including the most common pushing (corruption in Mexico) and pulling factors (demand for drugs in America) of DT activities.

Cartel Nueva Plaza (New Plaza Cartel)

It did not take long to see a splinter gang from the CJNG, and in 2017, a lieutenant in charge of the Guadalajara plaza, Carlos Enrique Sánchez, known as *El Cholo*, began a turf war with its former boss Nemesio Oseguera. The details that led to the dispute are unclear, but it seems to be similar to other cases of drug cartel fragmentation. A drug cell led by *El Cholo* cumulated enough power and autonomy to act on its own as enforcer of the CJNG. *El Cholo* ordered and killed a financial operative of the CJNG who lived in the coastal city of Puerto Vallarta, Jalisco. In retribution, the head of the CJNG put a price on *El Cholo*'s head, and since then, the two groups have been fighting yet another violent guerrilla war in Jalisco state, in particular adjacent towns to Guadalajara city (InSight 2018).

Drug violence and murder rates are so high in Jalisco that morgues are overflowed. To deal with the crisis, some cities have rented refrigerated trailers to store dead bodies while dealing with the situation. With not enough facilities to park the trailers, some of them have been moved to neighborhoods closer to the forensic medical facility. In early fall of 2018, one of these trailers, carrying more than 150 dead bodies, was left in at least two towns. In these towns, residents complained of dripping blood, flies, and putrid odor coming from the trailer (the refrigeration system of the truck did not work). The "rolling morgue" (as this truck was dubbed) became an international scandal and an embarrassment for the Jalisco government, and shortly after the incident became news, the state forensic chief was fired by the governor (McDonnell 2018). Experts consider that the increase in homicide rates and extreme violence in Jalisco are related to the infighting between the CJNG and its splinter group. Throughout Mexico there are similar situations of morgues that have been overwhelmed by dead people who were killed violently. Murder rates in Mexico reached record numbers never seen before in the past three years, and there is no hope that this trend will change at the short term given that the roots of the problem remain unaddressed (Ángel 2019; Instituto Nacional de Estadística y Geografía 2018).

MEXICAN DT FORECAST

Given the complexity of the current situation of DT in Mexico (and by extension in the United States), the problem will not be solved or improved in any meaningful way in the near future. The pulling and pushing factors that have contributed to growth and consolidation of DT for decades remain unchanged and there is no political will in Mexico or the United States to take a visionary approach to radically change the current situation. Among those pushing factors are chronic corruption in Mexico, poverty, unemployment, and lack of opportunities where drugs are produced, increased drug use in Mexico, deep embedment of the culture of DT, and a widespread disregard for the rule of law (Grillo 2011). Significant pulling factors are endless demand for illegal drugs in the United States, continuous reliance on the WOD as the only approach to tackle DT, and reluctance to reclassify drug use and addiction from a criminal to a public health issue.

The arrival of central leftist politician Andres Manuel López Obrador as new president of Mexico in December 1, 2018, brought high expectations that the problem of DT would be managed differently. He promised to reassess the WOD paradigm and invest in social and economic development to combat the roots of DT. However, it is reasonable to conclude that there will not be any substantial positive transformation of the problem soon. The reason being that DT is a transnational crime that involves a complicated network of stakeholders (farmers, traffickers, smugglers, dealers, users and so on) in multiple countries interconnected by the profitability of the drug trade. National government initiatives can only contain the problem for a limited time before drug traffickers reorganize and adapt to whatever circumstances appear as a result of law enforcement operations. In the best-case scenario, the new president of Mexico may be able to reduce violence and murder rates in Mexico in the medium or long term, but these efforts will not dismantle or undermine the huge infrastructure of DT that has been built for more than 100 years in Mexico.

Likewise, there is a puzzling realization in the fact that the leading strategy used in the past three decades to dismantle DT organizations—*leadership decapitation*—has not only failed to achieve its goal but also worsened the problem. As mentioned previously, in both Mexico and the United States, there has been an emphasis on taking down main kingpins of drug cartels (through arrest or murder) as a tactic to take apart organizations. Experts (Philips 2015) and the current situation in Mexico alone show that such tactic has only fragmented drug groups into smaller cells which leads to extreme violence as these gangs brutally fight each other to gain a piece of the drug business. It is difficult to believe how the DEA and other law enforcement agencies in both countries are oblivious to this reality and despite evidence that the leadership decapitation strategy does not work governments in Mexico and the United States still keep it in place.

Perhaps the most graphic example of how ingrained in the U.S. government the aforementioned strategy is, relates to the trial of the famous leader of the Sinaloa cartel Joaquin *El Chapo* Guzman in a Manhattan federal court in late 2018 and early 2019. The drug lord was sentenced to life in prison for DT charges, a predictable outcome given the amount of evidence (e.g. dozens of witnesses, informants, surveillance audios, documents) prosecutors submitted to the court to persuade the jury of the criminal charges. The trial offered the opportunity for news entertainment (and for those who are unfamiliar with DT) to have a glimpse of the inner workings of how traffickers handle the illegal drug trade. The media sensationalized details of *El Chapo*'s criminal life as the boss of the fearsome Sinaloa organization providing details of his corruption tactics, murders, betrayal, violence, extravagant lifestyle, and his relations with lovers. The entire story of the trial could easily be transformed into a movie script for another successful mafia film and several sequels (Grillo 2019; Winslow 2019).

For the U.S. government, the trial was held as a success of American law enforcement and the diligent work that federal agencies are capable of doing to bring to justice those who dare to harm America. The conviction of *El Chapo* was interpreted as a victory of the WOD and an alleged confirmation that it works. However, the trial failed to bring attention to the complex nature of DT activities and the pulling and pushing factors that feed the American drug problem. It also oversimplifies the complexity and nuances of drug use, demand, and DT because it reduces them to a criminal justice problem only. Finally, the trial reinforces the DT narrative defended by the DEA (and those who support strict drug control) that this is mostly a black and white issue with an "us vs. them" storyline. The good guys are "us" (the United States, American law enforcement agencies) while the bad guys are "them" (e.g., traffickers, dealers, foreigners, Mexicans). The fact is this tabloid-like narrative of *El Chapo*'s conviction does nothing to address the real problem of high demand for illegal drugs in the United States, the thousands of Americans dying every year from opioid overdoses, and the criminalization of drug use.

As if that was not enough, illegal drugs have become commodities in the international black market and its commercialization has supplemented the world's economy and the global financial system. This implies that in countries such as Colombia, Mexico, and the United States, the illegal drug trade contributes to their national economies directly or indirectly through money laundering schemes, investments from drug proceeds, employment, and growth of the local narco-economy (McDonald 2005; United Nations Office on Drugs and Crime 2018). It is evident that the economy of DT is monumental and intertwined with the legal global trade in a way that cosmetic or timid changes at the national level will do nothing to address the roots of the problem.

Unfortunately, DT will remain a complicated problem or even become worse in the near future before it gets better. There will not be substantial changes that could undermine it or reduce availability of drugs, violence, homicides rates, drug overdoses or any other negative effect associated with it in Mexico and the United States. To honor the truth, there are few options on the table, but most politicians and public officials do not dare to invest political capital on decriminalization or legalization of illegal drugs that could cripple the infrastructure of DT permanently. The final chapter will offer an explanation on these options and why and how they could be implemented, if any.

The next chapter delves into the origins and nature of narcoculture, a lesser-known phenomenon that has granted informal legitimation to the illegal drug business. Although narcoculture has existed for several decades, only until recently it has become a subject of study because of its influence to understand the culture of DT. This phenomenon manifests in multiple ways through music, lifestyle, religion, literature, and TV shows. One interesting aspect of this sociocultural event is how it has been endorsed by individuals who are not affiliated to DT activities, yet they have adopted similar values used by traffickers. Let us examine it.

Chapter 3

Narcoculture

Social scientists know that in every society there is a culture, and although there are multiple explanations for this concept, it can be broadly defined as the norms, values, attitudes, practices, ideas and rituals that regulate everyday social situations in a particular community (Bates and Fratkin 2003). When a group of individuals gets together within a society and identify themselves through another set of particular characteristics such as ethnicity, religion, ideology, or any other feature that differentiates themselves from the parent group, their identity becomes a subculture (Gelder 2007). Thus, a subculture usually preserves some of the norms and values of the main group, but it creates its own rules, principles, different codes, lifestyle, and even language. A subculture generally possesses some core features among its members that distinguish it from the parent culture. Some typical features of this subculture are the following: having a common identity that is usually labeled as deviant; sharing similar values, symbols, practices, and particular vocabulary among members; lacking a formal leadership and adopting a more informal and fluid social dynamic between members of the group; and resisting the hegemonic values of the dominant culture through passive or active behaviors that adhere to the principles and codes of the subculture (Gelder 2007). Thus, queers, swingers, and heroin users are just a few examples of a subculture because they have been able to get together and develop their own rules, code of ethics, and membership principles as a subgroup within our society.

If this criterion is applied to drug traffickers and those who are connected to the illegal drug trade in Latin America and the United States, it is possible to conclude that there is a whole subculture around drug trafficking (DT) activities and the people who engage in it. This subculture is usually expressed in multifaceted ways and includes multiple categories. From music (narco-corridos), lifestyles (narco-fashion), language (narco-vocabulary), and religious beliefs (worship of the *La Santa Muerte*—Holy Death), to cultural objects (lavish consumerism) and a unique worldview (machismo, use of violence, and so on) that are all shared among individuals who adhere to these values.

The culture of DT as a social phenomenon has become known as *narcocultura* (narcoculture), but there are other synonyms such as *sociedad-narca* (narco-society), and *mundo-narco* (narco-world). Because of its more widespread use and acceptance the word, "narcoculture" will be used in this book as the concept that embodies the culture of DT. Experts and those familiar with the phenomenon of narcoculture have defined it differently, depending on the emphasis meant by who gets to define it. For instance, Campbell states that narcoculture is "a cultural complex or whole way of life centered on drug trafficking" (Campbell 2009, 17). Ovalle defines this concept as "the code of conduct, lifestyles, and relationships of those who are involved in the 'narco-world'" (Ovalle 2005, 3). Morín (2015) says, it is "a subgroup or minority organized around the trafficking of illegal substances that keeps some components from the dominant culture while developing its own culture of seeing, being, and doing in the world based on a style known as narco" (Morín 2015, 204). The central idea about these definitions is that narcoculture is understood as the ethos and way of life adopted by those who engage in DT activities.

To provide consensus and a clear framework to better understand this phenomenon, I define narcoculture here as the *set of beliefs, values, ideas, norms, social practices, and specialized vocabulary associated with DT activities, its ideologies or lifestyles adopted by some individuals who may or may not be involved in the illegal drug trade.* A fundamental component of this definition is that it does not only include the people who actively participate in the illicit drug trade but also individuals who are not implicated in that activity but partake or share some ideologies, practices, or ways of life related to DT activities. This distinction is crucial since some aspects of narcoculture are now part of the dominant culture in some countries such as Colombia, Mexico, and the United States where they have been adopted by thousands of people who enjoy or practice a narcoculture lifestyle but have no connection with DT activities.

Although narcoculture began as a subset of the dominant culture decades ago, today this phenomenon appears more mainstream and has become socially accepted (or at least tolerated) in some regions or sectors of society in Latin America and the United States. As a result, more and more people have embraced some of the features of narcoculture or its ideology through music, religious practices, lifestyles, and a specialized lexicon even if these individuals have no connection with the illegal drug trade. Not just that, narcoculture has been glamorized in the recent past through movies, soap operas, and TV series that romanticize—if not blatantly glorify—DT. One common approach in this glamorization process is to present a heroic and superficial portrayal of drug lords such as Pablo Escobar and Joaquin *El Chapo* Guzman, famous leaders of DT organizations, while ignoring the complex nature of the phenomenon.

Similarly, media corporations have found a profitable niche by producing and broadcasting narco-films (e.g., Sicario I and II), narco-series (Netflix *Narcos*), and narco-dramas (*La Reina del Sur* is a soap opera in Spanish broadcasted by Telemundo) full of stereotypes. In general, the main scripts of these productions are based on a parochial depiction of the narco-life loosely based on real or fictional characters related to the illicit drug trade with the idea—allegedly—to entertain viewers. The audience and ratings for these commercial products have been successful and lucrative for those media companies, which makes it difficult to take another approach (Grillo 2016). However, it is not clear whether these media productions are just meant to gain a broad audience to capitalize in ratings or they indirectly and subtlety are endorsing drug traffickers while implicitly providing a media platform that presents narcoculture as a harmless and lucrative phenomenon. Perhaps it is both since Hollywood companies and TV producers have always had a fascination for criminals, their exploits, and their personal stories as a selling point to catch the attention of viewers. This is something that will be analyzed further down in this chapter. Thus, the discussion should begin with the origins of narcoculture and how it became what it is today.

NARCOCULTURES RATHER THAN NARCOCULTURE

Narcoculture is not a rigid and fixed phenomenon that exists and manifests itself in the same way everywhere and always. Rather, narcoculture is a multifaceted expression of the culture of DT that represents the dynamic nature of the illegal drug trade and the people who are involved or have been influenced by it. There are urban versus rural expressions of narcoculture regarding fashion, music, and lifestyles. There is also an international variability of this phenomenon depending on countries (such as Mexico, Colombia, and the United States), as well as regional or geographical differences within one single country. Narcoculture can be similar in some towns but it can change from individual to individual. Even the type of work performed by members of a cartel within the long production chain of DT activities can influence how traffickers would adopt and display features of narcoculture (Astorga 2015; Castellanos Valdéz 2013; Grillo 2011).

There are also chronological distinctions in how narcoculture is understood and defined in the sense that this phenomenon has evolved throughout time to reflect the dynamic nature of DT and traffickers. Thus, early narcoculture lifestyles and attributes that characterized drug traffickers decades ago have been substituted, expanded, or transformed into new practices by contemporary practitioners of narcoculture (Astorga 2015; Grillo 2011; Zavala 2018). For instance, the way narcoculture existed in the mid- or late twentieth century (e.g. clothing, music, slang, and practices) is radically different from today's narcoculture that exists in urban settings like Mexico City, Los Angeles, or Bogota, Colombia. There is a broad spectrum of people who practice or adhere to the multifaceted elements of narcoculture—whether or not they are involved in DT activities—and these individuals may or may not share the same practices among themselves, but they indeed conform to the narcoculture ideology.

I argue that there are three main varieties of narcoculture: *Proto-Narcoculture; Gangster-Narcoculture* and *Adopted-Narcoculture.* The first one, *Proto-Narcoculture*, refers to the cultural manifestations of this phenomenon that originated in Sinaloa in the first half of the twentieth century with the initial values, norms, and customs of those who engaged in early DT practices. The second one, *Gangster-Narcoculture*, encompasses the beliefs, attitudes, and behaviors of drug traffickers that embrace (extreme) violence as a major component of their ideology, principles, and actions in their everyday life as traffickers. And the third one, *Adopted-Narcoculture*, refers to those practices, rituals, and ways of life that have been adopted by some individuals or groups of the dominant culture, but they are not associated with DT activities or drug cartels directly.

Proto-Narcoculture is centered on those traffickers and criminal groups that emerged first in the mountains and countryside of Sinaloa state and the streets and neighborhoods in Medellin Colombia where low-level classic drug traffickers' identity became known throughout the second half of the twentieth century. The main features of this narcoculture in Mexico and Colombia were—among other things—that traffickers came from a humble upbringing, were low-class, uneducated, and ambitious workers, and they depicted a masculine identity of macho and brave men (Campbell 2009; López López 2008; Wald 2001). As a result, those involved in DT activities developed a particular lifestyle and code of conduct based on their own sociocultural context. For instance, in Mexico, sporting a good quality and fancy sombrero along with a hand-made decorated (*pitiado*) belt and an ornamental buckle became a sort of early narco-fashion that was accompanied with cowboy boots to reflect an image of being a rancher or cowboy. Sometimes those who wear this outfit will also display expensive jewelry and gold accessories, such as golden bracelets, necklaces, rings, and luxurious watches, usually in an extravagant manner to make themselves noticed and to intimidate others (Campbell 2009; Wald 2001). Interestingly, this fashion style eventually became a stereotype of the traditional drug trafficker and many people who were not traffickers ended up adopting it as a personal lifestyle. Some of them also developed a ritual to exalt and worship Jesus Malverde as a saint (without the approval of the Catholic Church), a sort of Mexican Robin Hood who became the de-facto religious figure of traffickers—more on this later on—(Grillo 2011; El Paso Intelligence Center 2011; Wald 2001).

These traffickers would usually drive a pickup truck and would listen to *norteño* music and narco-corridos from well-known singers such as Paulino Vargas, Ángel González, and Chalino Sánchez (Wald 2001). The narcoculture associated with these types of drug traffickers was not the only one during the early years of expansion and consolidation of the illegal drug trade. There were other well-known drug traffickers, women included (Campbell 2009), in cities such as Tijuana, Mexicali, and Ciudad Juarez who developed their own type of narcoculture at that time (e.g., urban styles without adhering to the rancher or cowboy type of trafficker). However, there is no evidence that these traffickers were able to influence the main practices of those coming from Sinaloa which is considered the cradle of DT in Mexico. Once the values, principles, and lifestyles of Sinaloa traffickers moved into large urban settings, they became the default narcoculture and the most well-known identity to express adherence to narcoculture values. Among the most representative figures and organizations of this *Proto-Narcoculture* are Pedro Avilés Pérez, Ernesto Fonseca Carrillo, Rafael Caro Quintero, and most of the original leaders of the Guadalajara and Sinaloa cartels. All of the historical leaders and high-ranking traffickers of these two DT organizations came from the highlands of Sinaloa (Bodiguarato county and its adjacent areas in particular) and brought with them the narcoculture that originated in that state and that eventually spread out exponentially throughout Mexico and the United States.

Gangster-Narcoculture appeared much later on than *Proto-Narcoculture* given that early DT was mostly a family enterprise and drug producers knew each other well, to the point that conflicts and disputes were settled without violence as Astorga (2015) has fully documented it in detail. This does not mean that violence did not exist at all during those early years of drug cartels' consolidation. To the contrary, violence has always been a handy tool for traffickers to deal with rivals, betrayals, and officials who refuse to be corrupted by drug traffickers. Yet, the use of extreme violence and to brag about it (through music, messages, images, and mass media) was not part of the identity of early traffickers. *Gangster-Narcoculture* became more prevalent in the late 1980s and early 1990s when large DT organizations were labeled as cartels by the government as they consolidated their power and influence. This type of narcoculture cemented its roots at the beginning of the twenty-first century as old cartels fragmented into smaller criminal groups and they began a vicious cycle of extreme violence to impose dominance against rivals. *Gangster-Narcoculture* has been epitomized by Los Zetas cartel and other criminal groups that copycatted their gruesome use and display of extreme bloodshed as a powerful tool to advance their criminal activities. Traffickers who represent this type of narcoculture are not from Sinaloa and they were remarkably entrepreneurial by adopting new technologies (e.g. sophisticated Intel and weaponry, use of mass media, and terror tactics to conduct their business). They also expanded their portfolio of criminal activities to kidnapping, extortion, and human smuggling, beyond the DT business (Fernández Menéndez and Ronquillo 2006; Osorno 2017).

Adopted-Narcoculture encompasses those individuals who are not related to DT activities at all but practice or display some elements of narcoculture because they identify with them as a result of sociocultural exposure to it or enjoy the unconventional and rebellious nature of narcoculture practices, sometimes both. In places where DT has become deeply engrained in the community due to its powerful influence in the local economy and decades of tolerance by law enforcement agencies, being a trafficker is not an anomaly and the illegal drug trade turns into a normal and accepted activity. In some regions in Mexico and Latin America, the drug business is a dominant component in the political, social, and economic infrastructure of the community because it provides employment and brings jobs and wealth to people and local businesses (Astorga 2015; Grillo 2011; Valdés Castellanos 2013). Accordingly, those individuals who not are involved in DT are exposed and influenced by the broad range of activities, operations, and effects of the illegal drug trade because they live in the neighborhoods, communities, and towns where traffickers operate.

Community members then witness and experience first-hand drug traffickers' lifestyles, violence, power, and criminal influence in their everyday life. Thus, willingly or unwillingly, all of the expressions of the subculture of drug traffickers (e.g. music, fashion, and rituals) begin to be reproduced by mass media and society (mutually influencing each other) to the point that it becomes normalized over a period of time. Ultimately, narcoculture has transcended the exclusive realms of drug traffickers and ended up being adopted by some members of the parent culture because they identify with traffickers' lifestyle, ideology, or practices and want to imitate them.

ORIGINS OF NARCOCULTURE

The genesis of narcoculture is inextricably connected to DT and its consolidation as a major economic, social, and cultural activity in Latin America and the United States. Narcoculture has granted traffickers a gate to legitimize and socially express their illegal enterprises at the eyes of the community where they have lived because it takes away the stigma of criminality and it blends in illegal and legal practices. There is no one single cause of why and how narcoculture turned into what it is now. Rather, a combination of social, economic, political, and cultural factors have been the engine of this phenomenon where DT and narcoculture have grown, nourished, and mutually influenced each other in a transformative and dynamic process over the past decades (Astorga 2015; Castellanos Valdéz 2013; Grillo 2011).

In the early twentieth century, the first drug traffickers in Mexico were independent traffickers and regional bosses located in the mountains of Sinaloa state and northern Mexico along the U.S.-Mexico border. They conducted their operations at a small scale and mostly as a family business energized by the demand of drugs in America and the profitability of smuggling them (Astorga 2015; Valdés Castellanos 2013; Grillo 2011). As drug traffickers began to solidify their activities through stronger distribution networks, safe shipping routes, and successful smuggling operations, their businesses expanded. Along with this consolidation, traffickers adopted new behaviors, identities, values, ideologies, beliefs, and lifestyles that reflected their new wealth, status, and mindset as "successful and rich" members of the community. Slowly but steadily, they built their own status as entrepreneurs of a business that may have been illegal, but it was tolerated and admired by the rest of the community because it was a path to get out of poverty, make quick money, or gain social, economic, and political status. Altogether, this led to a new (sub) culture in Mexico and other places such as Medellín Colombia and along the Southwest border that was built on DT activities and shared by those who participated in the illegal drug trade, including their families and communities (Muehlmann 2014; Salazar and Jaramillo 1992).

Like any new subculture that appears in society, narcoculture's presence in society first felt subtle, marginal, and many times oblivious to the dominant group. Eventually, this subculture reinforced itself as it expanded along the DT business adding new members while its main features and practices as a subculture became recognized and singled out by the parent culture. In the case of early drug traffickers of the twentieth century, their subculture (*Proto-Narcoculture*) was little known because of the isolation of DT in rural areas and the basic and simple nature of the illegal drug trade during those initial years. Those who cultivated, harvested, and trafficked opium at that time in Sinaloa were called *gomeros* (opium producers). The term *gomeros* derived from the word *goma* (the dark brown paste extracted from the poppy pods to produce morphine and heroin) because these farmers and traffickers were in charge of slashing the poppy to collect the paste. They came from the mountains of Sinaloa, mostly from the town and municipality of Badiguarato, now famous for being the birthplace of many drug lords such as Joaquin *El Chapo*

Guzman. These traffickers wore hats and a cowboy-like clothing in their everyday activities, drove pickup trucks and displayed a peculiar demeanor (e.g. machismo attitudes, courage, personal independence, entrepreneurship, and street-smart behavior) that contrasted with the practices of the dominant group (Astorga 2015; Edberg 2004).

Being a labor-intensive activity, DT demands numerous individuals to be involved in the large production chain of manufacturing, transporting, storing, smuggling, and selling illegal drugs. There is an extensive network of people who collaborate together throughout the different stages of the DT business (farm-to-arm model) to make drugs available to consumers: drug lords, farmers, workers, drivers, watchmen, lookouts, foremen, enforcers, hitmen, money launderers, accountants, lawyers, corrupt officials, and so on and so forth. Unlike traditional street criminals, drug traffickers have never been isolated or alienated from social interaction and community building but quite the opposite. They are supported by their communities, families, and networks of associates in their illicit activities (openly or tacitly) because DT in those areas is understood first as foremost as a business and an opportunity to bring home resources, earn money quickly, get out of poverty, or simply to make ends meet. Crucial to this reality was the fact that violence and drug consumption was minimal or insignificant in the communities where DT flourished those early years, not to mention that there was little risk of incarceration since corruption kept officials on the side of traffickers (Astorga 2015; Edberg 2004; Valdés Castellanos 2013; Wald 2001).

Moreover, there is an intense socialization process in all this illegal activity that leads to extensive social network building in the communities where it occurs. Why? Because hundreds, if not thousands, of people who are part of these networks benefit—directly or indirectly—from DT. This socialization is extended to family, peers, friends, business, media, and the public at large through commercial, social, and political interaction, even if many of those actors are not directly involved in the drug business. As a result, over time the stigma and negative image of DT was taken away (at least in practical terms) because the illegal business became normalized and accepted as an ordinary lifestyle in the communities where it took place. Narcoculture then was the result of this acceptance and embracing (willingly or unwillingly) of DT activities and its economic and social benefits brought to individuals, families, communities, and cities in the years of its development and consolidation. But readers should not interpret this acceptance as a cold calculated decision made to earn quick and easy money. Rather, narcoculture and DT in particular should be understood within the larger sociocultural context of many Latin American societies where poverty, lack of economic opportunities, unemployment, absence of law and order, and discredited official institutions have pushed many people to accept and embrace lawlessness and narcoculture as a lifestyle and an inextricable part of their identities because there is no other way to make a living (Astorga 2015; Edberg 2004; Muehlmann 2014; Valdés Castellanos 2013; Wald 2001).

That being said, it should not be ignored that narcoculture is a modern concept that did not exist in the early developments of DT for most of the twentieth century. It was not until the mid-1970s that the term narcoculture was coined to represent the culture of DT. Although it would not be totally accurate to say that narcoculture has been always part of a drug trafficker's lifestyle and practices, this concept is the most representative of the culture of DT and for that reason it is adopted in this book as the most appropriate term to express this phenomenon.

DOMAINS OF NARCOCULTURE

As a product of social and cultural interactions attached to a segment of the population, there are multiple dimensions in which narcoculture occurs and is displayed privately, publicly and symbolically. These domains where narcoculture materializes are multifaceted and complex because they represent a broad range of the culture of DT and a large spectrum of people, whether or not they are involved in the illicit drug trade. Considering that the illicit drug trade is a labor-intensive enterprise and that many individuals are associated with it, there are different approaches and venues by which these people show their affiliation, adherence, or support to DT practices. Some of most common symbols and imaginary elements are masculinity, power, heroism, wealth, social mobility, economic status, and political statements. To present a thorough and proper analysis it is crucial to organize the domains of narcoculture into major categories to bring clarity and systematization while finding patterns and similarities of the several ways narcoculture is portrayed.

Thus, there are various domains in society where the culture of DT is revealed, produced, and re-created as a social, economic, and cultural phenomenon. Not only this, narcoculture as a social phenomenon has become commodified in the sense that it is used to generate profit. As a result, it has turned into a target of capitalistic production: movies, TV series, literature, music, clothing, and news about DT, traffickers, and their cultural artifacts are produced to inform and entertain as well as to make money (think Netflix series *Narcos* or the two movies *Sicario I* and *II* and you get the idea). The result is that narcoculture as such is affected by this commodification because its original meaning as the culture of drug traffickers has been changed and redefined by adding a commercial purpose into it that distorts narcoculture: either by romanticizing the phenomenon and presenting a sanitized version of it, or ignoring its complexity and seriousness due to oversimplification by mass media. That being said, the domains where narcoculture operates can be categorized as follows: music; language; lifestyle; religion; objectification and hypersexualization of women; literature; and television and cinema. Certainly, these are not the only realms where narcoculture unfolds, but they are the most visible, important, and well-known areas where it exists, so it is necessary to explore them in detail next.

Narco-Music (Narco-corrido)

Without hesitation the most notorious and visible manifestation of narcoculture worldwide is the narco-corrido, a music genre that chronicles the life, adventures, and culture of drug traffickers to the point of glorifying their lifestyles. Not only that, narco-corridos "often describe the exploits of, and situations faced by, those who are portrayed in some manner as outlaw heroes" (Edberg 2004, 25). However, narco-music is not just an apology or celebration of drug traffickers' lives but also a cultural and social manifestation of symbols and meanings (e.g., social bandits, heroic behaviors, social mobility, hyper-masculinity, and outsmarting law enforcement and rivals) that are intertwined with certain Latin American's ethos and lifestyles. This is one powerful reason why this music has an appeal to a broad audience in Mexico, the border culture, and the United States (Edberg 2004; Wald 2001).

Similar to other narco-vocabulary and language use in the DT jargon, the prefix "narco" has been added to the word "corrido," which is the original genre of music that gave birth to the narco-corrido. Corridos are songs with roots in Spanish ballad styles that the conquistadores brought from Spain to what is now Mexico during their conquest in the sixteenth century. Sometime during the nineteenth century, along the border region of Mexico and Texas, there began to appear songs that depicted the lives of cowboys and heroic outlaws (who move back and forth for what is now the current Mexico-U.S. border) along with stories of horses and dangerous journeys from one town or region to another (Edberg 2004; Quinones 2001; Wald 2001). These were the first corridos that Spanish speakers produced during those times and there is some controversy about whether these social ballads were a national phenomenon in Mexican culture or just a Mexico-U.S. border cultural artifact. There is no conclusive evidence to solve the controversy, but one fact is known for sure: the border region has always been a hub for corridos (and later on narco-corridos) where life, economic conditions, and social context have been the raw material that filled the lyrics and tales of those early ballad songs and ultimately narco-music in the recent past (Edberg 2004; Quinones 2001; Wald 2001).

The social, political, and economic context along the Mexico-U.S. border is complex, dynamic, culturally rich but usually misunderstood by those who are unfamiliar with the area. It is known that the border experiences widespread poverty, transient population, endless migration, intense border-crossing, strong economic interdependence, and ubiquitous maquiladoras that made this boundary a unique location for both Mexico and the United States (Bender 2012; Edberg 2004; Casey and Watkins 2014). Given the contrasting (and sometimes contradictory) economic, historical, and cultural nature between Mexico and the United States, illegal activities such as contraband, smuggling, and trafficking have been predominant since the nineteenth century, right after the current border boundaries were established. It should not come as a surprise then that people living on the border are familiar with those unlawful activities and traffickers, and as a result the border music (corridos and narco-corridos in particular) have portrayed that reality in their lyrics and stories (Grillo 2011).

The corridos as a music genre is based on waltzes and polkas where the accordion is a major instrument and the themes represent the lower working and rural classes. They include topics such as immigration, labor conditions, border social context, love lost due to migrating to the United States, as well as smuggling activities, celebrating heroic adventures, and stories of gunmen and outlaws (Edberg 2004; Wald 2001). The major themes of those corridos that preceded narco-corridos have included murders and other types of crimes, *tequileros* (tequila smugglers) during the Prohibition era, and conflicts between Hispanics and Anglo Americans.

During the Mexican Revolution in the early twentieth century corridos became very popular throughout Mexico and there was a renascence of this genre that expanded beyond the border. This music became popular because it elicited feelings of identity and sentiments that resonated with the sociocultural background of the audience. It is not just the rhythms and musicality that made corridos attractive to some communities in Mexico and along the border but also the symbolic, social, and cultural meanings of disenfranchised people who lived in a context of violence and poverty where little appreciation for the rule of law existed. These elements remained crucial as narco-corridos became a new genre on its own and audience spread out in Mexico and the United States (Edberg 2004; Wald 2001).

The switch from corridos to narco-corridos occurred as DT became more prominent in the 1960s and 1970s, and powerful drug lords consolidated their strongholds. As more demand for drugs in America lured traffickers to smuggle drugs and profit from the illicit drug trade, Northern Mexico and throughout the border there was an increased presence of these illegal activities. As a result, slowly but steadily DT activities shaped and conditioned the modern notion of the Mexico-U.S. border as a contentious and disputed territory where rampant illegal activities cross the border back and forth. Correspondingly, *corridistas* (people who write and compose corridos) began to produce songs where drug traffickers and smugglers became the main characters. These songs also narrated stories of DT activities, betrayals, executions, and shootouts with rivals and law enforcement agents (Edberg 2004).

Unlike what the media and many people unfamiliar with the subject assume, narco-corridos are not just a glorification of DT and the individuals associated with it. Rather, they are a compilation of messages, symbols, meanings, ideas, indictments, ideologies, exposés, and rich narratives that are represented through music in a particular sociocultural context in the Mexico-U.S. border, and particular regions and states such as Sinaloa. This context where narco-corridos are produced and consumed is occupied by different stakeholders such as traffickers, musicians, listeners, consumers, and society as a whole. These stakeholders interact in a dynamic and mutually reinforced process to create the stories, characters, and details that are eventually represented in narco-corridos (Edberg 2004; Valenzuela Arce 2002; Wald 2001).

Narco-corridos' topics are abundant and diverse because they represent the multifaceted nature of DT; however, it is possible to find some general categories to organize them thematically. Among them, the most common topics in the lyrics of narco-corridos were: political statements; depictions of real events or drug lords; accounts of heroic stories or tragedies; description of social hardships; tributes to money, drugs, and consumerism; moral and ethical lessons; depiction of corruption, police protection, criminal networking, and complicity between officials and traffickers; economic benefits of DT; and contradictions of the U.S. Drug Policy (Edberg 2004; Valenzuela Arce 2002; Wald 2001). This catalog of themes should be understood as a descriptive rather than an exhaustive list since the topics presented in narco-corridos are extensive and diverse. However, a common theme that appears in most of these songs is the use of violence in different degrees (Muehlmann 2014).

Crucial to the comprehension of narco-corridos is that they should not be interpreted literally since the use of metaphors, euphemisms, allusive language, humor, nuances, periphrasis, and double meanings are hallmarks of these songs (Paredes 1958). As Edberg correctly points out "many narco-corridos are full of code words, or 'narcojargon,' which are usually double-entendre references to actors or objects within the narco world" (Edberg 2004, 72). This characteristic is also found in Mexican verbal communication at large where indirect language and wordplay are common to convey humor, satire, irony, or mockery such as the famous *albures* (a sort of subtle verbal competition using double entendre where one of the meanings refers to sexual nuances).

Unlike traditional corridos that never used this type of language, the first narco-corridos developed a strong reliance on narco-jargon, metaphors, nuances, and wordplay in order to communicate the hidden messages of DT activities and the "reality or true events" related to it. Why? Because of the illicit nature of the illegal drug trade and because what seemed obvious on the surface of DT activities and crime news presented by the media may or may not be the real thing. By using this linguistic trope narco-corridos introduced a crucial element that would shape this genre forever given that some of the most famous ones include this type of wordplay. For a detailed analysis and examples of narco-corridos using this kind of code word and narco-jargon, see Astorga (1995), Edberg (2004), and Valenzuela Arce (2002).

The original corridos were usually performed alone by independent and solo male singers in cantinas, family gatherings, or men-only celebrations to get drunk and say unpleasant things about women (called *Parrandas* o *Borracheras* in Spanish). The new corridos—narco-corridos—that celebrated the life and death of drug traffickers and other themes became produced on tapes first and then CDs. They were later played in cars, trucks, and even on the radio. Concerts, festivals, and nightclubs became new venues where singers could perform live and entertain large audiences (Edberg 2004). This visibility of narco-corridos in public spaces in conjunction with the high-profile nature of DT in past decades somehow have contributed to idea of narco-corridos as being narrow-minded and—allegedly—made for and consumed by drug traffickers. Although this is not necessarily a false assumption, it does not represent the true nature of the phenomenon. This assumption ignores the broad audience and appeal narco-corridos have in society at large where these songs are produced, reproduced, and consumed by a large segment of society that has no ties with DT activities.

While growing up in Central West Mexico I remember that as a child I liked to listen to a couple of *Norteño* songs played by the well-known band *Los Tigres del Norte* (LTDN). These two songs were *Camelia la Texana* (Camelia the Texan) and *La Banda del Carro Rojo* (The Red Car Gang). The lyrics of the first one depicted the story of a DT couple, Emilio and Camelia the Texan, who successfully smuggles marijuana from Tijuana into the United States and they drive to Los Angeles. After the operation is over, Emilo lets Camelia know that he is leaving her for another woman. Feeling betrayed, Camelia kills Emilio and disappears with the money. The second song narrates the journey of some drug traffickers who drive a red car and smuggle a hundred kilograms of cocaine through El Paso and then they are busted ahead in San Antonio by Sheriff deputies because of a tip by an informant (Edberg 2004).

Under academic and mass media criteria, no doubt both songs would be considered narco-corridos since they do celebrate DT and glamorize the heroic journey of *narcotraficantes*. However, as a child, my family and I never thought of this music as a glorification of the illegal drug trade, nor were I or the people I grew up with involved in DT activities. These and other narco-corridos were known as Norteño music in my hometown, and the band was made up of a trio of musicians that included an accordion, a small drum set, and a guitar. These songs were performed and sang during family or friend celebrations to provide entertainment and dance to the beat of memorable Norteño classics that now have become known as "narco-corridos." However, my family, friends, and social network who enjoyed them back then never thought of these songs a narco-corridos per se. Instead, they were simply understood—and enjoyed for that matter—as another type of Mexican music that depicted heroic and violent stories but mostly served the purpose of entertainment in social events.

I brought in this personal experience to highlight the complicated nature of narco-corridos and how they are experienced differently, inconsistently, and many times in contradictory ways by different segments of society in Mexico, Latin America, and along the Mexico-U.S. border depending on geography, social class, education, context, and family upbringing. While it is true that narco-corridos have been cultivated and consumed by many drug traffickers and those associated with their activities, they are not its only audience. For instance, Quinones (2001) provides a detailed account of one of the most famous contemporary corrido writers and singers in the United States, Chalino Sánchez. He was an immigrant from Sinaloa who had settled and married in Los Angeles in the early 1980s and became a famous artist throughout the Los Angeles area and Southern California after his assassination in Culiacan in 1992 (where he had gone to give a concert). Eventually, California became a worshiping mecca for this artist. This is where many of his followers live now and many of them have no connection whatsoever with the illegal drug trade, even though they consumed his narco-corridos (Quinones 2001).

This is just but one case among many others to point out that the audience for corridos and narco-corridos goes beyond the stereotyped image of drug traffickers as the only consumers, and instead the example brings a more complex and nuanced reality than mass media and its commodification of narcoculture has attributed to the genre. Yes indeed, it is true that people associated with DT enjoy narco-corridos but this reality is much more complicated in nature because many people who enjoy and are devotees of these songs are not criminals. As I was working on this chapter in spring 2018, the famous narco-corridos playing band *LTDN* announced their latest U.S. tour and it happened that they were scheduled to come to Corpus Christi (where I used to live back then) on March 23, 2018. I am not an enthusiast of multitudinous events such as concerts, but I decided to give it a try to experience this kind of show for the first time. So, I bought a ticket and attended the concert. I was not disappointed with the show nor were the nearly 2,000 people who showed up that night and enjoyed with friends and family the dozens of "narco-corridos" songs played throughout that evening by the band at the Old Concrete Street Amphitheater. Just to clarify, *LTDN's* repertoire of songs goes beyond the narco-corridos genre. Even if they became known for singing famous narco-songs, they play a broad catalog of traditional corridos, and their followers love them because of their Norteño music style. As a side note, after more than five decades in the business, *LTDN* still attracts thousands of fans to their shows due to the popularity of their music and the quality of their performance on stage.

New Narco-Corridos: Movimiento Alterado

It has been discussed earlier that DT and narcoculture are dynamic phenomena that are constantly changing their meanings, forms, and expressions to adapt to the demands and realities of society and people. Narco-corridos are not the exception and a new genre of narco-music has emerged called "Movimiento Alterado" (or "corrido alterado" in some circles) *Movimiento Alterado* (MA) means in English "Altered Movement" and it appeared in 2009 in the city of Culiacán, the capital of Sinaloa state. According to some sources, two twin brothers born in that city—Adolfo and Omar Valenzuela Rivera—invented the concept of *Movimiento Alterado*. Then with a scholarship they migrated to Los Angeles and created a company called Twiins Enterprises that developed a niche to promote and successfully commercialize this type of narco-corridos (García Palafox 2011; González Flores 2013; Sin Embargo 2013). MA is defined as a musical genre that celebrates extreme violence (e.g., beheadings, torture, gruesome bloodshed, and brutality), its associated effects, and the glorification of a lavish lifestyle for traffickers, in particular those born in Sinaloa. In a more academic conceptualization Aguilar, Castellanos, and Pérez (2013) have defined *Movimiento Alterado* as "a group of singers and bands that define themselves as such and are apparently associated among themselves by a set of common references, themes, and goals" (2013, 7).

The lyrics of *Movimiento Alterado* also glorify drug use and the operation of heavy weaponry in DT activities to carry out the violence produced by the current WOD in Mexico and Latin America in all of its brutal reality, literally. This makes *Movimiento Alterado* a more extreme version of narco-corridos that subverts the original songs of this genre. Instead of musicians singing songs to drug traffickers, the musicians (allegedly) are the new drug traffickers who are singing corridos to themselves. In the past, the main narrative of original narco-corridos depicted DT operations, well-known drug lords, shootouts, drug smuggling, among other related activities to the illegal drug trade using a conventional language and double meanings, humor, metaphors, and wordplay. Now, the new category of MA narco-corridos is more explicit in the language of violence in both their lyrics and the videos created to commercialize the music. This new genre hypersexualizes women, celebrates drug use, and exhibits assault rifles and handguns. The protagonists engage in extravagant behavior, and the music includes a narrative where torturing, beheading, and killing rivals using gruesome violence is promoted (García Palafox 2011; González Flores 2013; Sin Embargo 2013).

A feature that characterizes these MA narco-corridos is the rhythm of their songs which is faster, altering the traditional beat that corridos and narco-corridos had in the past; hence the name "alterado" (altered) because the lyrics are sung in a sort of hurried manner. The songs are usually accompanied by videos as an inextricable part of the theme of MA narco-corridos. These well-crafted videos displayed with the songs, show explicit visual images and scenes that reflect how and why these new songs are "altered" compared to original narco-corridos. Also, the songs of MA portray a particular type of hyper-masculinity (e.g. fearless, audacious, heroic, and experienced men that know how to kill and are not afraid of death) with a strong identity associated to being born in Sinaloa. For this reason, it is common that many words and argot of MA songs reflect the local language that comes from Sinaloa such as *Buchones* (local name for drug traffickers), *Culiches* (demonym for the natives of Culiacán city) and *Percherona* (bullet-proof vest), with a very distinctive Sinaloan accent (Aguilar, Castellanos, and Pérez 2013). A simple search on the website YouTube using the keyword 'movimiento alterado' will bring hundreds of examples.

There are dozens of bands and singers who usually have a local and regional profile where most of their fan base is located. Among those singers who have reached national and international recognition and who has become the iconic representation of *Movimiento Alterado* narco-corridos is a singer named Alfredo Rios, better known as "El Komander" (The Commander). He was born in Sinaloa and began a career as a singer in a band named Comando Norteño. Eventually he migrated to the United States and partnered up with the twin brothers Adolfo and Omar Valenzuela and through their company, Twiins Enterprises, El Komander has reached a broad audience and a profitable career as a singer of MA narco-corridos (García Palafox 2011; Sin Embargo 2013).

Although this music is not played on radio stations in many regions of Mexico because it is assumed that the lyrics promote violence and praise DT, the songs are mainly distributed and consumed over the Internet. In fact, this is another interesting thing about MA narco-corridos because bands and singers who specialize in the genre have made extensive use of IT and the Internet via YouTube, Facebook and other media platforms to release their material and connect with an established fan base. In 2011, then governor of the State of Sinaloa signed a law regarding the regulation of alcohol that prohibited businesses to play or disseminate music that glamorizes or glorifies criminal activities under penalty of having their alcohol licenses cancelled. It was meant to target narco-corridos without naming names. There was debate and disagreement about this controversial law and the Mexican Supreme Court ended up deciding against the governor as this was a case of him over-reaching his authority by stepping on a matter assigned to local jurisdiction (González Flores 2013). Despite that legal decision, most radio stations in Sinaloa and throughout Mexico have refused to play narco-corridos, in particular those songs from *Movimiento Alterado* bands. Yet, people still play this music in public areas such as markets, parks, plazas, and trucks and cars while cruising cities and rural towns with the understanding that listening to these songs is a personal choice based on cultural and social mores rather than a literal adherence to DT culture or activities.

All in all, it is controversial to claim that narco-corridos, even those from the *Movimiento Alterado* genre, should be classified solely as an anthem or celebration of DT or the lifestyle of those who are involved in the illegal drug trade. Instead, their nature, distribution, and consumption among non-drug traffickers occur as a sociocultural trend that comes from a complicated and elaborate process that allows people to rebel or challenge the official narrative of DT via this music. At the same time, narco-corridos are a crucial part of the identity of DT activities and the people who are part of this illegal business. As such, this music genre is a true manifestation of the culture of DT in a context where the influence of this music is widespread and tolerated.

In a new twist about the endless dynamism of narco-corridos, there is a new music genre called "Trap-Corrido" that corroborates the social power and influence of narcoculture. Trap-corrido is a mix of trap music and corridos, the former a genre of hip-hop that was born in the South—mainly Atlanta but other places too—and the latter referring to Mexican ballads from the nineteenth century as explained earlier (Drake 2012; Edberg 2004). Trap-corrido is a recent phenomenon that originated in Southern California created by second-generation Mexican-American kids. They grew up listening to corridos in their homes but were also exposed to urban music such as rap and hip-hop along with the hardship of living in the "hood" and the problems associated with gangs, drug dealings, street hustlers, and violence on the streets of California (Thompson-Hernández 2019). These personal experiences have become the lyrics of trap-corridos and as a new genre of its own, mixing black and Latino beats that reflect the new demographics and diversity of conflicting urban settings.

Similar to narco-corridos, trap-corridos describe the stories, lifestyle, and conflicts of people who engage in DT activities or other unlawful behaviors regarding young, male, people of color. Major differences is that trap-corridos do not use the accordion that is so pervasive in narco-corridos, the setting of the narrative is now urban rather than rural, and instead of cowboy boots and ranchero clothing, trap-corridos singers wear high-end clothing from brands such as Balenciaga, Gucci, and Nike Jordans (Thompson-Hernández 2019). Sold-out concerts in California, Mexico and other locations by bands such as *Arsenal Efectivo* and *Fuerza Regida* reveal the extent to which this genre is captivating people who are not associated with DT but enjoy the rhythms and lyrics of trap-corridos (Thompson-Hernández 2019).

Narco-Language

Like any other subculture, drug traffickers and narcoculture have generated their own slang that is used and shared by those involved in the illegal drug trade. Narco-language was born in Latin America (mostly in Colombia and Mexico) but it has become a worldwide phenomenon as a result of the commodification of narcoculture by powerful entertainment companies (e.g. Netflix), movie conglomerates, television soap operas, books, music, and mass media's extensive focus on DT news and the WOD.

Narco-language as a phenomenon has become a new semantic field where a set of words denote a particular subject (DT activities). I define narco-language as *a complex lexicon of words, concepts, and slang to describe the entire reality where DT and traffickers operate*. This language is mostly used by those involved in the illicit drug trade, but it is not exclusive to them. Unlike what most people may assume, some concepts and argot of narco-language have been invented by mass media, society, and people living in or near cartels' territories to identify traffickers' criminal behaviors and their activities in order to make sense of the dangers and risks they are exposed to in everyday life in those places.

The most common word to identify narco-language is through the prefix *narco* which means both a drug lifestyle (*lo narco*) and a drug trafficker (*un narco*). Most of the lingo of narco-language is morbid by nature (it refers to grim and brutal actions such as killings, violence, and crime scenes) but it is also descriptive and explicit to designate with precision a particular event, phenomenon, or action. As such, it is dynamic and constantly changing by adopting new words as means to keep up with the influential nature of DT. Most of the narco-language argot is relatively new because it has been coined as the battle between criminal gangs and DT organizations has intensified in the past decades, and the use of extreme violence has come to be normalized in some places. As a result, narco-language has evolved as a crude reality to portray the brutality and gruesome nature of how drug cartels and their successive factions conduct their businesses to keep influence in their strongholds or make gains against rivals, law enforcement agencies, and the government (Campbell 2009; Saldívar Arreola 2012).

A crucial question to explain this conundrum of narco-jargon is to answer the following question: How did narco-language come to exist? The answer to it is problematic because there is no one single factor contributing to this phenomenon. However, it can be explained by looking at the nature of DT and how it is accomplished. As a labor-intensive activity DT uses an extensive social network to carry on its illegal activities. As a result, there is a strong socialization process by which individuals in the illegal drug trade interact, talk, get together, meet, and do businesses as part of the crucial role of the large chain of production that DT activities require to exist.

As DT became socially accepted in many communities and towns, traffickers developed their own lifestyles, practices, mores, and principles to reflect their new roles (*Proto-Narcoculture*). From rural areas in Sinaloa, narcoculture traveled to large urban settings such as Culiacán and many cities along the Mexico-U.S. border. This expansion contributed to the consolidation of the illegal drug trade by which narcoculture and narco-language became mainstream. Additionally, mass media and society have both contributed to the production and reproduction of narco-language by adopting and imitating narcoculture in ways that sometimes are difficult to single out and explain.

On unpacking the concept of narco-language, it is possible to identify some clear patterns of this lingo. First, the words, concepts, and slang of narco-language refer to drug traffickers' illegal behavior, actions, or specific components of the illegal drug business (e.g. narco-tienda—drug dealing location where drugs are sold in small quantities). Second, the use of the prefix "narco" alludes to some concepts related to DT behaviors and actions; however, there is abundant narco-language and words with no reference to the prefix "narco" such as *levantado, encajuelado, plaza*, and so on. Third, some phrases, concepts, or slang may refer to a complex illegal behavior or activity from drug traffickers or a context where these individuals are the main characters, or they exert great influence in that context. Words such as narco-state, narco-corrido, or narco-religion are examples of this category. Fourth, drug traffickers are not the only authors of narco-language. Mass media, the press in particular, entertainment corporations, and society have also contributed to this phenomenon in a collaborative manner through the commodification and reification of narcoculture. Finally, narco-language absorbs the gruesome nature of (extreme) violence used by drug traffickers while making it easier to handle its content among people affected by this phenomenon and the media. Narco-language underplays the sordid part of DT, while at the same time helps to normalize DT by using words and concepts that are accepted and adopted by society at large in order to make sense of behaviors, events, and actions performed by drug traffickers (Blog del Narco 2018; Campbell 2009; Saldívar Arreola 2012).

Narco-language is not a new phenomenon, nor is it a Mexican invention. In the early 1980s, during the apogee of the Medellin cartel led by Pablo Escobar Gaviria in Colombia, cartel members developed some sort of narco-language and identity around their illicit activities. Words such as *parcero* (friend), *muñeco* (literally doll but meaning dead body), *parche* (gathering place) and *traqueto* (drug trafficker) became part of the vocabulary of these gangsters and many young people in the city of Medellin began to reproduce it after hearing it on the street, television or movies because it became fashionable (Millán Valencia 2017). Eventually, as the flow of drugs shifted from the Caribbean to the Mexico-U.S. border and drug cartels in Mexico cemented their strongholds, narco-language developed and consolidated in regions and places with heavy presence of DT activities throughout Mexico and along its northern border.

It is not the intention of this book to present a dictionary of narco-language; however, I consider it critical to include and list with some of the most well-known words and concepts of this lingo in order to inform the reader. The concepts and words listed here come from academic and non-academic sources given that many terms are restricted to some regions, people, or particular communities such as blogs, drug users, or smugglers, and therefore the words are difficult to find everywhere. Among the most frequent and used concepts of narco-language are the following, on the understanding that this list is meant to be descriptive rather than exhaustive (Blog del Narco 2018; Campbell 2009; Saldívar Arreola 2012; Valdez Cárdenas 2016):

Narco-abogado, an elite defense attorney who represents in court a well-known drug lord, with the assumption that he or she may or may not become a courier between his client and the DT organization. *Narco-beauty queens*, young women who participate and win beauty contests and eventually become girlfriends, partners, or lovers of drug gang leaders. *Narco-fosas*, mass graves where traffickers have buried rivals or their victims. *Narco-mantas*, narco-messages left in banners at public places such as pedestrian bridges, plazas, and highways to reveal police or official corruption or to intimidate rivals; among others (see Glossary for more narco-language).

The list of words with the prefix "narco" could go on and on since the activities and behavior that drug traffickers engage in are limitless. That being said, not all of the words and phrases of narco-language use the prefix "narco," to denote their activities. Many of these concepts have a unique spelling derived from an object, verb, or action that has no relation with DT activities (Blog del Narco 2018; Campbell 2009; Saldívar Arreola 2012; Váldez Cárdenas 2016). Among the most common and well-used of narco-language words without the prefix "narco" are the following examples:

Buchona, an extravagant and hypersexualized woman that is the girlfriend or partner of a drug trafficker. *Calcinado*, a burnt body usually found in a car. *Calentar la plaza*, literally means to heat up the public square, but in narco-language means to challenge the control of a criminal gang that rules a territory by engaging in high-profile brutal killings to attract the attention of federal law enforcement. *Levantón*, to kidnap someone to torture and kill him. *Pozolear*, literally means soup or stew, but in the context of narco-language refers to the disintegration of a human body in a 55-gallon steel drum using caustic soda, among other items.

This is also a specialized jargon among some DT activities such as dealing with journalists covering DT activities, consuming drugs, and even living in certain geographical regions such as border cities like Mexicali, Tijuana, or where DT activities are prominent (Saldívar Arreola 2012; Váldez Cárdenas 2016). Some examples of this particular lingo of narco-language are the following: *Arponear*, literally means to harpoon, but it refers to intravenous injecting of drugs like heroin. *Manitas*, slapping a journalist as punishment for reporting news against cartel's commands. *Piso*, to murder a journalist who has not followed the rules of a criminal gang. *Tijera*, to mutilate a journalist as punishment for not obeying cartel's orders (Váldez Cárdenas 2016).

There is not enough research to determine with certainty and statistics how widespread the use of narco-language is in Mexico, along the border, the United States and where the presence of DT occurs. However, some experts (Campbell 2009; Saldívar Arreola 2012) argue that it is somehow common among certain communities and people who are exposed to narcoculture or live in a place where DT activities are prevalent. For instance, according to Saldívar Arreola (2012), who conducted an applied linguistic analysis of narco-language in Baja California, Mexico used different sources (e.g. interviews, archives, and mass media outlets) to measure the presence of this lingo among some communities. Although his approach cannot be generalized since the sample of his data is not representative, it provides an idea about the inner workings of this phenomenon. He found that narco-language is more common among males than females but is equally present in both young and old generations (Saldívar Arreola 2012).

Additionally, being exposed to some of the most common manifestations of narcoculture such as music, narco-telenovelas, blogs, newspapers, and mass media can influence how much and to what degree someone uses any of these narco-words. It should be pointed out that many specialized terms of narco-language have no widespread or national recognition in Mexico (only among marginal communities or those who are directly involved in drug use or DT activities). This explains why it is difficult to keep track of words identified as part of this lingo, and why it is hard to create a final list of all narco-language terms.

Interestingly, given the ubiquitous presence of narco-language in Mexico and Latin America, the official institution in charge of overseeing the Spanish language, the Royal Spanish Academy (*Real Academia Española*) in affiliation with twenty-three independent academies in the Spanish-speaking world, the Association of Academies of the Spanish Language (*Asociación de Academias de la Lengua Española*), published in 2010 the first dictionary of Latin American terms (*Diccionario de Americanismos*). This dictionary included for the first time the lingo of narco-language and words such as *levantón*, *plomear*, and *narco-corrido* are now officially part of the Spanish language (Asociación de Academias de la Lengua Española 2015). This fact is revealing in itself, because it provides enough evidence that narco-language and narcoculture have left behind their marginal status and became mainstream cultural and social components in many communities and countries at large.

In sum, narco-language is here to stay and evolve with new concepts and words as it is inextricably connected to DT activities and the people who are exposed to narcoculture one way or another. Although the use of narco-language contributes to the normalization of drug traffickers' violence by providing euphemisms that put aside the brutality of their behavior, this lingo also helps to make sense of the complex, unpredictable, and dynamic nature of DT. Like any language, narco-language creates a new reality that allows its users (drug traffickers or anyone living in proximity to the illegal drug trade) to make sense of a world that is new, violent, unpredictable, and difficult to grasp. In addition, narco-language has become a global phenomenon thanks to mass media and a new genre of cultural artifacts such as literature, music, cinema, and TV series. Finally, the presence of narco-language in the mass media has shed light on the intricacies of DT activities, its perpetrators, and many of the most atrocious aspects of the War on Drugs in Latin America, albeit for a stereotyped perspective.

Last but not least, narco-language should not be confused with coded language used by drug traffickers over the phone or any electronic communication devices used to disguise their illicit operations from law enforcement surveillance operations. Similar to the police or first responders who use radio codes to simplify and provide accuracy to their communications, drug smugglers and traffickers use creative codes and words while communicating among themselves over the phone or other electronic devices to mislead or deceive potential surveillance from law enforcement agencies. These codes and words are not narco-language, nor are they related to narcoculture, instead they are meant as a simple strategy to play the cat-and-mouse game that DT has become. Drug gang members hope that by using coded words it will make it more difficult for law enforcement surveillance teams to identify cartel operatives' voices, operations, and plans to disrupt their criminal activities.

Narco-Lifestyle

Narco-lifestyle refers to the way in which drug traffickers experience their social and personal lives as well as the products, items, and merchandize used by them to appear in social settings. The stereotypical image of these individuals has been captured in many narco-corridos songs that depict traffickers as, "gunslinging machos, decked out in flamboyant outfits. The classic attire consists of an expensive Tejana cowboy hat, kilos of gold necklaces, medallions, bracelets, rings, and brightly colored silk Western shirt, and *cinto piteado* (woven ixtle fiber belt), Levi's jeans, and sharp-pointed boots made of exotic animal skins" (Campbell 2009, 24). There are other features that are immediately associated with this appearance such as driving the newest and most expensive trucks, having a lavish lifestyle, living in huge unpalatable mansions, and throwing parties ostentatiously with prostitutes, drugs, and feast-like celebrations. As Campbell (2009) correctly points out, this image is a caricature of drug traffickers because not all of them have the same hierarchical status within the cartels' organization (hence most cannot afford such a pricey lifestyle), nor can these outlaws be conflated into one single and homogenous category of trafficker, and therefore, one single narco-lifestyle is impossible to exist.

That being said, it is feasible to identify some features of drug traffickers' behaviors and style of living that exist in lesser or greater degree among many of them that can be defined as narco-lifestyles. With the understanding that in these categories not everyone is what they seem to be, neither do they seem to be what they are because of the complexity and diversity of a broad range of individuals who are part of the illegal drug trade. Nevertheless, being a male drug trafficker conveys some ideals or behavioral expectations such as certain type of toxic masculinity, flaunting wealth, displaying fashionable items (e.g. luxurious vehicles, upscale clothing, and expensive jewelry), having an eccentric taste, drinking high-quality liquor and using expensive drugs such as cocaine, and enjoying the company of hypersexualized women (narco-beauty queens or buchonas).

In addition, there is the use of some symbols such as having an entourage of bodyguards (but not always), admiration or deference by local and regional officials, and the enjoyment of impunity when breaking the law. Not only that, there is the production and reproduction of certain social rituals such as large parties, weddings, and other rites of passage that serve as shows to the public to advertise the economic, social and political power of the trafficker. This deployment of ostentatious wealth includes the possession of specific objects (e.g., an automatic pistol, a fancy truck or car, and specific apparel) that complements the social and cultural persona of someone who is involved in DT activities. Finally, there is also a strong celebration of consumerism that is brandished persuasively to other people in order to acquire a personal identity and social respectability based on their illicit wealth. So, once someone adheres to these standards of sociocultural behavior, it can be recognized as part of a community (a deviant one indeed) that reinforces the status, hierarchy, and narco-lifestyle of drug traffickers in the larger context of society (Campbell 2009; Sullivan 2012).

It should be noticed that the most glamorized part of a narco-lifestyle is reserved for drug lords and bosses who are in the higher ranks of the echelons while the rank and file of cartel employees and its lower status members adhere to a less expensive version of this narco-fashion according to their stature within the organization or as independent traffickers. Even more important is the fact that the vast majority of people who are involved in the DT business (think of farmers, lookouts, hitmen, drivers, smugglers, mules, street dealers, and couriers) do not have access to the narco-lifestyle depicted here simply because they live in poverty, are uneducated, or have no means to acquire it (Muehlmann 2014).

Furthermore, one must keep in mind that what journalists, academics, officials, or mass media outlets defined as narco-lifestyle or narco-look (either clothing, symbols, demeanor, or music) is just another way to express the cowboy or ranchero styles that are known as Norteño Mexican fashion. This Norteño genre is prevalent in many rural and mountain communities in northern Mexico and is associated with farmers and peasants whose style was brought to the city when early drug traffickers borrowed key components of it and moved to urban settings, meaning that some symbols, demeanor, or clothing may look like narco-lifestyle but do not necessarily belong to it (Campbell 2009). Consequently, one should not criminalize an entire community or set of individuals who may adhere to this Norteño or narco-look if they are not involved in DT activities. Certainly, this should be the case given that there is not an objective or scientific criteria to differentiate between a narco-look and a Norteño style (Campbell 2009).

Narco-lifestyles have changed and evolved over time to reflect the innovative nature of DT. Accordingly, the new generations of traffickers have abandoned the stereotyped clothing (e.g. boots, hat, and cowboy outfits) and demeanors that reflected the traditional image of old traffickers to embrace new fashion trends where luxurious brand names such as Versace, Ralph Lauren, and others are seen as more desirable by these traffickers. This trend is not exclusive of cartel members and sometimes some individuals in society (in both Mexico and the United States) identify themselves with these products of narcoculture because they like them without necessarily being involved in the illegal drug trade.

A notorious case that illustrates this phenomenon occurred in 2010 with the arrest in Mexico of several well-known drug traffickers over a period of three months. Among them were Edgar Valdez Villareal (a.k.a. "La Barbie" recently sentenced to forty-nine years in federal prison in the United States), Jose Jorge Balderas (a.k.a. "J.J."), and Victor Valdez (a.k.a. "El Gordo Varilla"), all of them leaders of criminal cells that had branched off from larger organizations after the killing or arrest of the kingpin. It turns out that all of these traffickers were arrested and photographed sporting the same short-sleeved jersey, with open-neck, and displaying the familiar horseman with a stick logo on the front of their Polo shirt. As a result, it led to a new fashion trend where young people among lower-class neighbors in Mexico began wearing polo shirts that became known as *Narco-Polo* shirts (Stevenson 2011). To clarify, rather than encouraging the sales of the original jerseys that can cost up to $100 each, the demand for these Ralph Lauren shirts was based on counterfeited merchandize sold in the streets of Mexico City for around $10 a piece by unlicensed vendors that exist ubiquitously as part of the informal Mexican economy. Still, this phenomenon reveals how embedded narcoculture is among some social groups and the power of the narco-look.

In another example of the influence of narco-lifestyle, before the notorious leader of the Sinaloa cartel Joaquin *El Chapo* Guzman was finally arrested for the last time in January of 2016 (and eventually extradited to the United States to face prosecution), the actor Sean Penn interviewed him in October of 2015 and took a picture of himself and the capo shaking hands. This photo was published later on in the Rolling Stone magazine as part of a journalistic article written by the actor about his encounter with the drug lord (Penn 2016). In that picture, *El Chapo* was wearing a blue and silver striped shirt made by a Californian company named *Barabas*. The website catalog refers to this shirt as "Fantasy: Decorative print shirt" and is listed at $140 a piece (Barabas 2018). This item, along with another shirt worn by the famous drug lord in a video interview released by the same magazine after the article was published became a hot fashion trend in the spring of 2016 and skyrocketed Barabas' sales of these two shirts like never before. The company cleverly captioned one of these items as "Most Wanted . . . shirt" in a picture posted on its website showing a photo of the *El Chapo* with Sean Penn along with one of the company's male models sporting the same shirt (Lancheros 2016).

The two aforementioned examples are not isolated cases but part of a larger trend of narco-fashion that happens in plain view in our society. The company *Twiins Enterprises* (https://twiinsstore.com/men/), headquartered in California and mentioned earlier as the powerhouse of *Movimiento Alterado* narco-corridos, also has a store in its well-developed website and sells printed baseball caps and T-shirts. One of the shirt designs includes a famous image of *El Chapo* Guzman in black and white and the inscription in Spanish *Jefe de Jefes* (Boss of bosses). Another one features a caricature-like image of the same drug lord resembling the iconic Super Mario Bros. character created by Nintendo with the words *Super Chapo.* And a third shirt, in a clever sense of irony, features the face of *El Chapo* and the message "Siempre existe una salida" (There is always a way out), which obviously is referring to the multiple prison escapes by which *El Chapo* drug lord is known, while stating that any difficult situation can always be worked out. Each shirt is priced between $28 and $30 plus a shipping flat rate of $10.

The connection between fashion and criminal activities is nothing new in our society and for decades there has been a social fascination about the clothing, personal belongings, and lifestyles of high-profile criminals in the United States (Lancheros 2016). The main difference today is that the ubiquitous influence of mass media and Internet makes it easier for criminals to flaunt their habits, pleasures, and lifestyles and then some people or communities want to imitate them as if they were celebrities. This is certainly the case with a younger generation of drug traffickers who use social media and platforms such as Facebook and YouTube to show off what they deem as their greatest achievement as drug traffickers. They do it as a manifestation of narcoculture since rivals, government officials, and a fan base are willing to consume—for whatever reason—their narco-fashion and in response, many ordinary citizens imitate and celebrate those narco-lifestyles.

Similar to celebrities such as Kim Kardashian, Beyoncé, or others who release personal information, pictures, and other media messages to their supporters to maintain their statuses as superstars, some drug traffickers send constant implicit and explicit messages about their narco-lifestyles, lives, wealth, and economic benefits of being traffickers. The audience or target of these messages are peers, employees, rivals, police, and the community at large using social media and the Internet. Those messages are part of the phenomenon of narcoculture intended to glamorize DT and meant to signal that their business is not deviant. Regretfully or not, the messages are usually echoed in society because traffickers have a base of supporters, fans, or impersonators that have no relation to DT but still like to consume narco-lifestyles. Somehow this trend shows that there is widespread social and cultural tolerance (and sometimes open acceptance) of narco-fashion that has contributed to normalizing its presence in society to the point that someone wearing a similar shirt as *El Chapo*, even if is a counterfeited product, can be interpreted as funny or tasteless but not necessarily deviant or criminal behavior in itself.

Narco-Museum (Museo del Enervante)

The use of narco-fashion or narco-aesthetics is nothing new. For decades drug cartel bosses and middle-rank members have created their fashionable items to express their adherence to the culture of their illegal drug trade. Unlike today where it is possible to have a peak of those narco-goods via the Internet, past items and personal belongings of old traffickers are difficult to find. However, there is a place that has meticulously collected and displayed many of those narco-fashion objects from decades and all of them are part of a huge compilation in the hands of the Mexican army. The headquarters of the Mexican Secretariat of the National Defense (*Secretaría de la Defensa Nacional*), the government office responsible for overseeing the Army and Air Force in Mexico, is located in Mexico City. This institution houses inside a very unique and astonishing theme museum where the only topic in display is a collection of objects, drugs, army operations, and all sorts of artifacts and information related to DT activities and its law enforcement by the Mexican army. The official name of the museum is *Museo del Enervante* (The Museum of Drugs), but it is better known as *Museo del Narco* (narco-museum). *Enervante* means drug in Spanish, but the name can be a misnomer since the museum is meant to show selected visitors the work done by the Army in its fight against DT and traffickers throughout the past four decades, rather than an institutionalized dissection of illegal drugs in Mexico.

At first, the museum was built to educate Army personnel in the strategies, behavior, and mindset of drug traffickers in order to train soldiers and Special Forces for their operations against cartel members. However, it has been transformed into a de facto educational (and propaganda) tool for the Mexican government and the Army in its moral, political, and legal justification for the Mexican War on Drugs. The museum is closed to the general public, but it is possible to pay an official visit for news outlets, journalists, scholars, and some students for educational and journalistic purposes upon written request. Upon learning this fact, I requested an official authorization to visit the museum during the summer of 2018, not knowing whether or not my petition would be accepted. Luckily, my credentials as a professor helped me and my petition was accepted. Thus, my appointment to visit the museum of drugs was scheduled for 3 July 2018 at 10 a.m.

I traveled to Mexico City the day before the appointment and I showed up on time at the headquarters of the Mexican Secretariat of the National Defense. Needless to say that this institution is heavily guarded by the military and its access is restricted. Everyone not working there must check in and visitors are required to wear a badge at all times. At 10:00 a.m. of that day, I walked into the entrance of the perimeter and went to a room full of people to check in and I lined up. Two soldiers were working on computer stations to review IDs and check people in. A few minutes later the phone rang and one of the soldiers spelled out my name. The museum was calling to see if I was already there, they were expecting me. I raised my hand and quickly the front desk checked me in. Soon, an armed soldier came in and he escorted me to the museum premises located on the seventh floor of the main building. Honestly, I did not expect this level of professionalism. Even more, once in the museum a colonel welcomed me on behalf of the Minister of the Secretariat with a short official message and some protocol at the entrance of the museum. Then he proceeded to introduce another soldier, this time a Mayor, who would be my guide (along with three female guards heavily armed) throughout the three-hour tour that I spent in the museum.

To begin with, the museum is full of cultural artifacts, guns, drugs, and personal and eccentric objects belonging to famous or important Mexican drug traffickers and kingpins that soldiers and Special Forces have confiscated in their homes and hideouts during their arrest. The collection is vast and has grown dramatically in the past decades since the launch of the Mexican version of the War on Drugs in 2006. The museum is divided into ten rooms or galleries (*salas*) with different themes. From the history of drugs, to the international context of DT, to interdiction operations, eradication of marihuana and poppy plantations, drug smuggling technology used by traffickers, and narcoculture. Each room is carefully decorated with a display of objects, pictures, charts, and written information to explain in detail a particular theme. For instance, hall number three focuses on Army operations to destroy drug fields in the mountains of states such as Sinaloa, Sonora, and Chihuahua known for having a heavy concentration of DT activities. There are charts and pictures depicting the tools and equipment used by traffickers to produce marijuana and poppies to make heroin. A diorama shows how helicopters—rather than airplanes—fumigate drug fields with the herbicide Paracuat to destroy them. Unlike other countries, in Mexico airplanes cannot be used for aerial fumigation because most drug fields are located in ravines or steep hillsides on purpose making it difficult for soldiers to spot the fields and destroy them (Museo del Enervante 2018).

Galleries four, five, and six are labeled as *Intercepción de Drogas* (drug interception) on land, sea, and sky. In the first one, there are numerous gadgets and multiple pictures of devices, items, and merchandise showing the most ingenious tactics used by smugglers to hide, transport, and traffic drugs using hidden compartments in objects such as dissected animals, soda cans, fruits, shoes, painting frames, books, tires, the human body, gas tanks, and in the most inconceivable parts of a vehicle (see figures 3.1 to 3.7).

Gallery nine centers on the topic of narcoculture and displays personal objects and property from many drug traffickers and cartels in general. Here it is possible to see first-hand the most curious and unconventional manifestations of the culture of drug traffickers such as handguns and automatic rifles that have been dipped in gold or silver including engraved personalized features. Several counter display cabinets show a collection of 9-mm automatic pistols (somehow drug lords have a fondness for this type of handgun and almost invariably there is one in their hands when they are arrested). One of those pistols has the initials "ACF" engraved in its grips, in reference to Amado Carrillo Fuentes—the deceased leader of the Juarez cartel. Interestingly, this handgun was confiscated to Joaquin *El Chapo* Guzman in 1993 when he was arrested for the first time in Guatemala. In those years, the latter was still a middle-rank figure in the echelons of the drug cartels, and my guide assures me that the leader of the Juarez cartel probably gave it to *El Chapo* as a present (see Figures 3.8 to 3.9).

There are other pistols that have their grips decorated with engraved diamonds, religious deities, animal figures, high-end brand names, and even saints such as La Santa Muerte, allegedly associated with criminals only. Among the many oddities of this museum, there is an old Nokia cell phone with a frame of engraved 24k gold and diamonds that belonged to a middle-ranking gang member of the Gulf Cartel named Daniel Pérez Rojas (a.k.a. *El Cachetes*) who was arrested in June 2007 in the city of Matamoros, Tamaulipas (across from Brownsville, Texas). Also, there is a pair of luxurious sunglasses with gold temples that belonged to Benjamin Arellano Felix, one of the leaders of the Tijuana cartel, that were confiscated among other items during his final arrest in 2002 in Puebla, Mexico. The list of these objects is vast and it is impossible to include them all in here. The point to highlight is that they provide a good peak about the narco-lifestyle that has become an essential part of the culture of DT but that has evolved as new drug traffickers choose different personal items to display their narcoculture preferences (Museo del Enervante 2018; Woodman 2017). Next, it is time to turn to another dimension of narcoculture.

Narco-Religion

Mexico is the second-largest Catholic country in the world (just behind Brazil) and the nature of its Catholicism is unique. After three centuries of Spanish colonialism, Mexican people developed a religious syncretism founded in the official teachings of the Catholic Church and the indigenous beliefs and traditions from Mesoamerican cultures. This syncretism led to everyday religious practices where many Mexicans attend Church and pray to the large collection of Catholic saints and virgins. Simultaneously, many churchgoers also believe in non-official spiritual forces such as evil eye, witchcraft, evil spirits, and black magic that can be warded off using *curanderismo* (folk medicine), cleansing ceremonies, and resorting to medicine men or women. These spiritual options are also used to deal with hardship, and solve economic, health, and personal issues when it is deemed appropriate to the situation (McKinley 2008).

It should be noticed that these practices are more common and prevalent among working-class Mexicans rather than a widespread phenomenon in Mexico. However, there are anecdotal accounts that unofficial religious beliefs and folk ceremonies are practiced by many high-ranking politicians who resort to these methods in order to secure office, maintain their political privileges, and fight off rivals and enemies. There is a famous town named Catemaco in the state of Veracruz (along the Gulf of Mexico) known as the epicenter of witchcraft in Mexico. Politicians and all sorts of personalities who want spiritual protection or who think they may have been hexed, travel to Catemaco to be healed by medicine men (McKinley 2008).

I am familiar with this sort of religious syncretism since, as a child in a conservative Catholic family, my parents would take me and my older brother to this small community several hours away from my hometown to visit this *curandera* (medicine woman) named Lupita that would give us a *limpia* (spiritual cleansing) using an egg and branches of pirul tree (California pepper tree or *Schinus molle*) to put away the bad spirits and improve one's wellbeing. My family did it for years until one day my mom discovered that Lupita—like a magician—was pulling out salt, needles, and other scary tiny items from her apron to mix them up with the egg used for the spiritual cleansing when she cracked it into a bowl to show her clients what the cleansing job had picked up from them. Despite this, other family members, friends, and acquaintances have embraced this kind of devotion and resorted to these religious beliefs, amulets, and talismans to ask protection against calamities, ill wishes, and misfortune as part of their world view to make sense of the supernatural.

This attitude is widely adopted in many Mexican homes, although there is reluctance to publicly acknowledge it because it is not seen appropriate and according to Catholic norms and people who do not participate on them spurn those who do. Interestingly, the Catholic Church knows about it and constantly reminds churchgoers to stay away from these witchcraft affairs—as the Church calls them—and demands commitment to official Catholic practices. Other countries in Latin American and the Caribbean hold similar versions of this syncretism and even profess particular religions or cults such as Curanderismo, Santeria, Vodoo, Candomble, and other Indigenous creeds that openly combine Catholic and local indigenous religious beliefs (Kail 2015; McKinley 2008).

For this reason, it should not be a surprise that many Latin American drug traffickers and people who engage in criminal behavior (it is not exclusive of traffickers), pray and ask all kinds of saints and religious deities for protection against law enforcement agents and keep them away from being arrested. In fact, the spiritual world plays a huge role in the world view of drug traffickers precisely for the uncertain nature of their illegal activities, not just superstition. First of all, DT is a risky and unpredictable illegal business. Besides law enforcement agencies, traffickers and criminals have to face rivals, betrayals, employees' mistakes, suspicion, and deep uncertainty every day. Even though traffickers are aware that such is the nature of their illegal enterprise, to handle this confusion and anxious reality they appeal to natural and supernatural forces to provide protection to themselves and their businesses. Also, the association between crime and religiosity is nothing new. It has been well documented by some authors (Grillo 2011; Kail 2015; Saviano 2006) that bosses of the Italian mafia and their rank and file as well, in both the United States and Italy, are devoted Catholics who perform most of the rites of passage demanded by the Church (e.g. attend Mass, baptize their children, wear crosses, and pray to the Virgin) in order to seek protection from God while conducting their criminal enterprise. Thus, drug traffickers are not alone in their devotion to religious figures.

Moreover, religion is a permanent point of reference to many criminals because of their chosen lifestyle where their lives are constantly under threat of sudden death. Not just that, drug traffickers' faith (or the faith of any criminal for that matter) becomes a spiritual force that often informs their decisions while committing crimes. And it is here when superstition plays a crucial role in their behaviors because each individual chooses a personal religious practice (e.g. rituals, amulets, prayers, offerings, and sacrifices) to obtain the favor or protection needed for the goal to succeed (Kail 2015). Finally, drug traffickers do not see any contradiction between the teachings of Catholicism (or their preferred religion creed) and the criminal and violent lifestyles they have chosen: criminals are often delusional between their wicked ambition and the reality of the world. As a result, the spiritual world turns into an instrumental tool to reach a criminal outcome and their religious faith becomes an amulet that protects them from harm or law enforcement because they have a flexible morality or no morality at all (Grillo 2011; Saviano 2006; Salazar and Jaramillo 1992).

Because drug traffickers are not a homogenous group, nor is there a mandatory religious adherence to belong to a cartel or criminal gang (an exception may be La Familia Michoacana cartel discussed in chapter 2), traffickers have a broad range of patron saints, religious figures, and creeds to pray to and request favors for their spiritual needs. Among the most solicited saints that drug traffickers ask favors from are *La Virgen de Guadalupe* (Our Lady of Guadalupe saint, the most venerable image in Mexico), *San Judas Tadeo* (Saint Jude Thaddeus, the saint of hope and impossible causes), *Juan Soldado* (Soldier Juan, mainly the Patron Saint of migrants), *San Miguel* (Saint Michael who comforts souls at the time of death), *San Martin Caballero* (Saint Martin is the source of hope and luck) among other religious saints (Bunker 2016; Kail 2015). Given the illicit and complicated nature of DT, it should not be difficult to understand why these religious figures are worshipped by traffickers and the underworld with such devotion. In fact, one should ask this instead: Who in the shoes of criminals would not do it? Yet, in the past decade mass media and law enforcement organizations fighting drug cartels have mostly associated two main religious images with drug traffickers: Jesus Malverde, and La Santa Muerte. Hence, they are examined in detail here.

Jesus Malverde

The first known religious figure that became associated directly with early drug traffickers in the second half of the twentieth century is known as *Jesus Malverde*. The origins of this folk saint are murky since there is suspicion that he might have never existed at all and instead be a legend or a total myth (Quinones 2001). According to his biographers the history of Jesus Malverde occurred at the beginning of the twentieth century during the dictatorship of Porfirio Diaz that gave rise to the Mexican Revolution in 1910. During those years rural areas and small cities were full of bandits and criminals. Jesus Malverde was one among them in the highlands of Culiacán, Sinaloa trying to survive poverty and difficult times by stealing from the rich to give to the poor, a sort of Mexican Robin Hood according to the legend. Eventually, his criminal behavior led to his hanging on 3 May 1909 (Bunker 2016; Quinones 2001).

There is no precise information about the origins of this religious figure, what exists is an extensive (and sometimes contradictory) narrative around Malverde among those who profess a deep devotion to him that became mainstream in the late 1970s. Needless to say, the worship of Malverde is not sanctioned by the Catholic Church. It is no coincidence that the fervor for this figure was born in Culiacán, Sinaloa (the cradle of DT in Mexico) where the first chapel to honor him was erected there four decades ago. Malverde's largest and most well-known shrine is located in central west Culiacán, standing in a rustic small building near the railroad tracks. Inside, there are several smaller shrines of him along with many of his images hanging in walls as part of worshippers' offerings. At the center of the building there is a small chapel with a metal security door and inside a bust of him painted in green, surrounded by smaller effigies of Jesus and other saints. Devotees from all over Mexico (including the United States) go there to pay their respects and ask for favors to Malverde using candles, prayers, pictures of him, and words of thanks for received miracles or blessings (Grillo 2011; Quinones 2001).

Interestingly, strong devotion towards this religious icon existed before it was associated with drug traffickers. Throughout most of the past century, poor people in Sinaloa venerated Malverde because of his so-called miracles and spiritual services to them such as helping to find lost cattle or bringing health to a loved one. These stories became known among the poor and lower class and the fame of Malverde as a miracle saint cemented with no affiliation to criminals. When the Mexican government conducted the large military operation coded "Condor" in the mountains of Sinaloa against traffickers, farmers, and peasants in the mid-1970s (under the pressure of the United States to disrupt marijuana and poppy production), thousands of them abandoned their land and towns and moved to Culiacán and other urban settings. It was during this time that the media and government officials began to label Jesus Malverde as a narco-saint (Grillo 2011; Quinones 2001).

To be fair, many drug traffickers do worship Malverde as a unique spiritual force that can help them conduct their illegal business in a successful manner. Personal artifacts, images, tattoos, amulets, prayer cards, and statutes have been found in the hands of drug traffickers after being arrested in both Mexico and the United States. They use these items to petition Malverde protection against law enforcement agents during smuggling operations and illegal transactions. Even more, many of these artifacts have also been discovered in vehicles, warehouses, homes, and clandestine laboratories during search warrants and criminal investigations. This explains to what extent the religious icon Malverde is considered a venerated figure among drug traffickers (Kail 2015; Quinones 2001). Nonetheless and similar to narco-corridos, it must be noted that Malverde is not worshipped by traffickers only but by a broad range of people (usually the working class, poor, and the disenfranchised) who resort to this image as part of the broad spectrum of deities who belong to the unique Mexican religious syncretism. Because of this, even if the Catholic Church does not officially recognize him as a saint, he is tolerated by priests and the clergy because of the importance it has for some people in Mexican society (Grillo 2011; Kail 2015).

La Santa Muerte (The Skeleton Saint)

In recent years, another iconic figure that has surpassed the popularity of Jesus Malverde and has become a well-known image associated with drug traffickers, criminals, and gruesome violence is La Santa Muerte (LSM). LSM is also known by other nicknames such as *La Flaquita* (The Skinny Lady), *La Huesuda* (The Bonny Lady), *La Niña Blanca* (The White Girl), *La Madrina* (The Godmother), *Santísima Muerte* (Most Holy Death), among others (Chesnut 2012). La Santa Muerte is represented by a skeleton figure dressed in saint clothing such as a virgin, nun, or a bride while holding a scythe in her right hand. The scythe symbolizes an instrument used to cut the evil as well as to open a path without obstacles for her believers. There are also two owls on her shoulders as guardians of La Santa Muerte representing symbols of higher wisdom and the ability to see what is hidden. The image of LSM is almost similar to the grim reaper who is known in other cultures across the world in charge of "reaping" human souls. Except that in the context of Mexico and the United States, LSM is referred to as *she* and has a more elaborated meaning and a broader audience of devotees throughout Latin America and the

United States. The media and public officials, however, have demonized LSM as a deviant and predatory cult associated with criminals and symbolizing only the architype of a narco-saint (Chesnut 2012; Neumann 2018).

Unlike Malverde, LSM is revered by millions of devotees in Central America, Mexico, and the United States, as well as other countries such as Guatemala (*Rey Pascual*), Argentina, Brazil, and Paraguay (*San La Muerte*) where there are similar folk saints resembling the grim reaper but portrayed as a male figure rather than female. Devotees believe in the spiritual powers of LSM for healing, protecting, and granting requests during hardship times. Among believers, LSM has been deemed as an effective force for conferring miracles for those who have faith on her spiritual powers because it is *the* saint of difficult times (*las causas difíciles*). According to this faith, LSM performs all sorts of favors for everyday life problems such as bringing back boyfriends and husbands, providing prosperity, abundance, healing, and resolving health issues. In addition, she is known for helping believers to fight back enemies, bring revenge, or give protection against law enforcement during the commission of illegal activity. Not only that, "The saint, who has a reputation for 'getting the job done,' has become the official patroness of numerous small business owners throughout Mexico and in parts of the United States" (Chesnut 2012, 24). Although mainly associated with criminals and the underworld by the official discourse, most devotees tend to come from lower socioeconomic status, be disenfranchised, poor, uneducated. However, followers come from all sorts of backgrounds such as "High school students, middle-class housewives, taxi drivers, drug traffickers, politicians, musicians, doctors, and lawyers all are among the ranks of the faithful" (Chesnut 2012, 11–12).

LSM is found in images, statutes, prayer cards, altars, gold medallions, and candles with different colors in makeshift street shrines, altars at home, and some unofficial sanctuaries devoted to the saint found ubiquitously throughout Mexico (see Figure 3.10). Devotees usually burn and offer a particular candle color that is meant to symbolize and summon the type of spiritual assistance needed from LSM to get a favor. Thus, white candles (the most popular of them) are associated with purity, protection, and gratitude. Red ones with love, passion, and broken hearts. Gold candles with financial success and prosperity. Purple candles with spiritual healing and breaking curses. Yellow ones to fight drug addiction. Brown ones for good judgement and spiritual guidance. And finally, black candles are associated with witchcraft, protection against enemies and to get help in conducting illegal activities. Most public officials unfamiliar with the devotion to LSM assume that black candles and their shadowy requests are the only kind of favors that worshippers ask from this saint, which is far from the truth, yet it is the connection with crime that has become the most well-known feature of LSM (Chesnut 2012; Neumann 2018).

Given the sort of spiritual and protective powers of this skeletal saint, it should not be a surprise how attractive this image results for individuals who make a living breaking the law or living an unorthodox life in the streets of Mexico and the United States. La Santa Muerte is believed to provide favors that official saints will not dare to do. This fervor has spread out to prisons in California and the southwest of the United States (Texas in particular), as well as in Mexican penitentiaries where inmates have makeshift altars or possess images, tattoos, and artifacts related to LSM. In an ironic twist of circumstances, some police officers, prison guards, prosecutors, and others who have risky jobs in Latin America where their life is constantly under threat of sudden death have also joined the cult of LSM because of its supernatural protection against harm and evil forces. However, this personal faith is usually kept private due to the negative reputation that LSM has in official circles (Chesnut 2012; Kail 2015).

Law enforcement operations have confirmed the devotion and worship to LSM from some suspected criminals. During search warrants or stop traffics, police officers have found paraphernalia related to this unofficial saint and her devotion in the hands and homes of suspects, in particular, drug traffickers (Chesnut 2012; Kail 2015). News reports and the crime beat in Mexico and the United States have disproportionally focused on these types of stories (to increase viewer ratings) that sensationalize and distort to what extent LSM is an exclusive religious icon for drug traffickers. Meanwhile, these stories ignore the complicated notion of this saint figure and why she has a broad appeal to Mexicans and Mexican-Americans who have no connection with criminal enterprises or DT activities (Chesnut 2012; Kail 2015; Neumann 2018).

This narrative of LSM as the saint of drug traffickers has been consolidated and exploited by TV series such as *Narcos* (Netflix) *La Reina del Sur* (Telemundo), and the film industry which magnify and distort some accessory components of narcoculture into big controversies to fit a predictable script. Just to prove this point, the movie "Sicario 2: Day of the Soldado," which was released at the end of June 2018, presents a Hollywood version (a blockbuster film to entertain and make money) of the WOD along the Mexico-U.S. border. The film included in its theatrical release a poster with a full skull and red flowers, adorned with a couple of LSM figures on the sides of the skull as a clever marketing strategy that explicitly makes the correlation of drug cartels and the skeleton saint, the implication being that they are the same. Previously, an episode of the famous TV show *Breaking Bad* featured a scene where two traffickers are shown praying to LSM. The series *Narcos* produced by Netflix has also several scenes where the skeleton saint is powerfully associated with drug traffickers. Of course, these media material are just meant for enjoyment and distraction, but unfortunately some people reify films and

TV shows as a real representation of the world, and after watching them, many of them connect cartel members with the skeleton saint as an automatic part of DT, even if this is not supported with evidence and facts. Such commercialization only increases the stereotypes of Mexico and its people as a crime-prone society that disregards the rule of law. The reality, though, is that not all drug traffickers worship LSM, and not all devotees of this figure are drug traffickers and criminals (Chesnut 2012; Neumann 2018).

Whether for her miraculous powers or because of the reputation for granting all kinds of favor, the truth is that veneration for LSM has grown and expanded dramatically in the recent years. Before her official affiliation with criminals and the increase of makeshift altars along the Southwest border and Mexico, the reverence of this skeleton saint was kept as a private matter in the homes of devotees. As more and more people openly began to light candles to her and visit provisional shrines in public places to ask for favors, the number of followers seemed to increase, and her cult became more mainstream. Even if worshipping LSM is informal, scattered, and decentralized, there is indirect evidence about its continuous expansion by looking at the popularity of her figure in dozens of folk medicine shops (called *Yerberías* or *Tiendas Esotéricas* in Spanish) in Mexico and the United States where La Santa Muerte paraphernalia is one of the most sold items (Chesnut 2012; Neumann 2018).

There are dozens (and possibly hundreds) of makeshift altars and worshipping shrines of LSM throughout Mexico and the United States. Near my hometown in central west Mexico, there is a famous shrine of her located in the tiny village named Santa Ana Chapitiro. The place is called *La Casa de la Santa Muerte* (House of Holy Death). It houses hundreds of colorful crafted images of this figure in all sizes, dresses, contexts, and situations. For instance, there is a figure of the skeleton saint in one of the altars that seems to resemble a transgender LSM. While visiting this place in July 2018, I noticed several gay and transgender devotees leaving offerings and flowers in front of this particular image, which I assume reflects the inclusiveness of her cult where everyone is welcomed (see figures 3.11 and 3.12).

The only recognized Catholic temple with an open affiliation to the skeleton saint (albeit not acknowledged officially by the Church) is located in Mexico City near downtown on number thirty-five of Nicolas Bravo Street. The formal name of this temple is *Santuario Nacional del Angel de la Santa Muerte* (Angel of the Death Saint National Sanctuary). I visited the place on 4 July 2018 and interviewed the priest in charge of the temple, whose name will remain confidential. According to him, LSM attracts many worshippers because of the nature of her accomplishments as a powerful saint. First, everyone is welcomed to the temple regardless of social class, ethnicity, sexual identity, profession, criminal record, or any other category. This makes LSM an inclusive religious figure unlike many other Catholic figures who reject same-sex couples, homosexuals, and anyone who is not heterosexual. Second, devotees can perform in this sanctuary all the Catholic sacraments (e.g. baptism, receive first communion, marriage, and so on) and obtain official acknowledgement for it. The temple even performs same-sex couple blessings (not marriages) for gay people who are Catholic, something no other official Catholic temple offers. Finally, LSM is known for allowing a personal connection with her devotees, meaning that she is equal and of the same status of anyone else (after all, everyone will face her at the end of one's life, right?). Such access to her creates a strong bond that encourages all types of requests or petitions by devotees without moral or ethical considerations (see figures 3.13 to 3.15). An example of this connection is the kind of offerings that believers leave at her feet in altars and shrines: from flowers, cigarettes, and food, to liquor (tequila in particular) and other alcoholic beverages that devotees assume she likes. All things considered and apart from her association with the underworld, for many believers LSM is considered a *cool* saint (Chesnut 2012; Neumann 2018).

It should be understood then that like any other manifestation of narcoculture, devotion to Jesus Malverde or La Santa Muerte is a complex and multifaceted cultural phenomenon that is deeply intertwined with economic, social, and religious components. For this reason, the assumption by many public officials to associate LSM to drug traffickers only is a narrow-minded and ethnocentric perspective that ignores the nature, history, and context of this skeleton saint in Native and Hispanic people in the Americas. Death in Latin American societies, and certainly in Mexico, has a different meaning and fascination compared to the United States (where it is usually understood as a taboo topic and mostly in negative terms). In Mexico, death is part of the cycle of life and there is even a celebration about it—*Día de los Muertos* (Day of the Dead)—that began thousands of years ago in Mesoamerican cultures. The 2017 Pixar-produced animated film *Coco*, which became a successful hit in terms of accolades and grossed revenue, provides a charismatic glimpse of this tradition.

The image of LSM is not a rare artifact in Mexican society given that the common symbol of the day of the dead is a skull (known as *Calavera* in Spanish). In the early twentieth century, the famous cartoonist and engraver, José Guadalupe Posada, created an image called *La Calavera Catrina* (The Elegant Skull) to parody upper-class Mexican women. That drawing has become ubiquitous in Mexico and Latin America, and is now a classic figure intertwined with the *Día de los Muertos* celebration in November of each year (Lomnitz 2008). Even the James Bond filmography franchise included an explicit reference to it in its 2015 film *Spectre*. All in all, then, SLM is but another expression of the obsession and attraction that the grim reaper has for Hispanics and Mexican Americans that must be appreciated in the larger sociocultural context of the idea of death, rather than a parochial and insular interpretation by law enforcement officials who tend to ignore the multifaceted notion of social phenomena.

Narco-Barbies (Buchonas Women)

Women are not excluded from engaging in DT activities. There are examples of women being drug bosses in their own such as Ignacia Jasso known as "La Nacha," the "dope queen" of El Paso-Juarez (Campbell 2009) and Maria Dolores Estévez known as "Lola la Chata" (Carey 2009) in the middle of the twentieth century. Both women were high-raking drug traffickers who could be considered within the ranks of *El Chapo* Guzman for the standards of their time. But beyond them, most women involved in the illicit drug trade have played indirect or adjacent roles as partners, spouses, siblings, and employees of male drug traffickers. More recently, however, women have been forced to become mules or engage in drug dealing as a survival strategy (Muehlmann 2014) and the WOD in both Mexico and the United States is considered one of the contributing factors behind increasing numbers of women behind bars (Alexander 2012).

That being said, in the world of DT where manhood, sexism, and hypermasculinity are deeply intertwined as part of the identity of what it means to be a trafficker, the objectification of women is a common practice. As such, women are perceived as trophies to be exhibited and bragged about, besides women's regular roles as providers of emotional support, sexual favors, and sometimes as partners in crime, literally. For drug traffickers, women are a sort of accessory item that is an essential part of the narco-style that is produced and reproduced in their daily routines (Nuñez González and Alvarado 2012; Proceso 2016; Roberts 2016). However, not every woman is considered worthy of this objectification though; she must be someone that has become known today as a *Buchona*: a female who has a particular type of beauty based on body attributes. Buchona is an extravagant and hypersexualised woman who is the girlfriend of a trafficker (*buchon*) and has become immersed in the lifestyle of their boyfriends, lovers, and husbands. These women are characterized first and foremost for one element: their physical appearance. The concept of Buchona comes from Sinaloa and it was there where the narcoculture of these types of women developed in the past decades. Yet, it has now expanded to other regions and cities of Mexico and along the Mexico-U.S. border. I called this paradigm of beauty *Narco-Barbie* style (Nuñez González and Alvarado 2012; Proceso 2016; Roberts 2016).

Narco-Barbies have to adhere to a particular prototype of beauty that includes, but is not limited to, being young, pretty, having a slim waist, having big buttocks and breasts (naturally or surgically altered through cosmetic enhancement), being sexually attractive and feminine, having long hair, eyelashes, and long nails, as well as wearing expensive and luxurious clothing brands in a provocative and revealing manner. In a nutshell, these women have to look like an artificial Barbie doll to grab the attention of drug traffickers. Of course, this is a stereotyped version of a *Buchona* since some of them may choose a slightly different look than this one. Yet, the difference would not be too far from the description given here because drug traffickers overwhelmingly prefer this prototype of beauty. That said, not all women who look like Buchonas are such or are associated with traffickers (Nuñez González and Alvarado 2012; Roberts 2016). On a side note, it should not go unnoticed that this description of women is patriarchalistic (it is a product of the male gaze) and reproduces the sociocultural objectification that women have experienced for decades in Western societies. It also reflects one side of the phenomenon given the lack of input from any of these women and the fact that experts on this topic are mostly (if not all) men. This section is meant to be informative to reveal the eccentricities of narcoculture, rather than pass judgment on the motivations and circumstances of why these women embrace the identity of Buchonas.

That being said, even if Buchonas may look physically similar among themselves, they are not all the same. There are distinctive groups based on their upbringing, social class, their relationship with drug traffickers, and even their beauty preferences. These differences are not necessarily rigid since it would be difficult and problematic to classify the diversity of these women into fixed roles. Instead, these groups are meant to facilitate the understanding of Buchonas as an expression of narcoculture and how their roles and influence operate as a result of male drug traffickers' desires. These women can be put together in three primary groups: those who come from a humble upbringing; those who were born in a family context of DT; and those who married a trafficker and then adopted the gangster culture (Nuñez González and Alvarado 2012).

The first group refers to girls who were born in poverty and they may have little or no prospects to go college, to have a job to make ends meet, or any other opportunity to climb the social ladder in their communities due to sexism, patriarchalism, widespread unemployment, poverty, lack of opportunities, or all of these. Thus, if they happen to be pretty and have a body according to certain expectations of beauty, they can decide to become a Buchona as a means of social and economic mobility. It is important to keep in mind that in a context where the illegal drug trade and drug traffickers are socially accepted and recognized as an acceptable alternative to get out of poverty and social climbing becoming a Buchona is not a deviant tactic (Proceso 2010). It is worth noting that many of these women do not have much personal agency to opt out of becoming Buchonas since there are few social opportunities for them to get out of poverty.

The second group pertains to women whose families have been involved in DT activities for a long time, even generations. Therefore, young girls born in this environment adopt the culture of DT because it is part of their education and upbringing. They are prepared and socialized to uphold the tenets of the drug business because it is their dynastic duty, so to speak. Since these women know that they are part of a criminal enterprise, even if it is tolerated or accepted by families and the local community, they cannot live regular lives. Accordingly, most of these girls and women fraternize only with other families and friends who are also part of the illegal drug trade, and the women must adhere to the standard of beauty that is already in the culture of DT—the narco-Barbie prototype—to look attractive to potential partners. Inevitably, many of these women end up becoming (or at least looking like) Buchona even if they themselves do not identify as one. Just to clarify, not all women born into a family of drug traffickers will automatically turn into a Buchona woman and defend the lifestyle of the family. However, the social and household pressure from their families is strong enough to force many of them to follow these rules. Since there is little-to-no research about this phenomenon, scholars have resorted to case studies and information from third parties to get a more accurate understanding of the life of Buchonas. A series of interviews in the mid-2000s by Mexican journalist Julio Scherer to an alleged female drug boss named Sandra Ávila Beltrán, better known as La Reina del Pacífico (the Queen of the Pacific), sheds some light about what is it to be a women born in a traditional family of drug traffickers (Scherer 2008). This woman argues that it was impossible to escape this family background and she ended up marrying several drug traffickers and eventually getting involved in the drug trade because it was the only way to make the kind of living she was used to (Scherer 2008).

The third group of Buchonas refers to women who, before turning into a narco-Barbie (and without having any previous association with the illicit drug trade), end up as formal partners or spouses of drug traffickers out of love or convenience. In time, most of these women surrender to the aesthetics of narco-style and become Buchonas to meet the stereotyped beauty that most drug traffickers crave for. These women may have been pretty and attractive in the first place (without necessarily fitting the category of a Buchona yet), to get the attention of the gangster. Once a committed relationship has been formed, many men demand their women conform to the narco-Barbie standard of attractiveness. Since those standards are unrealistic and difficult to reach naturally, they turn to cosmetic surgeries (money is never a problem) to enhance breasts, buttocks, lips, and even undergo liposculpture procedures to remove ribs for a thinner waist. Many of these women may or may not adopt the Buchona style in their own initiative and not always as a result of a partner's pressure because they want to look more attractive, desirable, or prettier (Nuñez González and Alvarado 2012; Proceso 2010; Roberts 2016). It must be pointed out that Mexico is placed third for plastic surgeries performed annually worldwide (just behind the United States and Brazil), according to statistics from international medical associations (Proceso 2018). Interestingly, states such as Sinaloa have one of the highest rates of cosmetic procedures in Mexico, to the point that women from the capital of that state sometimes are called *Las muñecas de Culiacán* (the dolls of Culiacan) because after undergoing plastic surgeries, their appearance looks like inflated dolls (Sputnik 2017).

Part of the lifestyle and identity of a Buchona is to exhibit their bodies and flaunt the luxurious lives they allegedly have. With that in mind, most of them are actively involved in social media through Instagram, Facebook, and YouTube accounts where they keep a personal profile and display selfies, videos, and pictures of themselves. The images and recordings are about them wearing attractive outfits, posing in sensual postures, partying, having fun, and sometimes holding assault rifles and guns. Images of Buchonas are widely available on the internet and a simple search in YouTube or Instagram with the word Buchonas will prompt a long list of images and recordings with images of these females. Moreover, Googling the same word under the category of images, hundreds of pictures of them will also appear with the stereotyped image of a Buchona: taking selfies, showing their prominent breasts, buttocks and slim bodies, their nails, bikinis, and physical appearance that characterized this culture of DT. Social media is also an outlet where some of them engage in conversations between themselves and discuss being a Buchona. Not just that, there are forums and discussions where Buchonas would argue, criticize each other, and vent about their lifestyles, and often they would denounce or admonish critics who have labeled them "narco-sluts" (Nuñez González and Alvarado 2012; Roberts 2016).

Buchonas play such an essential role in the identity of a drug trafficker and the world of narcoculture that they are regularly featured in narco-corridos as protagonists as well as stage settings to serve the needs of the macho identity of the gangster who needs to boast about seducing these females. As a manifestation of narcoculture, Buchonas are a sophisticated and diverse group of women that reflect the ideology and values of DT with its emphasis on materialism and hedonism as the sole engines that encourage many young men and women to join the illegal drug trade and adopt its principles. Despite the categories mentioned earlier, the identity of a Buchona is not a fixed model, and many women who adhere to this lifestyle do not consider themselves as such even if they look like one in appearance. On the other hand, there are some women who openly identify themselves and Buchonas and are proud of their identity, but they have no connection with DT or gangsters. Therefore, these categories of narcoculture are always shifting and it is difficult to capture all of the intricacies because, like any other fashion in vogue, the nature of being a Buchona is invariably to adopt new trends and adapt to new realities due to the influence drug traffickers have on how narcoculture is understood and displayed in society, be it Mexico, Colombia, or the United States (Nuñez González and Alvarado 2012; Proceso 2018; Roberts 2016; Sputnik 2017).

Narco-Literature

One should ask why the narco-literature genre is a manifestation of narcoculture, and the answer is because the prime protagonists of narco-literature books are drug traffickers, their lives, businesses, activities, and stories connected to the illegal drug trade. Narco-literature as a genre can be classified into two major categories: fiction and non-fiction works. The first one refers to crime fiction using stories and plots that focus on the WOD and its devastating impact on society. It also includes the narrative where drug cartel activities, their characters, their businesses and the drama around all of it are used to produce a story that resembles the reality of the world of DT. The second category pertains to investigative journalism, memoirs, essays, and academic books where the authors (usually journalists but also former officials, politicians, and social scientists) document the inner workings of the hidden underworld of DT, corruption, murders, and the context of the illegal drug trade through interviews, archival research, confidential informants, and personal experience.

In a narrow definition, only the first category—fiction narco-literature—would be included as part of this genre. However, for the sake of providing a broader understanding of this phenomenon as a domain of narcoculture, both categories will be included here as part of this concept. Accordingly, narco-literature is defined in this book as *the literary work that chronicles the world of DT, those who are part of it, or the context of drug use and abuse, using fictional stories or through investigative journalism, personal accounts, and other prose narratives*.

Although narco-literature is not a new phenomenon (it has been present for several decades), its popularity rose in Colombia and Mexico first, then worldwide, due to the expansion of the illegal drug trade, and the drug war in particular, becoming more prominent recently. It is not a coincidence that this genre is a truly Latin American invention, where most of its contemporary authors are from places with significant problems of DT and presence of criminal organizations. The country leading the creation of most works is Mexico (although there are several Colombian writers who have written on this genre) including a set of authors whose works have been prized for their powerful narrative as "intense literary experiments." Fictional works within the genre of narco-literature have also been labeled as "Mexican drug crime fiction" even if that is not totally accurate, but the birth of the genre has been attributed to Mexican writers overall (Smith 2013).

For some authors (Villalobos 2012) the concept of narco-literature is problematic because it can have a negative connotation on how the fictional works of this genre are narrowly labeled as "drug novels." Not all the works of narco-literature are certainly about DT in the broad sense of the definition. Some of these books employ the theme of DT or a correlated idea as a point of departure, and then develop a plot that explores other related topics, with plenty of literary experimentations from different approaches. Narco-literature as a genre includes a broad spectrum of stories and authors that may have the common denominator of DT or narcos, but not all of them approach the topic of DT in the same way. Finally, narco-literature also emphasizes the commercial side of the genre because it pigeonholes different literary styles into one single formula by using the prefix narco (Olvera 2014). The word "narco-literature" is controversial, and it does not describe as its best this kind of literary work. But the term has gained popularity in the media and among some academic circles becoming a de facto denomination to describe fiction, monographs, and investigative journalism about the complex problem of DT and the people who engaged on it (Smith 2018). Even if it is not the most appropriate name, for the sake of simplicity for this analysis, this book uses the concept narco-literature as an umbrella term that groups together different styles and categories in order to document this genre as a domain of narcoculture.

It is not the purpose of this examination to make an exhaustive list of all of the works that could be included within the genre of narco-literature, nor is this a literary study of narco-literature. Instead, my intention is to make a selective and discretionary list of some of the most significant titles available to the public in order to exemplify to what extent narco-literature has become a dominant component to disseminate the notion of "narcoculture" as a pop cultural event. At the same time, it needs to be said how this genre has contributed in its own way to amplify the knowledge, influence, and visibility of DT, criminal organizations, and famous drug bosses worldwide. For that reason, this examination begins with the category of fiction and then proceeds to discuss the non-fiction one.

Fictional Works of Narco-Literature

Having explained that it is not my intention to catalogue all the works of the narco-literature genre, I do want to expose how vast this literary style is becoming. As an emerging genre that experiments with new language, narrative, and plots, narco-literature has gained recognition on its own as a literary style. For that reason, I will make a short description of some essential novels and proceed to list its most renowned publications. Probably the first known work of narco-literature in Mexico was the novel *Nacaveva: Diario de un narcotraficante* (Diary of a Drug Trafficker) published anonymously in 1967. The book explores the confessions of everyday life of a man who becomes a drug trafficker and explains his experience from an insider perspective of someone who was born and lives in Culiacán, Sinaloa. The fictional book has remained forgotten for decades given that its style and plot is amateur and is not well-written.

One of the first contemporary works of narco-literature that won international recognition was the novel *La Virgen de los Sicarios* (Our Lady of the Assassins, 1994), by the Colombian-Mexican writer Fernando Vallejo. It portrays the life of young assassins in Medellin Colombia in the early 1990s during the rule of Pablo Escobar. This novel was adapted into a successful film that won several accolades. In the same decade, the novel *Rosario Tijeras* (1999) by another Colombian writer, Jorge Franco, became a success and was also adapted to a movie and TV series with acclaimed recognition. It tells the story of a woman who has suffered maltreatment by many men until she becomes a contract killer who seduces men to kill them.

In 2005 another Colombian author, Gustavo Bolívar Moreno, published the novel *Sin Tetas No Hay Paraiso* (Without Tits, There Is No Paradise) that became a best-seller book and was adapted to a telenovela series (soap opera) with ample success in several Latin American countries and Spain. It describes the story of Catalina, a teenager with small breasts who wants to have a boob job in order to be attractive for drug traffickers as a way out of poverty. This plot was an early exploration of how some women adopted the narco-Barbie image as a strategy to lure traffickers and have access to wealth to get out of poverty and have social mobility.

Among Mexican authors, the novels by Elmer Mendoza such as *Un Asesino Solitario* (A Solitary Assassin, 1999), *El Amante de Janis Joplin* (Janis Joplin's Lover, 2002), and *Balas de Plata* (Silver Bullets, 2008) are among the first contemporary works from someone who happens to be from Culiacán, Sinaloa. The author and his works are well-known as the best of this genre. A classic fictional work of narco-literature that cannot be left out is the novel *La Reina del Sur* (Queen of the South 2002) by Spanish author Arturo Pérez Reverte, which became an international best-seller as a book and as a TV series produced by Netflix. It portrays the life of Teresa Mendoza, a woman from Culiacán with a traditional role as a passive and submissive girlfriend of a drug trafficker until he is killed, and she has to escape to Spain to avoid the same fate, only to become a drug boss in her own account in a new country. The book became so successful that even *LTDN* band wrote a narco-corrido about the protagonist that in itself turned into a famous song.

Don Winslow is an American author who has become an international best-selling celebrity in the genre of narco-literature for several novels where DT activities, violence, and law enforcement are part of the main plot. The first one was *The Power of the Dog* (a realistic depiction of the violence and senseless WOD that has consumed Mexico and the United States in the past decades). *El Cartel* (a sequel of his first work *The Power of the Dog*, where some of those characters delve in the ongoing battle of the WOD). And the last one *The Border* (this is the final book of his trilogy within El Cartel series). He wrote other novels such *Savages* (a story about two young California pot growers who have to face a drug Cartel when it demands a share of the business) but the main work is his trilogy series.

Here is a short list of the most well-known novels of this genre and their authors: 1. *La Santa Muerte* (The Skeleton Saint) and *Sicarios* (Hitmen) by Homero Aridjis; 2. *Campos de Amapola antes de Esto* (Poppy Fields before This) by Lolita Bosch; 3. *Trabajos del Reino* (Kindom Cons) and *La Transmigración de los Cuerpos* (The Transmigration of Bodies) by Yuri Herrera; 4. *Cocaina: Manual del Usuario* (Cocaine: Manual's User) by Julio Herbert; 5. *La Biblia Vaquera: Un Triunfo del Corrido sobre la Lógica* (The Cowboy's Bible: A Triumph of the Ballad over Logic) by Carlos Velázquez; 6. *Fiesta en la Madriguera* (Down the Rabbit Hole) by Juan Pablo Villalobos; 7. *Perra Brava* (Brave Bitch) by Orfa Alarcón; 8. *Estrella de la Calle Sexta* (Star of the Sixth Street) and *Instrucciones para Cruzar la Frontera* (Directions to Cross the Border) by Luis Humberto Crosthwaite; 9. *Al Otro Lado* (The Other Side) by Heriberto Yepez, among many others.

Non-fictional Works of Narco-Literature

Along with a boom in novels on DT, there has been a surge of non-fictional works such as essays, memoirs, and investigative journalism written by pundits, public officials, press reporters, and scholars in the recent years as an effort to explain the War on Drugs and its aftermath. As drug cartels consolidated in the 1990s and 2000s and DT activities became more powerful, violent, pervasive, and noticeable in everyday life in Mexico and along the U.S. border, the number of non-fiction books published to understand, diagnose, and address the problem increased dramatically.

This bulk of books should be understood as a manifestation of narcoculture for two reasons. The first one is that drug traffickers and their activities are the main content of these publications, and two, these works have attempted to shed light and explain the complexity of DT activities and the perpetrators behind them while featuring the lifestyles and narcoculture of drug traffickers. As a result, the public at large has been able to become more aware of this growing problem, but at the same time narcoculture has been exposed to the masses creating a feedback loop of information that has brought the culture of drug traffickers and their businesses into mainstream society.

Investigative Journalism

For decades, honest and hard-working journalists in Mexico have been able to document, denounce, and condemn the corruption, crimes, and illegal activities of public officials, their liaisons with organized crime, and the clandestine arrangements between traffickers and those who protect them. Therefore, it is not a coincidence that Mexico is one of the most dangerous countries for journalists as explained in chapter 4 (Reporters Without Borders 2017). Accordingly, many quality non-fiction narco-literature works have been authored by journalists and here are some of the most representative. Like the previous listing this one is not exhaustive but descriptive, meant to inform the reader how prolific this style is.

One of the first books of this genre is *El Cártel: Los Arellano Félix: la mafia más poderosa en la historia de América Latina* (The Cartel: The Arellano Felix, the most powerful mafia in the history of Latin America) written by journalist Jesus Blancornelas. He was known for his incorruptible professionalism as a journalist and one of the first experts on DT and organized crime during the 1990s. The book is a detailed account of the origins, structure, consolidation, and operational capabilities of the Tijuana cartel, one of the most powerful criminal organizations that has ever existed in Mexico at the end of the twentieth century.

Another prolific Mexican journalist who published magazine article and has written several books on drug traffickers and their businesses is Ricardo Ravelo; among his most well-known works are *Los Narcoabogados* (Narcolawyers), *Narcomex: Historia e historias de una guerra* (Narco-Mexico: History and Stories of a War), and *Cronicas de sangre: Cinco historias de los Zetas* (Chronicles of Blood: Five stories of los Zetas). Daniel Enrique Osorno is another Mexican reporter who has found a personal style to document thoroughly the biographies and illegal enterprises of criminal organizations and their bosses. His books *El Cartel de Sinaloa* (The Sinaloa Cartel) and *La Guerra de los Zetas: Viaje por la Frontera de la Necropolítica* (Los Zetas' War: A Trip to the Border of Necropolitics) are exceptional accounts of two of the most powerful contemporary drug cartels.

The book *Los Señores de Narco* (Narco Land: The Mexican Drug Lords and Their Godfathers) by Argentinian-Mexican journalist Anabel Hernández is a detailed examination of the history of DT in Mexico and the complicity between public officials and drug traffickers, providing evidence, names, and sources to document the inner workings of DT and how Mexican public officials are systematic accomplices and perpetrators. Another important journalist that was a sharp critic of the Mexican corrupt system was Julio Scherer García. Although his overall writings focused on political corruption and wrongdoing he wrote about drug cartel bosses and their enterprises, in particular his books *La Reina del Pacífico: La Hora de Contar* (The Queen of the Pacific: Time to Talk) and *Historias de Muerte y Corrupción* (Stories of Death and Corruption), provide a detailed account of how corruption operates in the world of DT using first-hand information from traffickers themselves and informants.

This section would not be complete without the inclusion of Javier Valdez Cárdenas, a renowned journalist from Sinaloa who specialized on covering DT activities in Sinaloa and won several international awards. He was murdered in his hometown of Culiacán on May 15, 2017, in broad daylight. Among his most notable books on narco-literature are *Miss Narco: Belleza, Poder y Violencia* (Miss Narco: Beauty, Power, and Violence), *Huérfanos del Narco: Los Olvidados de la Guerra del Narcotráfico* (Orphaned by the Narco: The Forgotten of Drug Trafficking), and *Narcoperiodismo: La Prensa en medio del Crimen y la Denuncia* (Narco-Journalism: The Press Media in between Crime and Criminal Complaint).

An extraordinary case of investigative journalism is J. Jesús Lemus, a journalist from Michoacán state and founder of *El Tiempo* newspaper. While reporting on the complicity of local officials and drug traffickers, he was arrested, tortured, and sent to a super-maximum security prison in Jalisco state in May 2008 based on bogus charges. There he met several high-profile criminals, among them some drug bosses who were doing time. As word spread out in prison that he was a journalist, not a criminal, and that he has been framed by officials to get rid of him, high-profile inmates befriended him and shared their personal stories of criminality with him. As a reporter, he managed to keep notes of those conversations and once he was acquitted of all charges three years later, he wrote several books about his experience and the violence that sent him to prison. Some of his most known works are *Los Malditos: Crónica Negra desde Puente Grande* (The Damned: A Dark Chronicle from a Supermax Prison) and *Michoacán en Guerra* (Michoacán at War).

British journalist Ioan Grillo books *El Narco: Inside Mexico's Criminal Insurgency* and *Gangster Warlords* have contributed to expand the knowledge and details of this genre. For years Grillo has been reporting on Latin America and eventually settled in Mexico City. He interviewed dozens of public officials, traffickers, criminals, and informants to document the material for his work. The book *El Narco* in particular is an excellent and well-research chronicle of the WOD in Mexico.

American author Charles Bowden wrote about the horrific effects of the drug war on people living near or where DT occurs. His books *Down by the*

River: Drugs, Money, Murder, and Family and *Murder City: Ciudad Juarez and the Global Economy's New Killing Fields* are two of his finest works to detail the context of the Mexico-U.S. border and how the illegal drug trade impacts individuals in this region. He argues that the WOD is actually a misnomer because the war is not against drugs but against those who use drugs.

Impossible to list and describe all the works of this category, here are some of the most influential books on the genre of narco-literature written by journalists: 1. *Killing Pablo: The Hunt for the World's Greatest Outlaw* by Mark Bowden; 2. *Desperados* by Elaine Shannon; 3. *To Die in Mexico: Dispatches from Inside the Drug War* by John Gibler; 4. *Tierra Narca* (Narco Land) by Francisco Cruz Jimenez; 5. *Narcotráfico y Poder* (Drug Trafficking and Power) and *De los Maras a los Zetas* (From Los Maras to Los Zetas) by Jorge Fernández Menéndez; 6. *Fuego Cruzado* (Crossfire) by Marcela Turatti; 7. *Marca de Sangre: Los Años de la Delincuencia Organizada* (Blood Mark: The Years of Organized Crime) by Héctor de Mauleón; 8. *El Hombre sin Cabeza* (The Headless Man) by Segio González Rodríguez; 9. *Tamaulipas: La Casta de los Narcogobernadores, un Eastern Mexicano* (Tamaulipas State: The Political Caste of Narco-Governors, a Mexican Eastern) by Humberto Padgett; 10. *El Cártel Incomodo: El Fin de los Beltrán Leyva y la Hegemonía del Chapo Guzmán* (The Inconvenient Cartel: The End of the Beltran Leyva Organization and the Hegemony of el Chapo´s Guzman) by José Reveles; 11. *La DEA en México* (The DEA in Mexico) and *La CIA, Camarena y Caro Quintero: La Historia Secreta* (The CIA, Camarena, and Caro Quintero: A Secret Story) by J. Jesús Esquivel; among others.

Academic Works and Memoirs

Scholars and people who have been directly or indirectly involved in the War on Drugs (either as drug traffickers, public officials, or victims), have written memoirs and personal chronicles to voice their experiences while dealing with DT activities. A few of these works are truly eye-opening narratives providing an insightful inner perspective difficult to get otherwise. Some of these books present a personal account of how they understood and interpreted the complex issue of DT and the current War on Drugs policy from their personal perspectives. As mentioned earlier, the concept of narco-literature is a relatively new creation and some of books of this classification were written before this genre came to exist. Therefore, a few of these works may not explicitly "belong" to this category; however, for the sake of illustrating the abundance of this genre they deserve to be mentioned here.

Among academics who pioneered scholarly work on DT activities is Luis Astorga, a Mexican sociologist who specialized on this topic in Mexico decades ago. His seminal works are *Drogas sin Fronteras* (Drugs without Borders) and *El Siglo de las Drogas: Del Porfiriato al Nuevo Milenio* (The Century of Drugs: From the Porfiriato to the New Millennium). In the former, there is a thorough depiction of the beginning of DT activities in Mexico as well as a detailed chronicle of the most important traffickers of the twentieth century based on evidence and facts. The latter is a socio-historical account of the availability of illegal drugs in Mexico in the past century along with a depiction of the DT scene in the second half of the century.

A scholar from Sinaloa, Arturo Santamaria Perez, has written several books on the role of women in DT businesses, two of his most known works are *Las Jefas del Narco* (Female Narco Bosses) and *De Carnaval, Reinas y Narco: El Terrible Poder de la Belleza* (On Carnival, Queens, and Drug Trafficking: The Terrifying Power of Beauty). Next, a combination of journalism and academia are the books *Narco Historia* (Narco-History) written by Carmen Boullosa and Mike Wallance and *Viento Rojo: Diez Historias del Narco en México* (Red Wind: Ten Stories on Drug Trafficking from Mexico) by ten authors, among them Carlos Monsiváis, Jesús Brancornelas, Élmer Mendoza, and seven more.

A combination of memoir and academic work is the book *Historia del Narcotráfico en México: Apuntes para Entender al Crimen Organizado y la Violencia* (History of Drug Trafficking in Mexico: Notes to Understand Organized Crime and Violence) by Guillermo Valdés Castellanos. He is a scholar but also was the head of the Mexican civilian intelligence agency (CISEN, the equivalent of the FBI in the United States) for several years. This book provides a comprehensive explanation of the problem of DT since its inception, covering the most relevant facts until the current situation as well as a prognosis of the problem.

The book *La Maña: Un Recorrido Antropológico por la Cultura de las Drogas* (The Mafia: An Anthropological Journey on the Drug Culture) by Edgar Morín Martínez provides a different perspective on the issue. This is a well-documented work that presents a more holistic perspective of the problem of DT. As a Mexican anthropologist, the author uses different methodological approaches from an inner context to compile the information and present a broad and unique approach to the topic. The same can be said of the book *Nuestra Historia Narcótica* (Our Narcotic History) by Froylán Enciso who is a journalist and historian from Sinaloa that reassesses the history of DT and Mexican drug policy based on well-documented sources. Also the book *Los Cárteles no existen: Narcotráfico y cultura en México* (Drug Cartels Do Not Exist: Drug Trafficking and Culture in Mexico) by Oswaldo Zavala presents an interesting argument about how DT has been an invention by the Mexican government to pursue political goals and justify state policies that only benefit the political establishment.

Another refreshing book on the genre is *Más Que Plata o Plomo: El Poder Político del Narcotráfico en Colombia y México* (More Than Silver or Lead: The Political Power of Drug Trafficking in Colombia and Mexico) by Gustavo Duncan. This work brings the argument that DT is not just an activity that enriches traffickers and criminal organizations, but traffickers themselves also have the desire to influence and control the status quo, so they openly want to accumulate political power from the state (when the latter is weak or nonexistent) and use it in their own advantage.

From the viewpoint of someone who belonged to a large criminal organization, a unique account told by a former member of a feared Colombian drug organization called cartel del Norte del Valle is the memoir *El Cártel de los Sapos* (The Cartel of Snitches) by Andrés López López. Using first-hand experience, he reveals the inner workings of the cartel, the brutal fights between its members, betrayals, and demise of most of these men and women. The author became an informant and eventually was turned in to the DEA for his crimes and once in prison he wrote about his experience as a drug trafficker and the book is his personal account on the topic.

A short list of other works written by scholars or witnesses of DT is the following: 1. *Vacíos de Poder en México: Cómo Combatir la Delincuencia Organizada* (Power Vacuum: How to Fight Organized Crime) by Edgardo Buscaglia; 2. *Seguridad, Traficantes, y Militares: El Poder y la Sombra* (Security, Traffickers, and Soldiers: The Power in the Shadows) by Luis Astorga; 3. *En la Niebla de la Guerra: Los Ciudadanos ante la Violencia Criminal Organizada* (In the Fog of War: Citizens Facing Organized Criminal Violence) by Andreas Schedler; 4. *El Narcotráfico en el Contexto de la Relaciones México-EE.UU.* (Drug Trafficking in the Context of Mexico-U.S. Relations) by José Octavio Tripp Villanueva and Carlos Mendoza Mora; 5. *Drogas: Su Legalización* (Drugs: On Legalization) by Eduardo López Betancurt, among other works.

Narco-Mass Media

Another fascinating phenomenon that has been influenced by the abundance of narco-literature is the fact that many of the books of this genre that became best sellers eventually made it to TV productions such as soap operas, series, and ultimately movies. This transition from books (that tend to have a more limited audience) to mass communication outlets such as blockbuster films and TV series allowed narco-literature (and narcoculture by addition) to reach a larger audience. As a result, the topic of DT, drug organizations, and drug bosses has been transformed into a media sensation and a pop culture phenomenon (think about *Breaking Bad* by the time the series finale was over and you get the idea). Predictably, the depiction of the protagonists, characters, and plots of these shows and films have been more fictional than real considering that the purpose of TV and movies is entertainment and making money, rather than educating viewers. Most of this media content often romanticizes, if not frankly glorifies, gangsters and criminal organizations by distorting or mixing facts with fiction regarding DT and drug lords. As a result, many viewers become confused or misinformed about the problem of DT and uncritically embrace the mass media version of the drug war, believing that TV series such as *Narcos* (Netflix), *La Reina del Sur* (Telemundo) or the movies *Sicario I* and *II* (Lionsgate International) are the authentic depiction of how organized crime works.

I have countless examples from my own students who as criminal justice mayors try to understand and explain drug cartels, kingpins, or DT based on the "knowledge" they have gained from watching *Narcos* on Netflix or the movie *Sicario*. Analogous to what is known as the CSI syndrome (how the glamorized and superficial depiction of forensic science in television shows influences public perception on it), movies and TV series that portray DT and drug lords end up "educating" viewers by presenting a confused and oversimplified narrative of these phenomena. Not only that, TV series and films also introduce a reductionist and narrow-minded context of the drug war and traffickers that ignores the complexity of the problem and reinforces the narrative "us versus them." This black and white perspective reinforces the ethnocentric view that many Americans (certainly many law enforcement agents fighting the WOD) hold against foreigners, immigrants, and those who have a different standpoint about DT, drugs, and how to deal with these social problems.

Furthermore, this mass production and consumption of narco-stories have helped to consolidate worldwide the notion of narcoculture as a well-known cultural phenomenon produced by drug traffickers. Before this happened, most of the iconic products of narcoculture were confined to some people, regions, or cities where DT occurred, however, today narcoculture has turned into a global phenomenon. Certainly, some domains of this phenomenon such as narco-corridos were popular in Latin America and the United States before the massive commodification of DT but hardly as narcoculture is understood and consumed today.

In a sort of self-fulfilling prophecy, movies and TV shows have depicted clichés and distorted characteristics of drug traffickers who, upon watching them on TV or films, adopted them as part of their personas. In time, some of these clichés of narcoculture are identified by the media and then are attributed to drug traffickers while they were invented by the media in the first place (Monsiváis 2004). It has been documented by several authors (Grillo 2011; Saviano 2006) that some mafia bosses and drug cartel members widely admire underworld movie characters such as Tony Montana, Vito or Michael Corleone, wanting to imitate their lifestyles and image. Think about the phrase "it's not personal, it's strictly business" said in one of the Godfather movies that has been reproduced in countless TV shows and movies about organized crime and repeated by some criminals, and the reader gets the idea.

The content of these media materials blatantly ignores the human tragedy that has occurred in Mexico and other Latin American countries where the most deadly effects of WOD are experienced. There have been thousands of people murdered, disappeared, and buried in mass graves in Mexico because of the drug war, and yet none of these media productions meant to entertain audiences, include any of these atrocious facts that are currently taking place. Likewise, the plotlines of movies and TV series invariably depict blacks, Hispanics, Muslims, and foreigners as "criminals" while "cops and government officials" are mostly white characters. This stereotypical version of DT only reinforces the existing racism, discrimination, prejudice, and sexist assumptions that already exist in America and many viewers accept them uncritically as the norm (Albarrán-Torres 2017).

Just to provide an example of the former, in the two blockbuster *Sicario* movies (2015 and 2018), the Hispanic assassin Alejandro Gillick (played by Benicio del Toro) is portrayed as a sort of folk hero who kills systematically in order to bring justice to America. Thus, the extreme violence committed by this character (like many other Hollywood movies) is depicted as justified and sanitized for the audience with no consideration or responsibility for the consequences of his crimes. Of course, the public knows that blockbuster movies, TV shows, or any mass media production for that matter are created to entertain, not to engage in critical thinking. However, my point is to acknowledge the powerful role and message that these mass media contents have had in bringing a narrow-minded notion of narcoculture to mainstream society while helping to expand the culture of drug traffickers. Another major issue of this trivialization of DT and criminal gangs is blurring the distinction between what is fictional and what is not. It is not just difficult to sort it out; there is a moment where reality and fiction mutually influence each other to the point where one cannot distinguish one from the other.

Taking this into account, following is a list of the most popular narco-films that have turned narcoculture, DT, and the WOD into a more conventional and familiar phenomenon. Like previous lists, this one is not meant to be exhaustive but descriptive and only to inform readers unfamiliar with this genre about notorious DT movies available to the public. Because this listing is informative, and most films have been widely known in public for years, I will only include the title of the films and the year they were released.

Narco-Movies, Narco-Documentaries, and Narco-TV Series

I will classify the movies in two categories: American and foreign films. Among the former are: 1. *Scarface* (1983); 2. *Traffic* (2000); 3. *Blow* (2001);

4. *Once Upon a Time in Mexico* (2003); 5. *A Man Apart* (2003); 6. *Miami Vice* (2006); 7. *American Gangster* (2007); 8. *No Country for Old Men* (2007); 9. *Machete* (2010); 10. *Savages* (2012); 11. *Sicario* (2012 and 2018); 12. *The Last Stand* (2013); 13. *American Made* (2017); 14. *Superfly* (2018); 15. *The Mule* (2018); 16. *El Chicano* (2019), and others. Among foreign narco-movies these are the most popular: 1. *Our Lady of the Assassins* (2000); 2. *City of God* (2002); 3. *Maria Full of Grace* (2004); 4. *Elite Squad* (2007); 5. *El Infierno* (Hell, 2010); 6. *Miss Bala* (2011); 7. *Heli* (2013); 8. *La Jaula de Oro* (The Golden Dream, 2013); and others.

There are also some documentaries that have approached the topic of DT in different ways, some of them are as follows: 1. *Cocaine Cowboys* (2006); 2. *El Sicario, Room 164* (2010); 3. *El Velador* (The Night Watchman, 2011); 4. *The House I Live In* (2012); 5. *How to Make Money Selling Drugs* (2013); 6. *Narco Cultura* (2013); 7. *Cartel Land* (2015); 8. *Breaking the Taboo: The Truth about the War on Drugs* (2015); 9. *Drug Lord: The Legend of Shorty* (2015); 10. *Narco-Song of Sinaloa: El Chapo's Drug Cartel* (2017); and 11. *La Libertad del Diablo* (Devil's Freedom, 2017); among others.

Television shows in both English and Spanish have been creative and successful in the genre of narco-productions with series openly embracing the content of narcoculture, DT, and gang leaders, which have contributed to put drug traffickers and their lives as a cultural phenomenon in terms of audience and popularity. Probably the most well known of them is *Breaking Bad* (2008–2013) which, at its peak, became one of the greatest series of all times with dozens of accolades and awards. The show is an American version of drug traffickers who outsmart law enforcement and glamorize this illicit activity.

Another important TV show known for its more accurate representation of crime and social issues is *The Wire* (2002–2008). Although the series explores the illegal drug trade, it also includes a lot of the issues of urban life and its most common dislocations. *Weeds* (2005–2012) is another TV series centered on the main character, a widowed woman with two kids, who begins to sell pot to make ends meet in Southern California. Eventually she meets a Mexican drug lord and gets pregnant. Only a couple of seasons focused on DT activities and smuggling drugs from Mexico, but the show contributed to the continuous glamorization of the illegal drug trade.

More recently, the TV series *Narcos* (2015–present) brings back the life of Pablo Escobar, the famous leader of the Medellin cartel. The show has gained a large audience and it has continued with a fourth season now set in Mexico. As with similar TV series, the show does not depict the reality of DT but a romanticized idea of it. Netflix in particular has been keen in producing multiple narco-stories shows such as *Escobar: El Patrón del Mal* (Escobar: The Evil Boss, 2012), and *El Chapo* (2017), among others. In Spanish language, narco TV series have also been popular in Latin American and the United States, in particular telenovelas (soap operas). Most of these productions are based on fictional works or memoirs that are part of the narco-literature boom that came in recently. For instance, the best-seller book *Sin Tetas no Hay Paraiso* (Without Tits, There is no Paradise) by Gustavo Bolivar has led to three different TV series: the first one in Colombia (2006), the second one in Spain (2008–2009), which was later broadcasted to other Latin American countries, and the third one is an American-Colombian production (2016–present) still showing.

Another one is *El Cartel de los Sapos* (The Cartel of Snitches, 2008–2010) a popular series (in Colombia first and Latin America later) that was based on the memoir by former drug cartel member Andrés López López who wrote the book while in prison in the United States. Further, Telemundo Company produced *La Reina del Sur* (The Queen of the South, 2011–2019), one more popular soap opera based on the homonymous novel written by Spanish author Arturo Pérez-Reverte. Yet one more successful telenovela is *El Señor de los Cielos* (The Lord of the Skies, 2013–present), a fictional account inspired in the life of drug lord Amado Carrillo Fuentes, former leader of the Juarez cartel who died in 1997 after cosmetic surgery meant to change his appearance. *La Viuda Negra* (The Black Widow, 2014–2015) is a soap opera created by Univision, and unlike the previous series, the main character of this one is a female drug boss named Griselda Blanco. She was a high-ranking leader who smuggled in cocaine to Miami in the 1980s.

An interesting production is the documentary series *The Day I Met El Chapo: The Kate del Castillo Story* (2017). It is a bizarre experiment that illustrates how reality can become fiction and fiction can become reality when mixing DT accounts and TV. It tells the story of Kate del Castillo, a Mexican actress who was contacted by the head of the Sinaloa cartel, Joaquin *El Chapo* Guzman, to help him make a movie about himself. She contacts Sean Penn, and both go to visit the drug lord in the mountains of Sinaloa. A few days later *El Chapo* is captured for the last time and eventually deported to the United States (Penn 2016). These series tell the whole story about this event from the perspective of Kate del Castillo, explaining how and why she was accused of money laundering and having ties with the Sinaloa organization by the Mexican government as a smear campaign but was never charged with any crimes.

The list could go on, but the material described earlier proves beyond controversy that narco-cinema, narco-TV shows, and narco-documentaries have expanded exponentially the phenomenon of narcoculture worldwide. What is more, mass media productions have influenced and shaped how narcoculture and DT are defined, understood, and consumed in society by exposing to large audiences a superficial and simplistic notion of these phenomena. It is true that visual entertainment is not designed to explore complex social issues and create awareness among citizens. Just to be clear, I am not complaining or criticizing the proliferation of this mass media productions; my point is about the unintended effects of this exposure in America that trivializes and glamorizes a reality that is killing thousands of people and destroying lives in Latin America. In other words, narcoculture as it is known in society today is not just the effect of drug traffickers and their activities but also the result of overexposure to media content that somehow distorts, exaggerates, dramatizes, or underplays the nature of DT and the culture of traffickers. Therefore, to counterbalance the glamorized notion that most Americans have about drug lords, their business and activities, it is necessary to look at the real impact that DT has on the lives of people who live and witness this activity south of the border. Then, the following chapter presents a detailed examination of the aftermath of DT activities in the recent past in Mexico and the South border based on facts and evidence.

Chapter 4

The Price of the War on Drugs in Mexico

There is a particular narrative of the problem of drug trafficking in the United States that has been repeated and magnified for decades by the media and many public officials in charge of the War on Drugs (WOD) and dealing with drug abuse. This account is incomplete, narrow-minded, and half-true because according to it, drug trafficking is reduced to smuggling drugs from South to North, mostly by Mexican cartels or other Latin American gangs, with the implication that all of them are foreigners. According to this view, drug trafficking organizations (DTOs) bring drugs to America from foreign places to poison our youth and our pristine neighborhoods in order to make money and destroy society. In addition, it is assumed that DTOs have a free reign in Mexico to conduct their illegal business due to corruption and incompetence by Mexican authorities because the government does not tackle the problem of drug trafficking efficiently and effectively (DEA 2018).

The official interpretation of drug trafficking in America has marginalized or hidden crucial and dreadful events happening in Mexico (and other countries) where drugs are produced, stored, or transported before they are delivered to American consumers. These events include extreme violence, unprecedented high murder rates, disappearances, mass graves, domestic and international migration, narco-politics, vigilante justice, and state capture that are strongly correlated to the business of drug trafficking. This chapter addresses in detail the effects of the illegal drug trade in Mexico that somehow have been hidden in American society.

EXTREME VIOLENCE

In the past twenty years, Mexico and Central America have been immersed in an unprecedented surge of extreme violence connected to drug trafficking activities. Experts (Skarpedas 2001) know that violence is one of the most powerful tools used by organized crime syndicates to accomplish their criminal activities. Violence is necessary "[T]o establish, protect, and defend drug territory in an illegal market, and to build a name for being consistently terrifying so nobody tries to take your property or turf" (Hari 2015, 66). When co-optation, corruption, or threats do not work, drug cartels resort to violence against victims, civilians, and rivals to maintain a strong grip in their territories to develop and nourish their bad reputation. This reputation is based on the premise that drug cartels (or any type of mafia for that matter) are capable of exercising credible physical force to harm or kill individuals with total impunity to preserve or defend their criminal enterprise. Once a criminal syndicate earns a negative reputation of being capable of extreme bloodshed, it does not need to exert violence anymore since the reputation itself would suffice to achieve its illicit goals. Decades ago DTOs did not use extreme violence, nor did they target civilians because avoiding violence was understood to be a good business strategy to maintain a low profile and deflect unwanted attention from law enforcement agencies (Boullosa and Wallance 2016; Grillo 2011; Valdés Castellanos 2013).

Things changed in Mexico and other Latin American drug-producing countries in the early 2000s, however, when a combination of factors led to a surge of extreme violence. Earlier though in the 1990s, Colombia experienced an extraordinary wave of violence from the main cartels involved in drug trafficking (Pablo Escobar and associates in particular). Violence eventually subsided when drug smuggling shifted from the Caribbean to the Mexico-U.S. border and Colombian cartel lost prominence in favor of Mexican criminal organizations (Boullosa and Wallace 2016; López López 2008). Although the violence in Mexico increased dramatically from 2006 onwards, it did not begin as a random event nor was it a sudden occurrence. Instead, a combination of political, social, and government affairs created a context where extreme violence became a profitable commodity for criminal groups, state agents, and the government.

To begin with, the old political system that ruled Mexico for more than seventy-one years lost the presidential election in 2000 and its authoritarian grip dissolved, which created a vacuum of power that was filled in by organized crime. Also, a new type of DTOs such as Los Zetas was born where its members had wide knowledge of counter-insurgency tactics (e.g., surveillance, use of sophisticated weaponry, raids, propaganda). These tactics were adopted by the Los Zetas group because it brought efficiency, organization, and profits to them. Soon after, other DTOs copycatted the same behavior due to their success and this created a race to the bottom where cartels competed to prove which one had the worse criminal reputation in order to keep their strongholds intact (Boullosa and Wallance 2016; Grillo 2011; Valdés Castellanos 2013).

As violence emerged as an efficient criminal commodity, cartel members started using social media platforms such as Internet forums, YouTube, and Facebook accounts to streamline live or record videos of rivals, informants, traitors, and officials being tortured, murdered, and decapitated. Gruesome violence turned into a spectacle meant to threaten, instill fear, exhibit power, and advertise the total impunity of drug cartel members. Simultaneously, DTOs evolved into a new type of decentralized system by breaking into smaller components and quasi-independent cells that enjoyed more autonomy and freedom as explained earlier. This fragmentation made it harder for law enforcement agencies to pursue, arrest, and disintegrate drug gangs. On top of everything else, a new generation of drug traffickers entered the ranks and files of the cartels; they did not hide their criminal status as traffickers but instead flaunted it openly and proudly in the media, social networks, music (*narcocorridos*—drug ballads) and social media (Gibler 2011; Grillo 2011; Valdés Castellanos 2013).

To make matters worse, a flow of semi-automatic weapons and high-caliber firearms from the United States began to inundate Mexico in the mid-2000s as a result of Federal Assault Weapons Ban expiration in September 2004. This ban was a ten-year prohibition law passed by Congress in 1994 to prohibit the manufacture and commercialization of some semi-automatic weapons for civilian use. Since the ban was not renovated by the legislative branch before its expiration, it immediately lifted the prohibition and civilians were able to have legal access to an assortment of assault firearms. Some American buyers (known as straw purchasers) were able to obtain sophisticated weaponry from multiple gun dealerships located along the Southwest border—but mostly from Arizona and Texas—to supply the cartels' demand for guns in exchange for a fee (Grillo 2011).

Using different methodological approaches experts have conducted research to estimate the number of arms trafficking from the United States to Mexico. According to a mathematical model using demand for firearms based on the distance by road from the nearest point on the U.S.-Mexico border, McDougal et al. (2015) concluded that between the years 2010 and 2012 an average of 212,887 firearms were purchased and trafficked to Mexico (McDougal et al. 2015). Another study concluded that between 1990 and 2013 the number of firearms smuggled into Mexico was 24.6 million arms (although not all of them come from the United States). This staggering amount of guns is based on a conservative estimate and the real amount is probably higher (Carrazco Araigaza 2015). There are multiple strategies to buy firearms in the United States and smuggle them to Mexico (Harp 2019). They are well-known to U.S. authorities and federal agents; however, there is no political interest to change the status quo given how divisive and ideological gun ownership and gun regulation have become in America.

In an ironic twist, something that also contributed to the surge of violence in Mexico was increased border security after the September 11, 2001, attacks on the United States. When the Mexico-U.S. border was reinforced with more surveillance and tighter controls, it made it more difficult to smuggle drugs through remote and desolated regions of the border in the desert or mountains. As a result, the value of controlling any of the forty-seven legal border crossings between the two countries rose and drug cartels fought a brutal battle to occupy, retain, and control as many of them as possible because they were crucial points of entry to store, smuggle, and traffic drugs into the United States (Grillo 2011). Those organizations or groups that controlled these ports of entry on the Mexican side of the border perpetrated all sorts of crimes and violence (mostly with total impunity), to keep a tight grip on their strongholds. This control meant that drug gangs had absolute dominance over the local and state police, and sometimes over army commanders in the jurisdiction. The port of entry, territory, or drug corridor crucial for drug traffickers became known as *La Plaza* which refers to "the valuable real state of a particular trafficking corridor" (Grillo 2011, 53).

Altogether, these events coalesced to create the perfect storm where extreme violence became normalized in Mexico in the past two decades, more noticeable since 2006 when the then-president Calderón launched the Mexican version of the drug war. Like Mexico, Central American countries are plagued with chronic political and social issues such as poor governance, corruption, weak institutions, high unemployment and extreme poverty. DTOs took advantage of this context to thrive and impose their hegemony. The most visible ramifications of this extreme violence have been a dramatic increase in murder rates across Mexico and Central America along with the impunity enjoyed by the perpetrators where most of these homicides remain unsolved (Campbell 2009; Grillo 2011; Valdés Castellanos 2013; Wainwright 2016).

MURDER RATES ESCALATE

According to the International Institute for Strategic Studies (IISS), in 2017 Mexico became the second deadliest country in the world just behind Syria. Based on *The Armed Conflict Survey* conducted by IISS and published in 2017, an estimated 23,000 people died in drug cartel violence incidents in

2016 alone. The number of people violently killed that year in Mexico's drug war exceeded those murdered in war zones such as Iraq (17,000) and Afghanistan (16,000). This is a shocking number considering that in Mexico there is no war machinery (e.g. artillery, tanks, combat planes), instead most deaths are the result of small arms, the report said (The International Institute for Strategic Studies 2017).

Mexican government agencies released their own report with data arguing that on average, every twenty minutes one person was killed during the month of May in 2017, with a total of 2,452 official deaths for that month alone. These numbers set up a record as the highest murder rate ever recorded since the Mexican government began to track down rates in 1997 (this historic number of murders will be eventually surpassed by yet other records in 2019). Thus, the murders kept climbing and during the first five months of 2017 alone, the death toll from violent homicide reached 11,155 victims, meaning that the final figure for 2017 was even higher than it was for the previous year (Lotto Persio 2017). In fact, according to official data collected by the National Institute of Statistics and Geography, 2017 was considered the most violent year in more than twenty years with a total number of 31,174 homicides in Mexico (Instituto Nacional de Estadística y Geografía 2018). Things got worse, and in 2018 the number of murders hit a new record high with nearly 37,000 homicides, according to official data. For some experts (Hope 2018a), the number of murders will not go down anytime soon (even with a new president in Mexico who promised to reduce homicides), because the context that favors this level of violence and impunity is systemic and requires an overhaul of multiple institutions and policies difficult to make at the short term (Hope 2018b).

It is not surprising then that after six decades of positive gains, life expectancy in Mexico has decreased over the past decade because of the unprecedented rise in murder rates between the years 2007 and 2014, according to a study published in early 2017 in the *Journal of Epidemiology and Community Health*. The authors argued that acts of violence are so prevalent today that they have become a serious public health issue because of the remarkable effect on the well-being of Mexican society with the potential to become permanent in the population (Canudas-Romo et al. 2017).

The concentration of homicides has occurred in and around regions with chronic drug trafficking activities such as Sinaloa and Guerrero states where drug gangs are battling among themselves for controlling traditional trafficking routes and drug markets as well as territorial expansion and domination over other profitable criminal business such as extortion, kidnapping, and robbery. Although the official narrative of this escalation of homicides is that members of drug cartels and criminal gangs are killing each other, the Mexican government has not provided any evidence to justify this account. For the past two administrations (2006–2018), the Mexican government has engaged in a disturbing pattern of blaming the murdered victims of violence for their own victimization without having any conclusive forensic evidence of such claims. Instead, these claims have been based on political merits mostly to deflect official responsibility and failure to investigate and prosecute the perpetrators.

As the War on Drugs began to unfold in full swing after 2006 many government officials such as detectives, prosecutors, district attorneys, and politicians throughout Mexico developed a narrative to arbitrarily label most victims of violence and homicide as "members of drug gangs." The evidence, according to authorities, for such labeling was the circumstances of how violence and death were inflicted. Most prosecutors who dealt with criminal investigations of these cases provided an official script arguing that given the drug cartels' execution methods found in crime scenes such as use of high-caliber weaponry against the victim, signs of torture, dismemberment or beheading, body gagged, taped or wrapped in blankets and the like, the victim had to be someone involved in drug trafficking activities. The assumption was that if they are involved in the illegal drug trade, they should be blamed for their own victimization (Molloy 2013). Now, assuming that any of these murder crime scene factors could suggest the involvement of the victims in organized crime, it is difficult to conclude that the victims were connected to drug trafficking activities or cartels just because of how they were killed. Simply put, there is no concrete fact supporting such allegation. In a country like Mexico, where more than 95 per cent of crimes are never prosecuted or thoroughly investigated, it is difficult to accept that government officials could accurately determine when a victim of a murder has been involved in drug trafficking activities by just looking at the circumstances of how the victim was murdered (Schedler 2015). Even if the argument is true and the victims of those crimes had been involved in the drug trafficking business that is not an excuse for Mexican officials to ignore the duties of the criminal justice system to investigate those violent murders and punish the perpetrator.

Pundits and experts (Molloy 2013; Schedler 2015) in Mexico have instead given a more plausible explanation for the government's rationale to treat those victims of murders as criminals. Given the incompetence and systematic corruption of the Mexican government, it is easier for authorities to criminalize the victims and blame them for their own victimization. More often than not, officials in charge of investigating and finding the culprits of these gruesome assassinations refuse to fulfill their legal duties based on the assumption that the victims "deserved" their fate for being involved in drug trafficking activities. Unlike what the Mexican government argues, data shows that many of those victims are civilians (as opposed to organized crime militants) and when murdered, they have been found unarmed and killed in or near their workplaces, homes, or on the streets (Molloy 2013; Schedler 2015).

The dramatic escalation of murder rates began in 2006 when then-president Felipe Calderón launched his Mexican WOD without a proper assessment of the problem and having no official strategy to deal with DTOs and criminal gangs. Ten days after his inauguration, he sent thousands of military forces to states such as Michoacán where drug trafficking cartels were battling among themselves and targeting the population with extortion, kidnapping, and drug dealing. Under President Calderón, the number of troops patrolling the streets and conducting law and order activities went from 20,000 to more than 50,000 in cities and regions affected by the drug trade (Boullosa and Wallace 2016). Soon after sending troops to fight criminal gangs, this policy became the de-facto official strategy for Calderón's administration to deal with the increasing extreme violence and gruesome murders that began to occur every day across the country. In the short term, the president's strategy appeared to succeed, however, the tactic backfired because too many fronts were open (many regions and states throughout Mexico have become drug trafficking hubs) and many of the security forces at the local and state levels were infiltrated by drug cartels. The fact that drug gangs enjoyed the support of the local police made it more difficult for the military and federal police to contain the illegal drug trade and successfully keep DTOs at bay (Boullosa and Wallance 2016; Valdés Castellanos 2013).

An important aspect of this strategy was that soldiers were deployed to maintain law and order where drug cartels have infiltrated local security forces and traffickers had taken over the local civilian government. Yet, armed forces are not trained to police and serve the community but to kill and defeat the enemy. The fact that the federal government gave domestic law enforcement responsibilities to the military led to widespread extrajudicial killings by soldiers against drug gang members and civilians. The military is not trained to conduct criminal investigations and gather forensic evidence either. This lack of technical knowledge contributed to the pattern of impunity already in place in Mexico because many criminal cases investigated by soldiers did not adhere to due process. As a result, indictments against drug traffickers would have legal loopholes to be exploited by drug cartels' attorneys. Eventually, many drug traffickers were released or acquitted by the courts after being arrested by the army because soldiers in charge of investigating a crime scene either trampled the evidence or did not properly collect it according to the rule of law (Aguilar Valenzuela and Castañeda 2012; Molloy 2013; Schedler 2015).

By 2012, when President Calderón left office, more than 130,000 people had been violently murdered. This number is an unofficial estimate from non-governmental organizations (NGOs), scholars, and human rights groups since the government record has been inconsistent and tends to present a lower number of crimes in order to avoid negative publicity. Perhaps the most dramatic aspect of this reality is that the Mexican government back then systematically denied or hid its responsibility in prosecuting and convicting the perpetrators of these murders and bring justice to the victims. Previous administrations under Presidents Calderón (2006–2012) and Peña Nieto (2012–2018) argued that most victims of the War on Drugs (WOD) were drug cartel members, but these administrations never presented data or evidence to support their arguments. President Calderón in particular asserted that violence and its immediate outcome, murders, were the result of criminal gangs killing each other without affecting society. As mentioned earlier, the government's narrative implied that those citizens who were not involved in drug trafficking activities should not worry about the violence because it only occurred between and against criminals. In the same line, the president stressed that murders and violence were restricted to a few states or regions of the country and were not a widespread phenomenon. It seemed as if the president's statements were a permanent state of denial in an attempt to shift his own responsibility in the crisis because data and facts from that time showed exactly the opposite. In fact, several scholars now have concluded that President Calderón's arguments regarding these killings were deliberately untrue (Aguilar and Castañeda 2012; Molloy 2013; Schedler 2015).

Since 2007, when the Mexican government began its strategy to tackle drug trafficking relying mostly on the military forces, presidents Calderón and Peña Nieto engaged in a similar political discourse to minimize murders and crime (using media outlets that reproduce uncritically the official narrative). These arguments ran from "Mexico could be worse," "drug-related violence and deaths have always existed in the country" or "other countries have far more violence and murders than us," to "violence and death occur in a few regions of Mexico and they are decreasing." This sort of institutional rationalization pretended to minimize violence, crime, and murders by refusing to take official action to address the problem thoroughly while ignoring government accountability. The strategy of this government's approach was to remain silent about the high murder rates and violence hoping that the bereaved will get tired of demanding justice (Molloy 2013; Schedler 2015).

Only when a high-profile criminal case became breaking news in mainstream media the government was forced to break the silence and publicly admit that such as crime has occurred. The typical official response then was a promise to find the perpetrators and bring justice to the victims, but usually no significant government actions would be taken to change the status quo. This is emphasized in prominent criminal investigations where victims were renowned journalists such as Javier Valdez. He was a veteran reporter who wrote articles about drug violence and drug culture who was executed in broad daylight in

2017 in the city of Culiacán. The criminal investigation of his assassination took several months before some arrests were made but not of all the perpetrators were caught. Invariably, the government's approach is to deflect its responsibility to someone or something else as the culprits and dodge the public uproar with strategies using public relation campaigns (Molloy 2013; Schedler 2015).

It is crucial to highlight that DTOs are not the only entities responsible for the violent murders in Mexico. Credible reports from NGOs, human rights groups (e.g. Human Rights Watch), and independent media documented that security forces such as soldiers, police officers (at the local, state, and federal levels), and the Navy's Special Forces have committed many of these serious murders themselves while fighting organized crime. The army in particular has been singled out as the institution committing most of the human rights abuses in Mexico engaging in extrajudicial executions, torture, mistaken-identity killings, shooting innocent bystanders, enforced disappearances, illegal searches, and actively hiding its misconduct (Human Rights Watch 2017). A 2018 documentary titled "Hasta los dientes" (Armed to the teeth), directed by Alberto Arnaut, chronicles the killing by the Mexican army of two students from the Tecnológico de Monterrey, a private elite university located in the most industrialized city of Mexico. The appalling feature of this murder that occurred on March 19, 2010, is that these two male students were executed by soldiers who had them confused as hitmen. Instead of admitting its error the army planted assault weapons, manipulated forensic evidence, moved the bodies, and accused the students of shooting at the army. The truth eventually emerged when the National Commission of Human Rights issued the recommendation 45/2010 that provided a reconstruction of the events and concluded that the army was actually responsible for the assassination of these two students (Arnaut Estrada 2018).

Unfortunately the killing of these two students was not an isolated episode of violence and assassination by state agents against civilians, many more executions and other unlawful acts such as torture, arbitrary detentions, kidnappings, and disappearances have been regularly perpetrated by soldiers, federal and local police officers, as well as Mexican marines during the past decade (Jasso 2018). A common pattern among this criminal behavior has been the reluctance by government officials to investigate and prosecute perpetrators of these crimes or to delay, cover up or sabotage criminal investigations (Carlsen 2018). Following are some high-profile cases of extrajudicial executions and crimes committed by state agents fighting the WOD.

It is relevant to note that during the second half of the twentieth century, the Mexican army was involved in anti-drug campaigns against traffickers to destroy poppy and marijuana plantations as well as to conduct law enforcement operations against DTOs. Back then like today, many soldiers enjoyed impunity when committing human rights violations since their actions were under military jurisdiction and when prosecuted the punishment would be lenient (Enciso 2015). A few things have changed though and in 2014 the legislative branch reformed the Code of Military Justice to allow Civil Criminal tribunals (instead of the military system) to prosecute abuses by army forces (Human Rights Watch 2017). This, however, has not stopped abuses because there is not enough political willingness by the government to go after the perpetrators since the army is one of the most trusted security forces in Mexico and seen as the only one capable of confronting drug cartels and criminal gangs at a large scale (Boullosa and Wallace 2016; Valdés Castellanos 2013).

One shocking case of human rights abuse by the army took place on June 30, 2014, when—allegedly—soldiers responded with aggression against members of a criminal gang and killed twenty-two civilian gunmen defending a warehouse in the mountains of Guerrero state in a small town called Tlatlaya. There were some inconsistencies in the investigation report and after one of the surviving victims gave her testimony to the press, allegations of a military massacre surfaced (Carlsen 2018; Ferri Tórtola 2014). The National Human Rights Commission conducted a thorough investigation and found that between twelve and fifteen of the gunmen were shot to death after they had surrendered to soldiers and were unarmed. Because of public outcry, the military and federal government began an official investigation to look at the evidence and prosecute the abuses. Eventually, seven soldiers were charged, three with murder and abuse of authority and four with improper exercise of public service and concealment. However, all of them were subsequently acquitted by a federal judge based on legal technicalities because of due process violations in the trial against them. There have been other similar cases of human rights violations from military forces but impunity and lack of accountability by high-ranking members remain widespread in the Mexican armed forces, and soldiers who have killed civilians are rarely prosecuted (González Rodriguez 2015).

More recently another case of extrajudicial execution took place in the border city of Nuevo Laredo on September 5, 2018, when local police officers kidnapped and executed eight civilians, then the agents staged a false crime scene intended to show that the victims have died during a shootout after they had attacked security forces. However, pictures, crime scene evidence, and witnesses exposed these officers engaging in extrajudicial execution. The case is still unfolding but it reveals to what extent state agents are also responsible for high murder rates in the context of the Mexican WOD (*The Brownsville Herald* 2019).

DISAPPEARANCES: A PANDEMIC PROBLEM

Along with an increase in murder rates during the last decade, another problem that has also created affliction and anger in Mexican society is the phenomenon of forced disappearances. Every year thousands of people worldwide go missing—voluntarily and involuntarily—for different reasons such as kidnapping, human trafficking, accidental deaths, migration, and the like. In the case of Mexico, most people who have vanished are the result of *forced* disappearances, meaning that victims have been taken away against their will by direct intervention of security forces or their indirect participation or omission (Human Rights Watch 2013). The disappearance of people is not a new phenomenon in Mexico or Latin America given that during the 1960s and 1970s the dictators of South America and authoritarian governments, such as the one in Mexico, used to disappear political dissidents, rivals, or anyone who challenged the authority of those regimes (Illiadas and Santiago 2014). However, there are major differences between the current disappearances and those that happened during the war which became known as "dirty wars."

As mentioned earlier, an authoritarian government ruled Mexico for seventy-one years. During the 1960s and 1970s the Mexican state engaged in counter-insurgency to deal with political activists and leftist member of the communist party who challenged the government's oppression. State agents arrested, tortured, killed, and disappeared hundreds of civilians (mostly students, peasants, rebel suspects, and individuals labeled as "activists") based on their political affiliation and their opposition to the status quo. Among the perpetrators were soldiers, death squads, and militant groups trained by the government to blend as citizens and attack students and activists from within during demonstrations. Most of these disappearances were politically motivated and it was clear that the state, through its different clash groups and state actors, was behind them (Sierra Guzmán 2012).

Unlike fifty years ago, Mexico now has a democracy and is part of the twenty major economies of the world, it is the eighth most visited country by tourists, and it possesses a vibrant middle class and some independent government institutions. Yet, the inertia of crippling problems such as corruption, crime, and impunity has contributed to the current nightmare of disappearances. There is clear evidence that the problem escalated from 2007 when then-president Calderón militarized law enforcement operations against organized crime as a response to the Mexican version of the WOD. As a result, the number of disappeared has steadily increased every year. Similar to other visible and violent crimes in Mexico, authorities have regularly denied that such disappearances occur in a systematic way arguing the lack of evidence to support those claims. This despite reports from journalists documenting those events and families of the disappeared who have confirmed the disappearance of their loved ones.

Because of public officials' reluctance to address the disappearance problem proactively and the serious dimension of the issue, civil society groups and NGOs have stepped up to do the work that Mexican authorities have refused to do and have conducted their own inquiries to find out about this phenomenon. Thus, in February 2013 Human Rights Watch (HRW) published an incriminating report against the Mexican government pointing out how thousands of people disappeared during the administration of President Calderón. The document explained how public officials throughout the different bureaucratic layers have failed to investigate and respond properly to these disappearances while denying government resources to search for the victims. Although the report only documented nearly 250 disappearances, it highlighted the fact that thousands more have occurred, labeling the issue as a national problem and "the most severe crisis of enforced disappearances in Latin America in decades" (Carlsen 2018; Human Rights Watch 2013, 4).

To contextualize the problem, HRW reported a particular pattern well-known by the victim's families and the agencies of the criminal justice system (but hardly contested by the government's official account of this issue) about how these forced disappearances have occurred. Most of them began when security forces arrested individuals without probable cause or warrants of arrest in an arbitrary fashion. Immediately after, the detainees were taken somewhere else and then were disappeared. The arrests usually occur in public venues such as bars, checkpoints, workplaces, or in the homes of the victims—usually in the presence of relatives. Perpetrators invariably wear official uniforms of the police or the military. In some cases, evidence indicates that a particular group of government agents has executed multiple disappearances in the same region, within a particular time period and following a similar method (Human Rights Watch 2013).

According to the report by HRW, when looking at the official response on these disappearances by government officials a systematic attitude has characterized their work: overwhelmingly, institutions and agents of the Mexican criminal justice system have refused to take action when a victim's family submits a police report to denounce the abduction of a loved one even when it was still in process. Also, prosecutors, detectives, and personnel in charge of conducting criminal investigations on these cases have systematically committed serious omissions when performing their basic official duties. Among the most common negligent duties are failing to track the victims' cell phones, not looking at his or her bank transactions, and not securing surveillance camera records when available. Another serious omission has been the unnecessary delays to investigate the disappearance in order to deflect official responsibility. On a regular basis, officials misled the victims' families when confronted by them arguing that authorities did not have jurisdiction to investigate the disappearance, informed them that the police report could not be legally filed, or told victims' families to look themselves for their loved ones somewhere else (González Rodríguez 2015; Human Rights Watch 2013).

In the same way, public officials methodically conveyed a message to families that their disappeared loved ones had been targeted because they were involved in criminal activities even if there was no evidence of such a thing. As a result, authorities used that argument to justify their inaction in conducting the necessary investigations to locate the victim. Other times, officials encouraged families to conduct criminal investigations on their own arguing that prosecutors and the police did not have time, resources, or credible clues to find the perpetrators. To add insult to injury, many prosecutors and detectives made gross mistakes during criminal investigations such as misplacing evidence, failing to execute basic forensic steps (e.g., taking DNA samples or fingerprints when available), recording data inaccurately, or simply manipulating or destroying key evidence to make it easier for them to close the investigation (González Rodríguez 2015; Human Rights Watch 2013).

As a result, it is not hyperbole to say that Mexico is undergoing an epidemic of missing people who have been forcefully disappeared by the thousands in the past decade, and the number of them is growing every day. Unlike the disappearances that took place during the "dirty war" in the 1960s and 1970s where the perpetrators were clearly state agents, today disappearances have been carried out by a murky network of state and non-state agents. This network is being powered by a context of impunity and corruption where some local and federal security forces turn rogue and become enforcers of drug gangs or facilitate information and equipment to hitmen who conduct the disappearances (González Rodríguez 2015). This illegal behavior could not have happened without the collusion of government officials at the federal, state, and local jurisdictions who have facilitated and empowered (by action or omission) perpetrators knowing that their crimes will not be prosecuted. The triad of murders, disappearances, and mass graves have become common phenomena throughout Mexico and reflect the state of terror that the most vulnerable groups (women, poor, indigenous, uneducated, and lower-class Mexicans) have undergone in the past two decades (Wright 2017).

For years it has been difficult to estimate the exact number of disappearances because the government did not keep an official and consistent record until recently as a result of public pressure and political turmoil about the nature of the issue. According to the latest official account that the federal government now keeps in the National Registry of Information about People Lost or Disappeared, in the past ten years from 2007 to 2017, more than 33,500 people have officially disappeared. On average thirteen people disappeared every day in Mexico during 2017 according to official data (Registro Nacional de Datos de Personas Extraviadas o Desaparecidas 2018). However, these numbers are not reliable because in the past authorities reluctantly collected the information from family members who have filed a police report. Yet, many disappeared victims were not reported to the police by relatives or loved ones out of fear of reprisals by security forces or drug cartels' members who have co-opted the local government and control all civil life. Usually, the disappearances occur in locations where organized crime is rampant and criminal groups have substituted the rule of law with a strong criminal grip against the community and the local authorities. Additionally, many immigrants from other countries who have disappeared are not included in official statistics of the disappeared because of the fact that their relatives live somewhere else and they cannot file a police report with the local authorities in Mexico (El Universal Data 2015; González Rodríguez 2015; Molloy 2013).

Those who have disappeared often have a particular demographic profile: most of them are young, male, and between fifteen and twenty-nine years old. The bulk of the disappearances have occurred mostly in five Mexican states: Tamaulipas, Estado de Mexico, Jalisco, Sinaloa and Nuevo Leon (Registro Nacional de Datos de Personas Extraviadas o Desaparecidas 2018). A common factor that characterized most of these disappearances was the lack of interest from authorities to acknowledge the problem and address it accordingly, unless until recently. That attitude was not exclusive of government officials in charge of investigating the crime at the local or state institutions. At the federal level too, President Enrique Peña Nieto (2012–2018) blatantly ignored the phenomenon during his administration by maintaining a cold public silence about the disappearances. The same disdain was shown by the president to similar public safety issues such as the increase of brutal violence, crime, and soaring murder rates. However, the new central-leftist government of Andres Manuel López Obrador (AMLO) has criticized those policies and now it appears that from 2019 on the federal administration is taking a proactive approach to acknowledge the issue of disappearances and taking steps to tackle the problem (Reuters 2019).

Because of this context and the culture of impunity that has prevailed for decades in the Mexican criminal justice system, most local and state officials throughout the country have followed the same script regarding the disappearances: they regularly blame the victims for their own abduction or victimization, label them members of criminal groups to justify institutional inaction against perpetrators, and ignore or delay petitions by the families of the disappeared to investigate the crime. In addition, for the past two federal administrations until the end of 2018, there was no government strategy to look for the disappeared and tackle the problem in an organized and systematic manner. What is worse is that most local and state authorities do not know how to proceed when a police report has been filed when a person disappears nor there is a real government effort at any level to solve the disappearances (El Universal Data 2015; González Rodriguez 2015; Molloy 2013).

The new president of Mexico, AMLO, who took office in December of 2018, immediately distanced himself from previous government tactics regarding disappearances and for the first time the federal administration acknowledged that the state was one of the primary violators of human rights (*Reuters* 2019). In March of 2019 the Mexican government announced the re-establishment of the National Search System for Missing Persons in order to find nearly 40,000 people who are officially considered disappeared. Among them thousands of migrants who were crossing the country to reach the United States disappeared in their way up to the border. This new government position is a well-intended effort to tackle the problem but it remains to be seen if these measures will be enough to break the inertia of past administrations and truly find those who are missing while reducing the problem to minimum levels. To that end, in January of 2020 the government released a new figure of disappearances based on data from state prosecutors and the estimate is that more than 61,000 people have disappeared in Mexico in more than a decade (Sheridan 2020).

THE DISAPPEARANCE OF FORTY-THREE STUDENTS

The catalyst that brought the issue of disappearances to national and international headlines was the mass kidnapping and disappearance of forty-three students on September 26, 2014. These students affiliated to the Ayotzinapa Rural Teacher's College located in the city of Iguala in Guerrero state (Iguala is situated over 100 miles south of Mexico City). The exact details about what happened during that day and thereafter remain elusive due to contradictory statements from witnesses, survivors, and government officials. According to survivors, family members, journalists, and human rights activists, on the afternoon of that Friday, September 26 around 100 male students from the Teachers College travelled to the city of Iguala to commandeer buses from there to attend a march in Mexico City that would take place a few days later. It was not uncommon for these leftist students to engage in political activism actions such as appropriating public buses to mobilize from place to place and because of that, authorities have tolerated their actions for years (González Rodríguez 2015).

The students were driving a couple of buses and then commandeered two or three more at the local bus station after arriving in Iguala. Around 9:30 p.m. of that day, a group of municipal police officers intercepted one of the buses and clashed with the students in the middle of the city, shooting and killing three of them. One hour later, at least two police patrols attacked another bus on the city's highway as students tried to flee. The officers were dressed in black, hooded, they blew out tires and shattered the bus' windows. A third bus was also stopped by yet another police patrol in the outskirts of the city, and students were violently detained and taken somewhere else. The following morning, when authorities began to probe the violent events of the previous night, they found six people dead in three different locations, more than twenty individuals wounded, and forty-three students disappeared (Devereaux 2015; Gibler 2015; González Rodríguez 2015).

From here, the whole situation became murky in terms of what happened to the Ayotzinapa students after that night. According to the official account, the local police was instructed by the mayor of Iguala—José Luis Abarca—to arrest the students and turn them in to the criminal gang known as *Guerreros Unidos* (United Warriors). This is the same criminal organization mentioned in chapter 2, notorious for their ruthless tactics against rivals and civilians. Allegedly, the mayor thought that these students were there to protest and boycott his wife's annual public address as president of the municipal public institution of social assistance called *Desarrollo Integral de la Familia* (DIF). Once in the hands of United Warriors' thugs (according to the official investigation) the students were beaten up, murdered, and burnt to ashes in a huge pyre in a landfill near the town of Cocula, a few miles South West of Iguala. In line with this government narrative, the thugs took turns feeding the fire with flammable materials such as wood, tires, and plastic to make sure the bodies were totally cremated. The remaining parts of the students that did not burn were put into garbage bags and thrown into a river near the landfill. This again became known as the official version of the disappearance, but the narrative was highly contested by survivors, relatives of the victims, and independent forensic experts (Devereaux 2015; González Rodríguez 2015).

To support the official investigation of the crimes and disappearances, the government argued that the mayor and his wife—María de los Angeles Pineda Villa—had strong ties to drug trafficking groups and had been involved in criminal activities. Accordingly, the couple had given protection to the gang *Guerreros Unidos* in its fight against a rival group known as *Los Rojos* (The Red Ones). As the federal government was concerned, the couple was the mastermind behind the abduction and killing of the students on September 26, 2014. Immediately after the crime, the federal government was reluctant to take over the criminal investigation arguing that the nature of the case merited local jurisdiction. So the first steps to searching and collecting evidence, preserving it and interviewing witnesses and suspects were in the jurisdiction of state and local authorities of Guerrero state. Eventually, under a lot of political pressure, the federal government accepted jurisdiction over the case and the investigation was sent to the Attorney General's Office (*Procuraduria General de Justicia*—PGR, now called *Fiscalia General de la República*).

After several months of public protests, political turmoil, and civil unrest, on January 2015 the attorney general officially announced that the forty-three students had been killed and incinerated by the Guerreros Unidos gangs in a landfill in Cocula (as described earlier). The attorney general called this version of the disappearance *"la verdad histórica"* (the historical truth) because—allegedly—it was based on facts and evidence from the perpetrators. However, that assumption would be hardly contested and challenged in the months and years to come given the lack of conclusive physical evidence from the crime scene, forensic inconsistencies, contradictory testimonies, and the government's withholding of information that refuted its own investigation (Gibler 2015; González Rodríguez 2015).

To understand the true nature of this hideous crime, it is crucial to contextualize the social and economic reality of this part of Mexico where the students disappeared. Guerrero state is most famous for its port of Acapulco that thrived as an international tourist destination during the 1960s and 1970s. It is where the Clintons went for their honeymoon and the name has became associated with the famous Cannabis Sativa Acapulco Gold marijuana strain. It has been a large producer of weed and poppy for decades. In particular, the mountains near Iguala have become a trafficking corridor for the manufacture of heroin, turning this city into a crucial drug hub for many DTOs. Sadly, drug gangs and drug trafficking cells have maintained a strict criminal control of the region and have substituted the sovereign of the state in cities and towns, including Iguala. From a criminal perspective, such strong grip is necessary to preserve the illegal drug trade that connects the heroin business between that region of Mexico and the United States (Fernández Menéndez 2018).

The Government's Truth of Ayotzinapa Students Collapses

According to the government's account of the students' disappearance, federal investigators claimed that members of the *Guerreros Unidos* gang confused the forty-three students with rivals belonging to the *Los Rojos* gang (given that all of them were male, young, and were found clustered). Allegedly this was the ultimate reason why students were murdered and disappeared. To make matters worse, there is evidence that the municipal police of Iguala city, as well as its mayor and wife, had been bribed by and were under control of the *Guerreros Unidos* gang. However, as independent sources (e.g., investigative journalists, survivors, and witnesses) began to voice their findings and testimonies, the narrative of the official investigation collapsed because it was not supported with forensic evidence from the crime scene.

To begin with, the core of the criminal investigation presented a narrow plot by which the only culprits seemed to be local authorities who had conspired together to kidnap, murder, and disappear the students. Yet, there are testimonies and physical evidence (e.g., army reports and surveillance videos) indicating that soldiers and federal agents were present in Iguala before, during, and after the kidnapping and abduction of students, something that federal prosecutors strongly denied. Second, the government account was overwhelmingly based on confessions obtained from alleged suspects without any support from physical evidence. This is problematic given that the Mexican criminal justice system has a documented record of extracting confessions using torture or coercion. Third, the federal authorities were caught withdrawing important and crucial information to manipulate the public opinion regarding the credibility of the case. Meanwhile, the attorney general rejected calls to be transparent throughout the entire criminal investigation process and he was reluctant to share with the public and the victims' families key elements of the investigation on what had happened the night of the students' disappearance. Finally, intense media coverage by national and international outlets eventually exposed the endemic corruption that had eroded institutions of the criminal justice system in Iguala as well as the entire state of Guerrero (Devereaux 2015; Gibler 2015; González Rodríguez 2015).

As independent scientists and forensic experts looked at the evidence presented in the government's account, general skepticism about the investigation grew exponentially because forensic findings were not consistent with the government narrative. For instance, the Attorney General's Office maintained that all forty-three students were burnt to ashes together in the landfill of Cocula town right after they were abducted and killed. But in order to keep a fire big enough to incinerate so many bodies would have required 33 tons of wood if that was the only fuel used, according to experts. If car tires were the only combustible that perpetrators used, it would have required at least 1,000 of them to incinerate that many corpses, and the amount of smoke released from the pyre would have been large enough to be seen from miles away and visible to the naked eye for many witnesses around, yet there were none. Needless to say, there was no conclusive forensic evidence at the crime scene that scientifically confirmed or suggested that all the students had been burnt there in such a way, according to independent experts (Devereaux 2015; Gibler 2015; González Rodríguez 2015).

Considering that the government was hiding evidence and dragging the investigation, the parents of the students invited an international group of forensic experts to look at the case. This group was the Argentine Forensic Anthropology Team (*Equipo Argentino de Antropología Forense*), or EAAF, for its Spanish acronym. This was a not-for-profit scientific organization created in 1984 to investigate the disappearance of thousands of Argentinian citizens by the military government that ruled the country in the late 1970s and early 1980s. This forensic team began its work in early October 2014, a few weeks after the disappearance, and noticed a clear pattern of forensic negligence in the official investigation. The team observed a lack of objectivity by government officials who forcefully tried to match the confessions of the detained suspects with some evidence in the crime scene, and not allowing the EAAF full access to evidence. The team found gross inconsistencies in the official account of the crime, confirming eventually what other experts have suggested: the Ayotzinapa students were not incinerated in the Cocula landfill as the government stubbornly kept arguing (Equipo Argentino de Antropología Forense 2015).

Since the conclusions of the official investigation had lost credibility to the parents of the disappeared and Mexican society, the government decided to accept an independent and external investigation by international experts who would look at the facts of the case and clear up all skepticism. At the request of the Mexican government, the Inter-American Commission of Human Rights—IACHM (*Comisión Interamericana de Derechos Humanos*), an autonomous institution of the Organization of American States, designated a team of five international and renowned experts to launch a detailed inquiry of the Ayotzinapa students' disappearance. The team was named Interdisciplinary Group of Independent Experts (*Grupo Interdisciplinario de Expertos Independientes*) known as GIEI for its Spanish acronym and it was made up of a former attorney general, a social psychologist, a prosecutor, and lawyers, all of them with vast experience in these matters. To clarify, this investigation of the official case was a different and independent effort from the Argentine Forensic Team that had originally looked into the event and helped the parents of the disappeared students in the first place (Goldman 2015).

On September 6, 2015, six months after it officially began the investigation and almost a year after the students' disappearance, the GIEI group released its first report about the abduction and killing of the forty-three Ayotzinapa students. The report was called *Informe Ayotzinapa* (Ayotzinapa Report) and in its more than 500 pages, it debunked the government's account of the disappearance by asserting that there were serious mistakes in the official investigation, such as explicit actions to tamper with or destroy evidence, and many lines of investigation had been blatantly ignored and marginalized. Also, the report concluded that there was no physical or forensic evidence in the Cocula landfill where the alleged fire incinerated the forty-three students to support the official conclusion of the investigation that the government stubbornly defended. The international team of experts also documented that federal agents and the army were present in Iguala the night of the attack. Altogether, the report blasted the so-called historical truth of the case because it did not represent the disappearance of students as it really had happened. The document emphasized that the criminal investigation had been fragmented since the beginning, adding that there was an underlying government intent to close the case prematurely without truly exhausting all lines of forensic investigation (Inter-Disciplinary Group of Independent Experts 2015).

A second report by the GIEI was released in April 2016 that confirmed the original findings from the first report and documented even more inconsistencies in the government investigation and its handling. For instance, it confirmed that federal security forces were patrolling the streets of the city and that the army had recorded video footage and photographs of the students clashing with the local police but refused to share them with the GIEI team. Using a Freedom of Information request, some Mexican journalists got access to military records and discovered that a contingent of soldiers assigned to a military based in Iguala was tracking the students' whereabouts before their disappearance as they drove to the city for commandeering the buses. These soldiers knew of the shootouts against the students, witnessed dead bodies lying in the streets, and even went to a hospital to interrogate some of the injured students, yet the official investigation did not mention anything of this despite reports of it by survivors and witnesses. It was obvious at this point that these and other important facts had been purposely ignored or hidden by the federal government during the investigation in order to keep a tailored version of it to reinforce the official account of the disappearance (Goldman 2016).

Although the government publicly maintained that it was fully cooperating with the international experts, in reality it never allowed members of the group to interview the soldiers stationed in Iguala nor did it provide the necessary access and resources for a complete and independent criminal assessment of the evidence. In fact, it did exactly the opposite by torpedoing the work of the experts and instigating (or allowing at least) a smear campaign against the five members of the group to discredit their work through personal attacks in the media. As the last six months of GIEI mandate was about to expire, the government refused to extend it and doubled down on its defense of the official investigation, ferociously asserting that the experts' conclusion was similar and almost identical to the official investigation by the Attorney General's Office, which was not true at all (Goldman 2015; González Rodríguez 2016).

Given the magnitude of the crime, along with evident negligence in handling of the case, the disappearance of the forty-three Ayotzinapa students became the largest political scandal of President Peña Nieto's administration. The fact that the government tried to cover up the potential involvement of federal security forces in the disappearance added more skepticism about the true intentions of the authorities to bring justice to the victims and punish the culprits. As a result, the case led to widespread protests in Mexico and other countries where civil society along with national and international well-known figures condemned the government for the official response to the events and the botched cover-up of the case. Despite overwhelming evidence that the official version of the disappearance had many legal flaws and factual inconsistencies, the federal government inflexibly adhered to it rejecting other interpretations by experts and the available forensic evidence

(Fernández Menéndez 2018). This had dire consequences later on when in September 2019 those accused of the students' disappearance began to be acquitted and released from prison based on the fact that criminal confessions were elicited through torture and the legal flaws and contradictions of the official investigation (El Universal 2019).

An element that galvanized public opinion nationally and internationally was the fact that the perpetrator of these disappearances was the Mexican state. *¡Fue el Estado!* (It was the state!) became a common slogan during marches and protests to denounce the arbitrariness of the federal government in handling the Ayotzinapa case as well as its co-responsibility in the crime. There was no doubt, even in the official version of the case, that local security forces and elected officials were actively involved in the crime. As such, the abduction and killing of the Ayotzinapa students was an enforced disappearance with the active or passive involvement of state agents which violates international law because it constitutes a crime against humanity. In addition, this crime brought to light the degree and sophistication of how organized crime (DTOs in particular) had subdued local governments and substituted it with a parallel regime of violence, terror, crime, and impunity while the federal government did little or nothing to address it (see Figure 4.1).

The disappearance and murder of the students were not the only mass-scale tragedy that the denizens of Iguala and Guerrero state had witnessed in the recent past. For years, the gang *Guerreros Unidos* had terrorized the region with kidnappings, killings, and disappearances of those who opposed them or did not comply with their criminal activities. Weeks after the government version of the criminal investigation was released to the public, friends, peers, relatives, and community members of the disappeared students began to look for the remains of the forty-three students on their own in the outskirts of Iguala town and other places given the lack of government interest in locating them.

There was some unconfirmed information at that time that the Ayotzinapa students had been probably murdered and maybe illegally buried somewhere around Iguala. People living in this area knew that *Guerreros Unidos* had systematically killed and disappeared individuals in the recent past. What came next was astonishing for anyone unfamiliar with drug trafficking violence in Mexico but not for the people who live in Guerrero state. Eight months after the students' abduction, more than sixty mass graves were found in different locations around Iguala with nearly 130 corpses illegally buried but none of them belonged to the students. This number of graves was the official account kept by the prosecutor's office but it did not represent all of the existing gravesites in the area. Several of them had been dug up by relatives of the disappeared without the presence of the police and forensic personnel to document the exhumation (Mosso 2015).

An unintended effect of the forty-three students' disappearance was that the larger problem of disappearances in Mexico became national and international news and it could no longer be ignored or hid by the Mexican government. Not only that, this case also spotlighted another serious problem correlated to the murders and disappearances: the existence of hundreds of mass graves throughout the country where many bodies of the disappeared and murdered victims have been illegally buried, an issue that is discussed next.

NARCO-FOSAS (DRUG TRAFFICKING MASS GRAVES)

A *narco-fosa* is the name given to an improvised and clandestine hole or grave usually located in desolated places where drug cartel members bury one or more corpses of the people they murder so the victims cannot be found and identified. It is a portmanteau of the Spanish words *narco* (drug trafficker) and *fosa* (pit or grave) as explained in the previous chapter. The term has become common in newspaper headlines in Mexico in recent years as mass graves are regularly discovered in and near regions affected by drug trafficking activities. However, since the violence caused by the drug war expanded to most of Mexico, mass graves are now frequently found throughout the entire country (Guillen, Torres, and Turati 2018).

There are four main threads that connect mass graves in Mexico with high murder rates and people who have been disappeared: extreme and unprecedented violence; out of control DTOs; the drug war approach of strict drug control to deal with the illegal drug trade; and nearly total impunity for the perpetrators of violent crimes. When looking at the day-to-day drug-related crimes happening in Mexico, it is possible to infer that most of the victims who are killed and buried in mass graves are not murdered in combats between rival gangs. Instead, the victims are either executed in plain view (e.g., streets, homes, and workplaces) or kidnapped by thugs and assassins and murdered somewhere else (Universidad Iberoamericana 2017).

In contemporary Mexico organized crime and DTOs know that getting rid of their victims' dead bodies substantially reduces the possibility of being prosecuted and convicted of murder chargers. Without a corpse, there is no immediate criminal investigation of a homicide (at least not in Mexico). Therefore, hiding a body in a clandestine grave guarantees unwanted attention from the media and federal authorities. Not only that, mass graves reflect a premeditated intent to generate terror against rivals and civil society in order to maintain strict control of the territory by perpetrators while showing defiance about how much impunity these criminals enjoy in committing their crimes (Universidad Iberoamericana 2017).

Since the so-called Mexican drug war began in 2006, criminal gangs in Mexico have extensively been using mass graves to bury the people they murder. There have been cases where instead of burying the victims of murder, some cartel bosses had chosen a more disturbing method to get rid of the corpses: disintegrating them with caustic soda (sodium hydroxide), a powerful chemical used in industrial applications, then burying the remains in a pit. In January of 2009, the arrest of a man named Santiago Meza López known as *El Pozolero* (The Stew Maker) in the city of Tijuana made international headlines when he confessed to authorities that he had dissolved the bodies of at least 300 people in caustic soda as an employee of a key drug trafficker in the region (Grillo 2011).

El Pozolero's nickname came from a popular Mexican stew made with pork, ground corn, and spices called *Pozole*. This criminal became known as El Pozolero because he was responsible for dissolving the corpses of people killed by drug gangs. He explained in detail the nature of his job which consisted of dumping a body in an empty oil barrel, pouring in acid and waiting twenty-four hours to dissolve it. Then he would dispose of the pieces of bones and other parts by burying them in a pit (Grillo 2011). Nonetheless, this gruesome method to disintegrate human bodies is not a widespread phenomenon in Mexico. Rather narco-fosas have been the most prevalent form of disappearing those who are targeted by violent groups in the drug war because it makes it easier for criminal groups to dispose of dead bodies.

Until recently, there was no national database or official census about the mass graves discovered in contemporary Mexico, mostly in states where drug trafficking activities concentrate. Frustrated with the government's apathy to help them find their loved ones, families of the disappeared (mostly mothers of the victims) throughout the country began to take the task in their own hands (literally with shovels and picks) to find for themselves the remains of their relatives. These mothers came together, got organized, and created citizens groups and collectives such as *Solecito* (Little Sun) in Veracruz, *Familias Unidas por Nuestros Desaparecidos* (United Families for Our Disappeared Loved Ones) in Jalisco, *Fuerzas Unidas por Nuestros Desaparecidos en Nuevo Leon* (United Forces for Our Disappeared Loved Ones in Nuevo Leon state) among other organizations. These civil society groups exist throughout Mexico and their members regularly protest, march, and put pressure on authorities to force them do their job and locate mass graves. Since local authorities have not taken action, these groups began to locate narco-fosas by themselves in states such as Guerrero, Michoacán, Tamaulipas, Jalisco, Morelos, Baja California, and Veracruz, all of them known for having a strong presence of the violent DTOs (Guillen, Torres, and Turati, 2018).

At least 1,075 mass graves were found in Mexico between 2007 and 2014 with 2,014 bodies recovered from them, according to the 2017 report

"Violence and Terror: Findings about Clandestine Mass Graves in Mexico" (*Violencia y Terror: Hallazgos sobre fosas clandestinas en Mexico*). This document was published by Universidad Iberoamericana of Mexico City in collaboration with the Mexican Commission on Defense and Promotion of Human Rights. The data includes information collected from a triangulation of sources: statistics from official criminal investigations provided by District Attorney's Offices from at least twelve states, federal authorities, and news reports about mass graves generated by the media during these years. Data showed that most mass graves were found in Durango, Guerrero, Jalisco, Michoacán, Nuevo Leon, and Tamaulipas states, which confirmed what many families of the disappeared already knew: that there is a strong correlation between the presence of DTOs and mass graves (Universidad Iberoamericana 2017).

It should be noted that the amount of mass graves indicated by this report represents an academic estimation rather than the total number of them. First, not all authorities reported official data about mass graves, either because they did not have it or rejected to share it. Second, according to the report, some families of the disappeared have tips or knowledge where other mass graves are located in or near their communities, but they have not reported them to the police out of fear of criminal groups still roaming around those communities. Finally, given the powerful presence of DTOs in some regions of Mexico, it is improbable that all existing mass graves will ever be discovered and reported to the government. Thus, the final number of them will always be underestimated and Mexican society will never know the exact figure.

Another source of information on this is a year-and-a-half investigation by three female independent journalists published at the end of 2018; they put the number of clandestine graves at least up to 1,978, most of them located in twenty-four Mexican states. According to their findings, authorities have recovered from those pits "2,884 bodies, 324 craniums, 217 bones, 799 bone remnants, and thousands of other remains that belong to an as yet undetermined number of individuals" (Guillen, Torres, and Turati 2018, 1). However, these facts are only the tip of the iceberg since there are dozens, if not hundreds, of other graves that remain hidden. Many people believe the graves are located in isolated and abandoned locations, but these journalists found that sometimes bodies were buried closer to streets and in populated vicinities. Government inconsistencies in record-keeping, lack of resources, and legal uniformity to identify the pits, number of victims, and the dead bodies have all delayed finding mass graves and thus denying justice for the victims and their families (Guillen, Torres, and Turati 2018).

As a gesture to break with past authoritarian and corrupt regimes, the new government of AMLO announced in August 2019 that based on official records and data compiled by his administration there were more than 3,000 mass graves throughout Mexico and nearly 5,000 bodies had been found in them (Tuckman 2019). This public government acknowledgement of the problem is unprecedented in Mexico and it suggests that finally federal authorities are willing to admit negligence on this phenomenon and set up mechanisms and policies to bring justice to victims and tackle the roots of mass graves.

Unfortunately, as extreme violence, soaring murder rates, and clandestine graves expanded throughout Mexico, the people in charge of reporting these events and bringing information to the public about them, journalists and reporters, became a target from organized crime groups. The reader should keep in mind that the role of mass media in reporting criminal activity by drug cartels has been crucial to obtain a more accurate depiction of how DTOs work and the effects of the illegal drug trade. Journalists' work focuses on drug trafficking and its negative effects in the everyday life of people but they also report on the connections between traffickers and officials as well as the corrupt activities of police officers and security forces who are working for or protecting criminal gangs. Drug cartels do not want their business, connections, and activities to be exposed to the public so they began to silence the media and journalists systematically to protect their operations.

KILLING THE MESSENGER: MURDERING JOURNALISTS IN MEXICO

Since the late 2000s, journalists have become the target of kingpins and unscrupulous politicians who want to silence them through bribes or bullets. As a result, journalism has turned into the most dangerous profession in Mexico in the last decade with dozens of reporters being killed for doing their jobs. This is the price that many reporters and journalists have to pay for informing society about the inner workings of narco-politics, drug trafficking activities, and political corruption (Gibler 2011; Reporters Without Borders 2017).

According to the 2017 report from World Press Freedom Index, Mexico ranked as the most dangerous country in Latin America for journalists. In just fifteen years, Mexico went from being 75th to 147th in the index that Reporters Without Borders (RWB) compiles every year. This catalog rates the level of freedom that journalists enjoy while doing their job in 180 countries where the number one position is the most freedom available to them and the last with less freedom. Based in Paris, RWB is an international non-government organization and one of the world's leading institutions in defending and promoting freedom of information worldwide. RWB publishes this catalog as a sort of tool to bring public awareness on violations against freedom of information and attacks to the press while at the same time it evaluates media's independence, potential censorship from government officials, transparency, and infrastructure for a free press, among other things. RWB has compiled enough evidence to conclude that in Mexico, journalists who investigate and cover news on DTOs, political corruption, and organized crime are frequently threatened and attacked. Meanwhile the government ignores these crimes and delays criminal investigations meant to arrest and prosecute those who commit crimes against journalists. Not surprisingly, the murders of journalists in past decades remain unsolved, something that reflects the degree of impunity that reigns in Mexico (RWB 2017).

Between the years 2000 and 2019, at least 122 journalists were murdered in Mexico. Data show a strong correlation between the beginning of the Mexican drug war in 2006 and the number of murdered journalists rising up. During that period of 2000 to 2006, right after the authoritarian regime lost the presidency to the opposition and a new government took power, at least twenty-two journalists were assassinated. However, during the administration of President Calderón (2006–2012), forty-five reporters were killed for doing their job as communicators. At the same time, during the administration of President Peña Nieto (2012–2018) forty-seven journalists were murdered and the number rates keep climbing every year (Ureste 2019). Just in 2017 alone, twelve reporters were murdered according to Articulo 19, an independent and apolitical Latin American organization that promotes freedom and access to information based on human rights principles (Articulo 19 2017). In the year 2018 nine journalists were killed in Mexico and by fall 2019 at least twelve of them have been murdered, the world highest number and surpassing Syria as the deadliest country for journalists (Kahn 2019). This information does not include the hundreds of aggressions such as threats, arrests, intimidation, and physical harm against reporters and journalists that occur every year but are not reported to the police (Articulo 19 2018; Hope 2018b).

When analyzing the data of these murders, there is a noticeable trend on the geography of murders. The vast majority of them have been committed in states where drug trafficking is rampant but also where the local governments have been found colluded, co-opted, or subdued by criminal groups. This means that authorities actively protect perpetrators or passively ignore their official duties to take action against perpetrators of these crimes. Veracruz State—located along the Gulf of Mexico and a well-known corridor for human and drug trafficking—has become the most dangerous state in Mexico for journalists with at least twenty-six reporters murdered in the last seventeen years. It is followed by other Mexican states such as Chihuahua, Tamaulipas and Oaxaca with at least thirteen murdered journalists each during the same seventeen-year period and Guerrero with at least eleven reporters killed throughout that period (Articulo 19 2017).

Besides the threat of potential death, journalists also face intimidation, harassment, censorship, arbitrary detentions, and violence by government agents, security forces, and criminal gangs who see their reporting as a threat to their criminal activities and the pervasive impunity that has existed in Mexico for decades. Given the conditions under which Mexican journalists do their work, RWB has documented that the constant threat of violence against reporters has created a vacuum of news information that is known as *zonas del silencio* (silenced zones). Simply put, *zonas del silencio* refers to those regions, states, or geographical areas where journalists reporting on local violence, deaths, and shootouts have been suppressed to comply with orders from criminal gangs and organized crime that control the territory. This sort of media silence helps drug traffickers to avoid unwanted attention from federal authorities and from the army or navy, and thus facilitates control of their strongholds. For that reason, journalists are prohibited from reporting any news about murders, guns battles, violence, and even car accidents (including any incident that traffickers deem damaging to their interests). Those journalists or reporters who dare to challenge the cartels' orders will be kidnapped, harmed, and killed (Gibler 2011; Valdés Cárdenas 2016).

The same applies to photojournalists who want to document violence through their cameras. They are not allowed to take pictures of some crime scenes or events and if they do, those images cannot be published without cartels' approval. Criminal gangs have even selected spokespersons to speak on behalf of their organization and these individuals decide whether or not crime news or pictures are published in the local media. Anyone who challenges this censorship can be punished according to some arbitrary criteria that criminals themselves have created. Punishment varies and includes a few slaps on the face, hits on the back, limb mutilation, burning some parts of the body, torture, and death if the reporter has periodically violated trafficker's orders (Valdés Cárdenas 2016).

To maintain strict control on journalists' whereabouts and keep track of their work, drug gangs as well as local politicians have infiltrated newspapers and co-opted some journalists through bribes or credible threats of violence to force them into betraying their peers. Thus, these corrupt reporters (willingly or unwillingly) pass on personal and journalistic information directly to cartels' spokesmen about upcoming editorial decisions, who is conducting investigative journalism on what and where, and which crime news will appear on the front page of the newspaper the following day. With this inside information, criminals' spokesmen contact reporters, chief editors, or even top newspaper administrators to dictate what is published and what is not. Journalists and administrators alike have no other option but to obey the orders of cartel members under the threat of harm or murder if they dare to disobey (Valdés Cárdenas 2016).

As a result, there are some cities, towns, or regions of silenced zones where everyday crime does not appear in the media as long as it refers to or is associated with drug activities, criminal gangs, or political corruption. As mentioned earlier, states such as Sinaloa, Veracruz, Guerrero, and Tamaulipas—the ones where most journalists have been murdered—are known as *zonas del silencio* by media outlets, the police, and the governments: nobody knows anything, nobody sees one thing, nobody talks about it, is the non-written rule for communicators in order to survive their profession (De Mauleón 2017b).

Journalism in Mexico at a Dead End

The high number of journalists killed in Mexico reveals the risks and threats reporters have to face for doing their work. These communicators are usually targeted because they dared to report about the reality of violence, death, and political corruption that characterize many regions and states plagued with drug trafficking activities. Although this might be counter-intuitive, the most serious dangers for them do not come from drug traffickers themselves but from public officials such as police officers, politicians (from local, state, and federal institutions), and military forces who have been found responsible for more than 50 per cent of the aggressions. According to one report released on March of 2016 and produced by the Minister of the Interior (*Secretaría de Gobernación*), journalists have a higher risk to be harmed by any of the aforementioned public officials than by civilians, followed by non-identified perpetrators (Martinez 2016). The problem is that many times it is difficult to distinguish between state agents and non-state agents given that public officials can be easily corrupted by traffickers and they might work together in criminal enterprises. Other times, police officers go rogue and become traffickers themselves and when they threaten or harm journalists they do it under the role of both state agents and criminals. Anyhow, it is difficult to make this distinction because the line between the two has become blurred in contemporary Mexico.

To make matters worse, reporters are usually caught between a rock and a hard place when they conduct investigative journalism on drug trafficking and similar topics. In the mid-2000s drug criminal organizations began to use mass media and news outlets as tools to instill fear and threats to rivals, officials, and society, and they wanted to control what was published. To that end, a particular drug gang may want to publish a recent execution or a crime to make a public statement of their power against adversaries, while these may want to do exactly the opposite and keep that incident from being broadcasted. As a result, journalists can receive a phone call demanding a particular editorial action such as not publishing the news of a murder to favor a particular cartel while at the same time, a rival gang can call those same journalists to request the publication of those news in order to upset or discredit their opponents. Both gangs present credible threats of violence and harm against the communicators and the newspaper if the criminals' orders are disobeyed, which put journalists in a conundrum because they could face retaliation either way they choose. Given this scenario, many journalists and media outlets have ended up suppressing any news about drug cartels at all and even practicing self-censorship to avoid upsetting drug traffickers when they have become the "de facto local government" (Valdez Cárdenas 2016).

A dramatic case that symbolizes this dilemma and the plight of many local newspapers and their reporters in Mexico took place in Ciudad Juarez a few years ago. On September 19, 2010, *El Diario* (The Daily), a respected and well-known newspaper located in the border city of Ciudad Juárez, published a front-page editorial title directly asking drug traffickers a question: "What do you want from us?" A few days earlier a young photographer named Luis Carlos Santiago working for that newspaper had been murdered. This was the second time an employee of El Diario's covering the crime beat had been gunned down by traffickers because of reporting on the drug war. The editorial bluntly asserted, "We want you to know that we are communicators, not mind readers. We do not want more deaths. It is impossible to carry out our role in these conditions. Tell us therefore what is expected of us." "You are, at present, the de facto authorities in this city because the legally mandated authorities have not been able to do anything to keep our colleagues from continuing to fall, although we have repeatedly demanded they do so" (Carroll 2010; Gibler 2011; Villalpando 2010). This editorial made headlines around the world, not just because it reflected the powerlessness and despair of Mexican journalists and many local newspapers, but by the way it publicly denounced how local, state, and federal governments were incapable of providing minimum public safety and enforce the rule of law to protect journalists.

An aggravated feature that has made attacks against journalists more common and easier to carry out has been the passive role of the government to go after the perpetrators of those aggressions: there is almost 99 per cent impunity of crimes committed against them (Article 19 2017). Sometimes when a public official is behind the attack or providing protection to the perpetrators, it is not unusual that local authorities intentionally torpedo criminal investigations to make it difficult, if not impossible, to bring justice to the victim. The heartbreaking reality of the situation is that the passive or active attacks against journalists are not exclusive of local and state governments who want to keep their corrupt behavior secret but also at the federal level.

Some of the highest public officials, such as the president, have displayed reckless actions to interfere, sabotage, or prevent freedom of information and investigative journalism when it affected the interests of the president and his inner circle in the past two administrations of Presidents Calderón and Peña Nieto (Valdez Cárdenas 2016). It remains to be seen if the current president will distance himself from such practices and provide protection and shelter to journalists who are critical of his administration (Reuters 2019)

Just two examples of this presidential interference have been documented in separate but connected actions. The first one refers to a well-known and award-winning journalist named Carmen Aristegui who has been very critical of government corruption and has exposed several scandals involving public official and their inner circle. Working for the Mexican radio station *MVS Noticias* she and her team of investigative journalists uncovered in 2014 the conflict of interests and potential corruption of Mexican president Enrique Peña Nieto. They published an investigation on the purchase of a multimillion-dollar house by the president's former wife Angélica Rivera from a contractor who had obtained benefits from the federal administration. The scandal became known as "la casa blanca" (the white house) because of the color of the home at the center of the revelation. It led to widespread outrage against the president, seriously damaging the reputation of the administration as a corrupt one (Tuckman 2014).

In 2015 Aristegui was fired by the owners of the radio station where she worked—allegedly—for using inappropriately the radio's logo (MVS) from the company that owned the station. Although the justification for her termination was strictly legalistic, most pundits, academics, and independent journalists agreed that it was politically motivated and presumably the result of government pressure from the federal administration to her employer. There was evidence that in a previous similar situation the presidency had instigated labor harassment against this independent journalist because of embarrassing reports documenting wrongdoing or at least undisclosed conflict of interests by the president and his inner circle (Wilkinson 2015).

The second case of political meddling from the federal government against journalists was revealed in June of 2017 when the *New York Times* published an investigative report (Ahmed and Perlroth 2017) revealing that the Mexican government had been spying on several journalists, anti-corrupt activists, and human rights advocates who were critical of the administration. The report uncovered the fact that in 2011, at least three Mexican federal agencies had acquired from an Israeli cyber-weapons corporation a powerful software, known as Pegasus, to spy on individuals. This spyware was designed to infiltrate mobile phones and collect all the personal data of the user including calls, texts, emails, contacts, and internet browsing. The manufacturer (NSO Group) only sold the software to governments under the condition that they would use it to combat terrorism and crime only. The contract between the company and the government included a written agreement that the purchaser will not misuse the spyware to target other individuals, except those listed in the contract. Despite this, anti-corruption activists, human rights lawyers, and journalists such as Carmen Aristegi who have been critical of President Peña Nieto's administration were targeted with this sophisticated cyber weapon to sabotage their work and reputation as communicators (Ahmed and Perlroth 2017).

Cyber experts and software analysts confirmed that the victims had been targeted with the Pegasus software because the software left its digital footprints on the victims' mobile phones. Although there is no conclusive evidence that the government was behind the cyberattack (the software was designed to hide the identity of the hackers) it is unlikely that private individuals could carry on such sophisticated espionage. The company that invented the program explained that this technology is designed to be used by the country that bought it, only at the place where it was installed. The implication being that nobody else but the Mexican government had the motivation and resources available to conduct this cybercrime. Accordingly, it is hard to accept that someone else other than government agents had access to the program and spy on citizens who have exposed the wrongdoings of the Mexican federal administration at that time (Ahmed and Perlroth 2017).

Predictably, the president and his clique vehemently denied any responsibility on the espionage against those journalists. However, there have been previous cases of hacking activities by the Mexican government on political opponents and on those exposing the wrongdoings of the regime. This precedent suggests this practice is not an exceptional event but a routine behavior of some high-ranking Mexican officials to monitor critics and restrict the publication of unsavory news about their public performance. In fact, for decades the authoritarian Mexican government intimidated, harassed, threatened, and murdered those who were critical of the political system and challenged the status quo, among them journalists and activists. With the new democratic process that began in the early 2000s these repressive measures seemed to be part of the past. Yet, the administration of President Peña that ended on December 1, 2018, resorted to undemocratic and shadow tactics to preserve political stability and silence journalists and detractors (Boullosa and Wallace 2016).

In the current context of the drug war and the government emphasis on law enforcement operations with military forces, most Mexican journalists (foreign correspondents are somehow spare from these threats) who dare to report the reality of the situation by unmasking wrongdoers and denouncing atrocities have no guarantee of any legal or physical protection against attacks. For decades, the Mexican government was not on the journalists' side to defend freedom of information but to punish and censor those who speak truth to power, unless journalists were on the payroll of officials. The corollary being that in a country that has been affected by endemic corruption for years, exposing the dishonesty of public officials still continuous to be a dangerous activity.

The nature of the drug war is such that it is extremely difficult for governments in countries where drugs are harvested, manufactured, trafficked, and smuggled to enforce the rule of law effectively. Drug cartel organizations behave like corporations (Wainwright 2016) and they deliberately prefer weak states that suffer from systemic poverty, inequality, high unemployment, corruption, and underdevelopment because it is easier for them to conduct drug business there. In the case of Mexico, its proximity to the world's largest consumer of illegal drugs, chronic issues of corruption, authoritarian rule, and poor governance have resulted in a context where lawlessness occurs in some regions of the country. As a result, vigilante groups and militias have emerged in isolated areas in response to confront criminal gangs and bring informal law and order to their communities.

VIGILANTE GROUPS (*AUTODEFENSAS*)

The arising of vigilante groups in different regions of Mexico in the recent past is directly correlated with drug trafficking activities. As criminal groups have decimated the social and economic fabrics of local communities, citizens are forced to take justice in their own hands given the absence of state authority and the rule of law. Vigilantes or militias are not a recent phenomenon in Mexico though. During the eighteenth and nineteenth centuries, peasant and community insurrections against injustices in central and southern Mexico were not uncommon during the Colonial Times (Taylor 1979). The Mexican Revolution (1910–1920) itself has been defined as the great upheaval where peasants, indigenous people, and other citizens fought to overthrow the oppressive dictatorship of Porfirio Diaz who ruled Mexico for nearly three decades (Boullosa and Wallace 2016). More recently, during the 1960s and 1970s, vigilante groups in Mexico sprung up to fight the authoritarian government and transformed into guerrilla factions that demanded social justice from the regime. It is not a coincidence then that most of these armed rebellions occurred in regions where poverty, lack of communication, underdevelopment, and lawlessness were rampant and where caciques (strongmen) imposed their own local government and rules because the state was absent (Illiades and Santiago 2014).

Accordingly, armed groups have existed in regions where the presence of federal and state law enforcement is weak or nonexistent and the local authorities have been co-opted by criminal gangs or strongmen. Under those circumstances many vigilante groups have organized themselves as community police officers (*policia comunitaria*) to defend their villages and maintain law and order based on customs and traditions (*usos y costumbres*). *Policia comunitaria* (a sort of euphemism to name vigilantes by another term) is a more socially accepted designation among public officials and society at large because it does not have the stigma of being an insurgent or armed group and designates instead a small-town law enforcement unit to maintain peace. Sometimes these groups called themselves *Policia Rural* (rural police) for the same reasons. Many of these groups are legitimate efforts from local communities to address violence, extortion, and crime from organized crime but also from strongmen and gangs of illegal loggers who target their natural resources or want to take their land (Illiades and Santiago 2014).

With the uncontrolled rise of extreme violence during the past two presidential administrations (2006–2018) as a result of the Mexican drug war, communities began to arm themselves. Tired of being exploited by criminal gangs and the lack of public safety in their villages (usually located far from main urban centers and difficult to access) more and more of them decided to fight violent crime and bring provisional peace in their own using vigilante groups. These groups (called themselves *Autodefensas* literally self-defenses, meaning vigilantes) arose predominantly in regions and states where criminal gangs have subdued the local government through bribes or violence. In early 2013, investigative journalism (Olmos 2013) revealed that at least thirty-six vigilante groups existed already in Mexico distributed among eight states: the vast majority of them (twenty) were in Guerrero state—where forty-three Ayotzinapa students were kidnapped and disappeared in 2014—followed by Michoacán state (three), Morelos (three), Oaxaca (two), Veracruz (two), Chihuahua (two), Estado de Mexico (two), and Jalisco (one) (Olmos 2013).

The crisis of vigilantism would reach its highest level of intensity in Michoacán Mexico where several Autodefensas groups made up of avocado farmers, cattle ranchers, landowners, and lime pickers began to appear in different cities and towns of Tierra Caliente (Hot Lands). These groups were fed up with the local cartels that had controlled and dislocated their entire communities for years. At the end of 2013, the different factions met and formed the General Council of Self-Defenses and Communitarians of Michoacán (*Consejo General de Autodefensas y Comunitarios de Michoacán*) that included at least twenty-two municipalities to battle the powerful drug cartel known as *Los Caballeros Templarios*—The Knight Templars are splinter criminal gangs of *La Familia Michoacana*, described in chapter 2 (Boullosa and Wallace 2016; Valdés Castellanos 2013).

Many Autodefensas members called this movement the Uprising (*El Alzamiento*) because it was a coordinated effort by citizens without the support of the government to eradicate a criminal organization that had terrorized the local communities not just with drug trafficking activities but also extortion, kidnapping, murder, rape, dispossession, illegal mining, and other crimes for years. The vigilantes proceeded in a systematic way from town to town to "clean them up" (eliminate) cartel members known as *Templarios* using violence, setting up highway checkpoints, and displaying assault weapons such as AK-47s and handguns publicly. By March of 2014 the Autodefensas reached the largest and most important city of the region in Michoacán and the headquarters of the cartel: Apatzingan. Although every town or municipality had its own leadership and members, the authority of the movement coalesced in the figure of a local physician named Juan Manuel Mireles Valverde for a few months before the movement collapsed and disbanded (Illiades and Santiago 2014).

The Autodefensas movement was a successful social movement that dismantled the main infrastructure of the Knight Templars' leadership and temporarily freed their communities from the criminal grip the cartel had enjoyed. These actions allowed vigilantes to recover some of the real state, land, and resources that cartel members had stolen from the locals. Because of their success and the fact they had taken justice on their own hands by doing what the government could not do for years, the vigilantes gained national and international notoriety, something that the federal government feared and resented. The idea that militia men were making inroads in providing public safety and restoring social peace while successfully battling DTOs was troublesome for the government that looked incapable of accomplishing its basic duties. The vigilante movement clearly reflected the reality of violence and crime in Mexico that the federal administration wanted to hide from international scrutiny because it exposed to what extent those communities had been out of government control for years. To avoid being seen as a weak administration, President Peña Nieto sent more soldiers and federal agents to patrol the region and major highways where Autodefensas were present to signal that the central government was taking action now and about to gain control of the situation (Tuckman 2013).

The vigilante groups were not a monolithic entity nor did they have strong leadership to control the cohesiveness within the movement and the communities they approached as they advanced from town to town. The vigilante movement had been an organic uprising, and there were ideological and political discrepancies about how the different groups of the movement should consolidate and justify their legal presence in the eyes of civil society, locally and nationally. As the vigilantes became more powerful they began to exert more local influence through violence, abuses, and even extrajudicial killings against former cartel members to take revenge. As a result, some of them looked more like mercenaries rather than citizens defending their communities. Just a few months after they had started their movement, disagreement and old personal rivalries spread out between them and eventually they began to fight each other and a turf war erupted (Illiades and Santiago 2014).

The vigilantes made the mistake of accepting among their ranks and files former cartel members who had repented from being involved with the local drug cartel and had demanded forgiveness from the vigilantes to join them. These individuals became known as *arrepentidos* in the movement and their sudden affiliation and welcoming, negatively affected the legitimacy of the vigilantes' cause. There was no full consensus among the militia men whether or not former criminals should be pardoned by the community and allowed to be part of the vigilante movement, and this led to even more divisions and the eventual disintegration of the vigilante groups (Miroff and Partlow 2014).

Because the existence of the vigilante uprising had challenged the rule of law as well as the authority and credibility of the Mexican state, the federal government set up a strategy to undermine this social movement by forcing them to demobilize and give up their arms through a government plan to transform the militia into an official and regulated local law enforcement agency (Miroff and Partlow 2014). To carry out his plan President Peña Nieto appointed a close subordinate named Alfredo Castillo to handle the government-induced reconciliation effort. The goal was to replace the vigilantes with a new Rural Police using the militiamen themselves as official agents while forcing them to register their weapons (including assault rifles) in a government registry managed by the army. This in itself was controversial since according to federal law only security forces were allowed to carry sophisticated weaponry such as assault rifles and civilians were strictly prohibited to do so (Mexico has one of the most restrictive gun laws in Latin America). Since the movement was divided by many core issues, the president's appointee used this internal antagonism to lure a particular group of militiamen that eventually sided with the government's initiative to end the vigilante's movement. These militiamen ended up becoming the Rural Police that the president sought to create while other vigilante factions that were suspicious of the government's intentions denounced the reconciliation plan as a strategy to seize their weapons and dissolve the vigilante movement once and for all (Miroff and Partlow 2014).

To make matters worse, drug cartels from neighboring states saw an opportunity to expand their operations and influence in this part of Michoacán state and some of their members began to support and infiltrate the real vigilantes to make inroads in drug corridors once controlled by the former cartel disguised as Autodefensas. The vigilantes clashed between them and shootouts took place in the following months where members of all fractions were killed. After these events, the government cancelled the Rural

Police, demanded vigilantes to turn their weapons in to the army, and stop their checkpoints and patrols, otherwise they will face arrest and incarceration. Most leaders of the movement were eventually arrested, killed by rival groups, or exiled themselves when the army and federal agents ramped up their operations in the region and the vigilantes movement, as it was known, came to an end (Illiades and Santiago 2014; Miroff and Partlow 2014).

In 2015 the American documentary *Cartel Land* directed by Matthew Heineman (and nominated for an Academy Award for Best Documentary Feature) provides some details about the Mexican drug war by shedding light on vigilante groups in both Mexico and the United States. The Mexican side of the story was shot in Michoacán state and it featured the main leader of the *Autodefensa*s Jose Manuel Mireles. The film follows him around during the peak of the vigilante movement as he tries to maintain a coherent discourse among his fellow militiamen, looking for support from the communities while trying to dodge the government's attention. The film contributed to bringing worldwide public attention to the plight of communities affected by Mexican cartels and their uprising of militia men to fight drug traffickers.

Most vigilantes did not surrender their movement; they only became more reclusive, go underground, and avoid displaying their guns on public. As the Mexican WOD and its militarized approach continues to linger, vigilante groups have expanded throughout Mexico in different degrees and nature. In places where drug gangs rule and fragmented drug cartels battle each other for control of drug corridors and strategic hubs for drug production and manufacture, many communities have no other option but to take justice in their hands to protect themselves against criminals. A dramatic reality is that sometimes vigilantes are supported or infiltrated by criminal gangs who pretend to be part of the community in order to maintain their grip on power and control over those same communities by using a clever disguise as vigilantes. This has created a chaotic situation where legitimate civilians tired of being extorted and abused take up arms to confront the criminal gangs but end up engaging in criminal acts or pursuing vigilante justice.

As for the vigilantes in Michoacán, Mexico where the movement got international attention, most of them still exist and as of spring of 2020 gruesome violence, killings, and regular shootouts between factions have returned to the regions of Tierra Caliente. In fact, very little has changed in those communities in the past five years regarding drug gangs and crime; it remains the same only with new names and faces. Why? Because the vacuum of power left by the Knight Templar cartel was eventually filled out by other criminal gangs that splintered from the previous drug organization that ruled Michoacán. In particular, the Jalisco New Generation Cartel (mentioned in chapter 2) has rapidly expanded into many towns and regions once controlled by previous DTOs. The government has been incapable of preventing organized crime from settling there and conducting illegal activities in these drug hubs. Accordingly, the vigilantes remain alert about this threat and have organized themselves again as a militia to protect their communities and fight off hitmen from criminal gangs. As a result, violence and murders have raised throughout Mexico as new data reveals that homicide rates have reached yet another record number in 2019 and there is evidence that this trend will continue for the near future (Hope 2018b).

It should not be ignored that all of this social chaos has been taking place while the government at all levels of the administration does little to address the problem in a swift and efficient manner. When a democratic government abdicates its responsibility of protecting citizens from violence and crime and ignores justice issues, it creates a context where everything is up for grabs, and criminal groups fill in the vacuum of power. As a consequence, criminal groups have become the de facto government in many jurisdictions and carrying out illegitimate activities because there is no functional government capable of enforcing the rule of law. What prompts a situation where a nation-state willingly or unwillingly abandons its duty to guarantee law and order? This is a crucial but complex question to answer and there are different explanations about the circumstances that has led the Mexican state to neglect and openly evade its fundamental responsibility. By not guaranteeing the rule of law and allowing criminal groups and DTOs to thrive and substitute the power of the state, the Mexican government has allowed systematic impunity to reign. The next and final section of this chapter provides an in-depth examination of this problem.

MEXICO: WEAK, FAILED, OR CAPTURED STATE?

In early 2009, the U.S Joint Forces Command published a report suggesting that Mexico—along with Pakistan—had the potential of experiencing a "rapid and sudden collapse," meaning that it could become a failed state in the near future. The argument was that the main institutions of the Mexican criminal justice system (e.g. police, judicial system), as well as the government itself and the political infrastructure, was under attack and pressure from DTOs and criminal groups that could send the country into a downward spiral of violence and chaos that could spill over to America (Debusmann 2009). The Mexican government and national security experts immediately rebuked this assessment by explaining that Mexico had some failing institutions here and there, but overall the entire country was stable and its central authority intact in most of its territory.

The concept of "failed state" is controversial, to say the least, because there are no objective criteria to determine when a nation reaches this point.

Whether it is the collapse of a nation's economic and political systems, its inability to control the territory, the erosion of legitimate power to enforce the law, or failure to provide basic services, Mexico is not a failed or weak state. It is true that systematic corruption is a common issue and there is serious red tape in most of its government institutions that correlates with that corruption. Also, Mexico has had unprecedented violence in the past decade with high murder rates that have increased every year. In recent years DTOs have taken control of some regions and cities in parts of the country. However, Mexico has one of the twenty major economies worldwide; it is listed among the ten most visited countries in the world, its main political and legal institutions operate (imperfectly but they work) throughout most of the country, and it has a democratic infrastructure that guarantees free elections and free speech for the most part as shown in the past presidential election of July 1, 2018, where a center-left politician overwhelmingly won the election in a free election without violence.

What Mexico has experienced since the early twenty-first century is "state capture." This idea refers to external and non-government entities that have gained control of some parts of the state. The term was used first to explain deep political corruption in Eastern European countries when rich mafia-like groups used their influence to gain internal control of the decision-making process within the government to benefit organized crime gangs (Valdés Castellanos 2013). In the context of Mexico and narco-violence, state capture refers to DTOs or criminal gangs that have appropriated a territory to become a parallel or shadow authority where citizens, businesses, news media, and local officials have to answer to criminals because they have gained control of the entire jurisdiction (Grillo 2011; Valdés Castellanos 2013). How Mexico got into this messy national security problem is a combination of political, economic, and criminal factors that have overlapped at least in the past two decades, beginning with the decline of the former authoritarian regime.

Experts on theories of organized crime have pointed out that breeding grounds for criminal groups and mafia to thrive are usually based on multiple causes. Prominent among those are political changes, demand for prohibited goods, inability to retain absolute control of a territory, and economic or social alienation derived from poverty, high unemployment, and chronic institutional marginalization (Skarpedas 2001). In the case of Mexico, the vacuum of power left by the authoritarian regime at the beginning of this century was a crucial event that contributed to the solidification of DTOs, although it was not the only one. Chronic social dislocations such as widespread corruption, poverty, abandoned communities, impunity, and the persistent demand for drugs in America formed the perfect conditions. Thus, this led to a context where the Mexican government could no longer apply the rule of law in some parts of the country and criminal groups stepped up to fill the gap. As a result, local government will eventually become privatized—so to speak—in the hands of strengthened and violent criminal gangs and DTOs throughout Mexico (Grillo 2011; Valdés Castellanos 2013).

Out of the three government jurisdictions (local, state, and federal), the municipal police have always been the most susceptible security force to be lured and influenced by organized crime in Mexico. Regularly local police are co-opted and infiltrated by strongmen, criminal gangs, and some of their officers directly work as employees to drug trafficking groups because of historical negligence by the authoritarian old regime (Boullosa and Wallace 2016; Gibler 2011; Grillo 2011). What makes local law enforcement agencies more susceptible to be corrupted? It is complicated to discern but most experts agree on the following causes. First of all, most local police officers are generally underpaid and they have little or no training to confront armed groups. Second, they are not allowed to carry sophisticated weapons since their main task is to prevent crime rather than investigate or confront perpetrators. Finally, job security is precarious because the patronage system permeating every layer of the state bureaucracy has substituted civil service with cronyism and favoritism. As a result, most officers can be fired anytime for any reason because there is no meritocratic service system in place to protect labor rights. This is correlated with the fact that Mexico has a decentralized multiple uncoordinated police system where the municipal police are trained to provide preventing functions where officers are uniformed to control and deter crime only (Reichel 2018).

DTOs have been aware of the conditions of local police forces and many of these officials end up working for the cartels when they are fired or just leave their jobs to join them because of the appeal of criminal life and its immediate illegal benefits. Thus, drug gangs have escalated their offensive to lure more municipal officers to work for them because it is cheaper and easier to bribe the local police than federal agents or soldiers. When corruption is not enough (there are honest law enforcement agents in Mexico) or police officers are working for rival cartels, criminal gangs simply murder these agents to clear their way and recruit new ones to gain dominance. The executions of police officers in fact increases the bad reputation of the perpetrators as ruthless criminals and make it easier for them to subdue officers to work for them (Grillo 2011; Valdés Castellanos 2013).

Local police departments are not the only target of drug gangs in their strategy to control and capture local jurisdictions. Mayors, council members, and other municipal officials have become valuable assets to their criminal activities in order to operate competitively against rivals while guaranteeing impunity for traffickers. This is a brand new criminal approach where drug gangs have seized and controlled every aspect of public affairs in some local towns, not just the police (hence the name *state capture*). From finances, taxation, social services, and building projects to budget disposal, are all targets for these criminals (Finnegan 2010; Grillo 2011). When organized groups are in absolute control of a municipality, all economic activities are taxed by them including salaries of high-ranking local authorities whether or not they are working with the organization. DTOs also extort people and businesses in the community, from taxi drivers, street vendors, and landowners to mining companies and even transnational corporations through their franchised stores locally doing business in the jurisdiction. For instance, conglomerates such as Coca Cola and Pepsi among other companies have closed distribution centers in Altamirano, Guerrero in Southern Mexico, a city neighboring Michoacán state that has been plagued with drug gangs in the past decades. The reason: growing extortion demands from criminal groups who target facilities and personnel if their demands are not met. This is not an isolated event since other small towns in states where drug traffickers are the de-facto government have also seen some business leave but more quietly to avoid unwanted negative attention (Associated Press 2018).

A former governor of Michoacán explained how cartels would take control of a city:

> I would get a call afterward from the mayor. Ten pickup trucks full of armed men had arrived at the municipality. The local police could do nothing. They were outgunned. But the criminals were very respectful. They would tell the mayor, "We want to work here. There will be not trouble, no crime, no drunkenness, nothing." Then they would take over the town, and enforce their rules. (Finnegan 2010, 48)

The cartel *La Familia Michoacana* the precursor of the Knight Templars organization in Michoacán is credited as the first criminal group that undertook this gangster approach to substitute the local government and impose a shadow regime. However, other drug gangs such as Los Zetas and the Juarez cartel eventually imposed similar demands using violence and terror in their respective strongholds (Gibler 2011; Grillo 2011; Valdés Castellanos 2013).

Not unexpectedly, criminal groups have also seized the political structure of the municipal institutions to influence elections and appoint corrupt officials who are under control of drug trafficking groups. This influence even expanded to governors and state officials by bribing key cabinet members of state governments or even governor candidates directly to obtain protection or classified information. In some places, the cartels were able to corrupt the entire political system to its basic foundation to form a criminal state within the state (Boullosa and Wallace 2016). Corrupting politicians (or narco-politics as it is known) is not new in Mexico. Evidence shows that a century ago some governors were directly involved or benefited from the illegal drug trade (see Astorga 2015, 2016). The novelty is that for the first time drug gangs are in absolute control of the whole business of drug trafficking and many politicians or public officials now have to obey (or at least ignore the actions of) drug gangs, not the other way around as it used to be decades ago. This was unthinkable back then when the central government had total control of the drug trafficking business, not anymore, and state capture is correlated to this new reality (Gibler 2011; Grillo 2011; Valdés Castellanos 2013).

By the 2000s, DTOs were out of control targeting civilians, officials, and politicians who interfered with their criminal activities. The obvious effect has been the large number of civilians killed and disappeared in the recent past. Even worse, an increasing number of security forces and public servants have been targeted and murdered by traffickers, too. From 2005 to 2017, more than one hundred politicians have been executed throughout Mexico, the vast majority of them mayors but also lawmakers and even a former governor (Jesús Silverio Cavazos Ceballos of Colima state) in 2010. As usual, most of these murders have occurred in states with a strong presence of drug gangs such as Guerrero, Jalisco, Michoacán, Tamaulipas, and Veracruz, and only a few of these murders have been solved, perpetuating the ominous trend of impunity (Gibler 2011; Grillo 2011; Valdés Castellanos 2013).

This climate of lawlessness has been repeatedly denied or downplayed by former federal administrations and several state governments when it is brought to light by media and critics. The reason: it attracts bad publicity to the authorities and exposes their failures. The fact that some drug gangs have controlled large portions of the Mexican territory such as entire cities (e.g., Acapulco, Culiacan, Reynosa, Nuevo Laredo), states (e.g., Guerrero, Sinaloa, Tamaulipas), or drug corridors (e.g., Tijuana-San Diego border or Texas-Tamaulipas region) has led to believe that an insurgency has effectively challenged the Mexican state. This control of territories fluctuates from time to time (depending on in-fights among drug gangs and law enforcement operations by federal security forces). This situation of lawlessness has uncovered the rampant corruption existing among public officials at all levels of government and how little has been done to address the problem.

The capture of the state by criminal groups has also exposed the inefficiency and futility of the drug war because no matter how many law enforcement operations are conducted, how many traffickers are killed or arrested, or how much drugs and money are seized, all of it is futile. At the end the entire illegal drug business continues unchanged and drug gangs remain the de facto power in some jurisdictions. With no alternative options to tackle drug gangs and the illegal drug trade besides the same policy of reactive police operations, drug cartels will keep their strategy to control territory and bribe or murder anyone who opposes them because it is profitable and a cheap investment in the world of organized crime. Then what? Can anything be done to change the status quo and make a significant and meaningful improvement in the fight against drug trafficking besides the WOD approach? To answer these and other questions is necessary first to examine the essence of current drug policies by breaking them down into pieces and provide a detailed analysis of why they do not work and what else can be done besides drug control.

Figure 3.1 Mural: Mexican Army Fighting Drug Trafficking. Lobby of Museo del Enervante. Picture by the author on July 3, 2018.

Figure 3.2 Samples of Different Prohibited Drugs Displayed at the Mexican Drug Museum. Museo del Enervante. Picture by author on July 3, 2018.

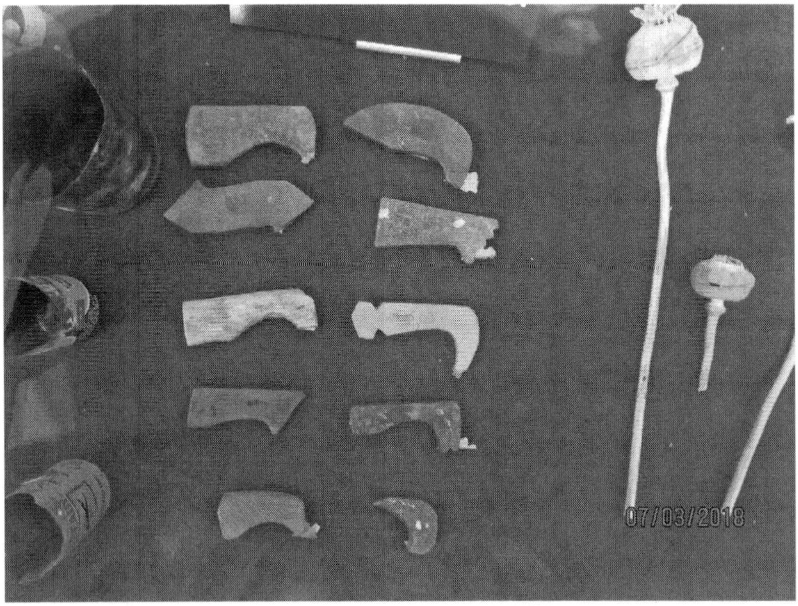

Figure 3.3 Seized Handmade Knifes (*rayadores*) Used to Split the Pods of Poppy Plants to Extract Opium Paste by Mexican Farmers. Museo del Enervante. Picture by the author on July 3, 2018.

Figure 3.4 Diorama of the "Typical Drug Trafficker" Guarding Poppy Fields in the Mountains of Mexico According to the Mexican Army. Museo del Enervante. Picture by the author on July 3, 2018.

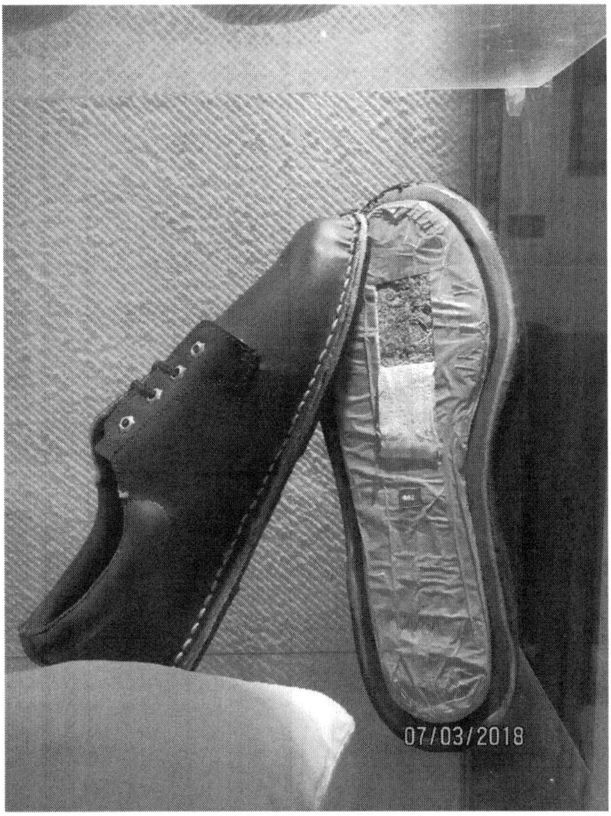

Figure 3.5 A Pair of Footwear Used to Smuggle Marijuana in the Sole of the Shoes Displayed at the Mexican Museum of Drug Trafficking. Museo del Enervante. Picture by the author on July 3, 2018.

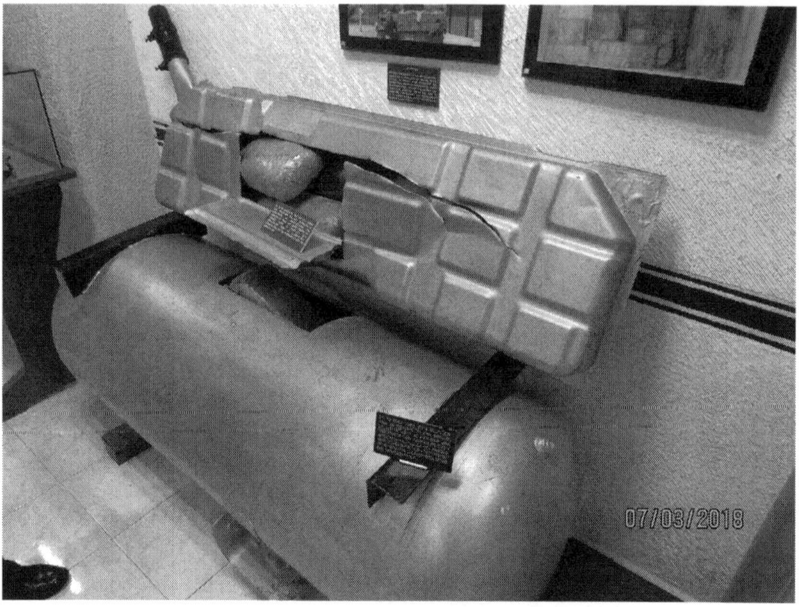

Figure 3.6 Gas Tanks Used to Hide and Smuggle Marijuana Displayed at the Mexican Museum of Drug Trafficking. Museo del Enervante. Picture by the author on July 3, 2018.

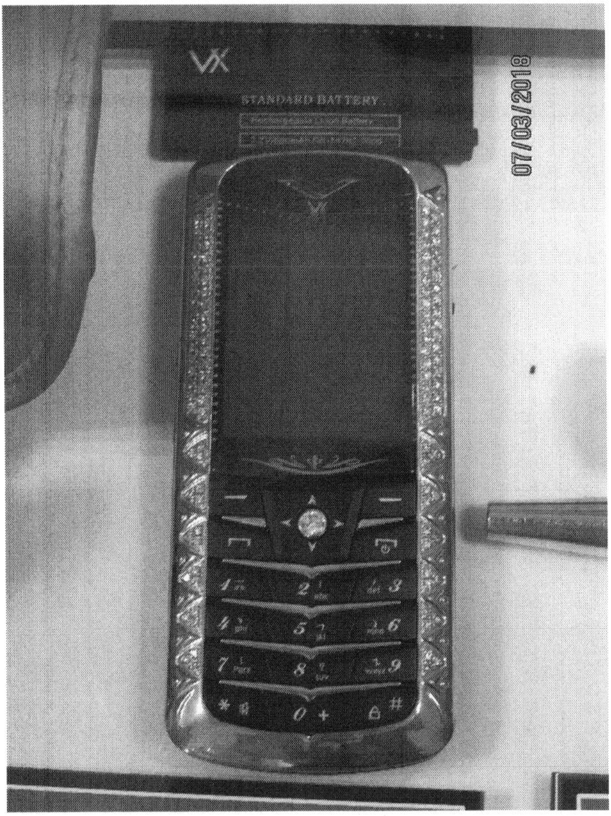

Figure 3.7 Mobile Phone Seized in Matamoros, Mexico, from a Drug Trafficker Belonging to the Gulf Cartel. The phone is covered with 24k gold and encrusted in diamonds. Museo del Enervante. Picture by the author in July 3, 2018.

Figure 3.8 Collection of Semi-Automatic Pistols with Decorated Handgun Grips and Engravings Seized by the Mexican Army from Drug Traffickers and Displayed in the Museum of Drug Trafficking. Museo del Enervante. Picture by author in July 3, 2018.

Figure 3.9 Semi-Automatic Pistol Seized by the Army with Handgun Grips Engraved with the Expression in Spanish "Only the Death Have Seen the End of the War." Museo del Enervante. Picture by the author on July 3, 2018.

Figure 3.10 Wooden Table and Chair Seized by the Army with a Painting of La Santa Muerte and Motifs of This Deity Meticulously Carved onto the Surface of Both Items. Museo del Enervante. Picture by the author on July 3, 2018.

Figure 3.11 Main Entrance at the House of the Holy Death in Santa Ana Chapitiro, Michoacán. Picture by the author on July 2018.

Figure 3.12 Transgender Figure of *La Santa Muerte* at the House of the Holy Death in Santa Ana Chapitiro, Michoacán. Picture by the author on July 2018.

Figure 3.13 *La Santa Muerte* Shrine at the Unofficial Angel of the Death Saint National Sanctuary in Mexico City. Picture by the author on July 4, 2018.

Figure 3.14 Jesus Malverde and Two Figures of *La Santa Muerte* with a White Candle at the Angel of the Death Saint National Sanctuary in Mexico City. Picture by the author on July 4, 2018.

Figure 3.15 Assortment of *La Santa Muerte* Figures for Sale at the Angel of the Death Saint National Sanctuary in Mexico City. Pictured by author on July 4, 2018.

Figure 4.1 Monument to the Forty-three Disappeared Ayotzinapa Students on Reforma Ave. in Mexico City. Picture by the author in summer 2017.

Figure 7.1 According to the Author of This Book, This Image Would be a Symbolic Representation of the DEA and Its Futile and Meaningless Mission of Fighting the War on Drugs. Sculpture known as 'The Unknown Bureaucrat' by Magnús Tómasson, located in downtown Reykjavik, Iceland. Picture by the author on May 2017.

Chapter 5

Drug Prohibition and the War on Drugs Revisited

DRUG TRAFFICKING AS A TRACTOR-TRAILER

Let us imagine that the business of drug trafficking could metaphorically be depicted as a huge tractor-trailer. Drug trafficking organizations would be the driver and in charge of where the truck is heading to with a large cargo of commodities (drugs) in its trailer. The wheels that support the chassis of the tractor-trailer would be prohibition and drug laws that criminalize drug use and define addicts as criminals because this is what makes drug trafficking move as a profitable business. The War on Drugs (WOD) and all law enforcement agencies implementing drug laws would be the tractor's transmission that enables power from the engine to go to the wheels and move the entire truck. Finally, the powerful diesel engine that keeps running the trailer (the most important piece) would be drug demand and addiction because consumption of illegal substances is the motor that pushes drug trafficking to exist. See figure 5.1 for a visual representation of this metaphor.

Indeed, there would be no trafficking, smuggling, and drug trafficking organizations (DTOs) sending illicit substances to the United States without the huge appetite America has for illicit drugs. However, to understand the complex dimension of drug trafficking as a global business, the metaphor of a tractor-trailer requires a more complex notion (to communicate the sophisticated nature of the problem) that includes a network of roads and highways to transport far away those drugs to satisfy the demand for them. One should notice that criminals and smugglers are not the only cause of drug trafficking but only an instrumental part that complements the complex machinery of this phenomenon. In fact, when examining the nature of drug trafficking it

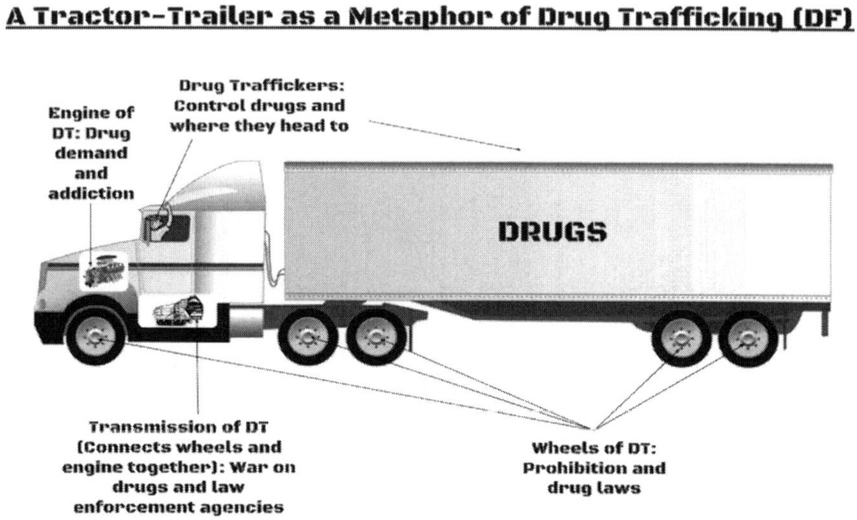

Figure 5.1 A Tractor-Trailer as a Metaphor of Drug Trafficking. Concept idea: Dr. Gabriel Ferreyra. Design: Melisa G. Castillo.

appears clear that three overlapping occurrences are needed for the conditions necessary for drug trafficking to exist: availability of drugs; drug laws; and strict drug enforcement (the drug war). Unintendedly, these three phenomena have become contributing forces to aid traffickers and drug groups to keep the drug business running.

Without any of these three components (drugs, prohibition, and law enforcement) drug trafficking would collapse like a house of cards because the size, sophistication, and nature of the illegal drug trade are such that it requires all of its gears to work in perfect tune to produce the desired results. Or in the case of the tractor-trailer metaphor, it requires all of these depicted parts to operate simultaneously and efficiently to allow DTOs to move the truck and the drugs worldwide. Although these three factors are apparently well-known and understood by many people familiar with the dynamics of drug trafficking, there are also serious misconceptions about why and how they facilitate and even promote drug trafficking. If only those who fiercely defend drug prohibition and the WOD would recognize the factual nature of illicit substances, why drug control will never solve drug use, and how strict law enforcement makes the problem worse, there would not be the need to re-examine these three occurrences here again. Let us begin by explaining the nature of drugs at its most basic principles and why it is naïve, if not blatantly foolish, to think that drug use can be stopped by attempts to cut the supply of drugs.

ON DRUGS

Many of the substances that today are defined as drugs by the international community have been part of the human experience for millennia and used by people since prehistoric times for different purposes such as rituals, ceremonies, religious festivities, recreational experiences, sacred cults, and other sociocultural and personal reasons (Escohotado 1999). Archaeological evidence has also found that drug plants and fermented beverages were consumed as far back as 8,000 years ago in South America, as well as in other parts of the world such as China, Italy, Argentina, and even in South Texas (Guerra-Doce 2015). Other ancient written sources such as Sumerian tablets, Babylonian cylinders, and Egyptian hieroglyphs have documented the use of poppy plant for enjoyment some 3,000 years ago and even earlier, as well as the use of marijuana (Escohotado 1999).

One prominent feature of all drugs—legal or illegal—is the fact that they have physical, psychological, and social benefits to users and this characteristic incentivizes drug demand and addiction. From time immemorial, people have resorted to drugs to increase performance or deal with fatigue (coca leaves and amphetamines), to address stress and social awkwardness (alcohol), to raise energy (caffeine), to experience euphoria (heroin), to combat pain (opioids), and to engage in ritual celebrations or spiritual journeys (peyote and magic mushrooms). This is a fact that has been well-documented by experts (Escohotado 1999; Guerra-Doce 2015; Walton 2002), yet it has been conveniently ignored by many public officials, politicians, and ideologues in America who systematically denied the benefits of drugs based on moral or dogmatic grounds. Just to be clear, I am not advocating drug use or suggesting that all drugs should be free and available to anyone in society; my point is to emphasize the complexity of the American drug problem and the contradictions between current drug policies and the historical availability and use of many drugs.

When considering all drugs together, alcohol has a special place as a drug of choice given its ubiquitous presence in most civilizations and because it is still the most used and abused substance in the world (Walton 2002). Alcohol intoxication and ingesting drugs to alter people's minds is as old as civilization. This desire to become intoxicated has only increased in the past centuries as more substances have been made available in our modern world. People seek out new experiences for multiple reasons such as pleasure, to deal with pain, to look for spiritual healing, religious enlightenment, and ritual purposes. To ignore or deny this reality is futile and it blinds us to understand the nature and dynamics of drug use and addiction in our current world and, more importantly, how to tackle drug trafficking more efficiently (Escohotado 1999; Walton 2002).

The legality or illegality of drugs in the United States is arbitrary because it is not based on medical criteria or the harm produced to consumers. For instance, dangerous drugs such as opioids have been easily accessible to Americas for decades as the current epidemic of opioid overdoses and deaths shows us. Meanwhile substances such as marijuana, peyote, and LSD are still illegal at the federal level and considered highly addictive when experts and evidence suggest otherwise (Escohotado 1999; Gupta 2015). Drugs are defined here as any substance that influences the central nervous system (Kuhn, Swartzwelder, and Wilson 2014). Interestingly, the concept of drug as a potentially dangerous substance is a relatively modern idea that developed with the origins of pharmacology as science in the nineteenth century. Previously, millennial substances categorized today as drugs were harvested, manufactured, and consumed by humans in social and religious celebrations without the stigma that many drugs have today. Not only that, in times of war governments and armies have resorted to drugs to encourage soldiers to fight and engage in the atrocities that all battlefields produce. And afterwards, to numb or treat soldiers who are injured or mortally wounded. There is an inextricable link between drug use and going to war (Bergen-Cico 2012). During the American Revolution and Civil War, soldiers used alcohol before and after combat to make soldiers shoot the enemy first. After the battle, alcohol was used to treat injuries and help wounded soldiers to withstand amputations, cope with pain (physical, emotional, and psychological), and soothe the trauma left by the war (Andreas 2013).

Fast forward to the present and there is a shocking reality in the United States that has been conveniently ignored by many politicians, public officials, and mainstream media, or at least there is no political willingness to openly discuss and accept it. The fact is that America is the world's largest consumer of illicit drugs by volume. To be fair, there are other countries that have a greater per capita use of illegal drugs than the United States, which is a more scientific way to compare different nations that share similar social, economic, and cultural development. However, the fact that America is the third most populous country in the world (just below China and India) should give the reader an idea about the size of the lucrative black market for illicit drugs that exist in America and why drug trafficking is such a prominent activity there. Thus, the United States is the top consumer of these illegal drugs, but use and abuse of prohibited drugs do not occur always and all the time across the board in America. It fluctuates from drug to drug and from place to place, meaning that marijuana use may be more widely consumed in California compared to Texas, but Alaska has the highest percentage of teenage drug use compared to Utah, which has the lowest in the same category. Therefore, it is crucial to differentiate between drugs (Kiernan 2018). Also important is to acknowledge that given the illicit nature of prohibited drugs it is difficult to calculate with precision to what extent illegal substances are consumed and the habits of users.

That being said, the most widely used illegal drug in the United States (and the world) is marijuana. A Gallop poll published in 2016 revealed that more than 33 million Americans defined themselves as marijuana smokers. This is one in eight adults admitted to smoking marijuana (McCarthy 2016). A more recent scientific survey titled "Weed and the American Family" conducted by the Marist University and Yahoo News found that more than half of the adult population in the United States have experienced marijuana at least once in their lives. Similarly to the Gallop poll, this study also revealed that nearly 35 million use pot at least one or two times per month, behavior defined in the survey as "regular user." This study also found that around 56 percent of Americans admitted that marijuana is socially acceptable (Romano 2017).

Prescription drugs are overwhelmingly misused by millions of Americans. But, how about other addictive drugs such as heroin and cocaine? Cheaper, more powerful, and available across the nation as never before, heroin has brought devastation to many communities, cities, and governments in recent years. As DTOs lost foothold in the marijuana market due to legalization of this substance in several states, they began smuggling purer and cheaper heroin all over the United States as the government cracked down on prescription opioids. So users transitioned from taking Oxycodone, Vicodin, and Percocet pills to snorting, inhaling, and finally injecting heroin since in many places a batch of this substance was cheaper than a package of cigarettes (Quinones 2015). The problem has gotten worse as users again transitioned to another drug and they began to use synthetic opioids such as fentanyl to substitute heroin, which has contributed to the epidemic of opioid addiction and overdoses in America (Centers for Disease Control and Prevention 2018; Tinker 2019).

Regarding cocaine, for nearly five years from 2005 to 2010 the use of this drug declined by nearly 50 percent in the United States (Kilmer et al. 2014). There is no consensus among experts about the reason why this occurred. Multiple factors such as law enforcement operations, users aging out, switching to other drugs, and all of these combined have been given as explanations (Kilmer and Midgette 2017). However, new data from different sources suggest that cocaine use is on the rise again in America. How do we know this for sure? First, the overall production of cocaine in Colombia has grown significantly in the past years (United Nations Office on Drugs and Crime 2018). Second, cocaine overdoses have also increased in the United States recently. Finally, an increased in prevalence (people reporting use of cocaine over the past month or year) has apparently increased, too. All this information is circumstantial and not very reliable since it takes time (sometimes years) to put together the data in a scientific manner that reflects the reality of drug consumption (Kilmer and Midgette 2017). However, it is a fact that global cocaine production increased dramatically by 56 percent in three years (2013–2016), according to the 2018 World Drug Report (United Nations Office on Drugs and Crime 2018). This suggests that if manufacture of cocaine expanded, demand and use of it also did.

All things considered, it is not difficult to realize how complicated the whole situation of drug use and abuse in America is given the huge demand for illegal drugs. This reality in itself should be enough to look at drug trafficking and addiction with an objective perspective and leave aside political and ideological claims, and instead apply evidence-based information in drug policymaking. Better still, the fact that now it is possible to know scientifically and with certain accuracy the nature of most prohibited drugs and their most serious effects, this knowledge should give politicians and anti-narcotic agents plenty of arguments for a commonsense approach to deal with drug trafficking and use of illegal drugs in the most efficient way.

Yet, the Controlled Substances Act that regulates federal U.S. drug policy still keeps in the same category (Schedule I) heroin, marijuana, and other hallucinogens such as peyote and LSD (Lysergic acid diethylamide) (Controlled Substances Act 1970). Regrettably, this distorted classification of drugs has been used as legal justification to enforce the drug war and drug prohibition policies even when these strategies have made drug trafficking and drug abuse worse rather than addressing the problem. To provide a more nuanced but easier understanding of drug trafficking in America, it is necessary to discuss important historical contexts regarding America's relationship with illegal drugs.

When Hard Drugs Were Legal in America

When America gained full independence from Britain, there were no drug trafficking activities because substances such as opiates, cocaine, heroin, and cannabis were legally sold and consumed throughout the eighteenth and nineteenth centuries. "Before 1800, opium was available in America in its crude forms as an ingredient of multidrug prescriptions, or in such extracts as laudanum, containing alcohol, or 'black drop,' containing no alcohol" (Musto 1999, 1). As incredible as it may sound, Americans in the late nineteenth century could buy in stores or order by mail medicine containing cocaine, laudanum (an extract of opium alkaloids used for treating common maladies such as diarrhea or pain), and morphine. The most famous sugary beverage in the world, Coca-Cola, contained cocaine until 1903, and then cocaine was replaced with caffeine (Musto 1999, 3).

Opiates were commonly used in the nineteenth century through a variety of medical patents available to anyone in the market under names such as "Mrs. Winslow's Soothing Syrup" and "Ayer's Cherry Pectoral." It is worth mentioning that before 1906, labeling requirements were not mandatory in patent medicines so many of those products did not list drug content and sometimes manufacturers even advertised their brands in a positive manner denying the presence of addictive substances. It was not until the first consumer protection law—the Pure Food and Drug Act—was passed in 1906 that the federal government began to regulate those products (Musto 1999).

Most of the opium available in America was legal and usually imported from overseas. However, opium production occurred in the United States in states such as California, Arizona, Florida, Vermont, Connecticut, and New Hampshire. It is not a surprise then that during the Civil War and afterwards consumption of opiates was widespread and many doctors commonly provided them to soldiers. In fact, the rates of chronic morphine use among Civil War veterans were so high after the war that their addiction was known as the Soldier's Disease (Bergen-Cico 2012). As Edward Brecher correctly describes, the American sociocultural context towards drug use two centuries ago was extremely lenient for our current standards. He explains, "the United States of America during the nineteenth century could quite properly be described as a 'dope fiend's paradise'" (Brecher 1970, 15).

A distinctive feature of this accessibility to addictive substances at that time was that drugs were not portrayed as a menace to society, nor were they associated with deviant behavior and a road to perdition. Drugs were indeed believed to be immoral and a vice similar to sexual dissipation, gambling, or smoking, but drug users did not lose their jobs, spouses did not get divorced if one of them had an addiction and parents did not lose custody of their children if suffering from chronic opium use. As strange as it may sound, American society in those days generally understood that opium addiction was difficult to quit and that the sudden withdrawal from chronic opium consumption could harm or kill the user. This perception was so embedded in society that there was little support to prohibit those drugs, although things would change soon (Brecher 1970).

By the early twentieth century, a noticeably large number of people in the United States have become addicted to some of the aforementioned drugs and a legal market existed. There is the assumption that drug use was evenly present among all demographic groups; however, addicts were generally singled out as belonging to minority groups (blacks) or being foreign (Chinese), but this was not the case (Musto 1999). The former was associated with cocaine and the later with opium use. These two groups were feared mostly because of their ethnicity and race rather than their inclination for drug use. As a result, blacks and the Chinese began to be associated with drug use, addiction, and immorality due to fearmongering and because they were minorities (Musto 1999). Even if it is true that the Chinese brought with them the practice of opium smoking in the mid-1800s when they helped to build the railroad network in the United States, anti-Chinese sentiment grew stronger in the West Coast, California in particular, due to economic debacle. By the early twentieth century this sentiment picked up and laws were enacted to target it, but the reality was that opium smoking had already been adopted by many Americans besides the Chinese (Musto 1999).

Cocaine use on the other hand was associated with black people, mostly in the South. This fear against African-Americans led to many myths and fantasies about them such as having superhuman strength or the myth that they could stand .32 caliber bullets without dying when under the influence of cocaine (Musto 1999). These were mostly white anxieties about drug use in America that originated from racist beliefs rather than legitimate assumptions about the true effects of cocaine issue. The demonization of black men and the subtle but persistent effort to associate them with crime, deviance and violence was not an accidental belief based on facts or reality but a continuation of racist and discriminatory practices after the abolition of slavery. Thus, it is not a coincidence that "[t]he fear of the cocainized black coincided with the peak of lynching, legal segregation, and voting laws all designated to remove political and social power from him" (Musto 1999, 7). It is worth mentioning that during this time in the early twentieth century, the Debt Peonage system and black codes (laws passed in the South meant to restrict African-Americans' freedom after the Civil War) began to collapse. Therefore, associating cocaine use to blacks and their allegedly supernatural powers was just another way to characterize them as primitive and uncivilized and maintain a strict social control over them, but now using the criminal justice system as a tool against them disguised as a law and order problem (Alexander 2012).

As science progressed more conclusive evidence suggested that opiates, cocaine, alcohol, and other substances led to addiction, and consensus grew in the medical field that those substances should be regulated. However, scientific development was still in the making in the early twentieth century, and there were still many unknowns and misconceptions about these drugs and their long-term effects. Without the availability of scientific information, misconceptions on drugs and their effects followed. For instance, in the 1910s, major newspapers, experts, and some politicians truly believed that cocaine and opiates made chronic users to commit crimes or become maniacs. This association between drug use and criminal behavior had no scientific foundation, yet this assumption would eventually became a dominant force to justify and push for drug interdiction, and eventually implement draconian punishment against drug users. Along with those ideas there was the belief that drugs were mostly used by the underclass, immigrants, and the undesirable.

Thus, American society began to consider whether or not to regulate or prohibit addictive substances; ultimately those efforts merged in the movement that led to alcohol Prohibition in 1918 and drug prohibition later on (Inciardi and Mcelrath 2014; Musto 1999)

DRUG PROHIBITION

Drugs have been a crucial component of American society since the country became an independent nation. The existence of drugs and trafficking in the United States is not a contemporary or new phenomenon because historical evidence suggests otherwise. When America was at the verge of its revolution, fighting for independence from the British Empire, it engaged in smuggling and trafficking of illegal trade goods (alcohol among them) in order to finance its independent movement (Andreas 2013). It has been widely documented that smuggling and illicit activities have been two primary characteristics of American history that helped to win its emancipation from the British Empire (Albertson 1950; Boullosa and Wallace 2016; Brecher 1970; Musto 1999). If illicit substances and smuggling have been part of the making of America, why have drug trafficking and drug use become such a confused, tortuous, and insoluble problem in the past century? The straight answer is: drug prohibition.

The prohibition of drugs in the United States has been a slow but steady process that officially began more than 100 years ago when the Harrison Narcotic Tax Act put a de-facto ban on narcotics, as drugs were labeled back then. Passage of the first law regulating and taxing derivatives of coca leaves and opiates took place in 1914. As its name suggests, this law was intended to reduce opium and cocaine consumption in the United States by imposing a special tax on anyone who produced, imported, distributed, sold, dispensed or gave away any of the aforementioned drugs or their derivatives. Important to note is that this legislation did not prohibit the trade, distribution and use of opium and cocaine, rather regulation and taxation was the main goal. Physicians, pharmacists, and the lawyers of pharmaceutical companies producing legal narcotics strongly opposed this law and when its passage was inevitable, they lobbied to create exemptions (Musto 1999). A particular clause in the law allowed physicians to dispense opiates "in the course of their professional practice only," meaning that doctors could prescribe them to their patients. However, this clause was eventually interpreted in 1919 by the Supreme Court in *Webb v. United States* and concluded that physicians did not have privileges to dispense opiates to drug users according to the Harrison Narcotics Tax Act (Musto 1999).

The Harrison Narcotics Tax Act was the first legal step into a prohibition era that swept America at the beginning of the twentieth century. Similar to narcotics interdiction, the prohibition of alcohol created a black market, alcohol trafficking, moonshining, and syndicate crime. The social and criminal backlash was so severe that prohibition lasted only thirteen years and it had to be abolished in 1933 after all the unintended consequences of this policy were finally acknowledged (Okrent 2011; Musto 1999). It is true that alcohol use had been a controversial issue since the American Revolution due to Puritan concerns and ideological beliefs. However, its regulation had been kept behind doors because most alcohol was consumed in the privacy of one's home rather than in public before the 18th Amendment was passed. The pioneer spirit that contributed to the expansion of the West and the arrival of the Saloon were crucial factors that changed the social perception of alcohol in public. As a result, alcohol consumption and its role as part of the socialization process became part of the American lifestyle by having more tolerance towards it and eventually by being adopted as a mainstream practice (Okrent 2011).

Prohibition Paves the Way to Drug Trafficking Infrastructure

One of the most dramatic effects of alcohol prohibition was that it consolidated modern organized crime in America. Criminal organizations such as the Mafia existed before alcohol interdiction and they engaged in illegal activities such as gambling and prostitution. Yet, prohibition created an artificial scarcity of alcohol that soon led to a profitable black market, encouraged by the fact that drinking alcohol was not illegal during the thirteen years that prohibition lasted, only its production, transportation, and commercialization. Thus, criminal organizations filled in the void by reaping the benefits of alcohol demand producing mass quantities of it as well as stronger liquor than ever before. Meanwhile, competition to control and monopolize the black market grew between Mafia groups to the point that it generated never-seen violence and lawlessness in the United States. Crime in particular skyrocketed in major American cities and law enforcement was unable to confront it successfully due to corruption, high costs of enforcement, and the pervasive nature of the problem. A considerable headache was that suddenly thousands of law-abiding citizens became criminals for making, selling, storing, or transporting alcohol when those activities were perfectly legal just before prohibition started (Recio 2002; Okrent 2011).

Considering that alcohol was never illegal in Mexico, many American distilleries and beer companies moved in to Mexico on the verge of prohibition and opened businesses throughout the Mexico-U.S. border. Some alcohol businesses even sent millions of gallons of liquor in trains south of the border to save them from being wasted before the 18th Amendment took effect, avoiding huge economic losses (Recio 2002; Okrent 2011). Eventually, all that liquor was smuggled back to the United States where demand for alcohol was increasing in the black market. Mexican entrepreneurs also took advantage of this economic opportunity and built beer factories along the border to profit from the new policy of alcohol interdiction. Understood as a new economic opportunity opened by prohibition, smuggling alcohol to America became a prosperous business, even more so than drug trafficking (Recio 2002).

Prohibition consolidated smuggling activities along the Southern border because it created a criminal infrastructure in both countries that it did not exist before for the simple but powerful reason that it was profitable to smuggle alcohol into the United States and demand was permanent and consistent. Certainly, when alcohol prohibition was finally repealed in 1933, it ended the bonanza of alcohol smuggling, but soon after, the Marijuana Tax Act of 1937 imposed a de-facto prohibition of cannabis and this new interdiction policy greatly contributed to the early development of drug trafficking of marijuana between Mexico and the United States (Recio 2002). Besides the regular construction of factories, storage, cheap labor, and transportation equipment to produce and smuggle alcohol, the business' infrastructure included a broad distribution network. Those in charge of smuggling alcohol (by land, sea, and even aviation at some point) used political connections, and enticed people and communities on both sides of the border to take part and benefit from alcohol smuggling. This smuggling infrastructure contributed to produce income and employment for many communities that became dependent on alcohol prohibition for their subsistence over the years (Okrent 2011; Recio 2002).

As a result, prohibition of alcohol (and later on illegal drugs) was a crucial component in the development and consolidation of drug trafficking in Mexico and the United States because it created the economic and social conditions for a prosperous illegal business. First, prohibition generated scarcity of a product that already had public demand in society since it was previously legal. Second, prohibition led to a monopoly of the drug market in the hands of traffickers who had to fight each other to control it using violence, corruption, and illegal methods. Finally, prohibition did not address the main problem that promotes drug trafficking: stopping people from using drugs. Rather, it sent consumption underground creating a huge and profitable black market (Recio 2002).

When the Volstead Act was repealed in 1933, alcohol smuggling from Mexico to the United States collapsed, but the entire infrastructure that was built upon this activity remained in place because alcohol was never prohibited in Mexico. Therefore, all the groundwork that existed to trafficking alcohol to the United States switched to smuggle now opium and marijuana because it was profitable and there was demand for these drugs. This transition from smuggling alcohol to smuggling opium and marijuana cemented the logistical conditions that eventually would expand and consolidate drug trafficking throughout the Mexico-U.S. border in future decades. Indeed, the routes, the border crossings, the enclaves, the human resources, the connections, and the political and social capitals indispensable for alcohol smuggling were all now available for drug trafficking after alcohol prohibition was repealed in 1933. Another crucial factor that also precipitated the transition from trafficking alcohol to illicit drugs and the arrival of early criminal gangs was the institutionalization of drug control policies as a bureaucratic program. Legislative attempts to create an independent office of drug prohibition finally came to fruition in July 1930 when the Federal Bureau of Narcotics (FBN) was created as part of the Department of Treasury. The first commissioner of the Bureau appointed by the president was Henry J. Anslinger, a zealot administrator who officially became the first drug czar too.

Anslinger's Crusade: Drug Prohibition Cements

To grasp the scale of influence and significance of Harry J. Anslinger as the first American drug czar in shaping drug control policies for decades, it is necessary to revisit why and how he was able to do so. First, it is worth noting that Anslinger was commissioner of the FBN for thirty-two long years under six different U.S. presidencies until 1962 when he retired. Second, the FBN has been acknowledged as the first law enforcement agency to engage in strict drug control policies for decades, in particular addressing drug trafficking in America. This was the result of Anslinger's work and emphasis on this approach because he truly believed that "the primary enforcement challenge was to control the drug supply, particularly from abroad" (Bertram et al. 1996, 79). In turn, the bureaucratic apparatus that cemented the FBN as the agency in charge of drug prohibition became the predecessor institution of the Drug Enforcement Administration (DEA), bringing with it the drug control zealous mindset that the FBN successfully built to remain relevant (more on this later). Third, what made Anslinger most famous was not the longevity of his tenure as much as his approach and policies based on extreme views, ignorance of science, radical ideology, and blatant racism to carry out his job (Bertram et al. 1996; Hari 2016; Sloman 1998).

As the first commissioner of the FBN, Anslinger's main policy was drug control. His agenda became increasingly intolerant and oppressive against drug users mostly because they were associated with minority groups. Without any scientific evidence and using sensationalism, far-fetched newspaper articles, and misinformation, Anslinger depicted marijuana as a monster drug that was destroying American youth and undermining U.S. society of its core values. He was outspoken on his views and frequently did radio broadcastings, appearing in public venues to lecture about the evils of marijuana, and arguing like an ideologue in a propaganda campaign. Anslinger even wrote melodramatic magazine articles with titles such as "Marijuana: Assassin of Youth," this one published in the *American Magazine* in 1937 (Bertram et al. 1996; Hari 2016; Inciardi 2008).

Aware that the bureau was small and exposed to potential budget cuts and reorganizational measures (the Great Depression was unfolding), Anslinger pushed for a tough strategy to ban all drugs—marijuana in particular—and criminalize users. Ultimately, his goal was to influence public opinion and instigate support for a draconian drug control strategy in order to increase the size, budget, and importance of his agency (Bertram et al. 1996; Chasin 2016; Sloman 1998). Such aggressive institutional approach resulted in the proliferation of black markets for marijuana, opium, and other illegal substances because there was already a steady demand for them in America. Bear in mind that regarding drug control, most experts have concluded time and again that anti-drug policies do not end consumption and demand for drugs, it only sends the market to clandestine operations and gives the monopoly of illegal substances to organized crime.

Anslinger went even further in his gospel against marijuana and ordered that field agents of the Bureau of Narcotics collect gruesome crime stories from across the country and arbitrarily link them to offenders claiming they were under the influence of marijuana when committing their crimes. Many of these crime stories were real, some invented, but there was no direct evidence of marijuana as the ultimate reason for these offenders to engage in criminal behavior. Of course, some criminals use marijuana or other drugs while committing crimes, but correlation is no causation. However, Anslinger distorted these media stories to make them look as if marijuana led people to commit crimes. He used these documents to give official credibility to his assertions about the nature and dangers of marijuana without providing evidence, facts, or data. For him, the most critical component of transforming these sensational stories into official documents of the FBN was to ignite a mass hysteria campaign to create consensus and momentum for a total banishment of marijuana (Bertram et al. 1996; Hari 2016; Sloman 1998).

These exaggerated crime stories became known as the *Gore Files* and Anslinger used them to openly argue that marijuana consumption made people to commit murder, sex crimes, and drive them to madness. For instance, in an article he wrote it said:

> How many murders, suicides, robberies, criminal assaults, holdups, burglaries, and deeds of maniacal insanity [marijuana] causes each year, especially among the young, can be only conjectured … No one can predict its effects. No one knows, when he places a marijuana cigarette to his lips, whether he will become a joyous reveler in a musical heaven, a mad insensate, a calm philosopher, or a murderer. (Anslinger 1937, 18)

Literally, marijuana was framed as an evil substance that led to extreme violence and insane criminal behavior. Perhaps for some readers these arguments may seem preposterous, comical, and difficult to believe today, but in the early 1930s they were believed by most citizens and that is why these stories were broadly used by Anslinger to implement his messianic message of saving the world from marijuana (Boullosa and Wallence 2016; Inciardi 2008; Sloman 1998).

Anslinger exploited white anxieties, high unemployment, and the economic despair caused by the Great Depression of 1929 that collapsed the world economy. Using mass media such as newspapers, magazines, and even movies (e.g., the film *Reefer Madness* released in 1936), he reinforced and magnified the message that marijuana was on the verge of ruining America. Within this narrative, there was an explicit effort to associate marijuana use with Mexican-Americans and immigrants. It is not an accident that the drug was also called the *Mexican dich weed.* The impact of the overall message was such that this false but widespread assumption that the Mexican community and Mexican-Americans (there was no distinction between them for the media and Anslinger) used marijuana indiscriminately contributed to the repatriation and expulsion of nearly one million of them (many were American citizens) in the 1930s (see Balderrama and Rodriguez 2006 for a detailed account on this event). Mexicans and Mexican-Americans became an easy and convenient target to be blamed for the moral panic that Anslinger and his henchmen created to pursue their own political and ideological goals within the FBN (Boullosa and Wallence 2016; Inciardi 2008; Sloman 1998).

The scary message from Anslinger was so powerful that it created enough public hysteria to force politicians and public officials to "do something about it" even though marijuana was not a major crime issue. Consequently, based on a distorted and ignorant view of the plant, the Marijuana Tax Act was enacted on August 2, 1937, changing the classification of marijuana as a narcotic, and equating it to opiates and cocaine in terms of dangerousness. This law created an immediate and de-facto prohibition that led to the criminalization of marijuana possession throughout the country. Infamously, Samuel R. Caldwell, a citizen of Denver, Colorado, became the first person to ever be convicted of a marijuana charge under this law just a week after it was passed by Congress (Chasin 2016; Schlosser 2004).

Anslinger's obsession with America's drug problem developed into some sort of McCarthyism, and similar to FBI's director Herbert Hoover, Anslinger kept files of well-known artists and musicians (mostly black) who he identified as drug users to harass or arrest them by agents of the FBN. Among those artists were Billy Holiday, Louis Armstrong, Cab Calloway, Count Basie, and many others (Hari 2016; Inciardi 2008; Schlosser 2004). He even claimed without any scientific evidence that Latinos and blacks were the main users of marijuana, which reveals to what extent his propaganda campaign was shaped by a racist ideology. In retrospect, most biographers and scholars now agree that Anslinger was an ultra-right-wing conservative bureaucrat who used smear tactics and fearmongering as tools to gain himself political recognition and obtain bureaucratic privileges for the Bureau of Narcotics within the federal administration (Hari 2016; Inciardi 2008; Schlosser 2004). For a detailed and well-researched account of Anslinger's tenure and his effects on the WOD, see Chasin (2016).

The influence of Anslinger's crusade went beyond the United States and he was actively and successfully involved in imposing U.S. drug control policy upon the rest of the world. As the main designer of federal drug control policies, he pushed for international treaties that unified previous legislation regarding drug prohibition such as the Geneva Convention in 1931 and the Single Convention on Narcotic Drugs in 1961 that consolidated drug control and broadened the scope of prohibition worldwide (McWilliams 1990). Anslinger even took a personal stand on imposing his anti-drug rhetoric in America's southern neighbor. In 1937, Mexico defined drug consumption as a health problem and the Department of Health was openly against prohibition. The head of the Office of Federal Narcotics Leopoldo Salazar Viniegra was a well-respected physician with a solid reputation as a scientist. Based on research, he wrote a paper "The Myth of Marijuana" where he rebuked Anslinger's statements that marijuana was a Mexican problem in the United States. He also argued convincingly that the so-called killer weed had no relation whatsoever with crime and suggested that Mexico should regulate marijuana by allowing government clinics for addicts while educating consumers, rather than engaging in prohibition measures (Enciso 2015).

The Mexican Department of Health allowed the opening of some clinics and gave permits to users to obtain marijuana in pharmacies. What most people do not know is that Mexico actually legalized all drugs on February 17, 1940 under the administration of President Lázaro Cárdenas because addiction was understood as a medical, not a criminal, problem. Salazar Viniegra met Anslinger in an international meeting and read his paper. The American czar was astonished by Salazar's standing on marijuana and aggressively fought back his measures. The legalization of drugs in Mexico was short-lived since Anslinger lobbied with the federal administration to impose an embargo on all medical drugs to Mexico while launching a smear campaign to discredit the Mexican physician. Anslinger was well connected with many high ranking members of Congress and had direct access to the intelligence community, thus the State Department put pressure on Mexico to backtrack this progressive approach. Since World War II was in progress, it was impossible to bring medicine from Europe and eventually the Mexican government cancelled the legalization of drugs on June 7, 1940, only a few months after its authorization (Boullosa and Wallace 2016; Enciso 2015; McWilliams 1990). Anslinger then can be credited as one of the most fervent defenders of drug prohibition by setting up the foundations for what would be known as the WOD in the years to come (Bertram et al. 1996; Inciardi 2008; Sloman 1998).

This brief examination of Anslinger's work at the Bureau of Narcotics is crucial to understand the legacy that his ideological crusade had against drugs and the consequences left in American society. Not just because he dismissed science and used shoddy tactics to obtain bureaucratic prominence, but more importantly, because his approach was racist, extreme, and unjust against many Americans who happened to suffer from addiction. Ultimately, Anslinger created the foundations of the U.S. drug policy that would eventually give birth to the WOD. This drug policy merits meticulous review of the theoretical doctrine and policies that have supported its justification for half a century.

THE WAR ON DRUGS (WOD)

Instead of addressing the real problem of drug demand and trafficking in America, the WOD has done little in nearly fifty years to address the problem of drug addiction and drug trafficking in the United States. The WOD has produced precisely the opposite result by aggravating the issue with unintended consequences and wasting billions of taxpayer money in a war that it was lost decades ago (Payan, Staudt, and Kruszewski 2013). Based on criminal justice data and evidence, research on incarceration rates, and social work in communities where many drug offenders live, most experts (Andreas 2013; Baum 1996; Bertram et al. 1996; Coyne and Hall 2017; Grillo 2011; Payan, Staudt, and Kruszewski 2013) have overwhelmingly concluded over and again that the WOD has not solved the problem but made it worse. Many scholars, politicians, journalists, pundits, former law enforcement agents, public officials, lawmakers, and economists have all explained and concluded in nearly similar terms that the WOD is a "failed experiment." Dozens if not hundreds of books, academic articles, newspaper articles, and official reports provide a clear and detailed narrative supported with facts, data, and evidence denouncing why the WOD has never worked as it was meant to be and will never do (Andreas 2013; Baum 1996; Bertram et al. 1996; Grillo 2011; Hari 2016; Mallea 2014; Wainwright 2016).

To provide a visual example of how the WOD has been handled in America, the following argument reveals its absurdity. The quote "It became necessary to destroy the town to save it," was reported by the *Associated Press* reporter Peter Arnett in 1968 describing the Vietnamese town of Bén Tre that was wiped out by American soldiers with napalm, rockets, and bombs, in early February of that year, killing thousands of civilians living there (Cronkite 1971). The U.S. Army's official justification for this destruction was that the town had been infiltrated by Viet Cong soldiers, and an urban guerrilla-military engagement would have caused many American and civilians casualties. Therefore to avoid American casualties, the U.S. Army concluded that massive devastation by bombing the city with airplanes' raids was necessary and justified to recover the town. This quote exemplifies the absurdity of war by which any means justified the ends. Applying the same analogy to U.S. drug policy and drug prohibition, a fervent defender of the WOD would say: it became necessary to destroy drug users and minority communities to save them. Based on how the WOD has been fought in America in the past 50 years, it can be assumed that the same rationale that condoned the obliteration of Bén Tre in South Vietnam has been used to justify the WOD. Regardless of the costs and unintended effects of this drug policy that has affected addicts and drug users' lives, their communities, and families, the WOD is justified on legalistic, ideological, and narrow-minded grounds. This assertion is not hyperbole since it has been fully documented at length the dramatic negative outcomes this policy has had in communities of color, the poor, women, and the disenfranchised in the United States (Alexander 2012; Coyne and Hall 2017; Hari 2016; Mallea 2014). Here is why.

WHAT IS THE WOD?

Since its inception, the underlying government strategy that sustained the WOD paradigm (and its predecessor drug prohibition) was the assumption that by cutting or limiting the supply of drugs available on the streets, users will not find them easily, and if found, drugs will be extremely expensive and unaffordable to buy for most users. Along with that, there was the belief (no science or evidence supports this premise) that under the threat of harsh punishment (e.g. fines, incarceration, long sentences, and the stigma of being an ex-convict), drug users will be reluctant to consume drugs (Alexander 2012; Bertram et al. 1996). Other arguments in support of the WOD have been the beliefs that this approach disrupts and dismantles DTOs, that enforcing drug laws reduces overdoses and drug-related illnesses, and the assumption that crime drug-related offenses and violence will decline by having a strict drug control (Coyne and Hall 2017).

Since these assumptions were never supported with facts or evidence, not surprisingly, any of the alleged benefits that the WOD promised never occurred. In fact, the opposite happened because today there are more drugs available on the streets of America than ever before and prices for most illegal drugs are low, and hence, affordable for must drug users and addicts. Also, there are more powerful and addictive drugs than ever before such as fentanyl, purer heroin, and methamphetamine. Finally, most of these drugs are systematically smuggled and trafficked into the United States through ports of entry and widely distributed nationwide making them accessible to any American (Alexander 2012; Andreas 2013; Baum 1996; Bertram et al. 1996; Hari 2016).

A crucial strategy used by those defending the WOD paradigm has been the use of political slogans such as the rhetorical argument of "being tough on crime" and the strategy of fearmongering (all drugs are deemed equal and the same) to justify more punitive measures. Among the most well-known legislative measures that reinforced the WOD approach were the creation of mandatory sentencing guidelines, issuing three-strike laws (laws meant to drastically punish offenders who have committed three felonies but usually not violent crime), and truth-in sentences, that have contributed to mass incarceration. Before any of these measures became law throughout the country, the incarceration rate in America was similar on average to other industrialized nations worldwide (Alexander 2012).

THE CONSEQUENCES OF WOD

Since its inception, the WOD has costed billions of dollars to Americans, it has led to mass incarceration and racial disparities in the criminal justice system, and has spurred violence, corruption, and organized crime where drugs are produced, smuggled, distributed, or sold. Not only that, because of the criminalization of drug users, the WOD has also contributed to several public health crises throughout the years such as spreading AIDS, Hepatitis C, and HIV. Also, drug control prohibits needle exchange programs and as a result unnecessary deaths and infections occur among addicts. All things considered, following is a detailed list of the costs of the WOD.

Economic Cost

The economic cost of the WOD is staggering and a waste of taxpayers' money for two major reasons: first, this policy has done nothing to reduce the presence of drugs and drug demand in America, and second, the amount of spending has reached absurd levels for a government policy that does not work. On average, the United States spends more than $50 billion each year fighting drug trafficking and punishing drug users (Coyne and Hall 2017; Drug Policy Alliance 2019). Since the launching of the WOD, the estimated total economic cost of this policy has been more than $1 trillion dollars, despite its systematic failure (*The Economist* 2009). This colossal amount of money has been spent mostly in three primary categories: the criminal justice system (police, courts, and corrections) in charge of arresting, prosecuting, and punishing drug offenders and those who traffic illicit substances; efforts to eradicate the supply of drugs in foreign countries such as Afghanistan, Colombia, Mexico, and Peru by implementing law enforcement operations against producers, disrupting drug trafficking corridors, and intercepting drug smugglers' attempts to ship or transport drugs to America; and stricter border control measures along the 328 official points of entry (airports, seaports, and border stations) to prevent illicit drugs from entering the United States (Coyne and Hall 2017).

Trying to stop illegal drugs from entering the United States is a futile and insurmountable mission considering the size of America's territory. The United States has almost 7,000 miles of mutual borders with Mexico and Canada and 12,383 miles of coastline (not including freshwater coastline), according to the U.S. Census. Even using the most sophisticated and modern technology available today, it is physically impossible to search every person, vehicle, semi-truck, and container that enter the United States due to the volume of trade America has from being the world's largest economy (Benavie 2009). Yet, this is exactly what law enforcement looks like when guarding America's borders against drug trafficking: a Band-Aid solution. Why? Because it does not address the real problem of drug consumption, just its symptoms.

Law enforcement dealing with the WOD are mostly fruitless police operations where some drugs, money, and low-level traffickers are taken into custody, and sometimes there is the destruction of some marijuana, coca leaves, or poppy fields. Now and then, there is the dismantling of a drug cell, disrupting a drug corridor, or intercepting a shipment of cocaine and killing or arresting a drug lord. However, the core of the illegal drug trade that supplies the endless demand for drugs in the United States remains always basically the same (Andreas 2013; Benavie 2009; Coyne and Hall 2017). These government efforts to eradicate drug trafficking do not make any noticeable progress in reducing the availability of drugs, violence, and demand for drugs, yet this information has been conveniently ignored or kept hidden by those who justify the WOD. Why? Because law enforcement agencies in charge of implementing and defending this drug policy remain the primary beneficiaries of the bureaucratic structure and large budgets that come with it. Among these agencies are the DEA, DHS, the U.S. Customs and Border Protection, Department of Justice, and state and local police forces (Benavie 2009; Coyne and Hall 2017).

Mass Incarceration

In recent decades, many victims, experts, and scholars (Alexander 2012; Andreas 2013; Baum 1996; Benavie 2009; Bertram et al. 1996) on the WOD have persuasively put emphasis on a less visible but powerful force behind this policy approach: the WOD has become a method of social control against those who are deemed second class or inferior citizens in America. Arresting, processing, and locking up disenfranchised Americans serve influential economic and political interests such as the prison-industrial complex. Politicians who win elections use fearmongering to become elected, and law enforcement agencies that police for profit use civil forfeiture seizures to increase their budget, so they usually resist changes to the status quo.

The most visible effect of this official effort to employ the WOD as a formal policy of social control is mass incarceration. Mass incarceration (MI) is also known as prison boom, hyper-incarceration, and mass imprisonment. It is defined as the process of extreme incarceration where the U.S. government has sent thousands of its citizens to long-term imprisonment (mostly people of color), many of them for non-violent crimes (Alexander 2012). Once these individuals are labeled felons they become under strict control of the criminal justice system (police, courts, and and prisons) even after having served their sentences. MI targets primarily non-violent drug users (mostly African-Americans and Hispanics) who have been sent to lengthy prison terms since the early 1980s (Alexander 2012).

The phenomenon of MI in America has been well-documented by criminologists who concluded that until the early 1970s, incarceration rates were stable and similar to other developed countries worldwide. However, from the late 1970s and the 1980s up until the 2000s, the incarceration rate increased dramatically to unprecedented levels of nearly to a 700 percent increase. A common example used by experts to highlight the dramatic nature of this phenomenon is the fact that the United States has only 5 percent of the world population but nearly 25 percent of the prison population (The Sentencing Project 2019). To be fair, the WOD is not the only reason behind MI, but it has been by far the most important contributing factor to it in the past three decades (Alexander 2012).

Even today when more Americans support progressive measures to deal with the drug problem and public support for marijuana legalization has grown steadily in favor, arrests for marijuana possession and other drugs have increased in the recent past (Stellin 2019). According to a FBI database, 1,654,282 people were arrested in America in 2018 for drug charges where marijuana was the most common drug. Out of these arrests, 663,367 were for marijuana in 2018, a small but higher percentage compared to the previous year when 659,700 arrests were conducted (FBI 2019; Stellin 2019). The vast majority of these drug arrests were for possessing small quantities of drugs (usually for personal consumption) rather than selling or producing them. Thus, law enforcement data confirms that the WOD and incarceration are still the primary force to deal with the American drug problem, considering that many police departments define arrests as a yardstick to police effectiveness and this measure is thought as the only option for addressing drug use and abuse (Stellin 2019). As a result, increasing arrests and MI will continue to define how the government addresses drug use in America as long as drug prohibition remains the main policy in place and no forward-thinking measures are adopted in the near future.

Violence, Corruption and Organized Crime Abroad

The negative impact of the WOD has been felt beyond America's borders in countries where the production and supply of raw material for drugs occur or where drugs are transported, stored, or smuggled in their route to the United States from Latin American, the Caribbean or as far as Asia. For decades, the governments of these drug-producing nations have criticized the WOD approach because it does not address demand for drugs in America, which is one powerful motivation for drug trafficking to exist. Beyond this, the United States has used the WOD as cover for imposing its economic and militaristic interests disguised as law enforcement operations and law and order initiatives. As a result, corruption, violence, crime, murders, lawlessness, and social chaos have increased dramatically in these countries as a result of drug interdiction (Andreas 2013; Benavie 2009; Wainwright 2016).

It has been studied at length that DTOs thrive better under a context of a weak economy, high unemployment, poverty, and ineffective governments, leading to more serious challenges of political instability and narco-governments in entire regions. For this reason, the WOD has strengthened DTOs by giving them the monopoly of illicit drugs and keeping drug smuggling profitable. Instead of undermining drug gangs, the WOD has reinforced them and turned their business into a truly transnational enterprise, well interconnected but decentralized, and difficult to dismantle from a law and order perspective given the ubiquitous nature of drug use and demand (Andreas 2013; Benavie 2009; Wainwright 2016).

Social Cost on Lives and Health Issues

Besides the economic costs, MI, and racial disparities, the WOD has indirectly contributed to premature deaths of many American drug users and directly caused the worse epidemic of heroin and opioid addiction in American history as of 2020. This is the case because the WOD criminalizes the personal use of illegal drugs while ignoring a harm reduction policy that would provide drug users access to health care services such as clean syringes (thus avoiding transmittable diseases like Hepatitis C, HIV, AIDS) and keeping drug addiction manageable from a public health perspective. Facing potential long-term imprisonment due to their drug habits, opioid and heroin users have moved to the margins of society to maintain their addiction. This marginalization worsens their health conditions because they share needles among themselves and inject drugs under a context of unsanitary conditions created by drug prohibition and the nature of drug trafficking's black market.

Furthermore, until recently with little support from politicians, no effort has been put on rehabilitation, detoxification, or alternative legal options to help substance abuse dependents to overcome their addiction. Except for some local attempts to divert drug users to rehabilitation instead of incarceration using drug courts, which began to appear as alternative to incarceration in the late 1980s. However, these efforts have provided mixed results since relapsing is a common outcome before complete detoxification and the criminal justice system punishes those who use drugs while on probation or under drug court management. Therefore, the overall response from the WOD' advocates has been punishment, incarceration, forced withdrawal, and intense supervision that have been deemed costly by experts and highly ineffective (Benavie 2009; Hari 2016; Quinones 2016).

Racism, Xenophobia, and the Dehumanization of Drug Users

Another unintended social cost has been the manipulation of people's emotions using fearmongering, perceived threats to social order, and anxiety over diseases and crime disguised as a law and order problem. There is a false narrative being pursued by defenders of the WOD that if the government does not take a strong stand against drug use and the illegal drug trade through strict drug control, American society would collapse or disappear as we know it. The problem is that most of these official tactics have led to concealed racism, prejudices, and xenophobia against minorities, the lower-class, and underprivileged people who are usually seen as the perpetrators of drug trafficking and those addicted to illegal drugs, even if these circumstances are not true (Benavie 2009; Hari 2016; Alexander 2012).

Research has shown that all ethnic groups engage in drug use and abuse overall in proportional numbers according to their population size in society (Walker, Spohn, and DeLone 2018). There is some variability in terms of which drug is being abused by whom in certain contexts, setting, and the nature of addiction. Nevertheless, in general, ethnic groups use illegal substances in proportionate numbers (Belenko and Spohn 2015). Yet, most of the people who have been arrested and imprisoned are African-Americans, Hispanics, minorities, the poor, and disenfranchised and the WOD has become a self-fulfilling prophecy because somehow the ethnicity and background of drug offenders "confirm" the perceived threat that (allegedly) these social groups pose to America (Walker, Spohn, and DeLone 2018).

This view is constantly produced and propagated by official accounts on drug trafficking operations and arrestees, mass media (films, TV series, and shows like *Cops*), and the evening news. Media in particular has contributed greatly to this pernicious effect by disproportionaly reproducing and spending more time broadcasting stories where perpetrators are people of color and the victims are Caucasians, even when research and data show that the patterns of criminal behavior in America are exactly opposite to this view. Crime generally occurs intra-racially rather than inter-racially: black on black or white on white (Walker, Spohn, and DeLone 2018). However, how the WOD is being fought encourages racial injustice, bias, and bigotry in a subtle but deliberate way in the criminal justice system because it dehumanizes perpetrators of drug offenses while facilitating institutional racism and discrimination to operate and reproduce inequalities (Alexander 2012; Walker, Spohn, and DeLone 2018).

The bigotry and discrimination against drug users have been particularly vicious given that it led to their loathing and dehumanization in America (Benavie 2009). Since drug use has been stereotypically associated with minority groups (think of Anslinger's crusade and one gets the point), this aversion and antipathy for drug users have given people permission to blame them for their drug dependence and addiction. This assumption usually includes a subtle but firm belief that punishment not treatment or rehabilitation should be the best outcome for them. An attitude unthinkable of doing that against mainstream Americans involved in other addictive behaviors such as legal drugs (e.g. prescription drugs and alcohol), pornography, gambling, sex and other vices (Benavie 2009; Singer and Page 2014).

Economic and Political Incentives to Continue the Drug War

It is no secret that the WOD has created powerful incentives for many politicians, public officials, and law enforcement agencies in charge of fighting this approach. For politicians, judges running re-election campaigns, and public officials, the WOD has helped them to win elections by rhetorically using the slogan *tough on crime* mostly against poor and low-level offenders who are an easy target for police operations. For law enforcement agencies on the other hand, the WOD has given them an opportunity to expand in size and importance by growing their bureaucratic infrastructure, given the central role that this policy has had at all local, state, and federal agencies. Accordingly, emphasis on the WOD has brought large budgets, profitable salaries, and considerable political influence in government decision-making strategies for those institutions and public officials who strongly defend this drug policy and vehemently oppose any other alternative (Baum 1996; Benavie 2009; Alexander 2012)

A more pernicious effect has been the fact that many law enforcement agencies have engaged in what is known as *Policing for Profit*, the practice of seizing cash and property from anyone who is suspected of being involved in an illegal activity or committing crime even when this person is never charged with a crime (Benavie 2009). This police practice is legally known as Civil Asset Forfeiture, and the most bizarre aspect of this legal process is that the police accuses and charges the property of committing a crime (this is true and legal). As a result, owners of that property must demonstrate that their possessions were not involved in a criminal activity, shifting the burden of proof from the police to citizens (Ingraham 2017; Walters and McCullough 2018). This is a practice that has been criticized as illegal and unjust because it violates the right to property established in the Constitution while diluting the principles of due process because owners are presumed guilty rather than innocent (Sallah et al. 2014). There are other negative effects of the WOD but suffice it to say that all in all the balance is overwhelmingly unfavorable against this approach simply because it has not and will never reduce drug trafficking let alone eliminate it.

THE WAR ON DRUGS INDUSTRIAL COMPLEX

When looking at the literature on drugs, one cannot be but overcome by the amount of information available to anyone interested in the topic. Attempts to understand the nature of illegal drugs, a question, or problem about addictive substances from a scientific standpoint, should not be a difficult task given that there are plenty of data to satisfy everyone's curiosity about them with accuracy and scientific certainty (Escohotado 1999; Kuhn, Swartzwelder, and Wilson 2014; Walton 2002). Yet, having a common-sense and educated approach toward drugs for the American public has been difficult, to say the least, not for lack of information but because of partisanship, ideology, and political interests.

Despite the abundance of scientific information about the characteristics of drugs and the need to recognize their differences, effects, and nature, this information has been dismissed or overlooked by what I call the War on Drugs Industrial Complex (WODIC). I define the WODIC as *the institutions, groups, and individuals who profit (politically, bureaucratically, and economically) from the policy of drug prohibition and defend the War on Drugs approach ferociously as the only alternative to deal with drug use and drug trafficking in the United States despite its proved record of being a failed policy*. Among the most fervent members of the WODIC are the DEA, the Department of Justice (except for some agents who do not buy this strategy), the prison-industrial complex, and most local and state law enforcement agencies, politicians who adhere to being tough on crime and its law and order rhetoric. Other entities that should be included in this definition are some traditional conservatives, and pundits who are unable to question the WOD paradigm from a scientific standpoint and thus reject any alternative option to this approach.

Overall, the WODIC has uncritically embraced two models of defining and understanding drugs and their alleged consequences: the Addiction model, and the Gateway model. The former refers to the assumption that all illegal substances have the power to enslave anyone who dares to try drugs even once (Hari 2016; Watson 2002). The latter asserts that using soft or less dangerous drugs such as cannabis are automatically gateways to harder and more addictive substances such as heroin or cocaine (Belenko and Spohn 2015). Despite the fact that there is no conclusive evidence demonstrating that any of these models is correct, stubborn defenders of the WODIC have argued repeatedly the opposite without providing any facts or data to support their claims.

The Gateway model in particular has been used by many law enforcement agencies and officials to defend their aggressive stand on prosecuting and jailing people caught with marijuana for personal use. To this day, researchers have studied extensively whether using marijuana will automatically lead to consuming harder (more addictive and illegal) drugs and they have found no evidence of such phenomenon (Belenko and Spohn 2015). What scholars did find was a correlation between using marijuana and other illicit drugs as well as evidence that most users of illicit and addictive substances begin using marijuana as their first drug of choice, but as experts correctly assert, correlation is not causation. The fact is that "most marijuana users never progress to use more serious drugs, which would appear to undermine the gateway hypothesis" (Belenko and Spohn 2015, 23). Anecdotally, it is also possible to dismiss the Gateway model by just looking at our last three presidents before Trump and think on what they did: Obama (forty-four), Bush (forty-three), and Clinton (forty-two) publicly admitted using marijuana at some point in their youth, and yet they did not end up chronic users of more addictive drugs. Based on the logic of the Gateway model, arguably one could even reverse the rationale of this model and ask instead whether smoking weed is a requirement to become president of the United States. This is a silly question that nobody would seriously consider as legitimate, yet that is exactly what the defenders of the Gateway model pretend with the premise behind that model (Belenko and Spohn 2015).

That being said, I argue the WODIC is not ignorant of the scientific nature of drugs and the lack of conclusive evidence to support the Gateway model. For the WODIC crusaders those facts are irrelevant and only instrumental to hammer loudly that all drugs (certainly marijuana that is still the leading cause of drug arrests in the United States) must be demonized and labeled as addictive and dangerous drugs. That tactic is necessary to justify the institutions as well as the personal and political interests upon which the WODIC stands. As such, this is the primary and most crucial strategy the WODIC exploits to maintain the status quo of framing all prohibited substances and drug use within a narrow-minded narrative where the WOD approach is seen as the only legal, moral, and safer alternative to deal with drug use, abuse, and drug trafficking.

If the WODIC dared to accept the science and facts on drugs and drug use, its most prominent justification to exist would disappear along with the privileges and political/ideological profits that have sustained the WODIC for decades. I am not saying that defenders of the WODIC would disappear, rather the DEA and other law enforcement agencies that police for profit would lose prominence as drug law enforcers and instead, channelize their resources to other serious crimes while saving taxpayers' money. Accordingly, the WODIC's dismissal of science and evidence about the nature and dynamics of drug use and addiction is just a tactic to pursue their ultimate political and institutional ambitions.

Although the WODIC has many components and advocates, there is one prominent defender that for decades has made a living out of the WOD. It is not willing to relinquish any power, political and economic profits, or any other privileges achieved from fighting the WOD. This government agency truly believes in what it does even when facts, evidence, and science contradict its mission. In all honesty this powerful advocate of the WODIC in its origins probably thought that strict drug control would solve the American drug problem and assumed that a drug-free world was possible. But after years of embracing and defending the WOD, this agency has contributed dramatically to consolidate this policy by building a sophisticated bureaucratic infrastructure never seen before whose main purpose was to eradicate drugs from America once and for all at any cost.

As time went by, it became clear the WOD did not work as planned given the complexity of the American drug problem. However, this advocate has refused to change course and stubbornly continues on fighting a drug that was lost long ago. Like Anderson's short tale, everyone knows that *the emperor has no clothes* (read: the WOD does not work), yet this institution keeps telling us that is not true and the emperor does have clothes according to its standpoint. One could completely ignore this entity and let it go on its own journey. However, its influence, power, and privilege position affect us all and it is no longer possible to be oblivious to it. It is precisely because of how the work of this entity is inextricably connected to drug trafficking and the drug problem that it merits its own chapter for a careful examination.

The goal of this examination is to provide an in-depth analysis of this institution to better understand why and how it does what it does. It is not to demonize but to shed light on the dark side of the WOD and then offer suggestions in the conclusion on how this entity could reverse course and truly contribute to solve the drug problem with a twenty-first-century approach if it dares to embrace science, justice, and comprehensive drug policy reform. This institution of the WOD is none other than the DEA, and its analysis comes next.

Chapter 6

How the DEA Got Lost in the War on Drugs

The Drug Enforcement Administration (DEA) has been the most fervent advocator of the War on Drugs (WOD) policy because the agency was created to defend this approach as part of its core mission, and it evolved, grew, and expanded over the past five decades thanks to it. The DEA has also radicalized the WOD by adopting measures, policies, and practices that have caused more harm, deaths, and other social dislocations than all the illegal drugs combined could have never produced, according to experts (Alexander 2012; Coyne and Hall 2017; Wainwright 2016). In addition, the tactics and strategies used by the DEA to fight the WOD throughout the past decades have created a law enforcement environment where wrongdoing and misconduct by DEA agents appear to be more common and tolerated compared to other federal agencies such as the FBI, Secret Service, and U.S. Marshals. The DEA itself seems to be more concerned about protecting its brand and avoiding scandals related to its agents' misconduct when the agency's reputation may be tarnished. As part of this strategy the agency maintains such secrecy, poor accountability, and transparency in the name of national security that the American public does not know with accuracy the extent of wrongdoing, and some unethical and potentially illegal operations the DEA engages in. Understandably this agency has to maintain some confidentiality of operations, sources, and agents' movements; however, when misconduct and wrongdoing have occurred the usual response by the DEA has been to stonewall information, and sometimes even lying blatantly to Congress and the American public. Thus, by pursuing an agenda narrowly based on the principles of the WOD at all cost, and without adapting to the realities of the drug problem in twenty-first century, the DEA undermines its mission, worsens the situation, and wastes valuable and limited public resources on obsolete law enforcement efforts.

I argue that the DEA was lost in the WOD because the agency took drug prohibition to an extreme by using this drug policy as the only approach to deal with the drug problem. As a result the DEA and the WOD mutually reinforced each other over the years and both became the same. As today the DEA cannot be what it is without the WOD and the WOD would not exist without the DEA. Initially, when the WOD gave birth to the DEA it provided a purpose for its existence. However, over time the DEA turned the WOD into a Frankenstein-like entity that is devouring the institution from within, or at least, it has shifted and transformed the initial goal of dealing with the American drug problem comprehensively. This chapter is about detailing that journey and explaining what happened to the DEA and the unintended consequences of battling a lost war that has undermined this agency and worsened the American drug problem.

ORIGINS OF THE DEA

One of the most significant consequences of Nixon's declaration of the WOD in 1971 was the consolidation of federal law enforcement to implement the new political approach toward harsher drug control. I use the word "political" intentionally since there was no evidence that drug use was a serious threat to society (never has been) in the sort of disproportionate menace that Nixon (and previously Anslinger) used it to justify their personal agendas. Instead, the motivation was essentially political as a way to distract Americans from the Vietnam War and the context that would eventually lead to the Watergate scandal in the following months to the president's resignation in 1974 (Baum 1996; Bertram et al. 1996).

A persistent and long assumption among politicians and public opinion is the unproven association between crime and drugs. There is no scientific evidence that drug use causes crime besides the fact that drug users automatically become into criminals by possessing illegal drugs (Belenko and Spohn 2015). It is true that there is a strong association in some criminal offenses where drug use contributes (but not causes) to crime such as the lifestyle of a drug user that predispose him/her to engage in illegal activity to pay for more drugs. This, however, does not mean that drugs per se produce crime, only that there is a correlation between some type of drug use and some type of crime. Meaning than this is not a systematic and general phenomenon where all drugs and all crime are associated (Marion 2018). Yet, this myth linking drug use and crime has been a driving force since drug prohibition began in the early twentieth century, but it was Nixon who aggressively argued this false association to justify his political motivations. "From the beginning Nixon identified drugs as a major source of crime. His decision to place crime at the top of his domestic-policy agenda thus made drug control a central issue" (Bertram et al. 1996, 105).

Nixon designed the WOD as an instrument to fight crime, not drugs, and the subsequent decision to create a strong federal law enforcement agency led to the birth of the DEA. This agency was born in July of 1973 as an effort to accommodate and consolidate drug control in one single agency. President Nixon came up with a strategy known as *Reorganization Plan Number 2* that soon was approved by Congress. As a result, the Bureau of Narcotics and Dangerous Drugs (the office that substituted Anslinger's Bureau of Narcotics) along with the Office of Drug Abuse Law Enforcement and hundreds of other federal agents (who were performing drug control tasks for several other agencies) all merged to give birth to the DEA (DEA 2019; Marion 2018).

The DEA was purposely created as a superagency in order to put together all the available government resources to conduct drug enforcement successfully and according to the new political priorities. To avoid previous interagency rivalries, the DEA was designed to maximize coordination in federal investigations and prosecutions. As such, the DEA's original mission was twofold: first, to combat drug trafficking (DT) and drug sales within the United States in order to curb the availability of drugs nationwide; and second, to disrupt drug smuggling, cut off the financial incentives to traffickers, and prevent drugs from being sent to the United States from outside its borders. The latter implied that the DEA had to manage large field operations domestically and abroad in order to accomplish its extensive mandate, which provided the most important role to carry out the WOD on behalf of the government like no other law enforcement agency has done before (DEA 2019; Marion 2018).

According to its official mission, the DEA has "to enforce the controlled substances laws and regulations of the United States and bring [perpetrators] to the criminal and civil justice system of the United States" (DEA 2019, 1) that smuggle illegal drugs to America. This duty can be easily interpreted as a euphemism meant to enforce the WOD instead, given that since the DEA's inception the drug war became the dominant policy to deal with the increasing drug demand and trafficking in the United States. Slowly but steadily, the DEA evolved into a pivotal bureaucratic institution in the federal administration in charge of fighting DT within the United States and around the world (Marion 2018). This power to conduct operations in underdeveloped countries such as Latin America and Southeast Asia where drug production was prevalent, gave the DEA extraordinary influence and social status to receive government support that led to expansion and growth in the years to come. Thus, in the next decades after its inception the DEA cemented its role as one of the most active and mighty federal agencies in the United States almost equal in influence to the CIA and the FBI.

The DEA's bureaucratic expansion over the years has been justified by the government as a necessary measure to combat the complicated nature of DT and drug use. The best advocate of the DEA's work has been the DEA itself. The agency officially argues that its agents and employees "have fulfilled its mission over the past five decades, and the important work of our predecessor agencies during 'The Early Years' of federal drug law enforcement in the United States" (DEA 2019, 1). The DEA is also its best biographer to defend what it does and it provides facts and historical interpretations, albeit from the perspective of the agency solely, to prove it. To market and publicize the drug war and its strict drug control approach, the DEA (like any other American federal agency) has created a well-kept website available to anyone online with a history section described as *DEA History in Depth* that presents a detailed narrative of how, when, where, and why the DEA became what it is now (DEA 2019).

This official history begins with *The Early Years* before the agency ever existed referring to the times of alcohol Prohibition and Anslinger's work as commissioner of the Bureau of Narcotics as well as the first drug laws passed in the first half to the twentieth century. Then, there is another section addressing the creation of the DEA between 1970 and 1975 followed by eight more sections or segments divided into periods of five years on average that explain the WOD under the administrations of Nixon and Reagan, as well as the agency's growth up until the current state of affairs as of 2013 (DEA 2019). There is no need to repeat what the DEA says about its major law enforcement achievements. Suffice to say, most of these accomplishments refer to bureaucratic growth, describing primary drug flows, and how the drug menace is unstoppable (which—surprise—it fully justifies the DEA's work). Also, there is information about arresting drug traffickers, dismantling organizations, and major and minor law enforcement operations where the agency has seized money, arrested traffickers, and took down drug cells (DEA 2019).

This interpretation of drug control and the triumphant job on the WOD that the DEA thinks it is doing would be credible if in fact illegal drugs were not available in the amounts they are currently on the streets of American and if DT was not the colossal multifaceted problem it actually is. The DEA's perspective on the drug war is a remarkably narrow-minded exposition of its most accomplished works in nearly fifty years that have changed nothing to stop the flow of drugs and trafficking in America. For those who are familiar with the official narrative of the DEA, we know as a matter of fact that DEA administrators and agents tend to present a sanatized, self-congratulatory and heroic-like version of the agency that ignores the reality of drug addiction in the United States and the powerful dynamics of DT that have kept the flow of illicit drugs coming to America uninterruptedly available for the past half-century. But in truth, I am not sure if this narrative is intentionally misguided or it just reflects the degree of delusion that the DEA has trying to fit the reality of drug use and trafficking to its ideology of drug control.

Despite the celebratory tone that the DEA uses to justify its mission and the inaccurate argument of how crucial the institution is for America to keep the country safer and freer from drugs, none of these statements are accurate. This criticism comes from all corners of American society, from scholars, ex-politicians, former law enforcement agents, to human rights activists, experts, and those who are familiar with the costs of the drug war and the futility of drug control. This critique against the DEA's work and the collateral damage that its strict drug control approach has had in America (and other countries) is well documented and supported with evidence, facts, and data compiled in the past years (Alexander 2012; Andreas 2013; Baum 1996; Bertram et al. 1996; Gibler 2011; Grillo 2011; Hari 2016; Wainwright 2016; Walker 2015), let us examine them.

The WOD Shaped the DEA

It is no secret that the DEA has been dramatically shaped throughout its existence by the WOD approach to the extent that this drug policy has determined the nature and ethos of the former. Strong evidence indicates that the DEA has become so habitual and dependent on the WOD to conduct its official duties that the agency could not exist as it is today if not for this failed drug policy (Alexander 2012; Bertram et al. 1996; Levine 1990). Not only that, the expansion and consolidation of the DEA along with the influence it possesses today in American foreign policy, politics, and in Washington, D.C., circles is inextricably connected to how the DEA has tackled DT and drug use by pushing the WOD paradigm as its only mode of operation.

To understand why the DEA needs the WOD to exist, it is crucial to contextualize a few key facts about the agency regarding its origins, development, and current emphasis on strict drug control. On a side note, I want to clarify that my academic criticism to this federal agency is not meant to demonize it, nor do I pretend to deny the hard work that most DEA agents do in their everyday activities to genuinely combat DT and the presence of illegal drugs in the United States. I am aware of the risks and dangers DEA agents face every day in the field, working diligently to do the right thing (with some exceptions, though). There should not be doubt about their mission given that most DEA agents only do what they are being told to do. Most rank-and-file agents just follow orders from politicians in Washington, D.C., who handle U.S. drug policy based on ideological, political, and personal motivations but rarely based on the complex dynamics of DT and using evidence-based information.

Having said that, my academic goal as a criminologist and social scientist is to provide a scholarly examination and expose the futile work the DEA has done—and continues to do—based on the premise that the DEA's work does nothing to really solve DT and drug use in America, which turns its official mission into a senseless endeavor. Even worse, not only has the DEA failed to achieve its goals, it has made the American drug problem more complicated and deadly by causing more deaths, harm, incarceration, violence, and crime than all illegal drugs altogether. This is not a hyperbolic statement or a one-sided personal opinion, dozens of experts and scholars have systematically reached this conclusion after looking at the evidence, data, and information that overwhelmingly show how ineffective the work of the DEA is and why the WOD is a waste of taxpayers' money (Alexander 2012; Benavie 2009; Bertram et al. 1996; Coyne and Hall 2017; Gibler 2011; Hari 2016; Inciardi 2008; United Nations Office on Drugs and Crime 2018; Walker 2015).

The DEA Became Addicted to the WOD

The WOD not only shaped the DEA; over the years the agency became addicted to the former. How did this happen? The basics of this process began with the creation of the DEA and the fact that the WOD gave birth to it. Indeed, the drug war is the DEA's parent (metaphorically speaking) because its only purpose to exist derived from this drug policy. As President Nixon declared "an all-out global war on the drug menace" in 1971 (DEA 2019; Marion 2018), the DEA was launched two years later to eliminate drugs once and for all and to battle the roots of crime (according to the White House). Although other federal agencies had minor roles regarding drug control, the DEA consolidated its position as the most important agency in charge of DT over the next decade and it became the only federal agency to enforce America's drug laws (Marion 2018, 214). In the 1980s and 1990s, as politicians from both parties and public officials within the criminal justice system emphasized an ideology of *tough on crime*, the drug prohibition was critical toward that goal (Alexander 2012; Belenko and Spohn 2015; Inciardi 2008)

Another important feature that reveals why the DEA is addicted to the WOD has to do with the legacy of America's drug control pioneer Henry Anslinger, whose unrelenting work and attitude to defend drug prohibition at all costs were inherited by the DEA at the time of its foundation. As explained in the previous chapter, Anslinger's behavior as commissioner of the Bureau of Narcotics reflected the bureaucratic mindset of a crusader who used fear, intimidation, ideological assumptions, and the influence of mass media to impose an anti-narcotics agenda to achieve bureaucratic prominence. Similarly, the DEA has ignored science regarding the nature of drugs, conflated all drugs as dangerous and the same, and stubbornly persisted in waging the WOD despite overwhelmed evidence that this policy is a complete failure (Alexander 2012; Chasin 2016; Inciardi 2008; Schlosser 2004; Sloman 1998).

To be fair, the DEA is not exactly reproducing identical tactics as Anslinger did during his long tenure as commissioner. After all, we are in the twenty-first century and social media, civil society, and government accountability are usually able to counter blatant abuses of power in America. Notwithstanding, there is no doubt that the DEA has integrated to its ethos the mindset of prohibition and drug control that motivated and justified Anslinger's work for decades. Similar to Anslinger, the official policy of the DEA toward marijuana use and legalization is still founded in the reefer madness ideology that Anslinger fostered for decades. As of 2020, officially the DEA still considers marijuana a highly addictive substance with no medicinal benefits (DEA 2019). This attitude is but a reflection of Anslinger's crusade that gave relevance to his work as Commissioner while ignoring scientific facts regarding drugs, something that the DEA has willingly kept and endorsed to artificially maintain institutional relevance even when growing consensus says otherwise about marijuana and the WOD (Alexander 2012; Boullosa and Wallace 2016; Gupta 2015; Hari 2016).

Furthermore, over the years the DEA has developed tactics, policies, and law enforcement practices in its everyday work to implement the WOD but sometimes agents appear to cross the line between legality and illegality, yet they are justified in the name of fighting drugs and traffickers (Esquivel 2013; Levine 1990). This modus operandi has been the result of articulating field operations and strategies in accordance with the ideology of WOD such as seizure of drugs, disrupting drug smuggling corridors, and dismantling DT organizations. This approach has not only been unsuccessful—DT and drug use are thriving in America—but it has solidified the notion that the WOD is the only possible path to address the drug problem. As a result, the more the WOD defines the DEA's main duties, the more this policy becomes indispensable for the institution to perform its official work according to the DEA's official mission. This is the reason the DEA has become addicted to the WOD and why the agency as a whole ignores any possible alternative (such as decriminalization and legalization of some drugs) to deal with drug use and DT in a comprehensive manner.

THE QUESTIONABLE GRAY AREAS OF THE DEA'S WORK

It should not be controversial how the DEA does what it does; after all, like any other federal agency in the United States, the DEA only executes what it has been told to do by politicians in Washington based on the laws that regulate the agency. Also, to be clear and fair, all American law enforcement agencies perform similar tactics and law enforcement operations as the DEA does.

However, because of the nature of the WOD and its emphases on stopping drugs from coming to America by dismantling DTOs, the DEA has developed undercover work, spying strategies, and counterintelligence tactics that from time to time are questionable and often blatantly illegal. These strategies have become so normalized and standard in the DEA's everyday operations as part of its regular work that nobody would dare to challenge them at the risk of being labeled ignorant, and probably anti-patriot. Yet, from a perspective that looks at DT and drug use as a holistic and complex problem—outside of the drug war model—the DEA law enforcement methods are not meant to solve the drug problem, only to prolong it. Therefore, under a critical thinking analysis, the DEA's core performance becomes meaningless because data show that it does not accomplish the most important mission of the agency but rather the opposite (Benavie 2009; Coyne and Hall 2017; Hari 2015; Walker 2015).

What are these questionable strategies? First, to infiltrate DT organizations and collect intelligence to arrest and prosecute offenders is the DEA's best tool to engage in sophisticated undercover operations (Esquivel 2013; Levine 1990; López López 2008). Second, the DEA has invested heavily in building an extensive network of informants worldwide to assemble information on DT operations, drug lords, and criminal gangs. Although informants are recruited from all sorts of backgrounds (e.g., local police, public local officials, and anyone familiar with the illegal drug trade) the DEA relies considerably on criminals who pass on information about their own drug operations, rival gangs, bosses, officials who protect them, and trafficking activities (Esquivel 2013; Office of the Inspector General 2016). All American law enforcement agencies recruit informants, so this is not per se a questionable strategy. The criticism with the DEA's approach is its heavy reliance on this tactic and the large number of informants working with the agency, ethical issues and conflicts of interests, and poor accountability managing informants (Office of the Inspector General 2016).

Third, because of its heavy dependence on criminals to accomplish its mission some DEA agents have had to make a pact with the devil, so to speak. Agents pay criminals and work with them deliberately (many of whom are violent and serious perpetrators) instead of bringing charges against them (Esquivel 2013; Levine 1990; López López 2008). This strategy creates conflicts of interests as well as significant ethical and professional issues to say the least, yet the DEA justifies this approach on the rationale that it is necessary to achieve its mission. Finally, the DEA also conducts clandestine and undercover law enforcement operations in foreign countries, many times unbeknownst to the local governments (DEA 2019; Esquivel 2013; Levine 1990; Savage 2017). This extreme secrecy creates a context where there is poor accountability, lack of supervision, and high discretionary decision-making power that can be easily abused by some agents. Again, these law enforcement practices are also conducted by the CIA, FBI and other federal agencies to a lesser extent, so they are not exclusive of the DEA. The problematic nature with the DEA's work is the size and costs of these operations and the fact that they do not change at all the availability of drugs in America and the flow of DT activities.

Accordingly, the DEA has been accused of negotiating with dangerous criminals, allowing some of its agents to commit unethical behaviors (including violent crimes), covering up botched operations (there is a detailed list of these events in the following section), and even lying to Congress and the Justice Department to protect rogue agents or agency's mistakes, among other serious allegations of wrongdoing, all of them excused as necessary under the WOD policy (Esquivel 2013; Levine 1990; Savage 2017). All things considered, it should be noticed that these issues do not appear to be a common or generalized practice within the DEA. Yet, they exist, the accusations are true, and the American public ignores whether or not they are rare, periodical, or common given that DEA operations are kept confidential and hidden from public scrutiny. Incidentally, this secrecy is a common practice among all federal law enforcement agencies to tackle serious crimes and threats to national security and public safety. However, the overall scope of the DEA's work does not meet this criterion because of the failure of the WOD and the fact that defining drug use and addiction as a criminal problem has been politically and ideologically motivated, rather than based on scientific and objective principles. That being said, information about DEA's most notorious wrongdoings and blunders have become known mostly through investigative journalism, filtrations, and social uproar from victims when they raise their voice to demand justice from DEA's offenses. The next section lists some of the most well-known and documented misdeeds.

THE WOD PROMOTES DEA'S WRONGDOING

The need to maintain secrecy in its operations, undercover activities, and the entire nature of how the DEA performs its job allows it to enjoy a broad degree of self-government with little or no external scrutiny. There is indeed strict internal regulatory processes within the DEA that control every significant decision and operation by all agents and employees. Often, DEA agents in private even resent or complain about this micromanagement by the DEA and how cumbersome it can be to perform simple tasks (former DEA Agent 2019). Yet, this rigorous control is kept confidential and difficult to verify because there is no external scrutiny and transparency by American society to verify if the DEA's work is being performed according to the rule of law. Yes indeed, there are internal processes to regulate most DEA's works as an agency, but regulators are DEA employees and hence, they are part of the ideological world of their employer with little to none appetite to denounce wrongdoing (when it happens) because the agency is not open to self-criticism. Such practice is probably no different than other federal agencies (perhaps with the exception of the FBI), except that the DEA's work has negatively impacted the criminal justice system like no other institution and this should be enough to demand more transparency and accountability. Having said this, the following examination does not mean to cherry-pick the wrongdoings of the DEA but to document that behind those actions there is a pattern that reflects the ethos of this institution based on secrecy, discretionary decisions, and conducting a double-standard policy. This policy operates in contrasting principles because publicly the DEA conveys the message of being a law and order government agency fighting the WOD. Internally, the agency appears to conduct some operations and work as a self-governed agency with enormous political power (similar to how the CIA works) as suggested by indirect evidence (Esquivel 2013; Levine 1990; McCoy 2003; Office of the Inspectors General 2017a, 2017b, 2016; USA Today 2015).

The first questionable strategy has been that some DEA agents are prone to engage in wrongdoing in their everyday operations due to the practice of using criminals as informants. Not everyday petty criminals but often drug cartel members and drug gangs' employees who are violent, dangerous, and have committed serious crimes. As a result, working with criminals to accuse and prosecute other criminals can blur the line between legality and illegality because the DEA pays them money instead of arresting and prosecuting them. In addition, many of these violent and dangerous perpetrators feel protected by their role as informants and continue their criminal activities if they want to because they enjoy impunity from prosecution. Although negotiating with informants and paying them for their intelligence is legal and strictly regulated by the DEA, the practice is extremely common and subjected to broad discretionary control while in the field of operations by agents in charge of informants (Office of Inspectors General 2016).

The official name of informants is *Confidential Sources* (or CS as agents regularly call them), and the administrative unit regulating informants is named *Confidential Source Program* (CSP). Even though the American public has little access to how this program is handled, the Office of the Inspector General (OIG) within the Department of Justice, released in September of 2016 an audit regarding the DEA's CSP (Office of the Inspector General 2016). The document provides a peak to the nature of the CSP to understand its dimension and the costs of running it as well as an indictment of how the DEA manages informants. Among other things the OIG concluded that between 2010 and 2015 the DEA handled more than 18,000 informants (just within U.S. offices, excluding all of the sources located in foreign soil) and nearly half of those people received almost $237 million in payments for services or information (Office of the Inspector General 2016). This is a large amount of money and informants working for the DEA considering that in the grand scheme of things, the information these criminals provide does not change the status quo of DT and drug abuse, therefore it seems a costly waste of taxpayer money.

The OIG report exposed that the DEA does not supervise the payments to informants in a rigorous and professional manner, which creates a context for potential abuse of authority, waste of resources, and possible fraud by informants while receiving payments. To document this criticism, the OIG found many cases where informants have received payments even though they were previously deactivated (deactivation occurs when a source commits a serious crime or has an arrest warrant but it has to be documented, meaning that if informants' crimes are kept secret they remain under DEA payroll). Based on its own DEA's confidential source data, the OIG estimated that the DEA probably paid approximately $9.4 million to nearly 800 informants who had been formerly deactivated between the years 2011 and 2015 (Office of the Inspector General 2016). There is not enough information to assume if this kind of wrongdoing is widespread within the DEA, but little is known about the CSP (except for some snapshot information coming from sources like this OIG report) because of the secrecy in how the agency manages its business. If not released by the OIG's audit, this information would have never been known to the American public.

Overall, the OIG concluded that the DEA has poor management, tracking, and oversight of the payments given to informants by the DEA's Intelligence Division. Moreover, the agency is unable to track the activity of all the informants, meaning that if some of them commit crimes, the DEA will not know immediately. The OIG also discovered that "some Special Agents received tips by email or text on non-government private accounts established by the agents, thereby possibly compromising personally identifiable information, affecting government record maintenance requirements, and complicating the DEA's efforts to manage and access important case-related information" (Office of the Inspector General 2016, 3). Again, there is insufficient evidence to know with certainty if this degree of sloppiness is a rare occurrence or a hallmark of the program when handling informants and their intelligence. However, there is an extensive degree of discretionary power by DEA controlling agents (those in charge of handling informants) over their sources and this in itself creates opportunity for carelessness work.

Perhaps that is why the OIG report condemned the DEA's sloppiness in managing informants because there was inadequate accountability and transparency regarding supervision of sources along with high costs and serious irregularities about payments for informants who were deactivated and should not have received any money in the first place. The OIG report did not provide a thorough program assessment to determine whether or not the CSP (the use of informants and how to handle them) has accomplished the mission that is intended to accomplish. In other words, is the use of informants contributing to reduce drug availability and drug use in America? Based on the answer, is it worth keeping the program? Even without looking at the DEA's data, I argue that the answer would be an emphatic NO. Why? Because drug use, DT, and the availability of drugs in the United States have not been addressed or tackled in any significant manner in decades and the American drug problem remains a serious and challenging question.

Furthermore, the unethical and questionable handling of informants by the DEA extends to the safety of many of them who are criminals and belong to gangs but face the risk of being murdered by their own bosses or associates if the latter they find out about their betrayal. This is a serious danger that DEA controlling agents are aware of and take measures to protect active sources domestically, but in foreign countries those measures are more complex to take and informants are more exposed to be killed. This is an outcome that has occurred and the DEA does not assume any responsibility even if informants end up murdered for passing on information to the agency (Esquivel 2013).

Working with criminals as informants is not the problem. As previously acknowledged, all law enforcement agencies in America work with them to facilitate the prosecution of some offenders by allowing cooperating defendants to *snitch* on their crime associates or bosses. This strategy is widely used because it makes the job easier for the police and prosecutors. There is nothing wrong or illegal to convince defendants to cooperate with prosecutors to bring down kingpins and criminal networks. The problematic nature of recruiting informants and working for the DEA is because of how expensive and pointless this approach is given that it does not address the American drug problem. Also, the DEA tactics of recruiting informants has become a tool of the WOD paradigm to disrupt DT operations and dismantle or diminish criminal organization, but that tool and its frequent usage do not deal with the roots of DT and drug use at all.

Besides the use of informants, another questionable tactic used by the DEA is the practice of undercover operations. Espionage and undercover work requires that DEA agents become immersed in the lifestyle and social context of drug traffickers to be able to know first-hand the basic details of trafficking operations, drug bosses, and cartel organizations. In the DEA world, those agents who are able to infiltrate DT organizations or engage in long-term undercover work are known as *deep cover* and they are considered part of the DEA's elite agents (Esquivel 2013; Levine 1990). Undercover operations are just something that law enforcement agencies do to investigate crime and capture dangerous criminals, which it is strictly regulated to avoid risking officers' lives. Thus, it would be unfair and naïve to assume that this work in itself is a misconduct or unethical by DEA agents. The CIA, FBI, and U.S. Marshall's Office engage in this tactic to fight crime successfully. Yet, the context where DEA's undercover work becomes problematic is when its agents buy drugs from traffickers, socialize with them to develop trust (drinking, eating, and celebrating DT business), and become associates and partners in crime (literally) for the sake of collecting information to accomplish the mission of the DEA. The collaboration between criminals and DEA agents goes even further when traffickers pass on information on rival gangs and enemies so they are arrested and their criminal activities are disrupted while the businesses of the DEA associates remain intact while the association lasts. Just to be clear, I do not argue that undercover work is unethical or that the agents are inclined to misconduct. My criticism on the DEA is because such activity creates conflicts of interest by cultivating relationships with criminals and associating with them while providing protection to some of those perpetrators who supply intelligence on rivals, but they are not prosecuted.

Unfortunately, through the lenses of the WOD, the use of informants and undercover operations are praised as clever and skilled work that demonstrates the diligence and fine work the DEA does. Yet, even if undercover work is able to take down dozens of traffickers, seize millions of dollars, and thousands of pounds of drugs every year, such achievements are completely pointless and futile. Why? In the grand scheme of things they do not make a difference in the availability of drugs, drug use, and demand for drugs in America. Thus these efforts are a waste of taxpayers' money and resources and the DEA should try a different approach to genuinely tackle the roots of the American drug problem instead of dealing with its symptoms.

The DEA, along with the Departments of Justice, has also turned the WOD into law enforcement for-profit activity. Using Civil Asset Forfeiture (CAF) laws the DEA (and other federal law enforcement agencies) has taken millions of dollars in cash, seize bank accounts, property, planes, and all the wealth that traffickers acquire from selling drugs. This practice is also common among local and state police departments and prosecutors throughout the country. Although CAF is legal and it was designed to fight organized crime activities by taking the profits of crime away from perpetrators, it is a controversial practice. CAF has been deemed an abusive measure because it disproportionaly affects poor minority families who cannot fight back seizures in courts to recover their assets if they are innocent of a crime (Ingraham 2017; Sallah et al. 2014). Under CAF regulations, law enforcement agencies do not need a criminal conviction to seize a person's property, and unlike a criminal trial that presumes the innocence of a defendant, people affected by CAF seizures have to prove that their possessions are "innocent" of a crime. This means that the authorities bring charges against the property rather than the people. However, most individuals do not dispute the seizure (even if it is not legally justified) and they automatically lose their property by not challenging the case. Additionally, many CAF cases involve assets worth a few thousands of dollars, so it is not worthy to spend more money fighting the charges in the courts (Ingraham 2017; Walters and McCullough 2018).

Although CAF is a valuable tool to fight organized crime, this approach has become a routine operation of *Policing for Profit* by the DEA because the agency has earned billions of dollars over a period of years in cash from people who were never charged with a crime. A 2017 report issued by the Office of the Inspector General of the Justice Department revealed that in a ten-year period (from 2007 to 2017), the DEA seized more than $4 billion in cash from individuals allegedly involved in DT activities, but more than 80 percent of that money—$3.2 billion—came from people who were never charged with a crime (Ingraham 2017; Office of the Inspector General 2017b). This suggests that maybe those people actually were not criminals but easy targets by the DEA to take their wealth away. Among other things, the Office of the Inspector General revealed a lack of assessment of whether or not these seizures and forfeitures actually work to address the problem of DT (there is no data by the Department of Justice to know this important fact). Also, the report described the case of 100 seizures of cash conducted by the DEA without search warrants where no narcotics were found and less than 50 percent of these cases led to arrests and new or other criminal inquiries. The implication being that DEA's seizures of assets appear to be motivated more by collecting money and property rather than investigating crimes and prosecuting offenders (Ingraham 2017; Office of the Inspector General 2017b).

Besides undercover work, use of informants, and potential abuse of CAF, the DEA has engaged throughout the years in some practices, patterns, and behaviors that may be defined as unethical and deceitful at best and illegal and wrong at worst. A clear example of this behavior has been how DEA agents in plainclothes registered, searched, and seized property without search warrants among Amtrak passengers traveling in Amtrak Southwest (Martyn 2019). These controversial measures were revealed by *The Intercept* conducting a journalistic investigation where it was discovered that DEA agents would board empty Greyhound buses, pull luggage bags and press on them to (allegedly) detect money or drugs unbeknownst to their owners (surveillance footage captured these illegal searchers). Additionally, these agents would board the Amtrak train that runs from Los Angeles to Chicago every day in both directions to aggressively conduct interdiction operations.

The problematic and gray area of these operations has been that DEA agents use a legal loophole tactic known as "cold consent encounter" as a way to get around the Fourth Amendment of the Constitution (Martyn 2019). To that end, agents approach individuals suddenly and based on insubstantial evidence to pressure passengers to consent for searchers. These people do not know that they have the right to refuse the agents' searches and many of these passages are racially profiled. A previous investigation by the Office of the Inspector General regarding cold consent encounters found that these searches are problematic and raise civil rights concerns, to say the least. Also, these encounters are ineffective (they have only 11 percent success rate) and they tend to target minorities or people of color because of biases or stereotypes about who is a drug courier. Overall, these searchers were plagued with disorganizational issues (there was no central or coordinated management) and confusion training on how to perform them according to the law (Office of the Inspector General 2015a). In general, the DEA work on bus and Amtrak stations has become an opportunity for policing for profit since Civil Assets Forfeiture has been used to seize money (assumed to be drug proceeds) from passengers but never charging citizens with drug crimes as explained earlier (Martyn 2019). This is just but another instance where the DEA has stretched its jurisdiction to continue using the WOD as a justification for heavy-handed measures aimed to remain a significant institution even if what it does means nothing in terms of drug availability, use, and overdoses.

Likewise, there is a long list of misconduct, shoddy behavior, and mismanagement by some DEA agents and the agency itself while conducting their everyday business that has occurred in past decades. Because of this pattern one has to wonder if these actions are the exception rather than the rule. I want to believe that these cases of misconduct and mismanagement are not common and just exceptional situations. The fact is that they do occur and the American public becomes aware of them only after third-party agencies or journalistic reports expose them. This suggests that the DEA does not like and does not want to be scrutinized and be transparent about them (like any other American federal law enforcement agency, official confidentiality is a must). Nonetheless, I assert that given how the DEA's work and its WOD approach affect thousands of Americans and the criminal justice system, it has the duty to be more accountable and open than other agencies. Not to mention that at the end, the DEA work is totally futile (Alexander 2012; Bertram et al. 1996; Coyne and Hall 2017; Hari 2016; Walker 2016)

Accordingly, I have compiled a list of complaints against the DEA that includes agents who have committed crimes during their official duties such as botched undercover operations and the agency blatantly ignoring science and facts, and stubbornly defending the WOD against overwhelming evidence of its failure, among other issues. The following are some of the most notorious and shameful episodes that may or may not reflect a pattern on the DEA, depending on how this information is interpreted. I leave it open to every reader to decide his or her own conclusion about it. One should keep in mind that secrecy, lack of transparency, and classifying information as confidential for national security justifications are used by the DEA to keep control of internal information and why it is not released to the public. My own personal analysis is that the DEA has a pattern of avoiding public scrutiny on how its agents do their work and this has made it more difficult to research from external sources information to corroborate this assumption. Yet through reports provided by the Office of the Inspector General, freedom of information requests by journalists, and victims' testimony, it is possible to compile a fair amount of data that exposes some of DEA's misconduct and wrongdoing but not all of it.

DEA'S DARK SIDE WAGING THE WOD

Although the American public knows that the DEA is in charge of fighting DT and arresting drug dealers, few people really comprehend the scope of power, operations, and assets this institution has at its disposal in waging the drug war. The size of the institution, the power these resources provide, and government regulations to keep operations and information confidential have molded the DEA to do what it does. I argue that there is a dark side about the DEA, so to speak, because the agency and some of its agents have engaged in cover-ups, lies, unethical behavior, and questionable activities that may have crossed the line between legality and illegality. This is not my personal opinion but based on evidence and facts collected by different sources such as the Office of the Inspectors General, investigative journalism, government reports, and victims' testimonies. Among the most controversial and well-known cases and facts of these allegations are the following.

Demonizing Marijuana and Rejecting Science to Maintain the Drug War

A particular position by the DEA that has had devastating consequences in the criminal justice system is its stubborn approach of labeling marijuana as an addictive and dangerous drug for decades. Although this standpoint is not necessarily illegal in itself, it is clearly ignorant, indefensible, and immoral because it has led to the criminalization of millions of Americans who have been caught in possession of marijuana for personal use and being prosecuted for it (Alexander 2012; Benavie 2009). The DEA's attitude is based on how marijuana was classified as a Schedule I drug in the Controlled Substances Act (CSA) of 1970. Although the CSA was meant to categorize drugs based on science and medical needs, it was influenced by the political forces when the WOD was launched. As the DEA is in charge of enforcing federal drug laws, it has the power to schedule and re-schedule drugs, yet it has refused over and again to make marijuana accessible to scientists (to conduct research about it) and people in need of this substance for medical justifications (Drug Policy Alliance 2014). For nearly five decades the DEA has systematically dismissed scientific evidence that demonstrates marijuana has medical use and it is not as addictive as the CAS categorization alleges, yet the DEA has systematically refused to reclassify marijuana from Schedule I to Schedule II or III (Drug Policy Alliance 2014).

The DEA has used administrative chicaneries disguised as regulatory policies to maintain its iron grip approach on drug prohibition by obstructing legal efforts to move marijuana to a less strict categorization. For instance, in the 1970s and 1980s, the DEA refused to process petitions to re-schedule marijuana until federal courts forced the agency to take action but still did not comply. In one case, the DEA dragged its feet for twenty-two years before responding to this rescheduling by finally denying the request asserting that there was not enough scientific evidence to support the change (Drug Policy Alliance 2014). The catch-22 (as experts call this situation) is that by refusing to re-schedule marijuana, it was nearly impossible for scientists to conduct research on the plant and then produce the evidence needed to prove that marijuana is not as dangerous and addictive as the DEA officially claims. As a result, this so-called lack of evidence is used by the DEA to defend its stonewall approach and has kept the classification of marijuana as a dangerous substance for decades against scientific evidence showing the opposite (Gupta 2015).

To be fair, the DEA has allowed some minimal research on marijuana over the years but most experts agree this access has been a meager measure for research to really conduct meaningful experiments to demonstrate the medical and physiological value of marijuana. However, the DEA at least has changed its policy to increase the number of suppliers of marijuana to researchers and facilitate access to it. For decades the University of Mississippi was the only source of legal cannabis in the entire United States where few scientists doing research on marijuana could get it legally. This has been another hindrance in the battle to produce evidence-based data to counter DEA's claims that marijuana is dangerous because it was extremely difficult for experts to have access to the plant and conduct experiments and research (DEA 2016)

DEA's demonization of marijuana reached laughable levels in 2012 when then-DEA administrator Michele Leonhart appeared in Congress before the House Judiciary Subcommittee on Crime, Terrorism, and Homeland Security to give testimony as head of the DEA. She was asked by Congressman Jared Polis from Colorado if marijuana was a less harmful drug than methamphetamine, heroin, and crack. She repeatedly refused to answer the question by saying that all illegal drugs are bad and addictive, then she argued illegal drugs are illegal for a reason and it means they are bad. The exchange went on for several minutes (it can be watched on YouTube) but she never dared to admit that marijuana was less harmful than heroin or methamphetamine, and at the end she was ridiculed for her narrow-minded attitude given that now there is overwhelming evidence that indeed marijuana is less dangerous and addictive that harder drugs (Ingraham 2015; Gupta 2015).

Another embarrassing situation for the DEA took place in 2014 when President Barack Obama gave an interview to *The New Yorker* magazine and, among other things, he argued correctly that marijuana was less dangerous than alcohol in terms of how it affects users (an argument that is accurate according to science). A few weeks later the DEA administrator mentioned earlier, during a national meeting with sheriffs, launched an attack on President Obama for those comments, saying that Obama's government did not understand the science behind those statements (Ingraham 2015). These two examples reveal to what extent the DEA still defines marijuana within the *Reefer Madness* framework that Anslinger created almost a century ago.

DEA List of Agents' Corruption and Misconduct

The American public does not know with certainty to what extent corruption cases are prevalent among DEA agents since there is not willingness from the agency to be fully transparent about the levels of corruption or misconduct from all agents. I mentioned earlier that these cases are probably the exception rather than the rule, but the DEA does not contribute to show that is the case. Only those cases involving gross misconduct or flagrant corruption are revealed to the media and the public once formal charges against corrupt agents occur. The DEA repeatedly denies that corruption, misconduct, and scandals are regular occurrences and instead argues those cases are anomalies, defining the situation as a bad apple problem, rather than an institutionalized practice. But there is evidence that the DEA is reluctant to investigate with objectivity cases of wrongdoing and misconduct internally. And when there is an inquiry, the most common outcome has been an exoneration of transgressors. If found guilty, the penalty is usually mild but never a serious punishment. The DEA tends to protect its agents (perhaps for obvious reasons) and shields them from prosecution to avoid a public scandal unless the perpetrator commits a shocking crime (Ingraham 2015; Mustian and Goodman 2018; Office of the Inspectors General 2017a; USA Today 2015).

During the 1980s and 1990s, corruption by some DEA agents occurred, certainly among those agents who worked undercover or closer to drug traffickers with access to cash and drugs. A *New York Times* article from 1989 documented the case of at least seven DEA agents who were accused of selling protection to drug gangs, stealing drugs from traffickers or from vaults where seized assets were kept and then selling them to traffickers. In addition, some DEA agents engaged in other crimes such as bribery, embezzlement, perjury, DT, and conspiracy to help or protect drug gang members (Berke 1989). One of the reasons why corruption in the DEA was probably more widespread and common in past decades was the fact that the agency paid low salaries and moved agents frequently around the country. Also, agents were subjected to long hours of work with no pay differential for living in overpriced cities that affected the value of their income. All of these factors combined pushed some agents to "cross the line" (as corruption is known in the world of law enforcement) and engage in corrupt acts (Berke 1989; Peterson 1991). Although the DEA became more professionalized in the past two decades, corruption and misconduct still occur and some current cases corroborate this phenomenon.

For instance, a former DEA agent named Jose Ismael Irizarry who once was deemed as a *superstar* and model employee has now been accused of conspiring with one of his informants to launder more than $7 million from DT activities. After he was transferred to Colombia, he began to work with the criminals that he was supposed to apprehend. He resigned from the DEA after he was ordered to return to the United States in 2017 and was indicted in a federal court in Tampa, Florida, after the FBI and the Department of Justice launched a federal investigation and uncovered his crimes (San Francisco Chronicle 2019). In February 21, 2020 he was arrested for conspiracy to launder money, bank fraud, aggravated identity theft among other crimes (Levenson 2020). The case is a huge setback for the DEA because it is possible that the agent's misconduct compromised sources, informants, and undercover work for the Colombia field office, and by extension, other criminal investigations in the United States. The extent of the corruption by this seasoned agent is still under investigation and it went beyond enriching himself. This DEA agent actively assisted a top Colombian cartel aid who specialized in money laundering, and was a relative of his second wife, to funnel DT proceeds into the legal economy and avoid detention from the police (Goodman and Mustian 2019).

In another embarrassing case of corruption, a veteran and decorated DEA agent named Chad A. Scott, who achieved distinction as a tough and experienced anti-narcotics officer working a task force along the Interstate 12 corridor, was charged at the end of 2017 with multiple counts of federal crimes including stealing thousands of dollars, engaging in perjury and obstruction of justice (Mustian and Roberts 2017). The indictment argued that agent Scott took money for himself during drug raids, engaged in drug dealing, and falsified government documents to profit from it. Other law enforcement agents who were part of his task force were also accused of tampering with witnesses and selling illegal drugs. Two of them were deputies in the Tangipahoa Parish Sheriff's Office and have already pleaded guilty of federal crimes and they have testified against agent Scott (Mustian and Roberts 2017). After a seven-day trial in summer 2019 was found guilty of two counts of perjury, three counts of obstruction of justice and two counts of falsifying government records (Department of Justice 2019).

The DEA is partially responsible for the wrongdoings of this agent because public records have revealed that the institution received complaints of abuse against Chad Scott years earlier. Victims argued that agent Scott regularly ignored DEA policies and abused Confidential Sources for his personal benefits and yet the agency did nothing to stop him. This is but a confirmation of how the DEA tends to protect its employees when facing accusations of misconduct rather than conducting thorough investigations to sanction and deter lawbreakers (Mustian and Roberts 2017). To be fair, the conviction of this agent could also be interpreted as evidence that corrupt DEA agents, when caught, are brought to justice and they are punished. If only the DEA were always willing to come forward and transparent about its agents' misconduct and corruption. However, the agency has a culture (and pattern) of dealing with these issues internally rather than openly and with transparency to the public. The problem lies in the fact that most DEA operations and agents who have been linked to wrongdoing or misconduct have been exposed by other law enforcement agencies, journalists, third entities, or the Office of the Inspector General, not the DEA. Therefore, the core of the issue is that the DEA does not want external scrutiny at all and has a clear aversion to let American society how it really operates.

Another case of corruption involved a DEA supervisory agent named Nathan Koen who was arrested by the FBI in Arkansas in December 2018 for bribery and conspiracy charges to distribute illegal drugs and bring them to Florida where he was once based. The affidavit that led to this arrest documented in detail how Koen used his experience as a seasoned DEA agent to protect an accomplished drug dealer (who had been his former informant) from being arrested while providing substantial insider information to help criminals run successful DT activities. Not only that, the DEA agent also received thousands of dollars in bribes from that informant throughout the years as payments for providing critical information to him and his criminal associates (Satter 2018).

A different instance of misconduct became public in August 2018 when a supervisory DEA special agent named Joseph Michael Gill pleaded guilty in a federal court in Tucson, Arizona, for the illegal selling of firearms. Agent Gill was assigned to the Nogales DEA office and according to prosecution documents, he purchased several firearms from gun dealerships and sold them on the internet using the website Gunbroker.com. He had engaged in more than 600 transactions on the website alone according to court records. The plea bargain documents detailed information that Gill bought three high-caliber rifles online and then sold two of them to two different people who he knew would probably use the weapons for illegal activities (Nogales International 2010).

Likewise, on June 2017 DEA agent David Polos was convicted on false statements and conspiracy charges along with his colleague Glen Glover, a DEA telecommunications specialist, in a federal court in Manhattan. During a background check in 2011, these two DEA employees failed to report that they were running a strip club called *Twin Plus Go-Go Lounge* where topless female dancers were the main attraction, some of them undocumented immigrants, who engaged in sexual acts with clients and personnel. Polos was sentenced to community service, one year of probation, and a fine of $5,000. He was able to keep his monthly pension of $4,590 from the DEA though because—according to the DEA—Polos had retired from the agency just before he was charged (Raymond 2017). This practice of letting DEA maintain employee privileges despite accusations of wrongdoing is not uncommon, in particular for employees who have had a long career within the institution. One way to circumvent the DEA system is to allow accused agents to retire (after twenty years of service all DEA agents earn the right to do so) or submit their resignation and thus the agency does not have to deal with internal procedures to investigate and punish wrongdoing since agents are gone after resigning or retiring (Mustian and Goodman 2018; USA Today 2015)

Another high-profile case of DEA corruption is based on a criminal investigation by the Department of Justice that led to the indictment and arrest in December 2018 of DEA agent Fernando Gomez. He was accused of providing firearms to a Puerto Rican drug gang and conspiring with criminals to distribute cocaine while helping them to evade law enforcement prosecution for nearly a decade (U.S. Attorney's Office 2018). Before joining the DEA, Gomez was a police officer in Evanston, Illinois, a suburb in the northern part of Chicago. It was during this time that he began to work for drug traffickers in Puerto Rico by sending them firearms. According to the prosecution, he joined the DEA to help traffickers evade law enforcement and to smuggle illicit drugs into New York. The agent was arrested in Chicago and denied bail then sent to New York City to face charges there (Fieldstadt 2018). This DEA eventually pled guilty in a Manhattan, NY federal court to a narcotics conspiracy involving the distribution of cocaine and agreed that he supplied guns to a DT organization in Puerto Rico. As of the writing of this book, Gomez was waiting to be sentenced in the same court (The U.S. Attorney's Office 2019)

DEA's Scandals and Protection of Wrongdoers

Besides corruption among agents, the DEA has also been involved in some notorious scandals that confirm the pattern by the agency to resist transparency and accountability. A 2015 report by the Office of the Inspectors

General (the Department of Justice Supervisory authority) found that at least ten DEA agents deployed in Colombia had sex parties with prostitutes who had been paid by DT organizations for several years (this was not a one-time event), and some of these agents had top secret security clearances. The parties took place in government-lease premises and seven of the agents explicitly acknowledged to have attended the celebrations and took responsibility for it (Horwitz and Leonning 2015). What is more serious is the fact that the technology and personal equipment used by the agents to perform their everyday jobs—laptops, Blackberries, and the like—were available during the sex parties, jeopardizing the work and security of the DEA as well as risking the life of the agents who could be blackmailed or coerced if such devices were to fall in the wrong hands (Office of the Inspector General 2015b). According to the same report, former local Colombian police officers claimed that three DEA special agents with supervisory responsibilities were bribed with expensive presents, firearms, and money by drug cartel members but the DEA did not investigate these accusations (Office of the Inspector General 2015b).

What is telling about this scandal, besides revealing wrongdoing is the overall attitude of the DEA to own responsibility and instead oppose any outside investigation. The DEA defied requests by federal investigators to conduct a thorough inquiry into the misconduct allegations according to Inspector General Michael E. Horowitz. He revealed that the DEA engaged in dilatory tactics and resisted the inquiry by not sending relevant information or sending incomplete facts to the authority investigating these allegations. The Inspector General also found that the DEA did not fully investigate these accusations against its agents even though there was enough evidence to demonstrate their administrative or criminal responsibility and apply sanctions accordingly. Instead, the DEA gave supervisors full discretionary power on whether or not to report such misconducts to headquarters while lacking accountability and transparency on the matter because no explicit policy to deal with these events existed. All of which only reinforces the assumption that the DEA protects agents when caught committing misconduct (Heath and Hoyer 2015; Horwitz and Leonning 2015; Office of the Inspector General 2015b). On a side note, this scandal caused an uproar in Washington, D.C., because of the nature of the offense, yet the official response by the DEA was that most agents involved in the scandal only received a light sanction. Accordingly, in mid-April 2015, the House Oversight Committee issued a bipartisan "no confidence" vote against Michele Leonhart continuing as head of the DEA, arguing that she could not manage anymore the responsibilities of the agency. A few days later she resigned from her position (Ingraham 2015).

Allegations of misconduct seem to be prevalent in the DEA Colombia office though, considered a key post in the DEA's WOD efforts to control DT given that most of the cocaine that is smuggled into the United States comes from that country. For this reason it is disturbing to know that the DEA has not been able to have tight control of all DEA agents stationed there. After the scandal of sex parties described earlier, the DEA sent Richard Dobrich as a new regional director of the Bogota office to clean the mess of the scandal and restore order. However, at the end of 2018 this top-ranking official was himself involved in an investigation of misconduct allegedly because he had used DEA money to hire prostitutes, according to an anonymous complaint. Dobrich ended up retiring (the usual non-written measure to end these scandals) from the DEA during the investigation, but he was eventually cleared of any wrongdoing by the Inspector Office later that year (Mustian and Goodman 2018).

Even if this case did not officially reveal any misconduct, it exposes one of the most vulnerable features of the WOD approach, which is the power of drug traffickers to corrupt government officials, including Americans. It is not a coincidence then that the DEA Colombia office suffers from wrongdoing and corruption from within given that it seats in a country that produces and exports most of the cocaine worldwide (United Nations Office on Drugs and Crime 2018). Drug gangs know how to lure some DEA agents to their side and corrupt them given the proximity between criminals and these officers through the use of informants, undercover work, and clandestine operations. Traffickers have unlimited access to cash to bribe the police and buy protection, and although most DEA agents are not susceptible to bribery, some are and drug cartels know it and proceed accordingly (López López 2008).

A different sort of scandal took place in 2004; a DEA agent named Lee Paige was delivering a speech on gun safety in front of classroom full of children. After lecturing them that he was the only person in the room with professional knowledge of the gun (he was handling a Glock 40.), he accidentally shot himself in the foot. The incident was caught on camera and eventually went viral after it was released to the public in a video posted in social media (Wing 2014). Gun accidents and federal agents committing such mistakes are not exclusive of the DEA. I guess every person in possession of a handgun could be exposed to it, accidents indeed occur. Yet, DEA agents (like all agents and police officers working on law enforcement agencies) are supposed to be professionally trained to be experts on handling guns, so this sort of incident arguably should have never happened. Certainly one would expect a higher degree of professionalism given that the DEA regularly allows DEA agents to visit schools and educated kids about the work the agency does to combat the American drug problem.

Finally, in 2012 a UC San Diego student named Daniel Chong was arrested at his friend's house after DEA agents conducted a drug raid. He was told that the agency would not charge him and would be detained for a few minutes only. However, he was thrown handcuffed in a cell in total isolation, with no windows or bathroom, and the agents forgot about him for five days, with no food or water. He was able to slip out one hand out of the handcuffs eventually and drank his own urine to survive. He was found incoherent and had to be hospitalized for several days and suffered post-traumatic stress disorder (Phelps 2015). The DEA eventually settled the case and paid Chong a $4.1 million settlement. The agents responsible for this incident received light sanctions: four agents earned a reprimand, one a five-day suspension without salary, and the supervisor in charge of the office during the event received a seven-day suspension. The incident was not immediately reported to the agency and the punishment was not swift. A report written later on by the Inspector General's Office denounced the DEA leadership for the incident and how it had been handled. Other lawmakers also criticized the light sanctions of the agents involved in the case and requested a change in procedures to avoid similar outcomes in the future (Phelps 2015; Wing 2014).

DEA Agents Killing Innocent People

There have been more serious cases of gross misconduct where special agents have killed innocent people while conducting operations under questionable circumstances, to say the least. The DEA has responded to these incidents with its usual position of denying any official responsibility and blaming the victims rather than punishing the agents responsible for the crime. One well-known case occurred in San Antonio in 2003, when fourteen-year-old Ashley Villarreal was shot in the back of her head by DEA agents who were watching her house to arrest her father Joey Angel Villarreal for DT chargers. She was driving a car around the house when agents showed up in an unmarked car at night and thought Joey Angel was in the car. When the agents tried to box the vehicle, the teenage driver—allegedly—tried to ram the DEA vehicle. Ashley died two days later. Witnesses' testimonies and later reports contradicted the official explanation of the event. Ashley's father was not in the car when the shooting occurred and the agent responsible for the Ashley's death was never charged or disciplined for the crime (Wing 2014).

In a more recent case, a series of deadly shootings involving DEA commando-style agents working on anti-narcotics operations in Honduras has shown how far above the law the DEA is willing to go to protect its privileges, brand, and questionable tactics. The first incident took place on the early morning of May 11, 2012 on the river Patuca near the municipality of Ahuas in north-eastern Honduras when sixteen unarmed civilians traveling by boat at night were shot by American and Honduran agents when their vessels collided. DEA agents were aboard a disabled boat carrying a large cargo of cocaine that had been previously seized from traffickers. The shooting left four innocent people dead, among them, two pregnant women Candelaria Trapp Nelson and Juana Jackson Ambrosia, a fourteen-year-old boy named Hasked Brooks Wood, and a twenty-one-year-old young man named Emerson Martinez. Four other villagers were seriously injured. Honduran police did not find any drugs in the taxi boat. A thorough joint investigation conducted by the Inspectors General Office of the Department of Justice and the State Department released a report in May 2017 that uncovered critical contradictions in the DEA official version of the incident and revealed unethical and illegal behavior of the DEA and its agents (Lakhani 2017; Office of the Inspectors General 2017a).

The DEA operation that originated the incident was part of a militarized program known as FAST (Foreign-deployed Advisory Support Team) that had been developed in Afghanistan to combat opium traffickers connected to the Taliban and later expanded to Latin America (Savage 2017). The program allowed DEA agents to work on foreign soil along with local agents to disrupt DT activities where the DEA provided the technology, equipment, and intelligence to choose targets and conduct operations, while the State Department provided aerial transport and air armed support with four helicopters owned by the agency (Savage 2017).

According to the joint report from the State and Justice departments, immediately after the shooting, the DEA recovered the officers and the cocaine from the disabled vessel and returned to its base while intentionally ignoring efforts to search, rescue, and help the people who were injured, dead, and stranded in the water taxi because of the shooting. (Office of the Inspectors General 2017a). To justify its action, the DEA officially argued that the victims were drug traffickers and that agents had fired against them in self-defense after being attacked. However, there was no evidence of such claim but rather the opposite as later was discovered by the Inspectors General's joint report. Also, The DEA claimed for months that the operation had been led by the Honduran government and the DEA was only providing guidance and mentoring local officials. However, the Inspectors General Office's report rebuked that information by asserting that the DEA did organize and was in full charge of the entire operation from beginning to end (Office of the Inspectors General 2017a).

The DEA also refused to cooperate with the State Department as it began to investigate the events that occurred in May 2012. Not only that, the DEA went further and deliberately lied to the American public, the Justice Department leadership, and Congress by insisting in the official narrative the agency manufactured after the incident (the report uses the words "incomplete and inaccurate information" provided by the DEA and avoids using the word "lying"). Stubbornly and against mounting evidence, the DEA double-downed in its narrative by saying that the victims were drug traffickers, that there was an exchange of gunfire, agents responded to an attack, and that DEA agents were not in control. None of these allegations were true according to the investigation by the Inspectors General Office, but the DEA would not give in. The report also revealed that the DEA had conducted its own internal investigation and did not find any wrongdoing in the official account of the incident (again an example of the culture of covering up misconducts). Yet the Inspectors General Offices exposed that the DEA engaged in obstruction of justice and witness tampering by putting pressure on an informant to tell barefaced lies on the accuracy of the events in an effort to support with false testimony the DEA's account of the event. The local witness eventually recanted his first deposition and later on acknowledged lying to investigators because of duress from the DEA (Lakhani 2017; Office of the Inspectors General 2017a; Savage 2017).

Two other deadly shootings occurred in June 23 and July 03 of 2012, where DEA agents from the same militarized program killed drug smugglers who allegedly refused to surrender when approached during anti-drug operations. Nonetheless, there were inconsistencies and contradictions found in the accounts of these incidents between what the local authorities investigated and what the DEA said had happened (including the fact that there was a gun planted in one of the crime scenes where a smuggler pilot died, according to one local witness). The Office of the Inspectors General did not find any wrongdoing on these particular events. However, the report was very critical of the DEA's performance regarding the FAST program and how the institution had attempted to block any investigation to find the truth and expose how DEA agents have acted during the first incident and its aftermath (Lakhani 2017; Office of the Inspectors General 2017a; Savage 2017).

Ultimately, the DEA ended up accepting responsibility for lying to Congress and the killing of four innocent Honduran citizens as a result of the DEA's botched operation in Honduras. Yet none of the agents involved in the shooting were ever punished, nor were the victims of the taxi boat ever compensated or assisted in any way to deal with their losses and injuries (Lakhani 2017; Office of the Inspectors General 2017a; Savage 2017). On a related note, the former DEA's administrator Michele Leonhart once said that the killing of hundreds of children in Mexico due to DT rivalries and violence was *a sign of success* (emphasis added) in the WOD (Ingraham 2015). Such disregard for thousands of lives affected and destroyed by the WOD is outrageous but not surprising coming from the DEA which is a fervent believer of that approach. Unfortunately, this way of thinking is not uncommon among some DEA agents deployed to foreign soil who, in their eagerness to uphold drug prohibition and "rescue" America from illegal drugs, are willing to sacrifice the lives of informants, innocent bystanders, and others as a price for the DEA's success.

Protection of the DEA Brand

Another potential problem in the DEA is how the institution and its agents are reluctant to proceed against colleagues committing wrongdoing or misconduct because there is culture of protection that runs deep within the agency and most agents are reluctant to turn peers in unless a serious or violent incident occurs (Berke 1989; Peterson 1991; USA Today 2015). This problem is prevalent in most if not all law enforcement agencies in America and it is known as the blue curtain, the blue shield, or the blue wall of silence. In the DEA it looks as if this phenomenon is even more common because some DEA decisions had sent the message that the institution is willing to bend the rules to protect agents. Those decisions have involved not firing agents who commit serious offenses and imposing soft penalties to wrongdoers, along with ignoring red flags on agents' behavior that should have expelled them from the DEA and they were not (Mustian and Goodman 2018; USA Today 2015).

An investigation by journalists, based on official records from the DEA, found that the vast majority of disciplinary files and investigations, including serious misconduct, did not conclude with the termination of the agent. According to records, the Department of Justice's Office of Professional Responsibility (OPA) handles more than 200 cases of DEA disciplinary processes each year and the most usual consequences are either a letter of caution or a short unpaid suspension (USA Today 2015). For those agents who are fired, they can appeal the decision and it is not uncommon that most of them will be reinstated by the U.S. Merit Systems Protection Board, a quasi-judicial independent institution that protects federal employees. Ultimately, the chances that a DEA agent faces severe consequences for misconduct or wrongdoing are extremely slim unless the agent commits a serious crime or has a long record of offenses (*USA Today* 2015).

I argue that one contributing factor to this apparent institutionalized protection of misconduct and wrongdoing derives from a *Cult Mentality* (CM) that permeates throughout the agency. Like any other organization with a cult-like philosophy, the DEA displays a fervent and undisputable mission toward a particular goal: the WOD and the assumption that a drug-free world is possible in this case. This mission is usually carried out in an aggressive approach and using proselytism (e.g. Red Ribbon campaign, press releases, media coverage). Also, the leadership and strategies of the DEA (e.g. strict drug control, undercover work, use of informants, anti-drug operations in foreign soil) are understood and executed as a dogmatic truth within the agency, even against evidence that they do not work. Thus, agents are not allowed to criticize the leadership and challenge what is wrong from within. As a result, skepticism toward the mission, disagreement, and questioning DEA's tactics and goals is discouraged or blocked internally (Richardson 1998). This is my personal interpretation of the DEA's ethos as an outsider and from a perspective of a social scientist. I do not intend to demonize or disparage the DEA or its agents for what they do or have done regarding the WOD. My criticism is meant to highlight why there is so much resistance to abandon drug prohibition and acknowledge the failure of the WOD and instead embrace forward-thinking to deal with the American drug problem where the DEA is a prominent stakeholder.

With that said, I interpret that as a result of the DEA's narrow-minded emphasis on mostly prohibition, it promotes a polarized mentality of "us vs them" while fighting the WOD where all drug users, traffickers, and anyone opposed to the drug war policy are labeled as "them" (read opponents) and considered immoral. On the other hand, DEA agents are defined as "us," the "good guys," those who protect our pristine cities and neighborhoods from drugs and who are virtuous and moral in the crusade against drugs. Finally, like any other cult, I argue that there is an intense brainwashing process within the agency to make everyone conform to the values, beliefs, standards, and practices around drug prohibition and the WOD approach. The indoctrination begins at the DEA training academy in Quantico, Virginia where new recruits have to undergo eighteen-week basic instruction program. Those in charge of training them are senior agents who have made a career in the DEA by cementing the principles of drug prohibition. Consequently, elder officers pass on to the new generation of DEA cadets the principles, beliefs, and assumptions of the WOD mindset and the indoctrination starts because it is extremely difficult for new DEA agents to go against this normalized narrative of illegal drugs.

I say indoctrination and brainwashing because within the DEA there is no room for publicly dissenting and criticizing the main strategies and doctrine that the institution wholeheartedly embraces regarding drug prohibition. Perhaps, one of the most revealing moments of this brainwashing occurs when the DEA and its agents react negatively against former colleagues (and police officers from other agencies) who once they have retired begin to criticize the WOD approach (Law Enforcement Action Partnership 2019). Or even worse, if some of these former DEA agents dare to join the "other side" and work in the now prosperous cannabis industry that is taking place across America such as ex-DEA agent Patrick Moen did (Ell 2018). There is a sense of betrayal and derision against those "traitors" because they did not uphold the values and policies of the DEA and have succumbed to the dark side, so to speak. All in all, it appears the DEA's Cult Mentality only reinforces its bureaucratic approach to try to solve the drug problem without really addressing the roots of the issue.

DEA's Questionable and Unconstitutional Criminal Investigations

As a result of the powerful role the DEA has acquired in the intelligence community based on its experience conducting undercover operations, drug raids, and using informants, it is in charge of a secret law enforcement unit called the Special Operations Division also known as SOD. DEA agents called this squad the "Dark Side" possibly because of the nature of the work and the power it holds. The unit is made up of agents from other federal agencies such as the DHS, National Security Agency (NSA), CIA, FBI, IRS, and of course the DEA. The SOD collects raw intelligence (e.g., wiretaps, espionage intercepts, social media and phone records) from the NSA and shares the information with local and state law enforcement agencies to support criminal investigations. In turn, the local authorities use conventional police strategies such as making a pretext traffic stop, conduct a search, arrest someone, or seize drugs based on that information (Aaronson 2018; Human Rights Watch 2018; Shiffman and Cooke 2013). However, the source of intelligence that comes from the SOD is kept secret because government officials cannot expose the NSA as the origin of that source. Instead, law enforcement agents (both local and federal) have to fabricate a scheme to justify before the courts how they found out a crime was being committed. Officials called this practice *Parallel Construction* and most times it involves sophisticated and secretive strategies to build a criminal case while protecting the methods and information from the SOD and the spying community.

Although the DEA's secret unit is not the only government agency that engages in this practice, it did pioneer this approach and it is one that is used prominently and regularly in criminal investigation throughout the United States, possibly every day according to a January 2018 report from Human Rights Watch (Aaronson 2018; Human Rights Watch 2018). The major problem with sharing secret information obtained by the NSA is that most of the criminal cases built upon it are drug crimes or minor offenses rather than national security matters as American society would expect from this involvement of the NSA and the spying community. Legal experts interviewed by multiple sources argue that using *parallel construction* to identify potential offenders and investigate criminal cases may be illegal because it violates due process and there is the possibility of even infringing their Constitutional rights (Aaronson 2018; Human Rights Watch 2018; Shiffman and Cooke 2013).

Parallel Construction (PC) means that defendants who are accused of using hidden NSA leads will not know how government operations were conducted to collect evidence against them. Thus, they cannot challenge the proceedings and the evidence from questionable criminal investigations if the real intelligence sources are concealed (Human Rights Watch 2018). Also, PC encourages misconduct and wrongdoing because any illegal actions by government officials while collecting evidence for a criminal case will not be subjected to judicial scrutiny and possibly be thrown out by a judge if it was illegally obtained (Human Rights Watch 2018). Even if PC helps law enforcement agencies to arrest drug traffickers and take illegal substances out of the street, the ends should not justify the means because government institutions and their employees must abide and comply with the rule of law to reduce the chances of potential abuses by government agents. All in all, the DEA's Special Operation Division is heavily used in the WOD, but its work and tactics appear to be in a gray legal area and at some point may be even illegal and unconstitutional. This heavy reliance on such strategies to pursue strict drug control policies at any price only confirms the DEA's rigid mindset to deal with drug use and DT at any cost using the obsolete model of the WOD.

Finally, a more subtle but unfortunate practice by the DEA is the hegemonic perspective this agency has on U.S. drug policy and the complete power to define the official narrative on the American drug problem. Considering that the DEA is supposed to be the agency with the most experience and knowledge regarding drugs, DT, and drug-related organized crime. Everything the DEA says, does, and publishes is accepted as universal truth. Data, reports, operations, and statistics released by the DEA and framing the problem in certain way are all reproduced uncritically by public officials and the media. American society accepts this as matter of fact because the DEA is expected to be remarkably qualified to know the American drug problem and respond accordingly. The issue with this practice is that the DEA has had indisputable power to frame the American drug problem on its own terms and that generates a monolithic idea of it with no dissension to challenge mistakes, bad policies, or potential abuses. Also, having the monopoly of the narrative on DT and drugs, leads to a narrow-minded perspective that emphasizes law enforcement and drug prohibition but ignores other options that could be more efficient and effective. Accordingly, being trapped in the WOD paradigm is one clear consequence of that situation. Finally, having total control of the narrative of the drug problem affects the objectivity and impartiality of the DEA because it is difficult to acknowledge mistakes and change course when needed and that is exactly what has happened to this agency.

Now what? If the DEA does not want to abandon the WOD and there is no willingness from the agency to try a different approach to address the drug problem, what can be done about it? It is a fact that drug prohibition does not work and this undeniable reality has already generated a wave of change that is cementing a new kind of approach to deal with DT, drug abuse, and drug demand. The legalization of recreational marijuana in several states in

America and in countries such as Canada and Uruguay is a small but significant step toward a more efficient approach. Sooner than later the DEA will have to re-evaluate its strategies and priorities to determine what changes are needed to meet the demands of a contemporary world that is totally different than the one when the DEA was born. These and other changes are currently on the making whether or not the DEA agrees, and they will be explored in the next and final chapter.

Chapter 7

Conclusions

A Paradigm to Mitigate Drug Trafficking

WHERE IS DRUG TRAFFICKING IN MEXICO NOW?

Given that the War on Drugs (WOD) continues to be the basic policy to deal with the American drug problem, it is not a surprise that drug trafficking remains a significant headache in the United States, Mexico, and the rest of the world. The situation is even worse considering all the economic, social, and public health ramifications that drug trafficking brings to countless communities everywhere as described in previous chapters. The amount of gruesome violence, drug gang-related murders, extortion, and corruption connected to drug trafficking endures and has gotten worse in Latin America, Mexico, and along the border with the United States. There is no sign that these circumstances will change in the near future given that the incentives and infrastructure built for drug trafficking are deeply embedded in society and they have not been addressed at all.

A new government took over in Mexico in December 2018 headed by Andrés Manuel López Obrador (AMLO). While campaigning, he promised to change course in the Mexican WOD and address the social roots of problem (e.g., extreme poverty, high unemployment, lack of education, among others issues) while reducing violence, killings, and organized crime activities. Despite these promises, as of 2020, none of the latter issues have changed in any form. Instead, they have exacerbated. Murder rates are higher than ever in cities such as Tijuana and Monterrey and other cities that had been spared from the wave of violence in the past (Mexico City, Cancun, and Guanajuato), are now experiencing extreme violence. Throughout Mexico, it has become normal to see daily shootouts, assassinations in broad daylight, disposal of decapitated and dismembered bodies on the streets, and high rates of criminal behavior overall (Linthicum 2019).

To prove this point, January of 2019 was the most violent year ever recorded in Mexico with a total of 2,929 men and women violently murdered in this month alone. On average, ninety-four people were killed daily or four every hour (Ángel 2019). Kidnappings (another high-impact crime strongly correlated to drug trafficking gangs who resort to it to diversify their criminal portfolio) also increased in January, with 140 cases and 164 victims. This rate is the highest number ever recorded for a single month. From January 2015 to January 2019 the percentage of violent murders rose 98 percent, according to official data (Ángel 2019). During the 2000s, most of the violence and drug-related murders were mainly concentrated in areas with drug trafficking activities. As of 2020, these activities have spread throughout Mexico (although with some differences) that reflect how drug organizations are able to take a de-facto control in entire regions.

Such situation is an unintended outcome of the DEA's strategy based on *Leadership Decapitation* to cut the supply of illegal drugs (Phillips 2015). When that occurs, the likely outcome has been more fragmented and decentralized smaller groups that fight each other in turf wars which actually generates more violence and criminality. Why? Because smaller drug gangs lack the connections and infrastructure to harvest, manufacture, smuggle, and distribute illegal drugs as old cartels have done it for years. To compensate for that, fragmented groups resort to extreme violence and intimidation against rivals and their communities to get the upper hand in controlling drug corridors and plazas. Additionally, these reduced gangs have turned to exploiting local economies through extortion, kidnapping, and a strong grip of drug dealing in neighborhoods along with other drug trafficking activities they deal with (Hope 2018b). Smaller cells are capable of doing anything in terms of crime because they understand their survival as a zero-sum game. Besides extortion and kidnapping, organized crime in Mexico has also expanded dramatically into other illegal activities such as theft of fuel (known as *Huachicoleo* in Mexico) from pipelines belonging to the government-owned oil company—Pemex. (Correa-Cabrera 2017; Stewart 2019).

In February 2019, the Mexican government approved a constitutional reform introduced by President AMLO to create a national guard as a strategic measure to counter crime, murder, and drug trafficking activities (Semple and Villegas 2019). Corruption and abuses by security forces have been rampant in Mexico in the past decade and this new law enforcement agency is meant to break that cycle of failure and abuse. Unlike other military institutions in charge of fighting organized crime, this one will have civilian command rather than military, and it will include a hybrid force of federal police members and army policing units (Semple and Villegas 2019). Unfortunately this new agency will not reverse the trend of crime and violence taking place in Mexico because it only reinforces the prevailing model of framing drug trafficking as a criminal issue while leaving untouched the pushing and pulling factors of the problem. Drug trafficking activities still are the most valuable source of illegal revenue for organized crime in Mexico and criminals are willing to engage in extreme violence, assassination, and corruption to reap a portion of the drug business.

Despite interdiction efforts by local, state, and federal law enforcement agencies, drug smuggling, selling, and consumption of drugs continue growing and expanding. Even with the latest technology, sophisticated operations, and state-of-the-art undercover work that the DEA praises to do (a lot of this work is done in Mexico), the flow of illegal drugs to the United States has not been stopped and will never be. Heroin, methamphetamine, synthetic opioids (fentanyl) and cocaine smuggling are at a record high as of 2020 in the United States. These drugs still have endless demand in America and this basic fact makes it impossible to cut their supply given how profitable trafficking these drugs is no matter how much law enforcement is spent against that illegal enterprise (Centers for Disease Controls and Prevention 2018; Stewart 2019).

WHERE IS DRUG TRAFFICKING IN THE UNITED STATES TODAY?

If the problem of drug trafficking in Mexico is worse than even before, how is the United States doing in this regard? Has America handled drug trafficking in a more effective and efficient way compared to Mexico? Are drug use and availability of illegal drugs in American streets lower than ever before? The categorical answer is no. America is not doing any better than Mexico, in fact, it is doing worse than before regarding its drug problem. Despite years of drug interdiction, the WOD, and billions of taxpayer's money spent on prosecuting and incarcerating drug users, the American drug problem remains a serious and complex one. If one takes into account the whole spectrum of the issue, it will be easier to realize that drug trafficking in the United States has reached unprecedented social, economic, and public health consequences like never seen before. The opioid epidemic that has impacted America since the 2000s (that has caused thousands of deaths every year) is a prominent example of how complex the problem is. Even though the levels of violence, murder, kidnapping, and extortion in the United States are nothing comparable to Mexico and other Central American countries, the United States has experienced an increase of drug-related deaths and criminality of its own. Here are a few facts to support this assertion.

Availability and consumption of illegal drugs are as high as ever before, according to the 2018 National Drug Threat Assessment report (NDTA). This document, published by the Department of Justice through the DEA, compiles information from local, state, and federal law enforcement agencies, public health data, and other sources. According to NDTA, availability and use of heroin have recently increased while its purity and prices are higher and cheaper respectively than ever before (DEA 2018). Cocaine, a narcotic that for nearly a decade lost predominance among American drug users has made a comeback. Today, cocaine demand and its availability have risen to levels similar to those seen in 2007 (DEA 2018).

The return of cocaine trafficking and use in America reveal an unmistakable feature of the economic forces behind the black market on drugs because it shows that drug use and demand cannot be defeated with law enforcement policies only. From the 1980s on, the United States invested billions of dollars in eradication programs, interdiction operations, and quasi-military aid in Colombia to destroy coca leaves fields (the row material to produce cocaine) and stop the flow of cocaine. Although demand and cocaine availability were reduced gradually and modestly in the 2000s, the drug has gained popularity once again. This revival of cocaine demand in America brings to question whether or not the billions of dollar spent decades ago to reduce its flow into the country were actually the reason for its decline or rather the result of drug users switching to other available drugs, a common pattern persistent among users and documented by experts.

The 2018 NDTA also reports how synthetic opioids, fentanyl in particular, have contributed greatly to thousands of overdoses and deaths throughout the United States in the recent past. Specifically, there is a strong correlation between the availability of fentanyl and the epidemic of opioid addiction and overdoses (DEA 2018). Synthetic drugs are nothing new in America given that designer drugs (substances with similar effects and properties to illegal drugs that are chemically modified to circumvent drug prohibition) have been widely available and used since the 1980s. Even before that decade, during the 1960s and 1970s LSD and later Ecstasy (MDMA) were associated with hippies, clubs, and raves respectively (Jenkins 1999). Fentanyl, a powerful synthetic opioid used in the medical field to deal with severe pain, appeared in the mid-2010s on the streets of America mixed with heroin. Fentanyl is 30 to 50 times more potent than heroin and it is usually imported from Asia, China in particular. This synthetic drug has been credited for thousands of overdoses and deaths in the United States and recently it has contributed greatly to the current opioid epidemic and overdoses (DEA 2018; Le Cour Grandmaison et al. 2019).

The nature of the opioid and overdose epidemic taking place in the country not only confirms how the DEA's work does nothing substantial to keep America safer and freer from drugs. It reveals why the DEA's approach of drug control has contributed to and prolonged the epidemic itself. This outcome is particularly true when considering the ramifications of police crackdown on prescription opioids in the 2000s, which instead of reducing addiction led to a heroin epidemic as users switched to this drug when unable to have access to prescription drug opioids. No other American problem encapsulates the unintended effects of the WOD. America's stubborn approach of strict law enforcement for drug control has worsened the current opioid epidemic. Such fiasco is most obviously noticeable in the fact that the drug problem remains a serious economic, social, and criminal issue in the United States (Quinones 2016).

The Opioid Epidemic Exposes the Failure of the WOD

In retrospect, experts begin to understand the dynamics of the opioid epidemic that has impacted American in the past decades and they have identified three different but interconnected opioid epidemics, not just one: prescription painkillers (1990s-2000s); heroin (2010-present); and synthetic opioids (2014-present). According to data available at the CDC and the U.S. Census, researchers were able to conclude that from 1999 to 2016 there were 351,630 opioid-related deaths in the United States. Throughout this period opioid deaths grew by 455 percent (Tinker 2019). Understandably, the opioid epidemic is a complex problem with multiple forces leading to this outcome. However, drug prohibition and the WOD have aggravated the problem for multiple reasons.

First, by criminalizing and punishing drug users, it forces them into the black market to find heroin and synthetic opioids to sustain their addiction. People overdose simply because they do not know the purity of the heroin they are taking or ignore whether or not the drug is mixed with synthetic opioids such as fentanyl (drug dealers cut drugs with other substances to make more profit). Drug policy experts know this predicament because it is a well-documented phenomenon known as the *Iron Law of Prohibition*. As law enforcement intensifies, more potent drugs are produced and consumed by drug users (Hari 2016). The more attempts the WOD makes to stop the epidemic, much harder opioids appear on the streets of America because enforcement does not address the root of opioid addiction, only its symptoms. This is one powerful factor why deadly overdoses have increased to shocking numbers in the recent years and why the epidemic will continue to worsen in the coming years (Coyne and Hall 2017; Hari 2016; Quinones 2016).

Second, there is scientific evidence (Frakt 2016; Hari 2016) that needle-exchange programs and supervised injection sites are associated with lower rates of overdoses and deaths because these two options allow drug users access to anti-overdose medication (naloxone) while reducing disease transmission by not sharing needles. Yet, the WOD makes it almost impossible to facilitate and create any of these harm reduction programs because it is against federal law to set them up. Local efforts to deal with the opioid epidemic exist but they are limited since federal law preempt state and local regulations. Despite this federal prohibition, some states such as Kentucky and Nevada, and cities such as San Francisco, Tacoma, and Seattle have allowed local health departments or NGOs to set up needle-exchange programs to reduce disease transmission rates and frame drug use within a harm reduction approach (Frakt 2016). In early October 2019, a federal judge ruled that a planned supervision injection site in Philadelphia does not violate the Controlled Substances Act because the place (called Safehouse) will allow people to bring their drugs and use them in a medical facility to reduce overdoses is meant to reduce drug use not to facilitate it (Allyn 2019). The federal government is expected to appeal the decision and it remains to be seen if the Department of Justice will ever allow these sites and needle-exchange programs to operate legally in the near future. Still, the vast majority of drug users do not have access to these effective health services throughout America.

Third, defenders of the WOD have systematically refused to re-schedule the classification of marijuana from a Schedule I drug to a Schedule II of The Controlled Substances Act. This rescheduling would allow less restrictions to conduct research on marijuana as well as its employment as an alternative painkiller with little or no side effects for certain individuals, according to research conducted in other countries (Berke 2016). Heavy users of prescription drug opioids could substitute them with medical marijuana to cope with chronic pain, a practice that has been reported to work well for some users. Although this still requires scientific studies to show conclusive evidence about it, the fact that a non-addictive, effective, and affordable option is already available could help to reduce the number of opioid overdoses. In the same vein, there is some evidence that marijuana can assist heroin users to deal with some of the withdrawal effects of opioid addiction and assist chronic opioid users to come down from their addiction. Yet, none of this can be done because of the inflexible attitude by the Department of Justice and the DEA to endorse a rescheduling of marijuana from Schedule I to II (Berke 2016).

Finally, most public officials who support the WOD approach (as well as many Americans) erroneously assume that drug use is mostly a problem of free will where users refuse to give up their addiction because they do not want to stop using drugs. This belief is based on the assumption that once people use drugs for a few times they will be automatically addicted and lose self-control. There is also the belief that substance abusers will become violent and irresponsible in their quest to satisfy their addiction once they are hooked on drugs. Even if these beliefs are widely accepted as true, they are not supported with empirical data. The reality of drug addiction is much more complicated because it encompasses the multifaceted nature of the human condition, meaning that social, cultural, economic, educational, and emotional factors intertwine with drug addiction. These factors cannot be excluded when assessing and understanding why people become addicted to drugs and what should be the best scientific method to help them recover (Lembke 2016).

The opioid epidemic reached such unprecedented levels that on October 26, 2017, President Trump declared it a "National Public Health Emergency" (NPHE) in order to bring government action at the federal level and address the situation in the most efficient manner. Some politicians and pundits criticized that the president should have declared a "National Disaster Declaration" instead, arguing that the funding and scope of the official declaration were limited and unable to change the nature of the current crisis given the size of the problem (Merica 2017). More than three years after the 2017 NPHE declaration, the problem has not improved at all. The opioid epidemic still kills more than 40,000 Americans annually as of 2020. The problem may have slowed down or stabilize in some regions, but it remains a serious national health issue if the yardstick is the number of Americans dying from overdoses each year. The death rates have steadily increased since the early 2010s (Tinker 2019).

The main question remains why the federal government has never implemented a comprehensive national approach to solve the opioid epidemic. Instead, the burden of the crisis has been left to state and local authorities for the most part. These governments have responded to the problem differently depending on local resources, political will, and how negative their communities have been impacted by the epidemic. This has resulted in a patchwork of responses varying from jurisdiction to jurisdiction because each city and county developed their own efforts to handle the public health consequences of these epidemics. For instance, some cities such as Seattle and Dayton started needle-exchange programs (discretely of course to avoid federal interference), others distributed opioid overdose reversal (Naloxone) among first responders and the police to reduce the number of overdose deaths. Other states and local officials pushed for an aggressive agenda to arrest and prosecute unscrupulous doctors and pharmacists who profited from OxyContin and other painkillers during the peak of the prescription drug epidemic.

There is a famous old phrase attributed to Abraham Maslow and Kaplan that says, "If the only tool you have is a hammer, you tend to treat everything as if it were a nail." This sentence summarizes with accuracy how drug control and the WOD have addressed the complex problem of drug use and abuse in America for nearly fifty years. The epidemic of opioid addiction and overdoses has not been the exception, and it remains a serious national health, social, and economic problem. American society would be pleased to support this hammer no matter its cost assuming there is evidence that it works. It does not. The approach has been proven inefficient, expensive, and inadequate to answer the opioid epidemic, and has made the crisis worse. What can be done then to move beyond this stagnation? Primarily, to put the hammer aside and evaluate possible alternatives to the drug problem. Then, it is crucial to reassess the entire nature of the American drug problem and began with a simple but powerful acknowledgement that drug prohibition does not work.

A NEW MODEL TO TACKLE THE DRUG PROBLEM

To tackle the American drug problem seriously, reverse the damage caused by the WOD, and reduce drug trafficking to minimum levels, it requires a new model that leaves behind old assumptions and embraces a fresh point of view that is comprehensive and versatile in nature. This model is not a silver bullet, nor will it guarantee that the problem will be solved once and for all. Such belief will only lead to disappointment and possibly to the sort of mindset that initially gave birth to the WOD paradigm. Any attempt to change the status quo of drug demand and drug trafficking can only be achieved step by step, using a trial and error methodology, and taking into account all stakeholders. Such endeavor will require patience, time, resources, and innovation. It will also demand accepting certain risks and understating that failures and setbacks are part of the learning process, not evidence of its failure.

Such model is actually not new in the sense that it has already been voiced long ago from multiple experts and stakeholders (Alexander 2008; Bertram et al. 1996; Drug Policy Alliance 2019; Hari 2016; Walker 2015) who are familiar with the negative effects of the WOD and the complex nature of tackling drug addiction. Nonetheless, the model suggested here is new to the extent that it includes a more comprehensive approach that incorporates recommendations to deal with the roots of drug trafficking in places where drugs are manufactured and exported. This model will make the WOD obsolete and gradually tackle other issues intertwined with the American drug problem such as the opioid epidemic, mass incarceration, drug-related violence, drug overdoses, and less violence and homicides.

This new model is not a single proposition but a multifaceted strategy that aims to make changes in the different layers and domains where drug use, abuse, drug trafficking, and all the ramifications of the drug problem manifest. These layers include—but are not limited to—the different components of the criminal justice system (police, courts, and corrections), the legislative and executive branches at the state and federal levels, federal law enforcement agencies (the DEA in particular), and other institutions that have some authority or control over drug prohibition, drug laws, or drug control by creating or enforcing these laws and prosecuting, convicting, and supervising drug offenders.

The new model is meant to persuade public officials, politicians, and society by and large that there are more efficient, cheaper, and practical alternatives to address the drug problem than the current approach. Among these alternatives are decriminalization and legalization of illegal drugs, evidence-based education, treatment, rehabilitation, and a harm reduction approach as it has been suggested by many experts (Andreas 2013; Bertram et al. 1996; Inciardi 2008). In addition, institutional and policy changes in the criminal justice system at the local, state, and federal are required as well as a reassessment that the drug problem in America is more than just a law enforcement issue. The new model has five paths toward its implementation: overcome resistance to forward-thinking; decriminalize drug use and possession of all drugs; create a path towards legalization of illegal drugs; overhaul of the DEA and its main mission; and redefine drug trafficking as a multidimensional phenomenon, not a criminal one.

OVERCOMING RESISTANCE TO FORWARD-THINKING

Resistance to forward-thinking is notably present when considering possible alternatives to the WOD such as decriminalization and legalization of drugs. Not because these options are extreme or a wasted effort—they are not—but because they are interpreted through ideological and dogmatic assumptions that dismiss research and data supporting them. It is this attitude that sustains the core of the resistance to change: no matter how much evidence experts and researchers present to expose the futility of drug control and prohibition, defenders of the WOD evade scientific arguments and reject alternatives options at once. Old habits die hard and the attitude "if it isn't broken, don't fix it" is common among supporters of the WOD. Then, the question is, how to overcome this resistance and promote a new model to transform the current state of affairs of the drug problem, if possible?

One obvious response would be to educate people but not the usual targets of anti-drug campaigns efforts such as children, students, drug users, and the general public. Instead education to overcome resistance to forward-thinking must be aimed at members of the criminal justice system (police officers, prosecutors, and judges) and public officials (e.g., District Attorneys, lawmakers, mayors, city council members, governors) to inform them about the scientific nature of drug use, harm reduction, and other options besides incarceration and punishment. To be more accurate, I would use the word *re-educate* public officials and politicians to raise their awareness and embrace pioneering drug policies and hopefully help them transform whatever preconceive personal negative assumptions and beliefs they may have about illicit drugs.

To that effect, there are at least two collective trends that reflect a push to change the status quo of drug control currently taking place in the United States despite ideological and partisan opposition to it. One is the decriminalization of marijuana and other drugs in many jurisdiction; and two, the legalization of the marijuana in eleven states (plus Washington, D.C.) and more of them joining the movement in the near future. The first one is a trend set up by some states but mostly politicians and local governments (e.g. cities, counties, tribe councils, district attorneys, mayors, chiefs of police, and city council members). They have finally adopted a progressive stand toward the WOD and began to decriminalize personal use of marijuana in their respective jurisdictions. Cities such as Manhattan, Philadelphia, Chicago, Brooklyn, Boston, Baltimore, New Orleans, Houston, Corpus Christi, Ferguson, and others no longer prosecute people caught with marijuana for personal use (Dewan 2019; Jouvenal 2018). In most of these metropolitan cities, forward-thinking prosecutors have been responsible for these changes motivated by the argument that enforcing marijuana laws wastes taxpayer money and takes away resources that are needed to address violent and serious crimes. These public officials represent a new generation of district attorneys who share a pioneering agenda to overhaul the criminal justice system regarding the most harmful effects of the WOD (Dewan 2019; Jouvenal 2018).

These officials have decided to decriminalize marijuana possession, invest in diversion programs to send low-level offenders to treatment facilities and educational classes, pursue less punitive and shorter sentences, and bring more accountability to cases of police brutality for more racial justice (Dewan 2019; Jouvenal 2018). These changes are not homogenous and every jurisdiction has had its own particular approach to generate decriminalization policies on marijuana. Some cities or counties have chosen diversion programs, while others have set up limits on the amount of marijuana needed to trigger an arrest. Some are giving away summons instead of jail time for those caught with minor possession of marijuana. In New Orleans for instance, the change came from the city council through an ordinance, while in Buffalo, Mayor Byron Brown ordered the city police department to stop enforcing low-level marijuana violations. In Baltimore and Corpus Christi, newly elected County District Attorneys were responsible for these changes. Overall, there is overwhelming consensus behind these policies to move beyond the WOD and adopt a new model that can address the American drug problem without the pernicious side effects of drug control. These local efforts are still a small step in the larger scheme of things, but they are evidence of a generational shift that will eventually make the WOD obsolete (Dewan 2019; Jouvenal 2018).

The second trend refers to changing attitudes in American society regarding public support for decriminalization and legalization of marijuana. This has been an organic process growing slowly but steadily in the recent past to embrace forward-thinking and adopt drug policies that are effective, affordable, and within a harm reduction logic. A recent poll by the Pew Research Center shows that 62 percent of the population (about six out of every ten Americans) endorse today marijuana legalization compared to only 32 percent in 2000 (Hartig and Geiger 2018). From a generational standpoint, there are even broader differences in support of progressive drug policies. For instance, approximately three-quarters of Millennials (74 percent) argue that marijuana should be legal compared to two-thirds of Generation Xers (63 percent), and roughly a little more than half of baby boomers (54 percent) concur with this statement (Hartig and Geiger 2018). These data are crucial to understanding that the legalization of marijuana is an irreversible trend and not a matter of "if" but "when" it will occur. The federal government will be forced soon to re-schedule marijuana and put it in a legal category that allows its medical use and eventual decriminalization and legalization of the drug nationwide.

All this implies that as the generational change occurs, more Millennials and Generation Xers will reach positions of political power that will tear down the legal, political, and economic infrastructure that has supported the WOD Industrial Complex (as described in chapter 5). In other words, if there are no government measures soon to legalize pot at the federal level, American society will just wait out for this course of action to occur independently of what the federal government and the DEA keeps doing about it. Legalization of marijuana will occur throughout the United States sooner than later. Such trend has been reinforced each election cycle in the past ten years, as more states move toward legalization of medical and recreational marijuana because it makes sense politically, economically, and socially (Drug Policy Alliance 2019; Ferreira 2017; Hari 2016; Ingraham 2016).

As of spring 2020 eleven states and the District of Columbia have stopped marijuana prohibition by legalizing this substance while thirty-three allow using marijuana for medical purposes. However, the number of states adopting marijuana legalization will grow soon as New Mexico, Connecticut, New York, Minnesota, Rhode Island, New Hampshire, and New Jersey are considering legislative bills to allow the recreational use of marijuana by the end of 2020 (Drug Policy Alliance 2019).

DICRIMINALIZATION OF DRUG USE AND POSSESSION

To tackle the American drug problem seriously, the new model demands forward-thinking which implies innovation and ideas for the future. One critical policy change to partially end drug prohibition and the WOD will be to embrace full decriminalization of drug use and possession of drugs throughout America, not only marijuana. Full decriminalization refers to those policies where illegal drugs remain prohibited but people are not arrested, prosecuted, or imprisoned if they are caught using or in possession of small amounts of any illegal drug (Belenko and Spohn 2015). Sometimes individuals can be arrested if caught with these substances, but they will face civil fines rather than criminal prosecution. A central tenet of decriminalization is that illegal drugs and selling them (even in small amounts) are still prohibited and those caught doing it are arrested and prosecuted. In other words, decriminalization of personal drug use and possession will be similar to a trafficking ticket where lawbreakers would face civil rather than criminal penalties (Belenko and Spohn 2015).

For decades, experts and scientists (Drug Policy Alliance 2019; Inciardi 2008) have demanded that drug use and possession of some drugs should not be criminalized. They have argued that most of those who have been arrested on these charges are low-level, non-violent offenders caught with small amounts of drugs mainly for personal consumption. The majority of such individuals are not a threat to society and the government wastes millions of dollars every year in law enforcement processing these individuals that bring no significant difference for public safety. On the other hand, those against decriminalization policies assert that detention, prosecution, and imprisonment of people who consume illegal drugs are necessary to deter others from using and selling drugs and to maintain law and order in our society. There is also legitimate concern that less or no punitive measures and absence of legal consequences for illicit drug taking could normalized drug use and increase the number of people who end up addicted to them (Belenko and Spohn 2015).

As legitimate and reasonable as these arguments can be there is no scientific evidence to support them and confirm with certainty that such outcomes will ever occur if full decriminalization is adopted. Simply put, most of the rationale against decriminalization is speculative in nature and difficult to demonstrate from a scientific standpoint. The debate on decriminalization implicitly distinguishes between marijuana and other illegal drugs, though. Most of the consensus in favor of decriminalization applies to the former, but there is little or no debate about the latter. The implication being that decriminalization of marijuana should be a reasonable option given the mild effects and no addictive nature of the plan compared to hard drugs such as heroin, methamphetamine, or cocaine.

This premise has been confirmed by the new wave of decriminalization policies recently set up by local government throughout the United States. City officials have given up arresting and prosecuting possession and personal use of marijuana as mentioned earlier. This does not mean that marijuana is a harmless substance, it is not. Research shows that it affects the brain of teenagers regarding cognitive development, has potential for addiction, among other health issues. There are also potential risks for psychosis and psychological addiction but far less severe compared to more addictive substances. It is important to acknowledge too that marijuana has great potential in the medical field to ameliorate health chronic problems and other psychological symptoms such as pain, seizures and insomnia (Gupta 2015).

I strongly argue that decriminalization of drugs should include all illegal drugs not just marijuana. This is one of the key suggestions of the new model proposed in this book to tackle the American drug problem earnestly. Decriminalization of marijuana is a critical first step to create a reasonable drug policy, but it is not enough to dismantle the pernicious outcomes of drug prohibition. Decriminalization of just marijuana excludes a large population of users and addicts in need of treatment and rehabilitation that are addicted to more dangerous substances. These individuals are in keen need of rehabilitation and treatment. By keeping marijuana as the only decriminalized drug reproduces the narrative of dealing with drug use and abuse as a criminal problem rather than a social, economic, and health challenge. Certainly, decriminalization of all illegal drugs would have to be regulated, organized, and gradually established to determine the best interest of society, public safety, and those impacted by this policy. But it can be done because other countries such as Portugal and Uruguay have already done it with positive results.

The DEA and diehard supporters of the WOD would immediately condemn any attempts to decriminalize all illegal drugs claiming that such step would unleash a wave of crime, increase drug use, instigate wrongdoing, and cause colossal health, economic, and public safety problems in America. These conjectures are publicly known because they have been told loudly for decades to depict an apocalyptic scenario if decriminalization ever occurs. Problem is that those behind these speculations also reject any possible alternative to drug prohibition besides strict drug control (DEA 2019). The reality is no conclusive evidence exists to support such claims. A few pundits who oppose decriminalization have found correlation between decriminalization and some of the allegedly negative effects of this approach but as experts know, correlation is not causation and for that reason, they should not be taken seriously.

Quite the opposite to those presumptive harms of decriminalization, research and empirical evidence from other countries that have defied catastrophic predictions for embracing full decriminalization of all drugs indicate that such progressive drug policy works and can be successful to confront the drug problem without experiencing any of the negative effects that allegedly would occur (Ferreira 2017; Hollersen 2013; Robinson 2016). There are many social, economic, and health benefits from decriminalization of drug use and possession. One is that it will reduce mass incarceration in America given than drug possession is the number one cause of arrest in the United States. Also, it will redirect law enforcement resources to address serious crimes and contribute to dismantle racial disparities in the criminal justice system. More importantly, decriminalization of all drugs will transform the American drug problem from a criminal one to a public health issue (Alexander 2012; Nadelmann 2018).

Research and practical experiments in other countries show that drug use and crime will not increase if decriminalization is embraced using an organized plan (Nadelmann 2018). Countries that have resorted to decriminalization as a sensible political strategy have been able to confront heroin epidemics, chronic drug addiction, HIV, AIDS, Hepatitis C, and other serious national health issues intertwined with drug use. The most well-known example of such approach is Portugal, a conservative nation that adopted a workable model of decriminalization drug policy in 2001 to fight a heroin epidemic and its additional social and health consequences (Belenko and Spohn 2015; Ferreira 2017; Nadelmann 2018).

Portugal's Decriminalization Experiment

In the 1990s, Portugal experienced a dramatic increase in heroin addiction, high crime rates, an unfolding epidemic of HIV infections (at some point it became the highest in Europe), and widespread drug use across the country. A decade earlier, cheap heroin from Afghanistan had inundated most of Europe, Portugal included, and this country did not have any experience dealing with drug use and addiction at all (Ferreira 2017; Hollersen 2013). At first, Portugal's government responded with the usual drug control policies common to Western countries, such as the criminalization of drug users, demonization of addicts, and anti-drug campaigns to encourage people to avoid or stop using drugs. In the meantime, at the local level, doctors, pharmacists, and other health care providers began to improvise different strategies to deal with the drug crisis but in a different manner, using harm reduction tools. They established unofficial needle-exchange programs, made substitution therapy available to drug users, and set up small clinics for detoxification. Among these providers was a young doctor named Joao Goulao, who pioneered a Center for Treatment of Drug Addicts (known in Portuguese for the acronym CAT). An unofficial network of these centers appeared throughout Portugal in the 1990s, and based on the experience he accumulated to treat addiction, doctor Goulao was appointed to lead the country's newest drug strategy of decriminalization (Ferreira 2017).

After a panel of experts considered the nature of the drug crisis in Portugal, they recommended the complete decriminalization of all drugs in the country. The recommendations were approved by the government and the new drug law known as 30/2000 took effect in 2001. This law gave Portugal the title of becoming the first country in the world to decriminalize drug use and possession of all illegal drugs. Joao Goulao was credited as the founder of Portugal's most progressive drug policy worldwide (Ferreira 2017). Among the most significant changes of this new path was that instead of arresting individuals who were caught with illicit drugs, the government would give users a warning. Users were required to visit a commission of professionals (a lawyer, a doctor, and a health care provider or social worker) within seventy-two hours to discuss options for rehabilitation in addition to treatment services available immediately for clients. More importantly was that these options were voluntary and there was no punishment for refusing them, stop treatment or drop any of these services anytime without a legal consequence (Ferreira 2017; Hollersen 2013).

To that end, the government invested resources to create the infrastructure needed to provide assistance to drug users throughout the country, including maintenance programs and needle-exchange sites while hiring new professionals to deliver the support needed by clients (Belenko and Spohn 2015; Ferreira 2017). Portugal is a relatively small country and had less than 10 million inhabitants during the beginning of this policy experiment, and this somehow made these efforts more manageable to carry out. As experts have predicted after decriminalization took place in Portugal, the heroin epidemic subsided and the national drug problem became manageable in the subsequent years (Ferreira 2017; Hollersen 2013). The overall effect was lower rates of drug overdoses, less HIV cases, a substantial decrease in drug crimes, and improvement in other criminal justice issues related to illegal substance abuse. Incarceration rates also plummeted given that now anyone caught with drugs would not be arrested and prosecuted.

The strong correlation between full decriminalization and the clear decline of Portugal's drug problem has been widely researched and proven to show that decriminalization has worked in this country. To be clear, illegal drugs such as cocaine, heroin, and marijuana are still illegal in Portugal but consumers can carry a minimum amount for personal use without fear of being incarcerated. If caught by the police, the situation is handled as if it was a parking violation, with no arrest, which avoids the cost of processing people through the criminal justice system and labeling drug users as criminals (Ferreira 2017; Hollersen 2013). A critical goal of Portugal's new drug policy was how much emphasis the government put to redefine the drug problem from a criminal issue into a social and public health matter. This meant a significant cultural and political turn to abandon old stereotypes and assumptions about drug use, addicts, and punitive measures. Instead, a reasonable and realistic strategy was adopted using evidence-based and empirical information to determine with accuracy what needed to be done. The first thing to change was official attitudes toward the drug problem by adopting a language that did not stigmatize drug use. Concepts such as "individuals who use drug" or "individuals with an addiction difficulty" substituted the label "drug addicts." Accordingly, institutions and personnel in charge of implementing the new decriminalization process underwent training to become sensitive to the damage caused by drug stigmatization and reflect the new policies and procedures (Ferreira 2017).

If Portugal did it, America can do it, too, because it has the resources, infrastructure, and necessity to implement such an approach. However, the main hurdles will be ideological and political rather than scientific or structural because many officials and law enforcement agents just cannot imagine to look at drugs and drug use from a different perspective other than being a criminal behavior. Here, too, the Portugal experiment offers another lesson. One of the premises behind Portugal's decriminalization as an innovative drug policy was that experts and politicians finally understood that a drug-free world was impossible to achieve. Being a traditional and conservative society, Portugal concluded that in order to confront earnestly its drug problem it had to prioritize citizen's lives and public safety over ideological, religious, and skeptical values. Decriminalization was seen as a pragmatic and humanistic process to face the nature of drug consumption and trafficking that all societies must face.

This implied also that Portugal had to accept the negative consequences of embracing decriminalization such as permanent drug use, some increase in illegal drug use, and an impact on the health care system with more drug-related diseases. But experts and the public sentiment was that the overall benefits of decriminalization exceeded by far the negative outcomes of implementing this policy. Decriminalization did not make the Portuguese drug problem worse but the opposite. Portugal continues to support its commitment toward a harm reduction policy because it is more effective than drug prohibition. America must look closer at this experiment to learn its benefits and maybe in the near future implement a similar policy at home (Ferreira 2017; Hollersen 2013).

The World Shifts toward Drug Liberalization

By no means is Portugal the only country that has decriminalized drugs. Several other nations across the world have taken steps to embrace this drug policy in recent decades because of the proven benefits of its implementation. Countries such as Canada, Costa Rica, France, Germany, Mexico, Holland, Switzerland, and Uruguay are among those experimenting with different measures to redefine drug use as a public health problem rather than a criminal one. For instance, since the early 1990s, Germany has taken a soft approach on prosecuting possession of marijuana. Although the drug is prohibited, legal loopholes have allowed its personal consumption as de- facto decriminalization since authorities do not prosecute people caught with small amounts of marijuana. The amount for personal possession of marijuana in Germany varies from state to state, where some authorize up to 6 grams, while others up to 15 grams (Schuster 2018). Additionally, Germany along with Canada, Denmark, the Netherlands, and Switzerland allow pharmaceutical heroin (diamorphine) to be prescribed as maintenance therapy to assist those people who are addicted to street heroin (Nadelmann 2018). This legal tolerance indicates how these nations have emphasized harm reduction and saving lives over punishment and imprisonment, a hallmark premise in drug legalization.

One eye-opening example is Uruguay, a country that became the first to fully legalized marijuana and has never criminalized drug use and possession of any drugs for decades. According to the Decree-Law 14.294 that took effect on October 1, 1974, individuals who were found with minimum quantities of illegal drugs for the purpose of personal consumption would not be prosecuted. The law is still in force and the country has moved to a full government-regulated market of marijuana (Robinson 2016). In 2009, Mexico also decriminalized all illegal drugs, although for minimum amounts. In summer of that year, the government passed a law that decriminalized small quantities of heroin, cocaine, marijuana, methamphetamine, LSD, and other drugs for personal use. Individuals caught with small amounts of these drugs will not face criminal charges anymore, and instead will be told to seek treatment. The new legislation allows users to carry 5 grams of marijuana, half grams of cocaine, 50 milligrams of heroin, 40 milligrams of methamphetamine, and 0.015 milligrams of LSD as a maximum to be considered personal use. Such thresholds are small given that drug addiction varies considerably from user to user, but still it is a first smart step to treat the drug problem as a health problem (Stevenson 2009).

International organizations and institutions are also embracing decriminalization as an effective measure that combines science and public health principles to end the draconian punishment and mass incarceration of drug prohibition. In June 2017, a joint statement by the World Health Organization and the United Nations called to end the discrimination practices in health care settings given how widespread this phenomenon is. The request included to review and repeal punitive laws such as those regulating drug use or possession of drugs for personal use because they oppose available scientific evidence and produce negative health outcomes (World Health Organization 2017; Nadelmann 2018). Clearly, this statement favors decriminalization of drugs based on a harm reduction approach because the rationale is that saving lives and providing health care should overrule legalistic and arbitrary concerns on drug prohibition.

A more specific global effort to repudiate the WOD and drug prohibition came when *The Global Commission on Drug Policy* was established in 2011. This international institution was created by a group of well-known political, economic, and cultural leaders, among them twelve former heads of state and government such as Ruth Dreifuss (former president of Switzerland), Kofi Annan (former secretary general of the UN), Fernando Henrique Cardoso (former president of Brazil), Ernesto Zedillo (former president of Mexico), César Gaviria and Juan Manuel Santos (former presidents of Colombia), among others (Global Commission on Drug Policy 2011). The first report published by this organization broke the taboo of drug control by denouncing the negative consequences of the WOD and demanding a new approach that favors public health and safety over penalties and prison. The report was a serious criticism of the WOD based on facts and evidence with a corollary that decriminalization of drugs is a viable and needed option (Global Commission on Drug Policy 2011). Given the experience and status of the Commissioners their report made the headlines of news media around the world because of its opposition to mainstream government drug policies. In the subsequent years there have been seven more reports by the Commission and in the last one from 2018, there is a call for regulation and legalization of drugs. The report addresses the implications of transitioning from illegal to legal drug markets under the auspices of the government as a viable and desirable option (Global Commission on Drug Policy 2018).

Support for decriminalization of all drugs has grown slowly but steadily across the globe in the recent years as more governments and people realize that drug prohibition is futile. Full decriminalization would be in compliance with international treaties and laws on drug control that most countries have adopted as members of the UN that prohibits legalization of drugs. If applied in America, decriminalization of all drugs would be a reasonable and practical drug policy for our times because it would contribute to tackle the most adverse outcomes of the WOD: mass incarceration, the opioid epidemic, racial disparities in the criminal justice system, and the criminalization of drug users. Decriminalization would be a reasonable and practical strategy if one takes into account that there is no conclusive evidence that any of the alleged harmful effects of decriminalization (e.g., increased crime, more drug use, massive public health care issues) have materialized in countries that adopted this policy (Global Commission on Drug Policy 2011; Nadelmann 2018).

Decriminalization of drugs seems to be a reasonable government policy that will be adopted by many countries sooner or later. Yet, one crucial issue with decriminalization is that the black market remains untouched because drugs stay illegal, and this perpetuates drug trafficking along with the unwanted activities that this problem brings. A strategic drug policy that actually would tackle the drug problem in a definitive manner is legalization of drugs. This progressive alternative has been debated for years by experts who see it as more appropriate policy than decriminalization and maybe is time to give it a chance and consider it as a serious option.

RECLASSIFICATION AND LEGALIZATION OF DRUGS

Marijuana Legalization: A No-Brainer

Legalization of marijuana in America and around the world is taking place at a speed that no one would have predicted a decade ago. Citizens and experts are witnessing that a government-driven regulatory market of marijuana has not produced the apocalyptic scenario predicted by opponents of this policy. For that reason, and because legalization reduces harm and incarceration rates, prioritizes law enforcement resources towards violent crime, and brings tax revenue, more and more local and national governments are moving toward adopting this policy. Data show that marijuana is by far the most used illegal drug worldwide, even though it has been prohibited for decades (United Nations Office on Drugs and Crime 2018). Regardless of where people stand on this political debate (against or in favor of legalization), the use of recreational marijuana (and other drugs for that matter) is part of societies' contemporary lifestyle. Understanding and accepting this truth will make it possible for governments to embrace marijuana legalization as appropriate drug policy to deal with drug use.

Perspective is important and one should bring attention to the double standards in society where alcohol is socially and publicly accepted as a normalized vice despite its health, social, economic, and criminal effects while marijuana has been prohibited and demonized. The latter does not have the potential for harm as the former, yet marijuana until recently was classified as an extremely addictive and dangerous drug which it is not accurate (Gupta 2015). Simply put, according to science and evidence marijuana is safer than alcohol (Fox, Armentano, and Tvert 2009). This does not mean that marijuana is a harmless substance, it has the potential for addiction and may cause dependency, psychosis, and other health issues in some people. But certainly it is not the reefer madness drug that the DEA and other critics argue and because of that its legalization is being embraced as an alternative solution to the WOD.

Complete legalization of marijuana will occur in America and other countries around the world in the years to come. In the United States alone (as of this writing), eleven states and the District of Columbia have already legalized marijuana for recreational purposes. Several more states are proactively working toward that goal and some of them will adopt it. Arizona, Minnesota, New Mexico, New Hampshire, New Jersey, among others, are considering legislative measures and will legalize marijuana in the short term (Drug Policy Alliance 2019). Perhaps the most revealing shift from prohibition toward legalization has been the regularization of medical marijuana in thirty-three states and four (out of five) U.S. territories. California was the first one that legalized marijuana for medical reasons in 1996, and since then gradually three dozen states have followed through the same path. The significance of this trend is how public and political support for marijuana legalization has grown over the years to the point that the medical and social benefits of marijuana are not controversial anymore for those who look at evidence-based and empirical data (Breaking the Taboo 2011; Global Commission on Drug Policy 2011; Gupta 2015).

Several countries around the world have also legalized marijuana within the past decade, among them Uruguay (the first to do so in 2013), Mexico, South Africa, and Canada. Other nations such as Spain and the Netherlands have had a de-facto legalization for a long time. Using legal loopholes, these countries allow marijuana clubs or coffee shops to dispense cannabis to members or customers legally as long as it is for personal use (Hassan 2018). Canada and Mexico are important cases because both countries neighbor the United States which still considers marijuana an addictive and dangerous substance according to federal law. Canada was the first industrialized country that adopted the complete legalization of marijuana for recreational purposes in 2018 through a legislative process. This is significant given that Canada is part of the Group of Seven (G7) advanced world economies and its decision has set a political precedent that legalization of marijuana is an acceptable policy to bring harm reduction policies as opposed to drug prohibition.

Interestingly, marijuana legalization in Mexico took place via the judicial branch rather than ballot initiatives or legislative work. Unlike the United States, to create jurisprudence is Mexico federal laws demand five consecutive rulings in different cases by the Supreme Court deciding the same legal matter with identical rulings. In 2015, drug policy activists began a strategic approach to challenge the constitutionality of the Health Code that prohibited the recreational use of marijuana. In October 2018, the Mexican Supreme Court decided the fifth case on this issue and declared the unconstitutionality of marijuana prohibition laws. The ruling set up precedent and it is now mandatory for all courts throughout the country not to block the recreational use of marijuana. To be clear, this decision did not make marijuana legal immediately, but it created a factual legalization process. It allows anyone who requests from the federal courts the right to use pot for recreational purposes to be protected against arrest and prosecution. At the end of 2018, the new Mexican government introduced a bill that will allow the commercialization of marijuana and its full legalization in 2020. This means that marijuana will be fully regulated and sold in Mexico very soon (Tallet 2018).

The path toward full marijuana legalization in the United States has also been encouraged by other political decisions that normalize this policy. By way of example, the federal government recently legalized hemp in America in a surprised bipartisan law called Farm Bill 2018. Hemp is a marijuana plant that has less than 0.3 percent of THC, meaning that it does not have any psychoactive power to make people intoxicated or stoned. Hemp is the raw material for more than 25,000 goods made out of it within a broad range of industries such as textile, food, and beauty products. Under the Controlled Substances Act (CSA), hemp was equated to heroin, cocaine, and LSD for half a century, a nonsensical categorization that resulted from the drug panic artificially created when the WOD began (Carpenter 2018).

That was not always the case since in colonial times, hemp was an essential economic crop and even the founding fathers grew the plant for economic purposes. The recent re-legalization of hemp reflects a timid but important new understanding of hemp and its agricultural value for America from the political and economic spectrum (Carpenter 2018). Such shift has also occurred regarding marijuana legalization because its commercialization and mainstream acceptance is now intertwined with capitalism. Besides benefits of harm reduction, marijuana (or *Cannabis* as it is called now) legalization has become an industry on its own and has the potential for job creation, tax revenue, and significant savings for the criminal justice system. There is potential for regulation and commerce with marijuana and for that reason pundits now call it the "Green Gold Rush" (Drug Policy Alliance 2019).

All things considered, the U.S. federal government has been left isolated in North America as the only entity that still holds a draconian prohibition legislation against marijuana. Considering that thirty-three states have medical marijuana, eleven of them allow its recreational use, and several more will adopt marijuana legalization soon, such position will be untenable in the near future. No matter which side of the marijuana legalization debate people stand for, the fact is that this progressive policy is here to stay. In the coming years, historians and politicians will look back to these days and ask themselves how come it took so many years to adopt full marijuana legalization in the United States.

Reclassification and Legalisation of Drugs

One of the reasons that marijuana is finally becoming legal and normalized is the general consensus that it is not a dangerous and addictive substance. It has some health risks of course, but the nature of marijuana is such that most people would agree to put it in a category along with tobacco and alcohol, if not less. What about drugs considered more harmful such as heroin, methamphetamine, cocaine, or hallucinogens? Should they be legalized at some point in the future? If they are, who and how would this regulatory process proceed? Should they be available to everyone or only to addicts? Will they be sold over the counter or with a doctor's prescription? What kind of regulatory processes should be adopted for those who use them? (Inciardi 2008, 286–288). These and other questions highlight the controversial notion of legalizing all drugs with few answers available so far. No country has ever adopted full legalization yet and according to experts, there are many potential risks and negative consequences that society should not dare to go this route (Inciardi 2008). However, these arguments should not discourage societies to implement gradual legalization of illegal drugs in the near future as a viable alternative.

The debate between those who support or are against drug legalization is extensive and goes from economic and political perspectives to moral, philosophical, and sociological justifications. Experts and pundits (Husak and de Marneffe 2005; Miller 1991) have spent rivers of ink on one side or the other of the spectrum to persuade people on the best approach. A simple Google search for the term "legalization of drugs" will bring millions of hits against and in favor of this policy. The most persuasive argument for legalization of all drugs is that the current approach to deal with the drug problem has failed (as clearly explained throughout this book). Not only that, such approach has caused far more damage (e.g., violence, organized crime, opioid epidemics, deaths, mass incarceration) than drugs themselves if they were legal. Therefore, the sort of potential harm that legalization of all drugs could bring will not exceed the harm already done by drug prohibition, period (Husak and de Marneffe 2005).

Also, it is naïve to continue drug prohibition when millions of people in America and around the world use illegal drugs anyway even if it is against the law (Inciardi 2008). If the criminal justice system were able to arrest and prosecute all Americans who consume illicit substances, the system would collapse. Therefore, the American criminal justice system goes only after the weakest link of those who consume or sell drugs such as the poor, disenfranchised, uneducated, and people of color, and this is another powerful argument why legalization of drugs should be a priority. The reality is that no legal system has ever managed to stop citizens from taking drugs (Hari 2016). Experts also argue that in a democratic society, the government should not infringe the right of people to put in their bodies whatever substance they want to consume whether that be sugar, fat, prescription drugs, alcohol, or heroin. The assumption being that if there is no harm caused to society or anyone except for the individual who uses the drug it should not be prohibited, or at least not criminalized (Husak and de Marneffe 2005; Miller 1991).

One significant problem regarding the legalization debate is that there is a profound ignorance of the true nature of illegal drugs and this lack of information distorts how to approach the problem. Because federal legislation has conflated all of them into the same category as dangerous and addictive drugs, most people assume they are. They are not. Based on scientific evidence, experience from experts, and those familiar with them, it is not difficult to differentiate that peyote, LSD, or marijuana are not equal to heroin or cocaine in terms of addictiveness and negative health consequences when used recreationally. However, there is not enough conclusive evidence about the consequences of recreational use of other illegal drugs such as methamphetamine or heroin to determine with accuracy how their legalization could affect people and society at large if adopted.

Regardless of who has the most convincing arguments to legalize or not drugs, the whole discussion misses the point that drug use, addiction, and dependency are quite complex problems. Politicians, pundits, and those in charge of drug control tend to have strong opinions against legalization, drug use, and addicts. More often than not, their opinion is just that, a view or judgment about these matters but rarely do empirical evidence or facts support their beliefs. This lack of knowledge has distorted the narrative on drug legalization and addiction because the debate about them and the corresponding government policies are motivated by ideological or political reasons rather than scientific data. The result has been failed government strategies disguised as well-intended measures that do not address the problem along with polarized views where stakeholders are incapable to compromise positions for the common good.

Obviously there is acceptable knowledge that heroin, methamphetamine, and cocaine are all addictive substances with potential health and personal risks for those who chronically take them. The greatest danger for users does not come from these substances themselves but from being prohibited. Drug maintenance programs and anecdotal information have shown that there can be individuals addicted to heroin and cocaine and still be functional as long as they have access to their drug of choice (Alexander 2008; Hari 2016). Even addiction to any of these three substances—methamphetamine, cocaine, and heroin—is remarkably different depending on the drug, frequency of use, dosage, route of administration and so on. In other words, the variables at stake to establish whether or not legalization of drugs will be beneficial or negative to society are complex but they can be figured out if experts, not politicians, were in charge of drug policies.

RECLASSIFICATION OF ILLEGAL DRUGS IN THE CSA

According to research and science not all illegal drugs are equal in nature, addictiveness, potential harm, and desirability from users (Alexander 2008;

Kuhn, Swartzwelder and Wilson 2014; Walton 2002). Understanding this notion about drugs is crucial to establish a depoliticized and dogma-free approach towards comprehensive drug policy reform to change the status quo. I do support the gradual legalization of most illegal drugs in America. This process should begin with a reclassification of the substances that are deemed less addictive and less harmful (according to science) such as a hallucinogens. Most hallucinogens (or psychedelics as some people call them) are still classified a Schedule I in the CSA which it does not reflect the scientific nature of them. Hallucinogens are defined as "psychoactive alkaloids that are capable of altering the cognitive functions of the brain, as well as inducing visual, auditory, olfactory, tactile, and gustatory sense-illusions" (Walton 2002, 284). Among the most common of them are peyote, psychedelic mushrooms, LSD, ayahuasca, and others. According to the message of this book I recommend that hallucinogens to be rescheduled in the CSA from their current category of Schedule I to Schedule III, to admit (as scientists now do) that they have accepted medical use, little potential for abuse, and mild to moderate risk of developing addiction.

This rescheduling will facilitate to conduct more research on hallucinogens and corroborate that they can be used to heal people. New evidence suggests the potential benefits of these substances to help people deal with depression, anxiety, PTSD, drug addiction, and other psychological issues (Sample 2017). Once they are reclassified and a new flexible legal context is available, governments at state and federal levels can begin a process for their legalization. To that extent, it is important to notice that the use of some of these hallucinogens, such as peyote and ayahuasca, are already permitted for religious purposes to Native American groups and the Union of the Plans Church (*Uniao do Vegetal* for its Portuguese name) respectively. Such exception and empirical evidence show that hallucinogens do not merit to be listed as Schedule I substances. In fact, the nature of hallucinogens is somehow similar to marijuana in terms of addictiveness, potential for abuse, dependency, and with low risk of producing psychosis, death, or serious harm (Escohotado 1999; Walton 2002).

Experts (Escohotado 1999; Walton 2002) argue that the most important variables to determine the risk of ingesting hallucinogens are set and setting. The first one refers to the mental state of the person experiencing hallucinogens. If someone is prone to violence or the opposite the substance may potentiate what is already latent in a person's head. The second relates to the circumstances surrounding the event of drug taken (e.g. quiet vs. noisy ambient, people present, their personalities, night vs. day) that may or may not influence how an individual reacts to certain hallucinogens (Kuhn, Swartzwelder, and Wilson 2014). In other words, hallucinogens like marijuana do not make people commit crimes or kill themselves, rather they may or may not potentiate and expose what it is in the head of drug takers. Of course there are other variables involved with these substances such as dosage, body type, someone guiding the experience or not, empty vs. full stomach, among others. When taking all of this into consideration, it should be clear to understand why rescheduling hallucinogens in the CSA should be a positive step to transforming American drug policy within a forward-thinking framework reflecting a twenty-first-century mindset.

As a more progressive approach is embraced at the federal level, other current illegal substances such as heroin, ecstasy, and methamphetamine should be rescheduled as well based on principles of harm reduction and a new paradigm to define and understand drug use and abuse as a public health problem. As radical as this change might look like to intransigent defenders of the WOD, it is not. The CSA was passed half a century ago under particular political, social, economic, and technological circumstances that do not exist any longer. Even though it has been amended many times to add new drugs to its catalog of prohibited substances, the essential classification of illegal drugs is obsolete, unscientific, and an obstacle to solving the American drug problem. If based on scientific evidence, harm reduction (strategies to reduce the negative implications of drug abuse), and aimed to shift the paradigm of drug use from a criminal justice issue to a public health problem, this reclassification of illegal drugs in the CSA can be legally, politically, and socially viable.

Another measure that seems more contentious on the surface but equally possible and necessary would be the gradual but total regulation of the black drug market. Rescheduling any of the most dangerous illegal drugs first (heroin, cocaine, methamphetamine, or hallucinogens) will not increase crime or drug consumption at all, rather it would create the opportunity to generate reliable scientific data to produce informed drug policy decisions in the near future. This rescheduling would also contribute to destigmatizing drug use and begin the official transition from defining the problem as a public health matter instead of a criminal one (Belenko and Spohn 2015; Hari 2016). However, re-scheduling of illegal drugs in the CSA should be understood as a small step towards a more progressive policy that is legalization of those substances to change in a beneficial way the American drug problem permanently.

THE CASE FOR DRUG LEGALIZATION

For decades, the debate on whether illegal drugs in the United States should be legalized or not has been contentious, extensive, and futile. Because of the strong opinions on both sides of the topic that rely mostly on ideological, political, and moral grounds rather than science to convey the benefits and disadvantages of such measure, it has been extremely difficult to grasp the essence of the debate. Also, there is confusion on what it means by the term 'legalization of drugs'. Often, legalization is confused with decriminalization. These two policies are similar in the sense that both promote the elimination of criminal charges against individuals arrested for possession and sale of prohibited drugs. But they also differ dramatically in the fact that decriminalization implies that all illegal drugs are still forbidden but drug users will not be punished for their use. Meanwhile, legalization refers to the context where illegal drugs are not prohibited anymore but regulated and taxed by the government and available to consumers (Inciardi 1991; Karel 1991; Nadelmann 1989).

For years, the legalization debate was understood as a utopian measure promoted by radicals and hippy-like advocates with no clear knowledge of the implications of such policy, which by the way, meant many things to different people (Walker 2015). That is not the case any longer as the legalization of marijuana has become a reality in America and other countries worldwide, the idea of regulating drugs that were prohibited in the past is becoming mainstream as a genuine alternative to the WOD. As more governments and public officials begin to recognize the futility of drug prohibition, legalization of illegal drugs is not a radical proposal anymore that under careful consideration could be gradually implemented in small steps and based on a trial and error approach.

Indeed, the legalization of drugs would be a revolutionary shift because of its implications and the fact that there is no point of reference to determine the extent to which this drug policy will change the nature of the American drug problem. There is no doubt that the change will be positive and less harmful compared to fifty years of the WOD, but there is a great deal of uncertainty about how this change would unfold. And this in itself has become a catch-22 situation because the lack of a precedent about having a regulated drug market has led those opposing this policy to anticipate an apocalyptic scenario if illegal drugs are ever legalized. Simultaneously, if governments do not dare to take the first steps to implement a gradual legalization (out of fear and hypothetical situations that may never occur), it will be impossible to realize whether or not drug legalization is a workable and optimal option.

In support of drug legalization, there are already some case studies (in Portugal and the United States) about drug liberalization that show in practice how the implementation of decriminalization and legalization of illegal drugs did not trigger the negative consequences that critics stubbornly argued would occur. As explained earlier, before Portugal decriminalized all drugs, pundits claimed that drug use and crime will increase dramatically, that the health care system will collapse, and that complete chaos will reigned due to drug decriminalization. None of these scenarios materialized but quite the opposite as multiple studies now prove that decriminalization reduced opioid overdoses, drug use, and lowered government spending associated with the criminal justice system (Ferreira 2017; Hollersen 2013). On the other hand, in the state of Colorado a report published in October of 2018 by the Colorado Division of Criminal Justice on the impacts of marijuana legalization written five years after a regulated market of this substance began to operate, showed that none of the most ominous concerns regarding legalization ever occurred. Juveniles are not smoking more pot as predicted, nor there has been a major increase in crime, and arrests for marijuana have dropped by half in a five-year period. True, there is an increase in organized crime, arrests for driving under the influence has surged, and higher rates of hospitalization for possible marijuana exposure are now common. Overall, this scientific report conducted by the government of Colorado confirms the benefits of marijuana legalization as compared to the decades-old approach of drug prohibition (Colorado Department of Public Safety 2018)

That being said, the full legalization of illegal drugs would be a more complex enterprise because of the uncertainty of the process and the controversy surrounding addictive substances such as heroin and cocaine. This, however, should not be a deterrence to embrace this new policy and instead governments should proceed with caution and small steps while learning as the legalization process unfolds. To this end, it should be clear that there is no one single path towards drug legalization but many options depending on multiple variables (Nadelmann 1989). But if alcohol and tobacco regulation are used as references to implement drug legalization in America, there will be less contentious components to implement this new drug policy paradigm. For instance, legalization will be strictly regulated regarding the sale and distribution of drugs only to adults (twenty-one years and older). Not all drugs listed as illegal in the CSA will be completely legalized. Those substances deemed by experts as extremely addictive (e.g., methamphetamine) will be decriminalized first and then allowed if needed to chronic adult drug abusers under strict medical supervision. Similar to prescription drugs, those individuals with chronic drug dependency on addictive substances could receive drugs as part of maintenance programs but in medical facilities where rehabilitation and detoxification services are available. Drugs would be distributed on pharmacies and hospitals and paid by public subsidies given that these costs will be cheaper than the current approach of drug prohibition. It is not the goal of this book to make a formal proposal on drug legalization, instead I refer to other authors such as Hari (2016), Karel (1991) and Nadelmann (1989) who have discussed at length how this legalization process can be implemented. Again, there can be multiple paths towards drug legalization and only a trial and error approach will provide the experience and knowledge to find out an efficient and effective course on this new drug policy.

A crucial component of this process would be to give states the power to create their own drug policy approaches (Walker 2015) as it has been the case with recreational marijuana. This decision will allow more creativity and innovation in the process by which the most effective and efficient trial and error approach to drug legalization could be eventually adopted by other states. For sure, there will more questions than answers because of the uncertainty of the policy and some negative consequences such as an increase in drug use, drug dependency, and crime will occur as well as other societal, economic, criminal, and political problem (Walker 2015; Inciardi 1999). Yet it is worth the effort given that the current WOD approach is obsolete and the harm it has produced by far exceeds any of the potential negative consequences that the implementation of drug legalization would generate. It is important to remember that based on science most illegal drugs are not as dangerous as they have been described in the CSA. Also, if a drug becomes legal it does not mean that everyone will rush to use and abuse it immediately and fully. In other words, if legalized, the use of most illegal drugs will not increase substantially (Hari 2016; Nadelmann 1989).

Regarding addictive drugs such as heroin, methamphetamine, and cocaine I would advocate for their legalization in a gradual and controlled process that must begin with a change in its legal categorization to move them from Schedule I to Schedule II or III in the CSA. This shift will allow these drugs to have a valid medical use but also and more importantly, scientists can request government grants and conduct research to find scientific evidence on the potential short- and long-term harm of such substances. As of today, it is this lack of evidence-based information that hampers the debate on drug legalization and the implementation of forward-thinking measures because U.S. drug policy makes it extremely difficult to receive funds and conduct experiments with substances listed as Schedule I (Baum 1996; Bertram et al. 1996).

COMPREHENSIVE REFORM OF THE DEA

There is an image that I think reflects with accuracy the current status of the DEA. This is a sculpture created by Magnús Tómasson in 1994 called *The Unknown Bureaucrat* located in downtown Reykjavik, the capital of Iceland. This is a statue of a man wearing a suit, walking somewhere with a left-hand in his pocket and a briefcase on his right hand. However, instead of a head and torso, there is a massive volcanic rock from the belly up covering his entire upper body that looks as if this person is bearing a huge load on himself (see Figure 7.1). This sculpture depicts the mundane existence of a faceless employee who seems to be just another gear in an assembly line or mechanism where he has not personal agency and performs a tedious job. I consider this statue to be the most iconic representation of a DEA agent and the agency itself because it conveys the meaning of a person or institution condemned to work each day senselessly and routinely with no direction, purpose, or mission to improve and change the world. In particular, I interpret the giant rock that covers half of the man's body to be the War on Drug mandate that politicians inculcated in this bureaucrat since the inception of its work. By analogy, the DEA and its agents execute every day a job that is meaningless, futile, and repetitive within the grand scheme of things because it does nothing to change the American drug problem at all, no matter how much work the DEA and employees do. As things stand now, the DEA is truly the American version of the unknown bureaucrat.

In view of this, the DEA has played an essential role in the crusade of drug prohibition in America as the enforcer and progenitor of the WOD for decades. Any meaningful change to drug policy must include an overhaul of this agency because its current format will not accept anything but drug prohibition. Considering how powerful the DEA's influence has been in shaping and consolidating drug control in the United States, the scope and depth of overhaul (or reform to be more appropriate) must be comprehensive. This should include, among other things, a reassessment of the mission and goals of the institution, acknowledgement that drug prohibition is a lost cause, a desire to redefine the DEA's future outside of the WOD paradigm, and willingness to downsize its operations.

I have argued in chapter 6 that the WOD shaped the DEA and this made the agency become addicted to such policy. Using the same metaphor here, the DEA must now go to rehabilitation and detoxify from the WOD, stay sober, and explore how it can keep doing its work without that addiction. This process does not mean that the DEA will disappear or become obsolete, quite the opposite. If the DEA is able to give up addiction to the WOD, it will become more meaningful to the extent that its work will confront the realities of drug use and demand in the twenty-first century with visionary policies rather than outdated approaches. Ideally this is how the detoxification process will go.

Overcoming Denial

Denial of addiction is a common attitude among drug users and is one difficult obstacle to overcome the problem. Denial refers to the decision of ignoring the truth of the addiction problem and engaging in delusion. The DEA has already experienced this denial for years by denying in absolute terms that it is addicted to the WOD and refusing to acknowledge that what the agency does is futile in addressing the American drug problem. To move beyond denial, addicts need to admit they have a dependence problem, and in this case, the DEA will have to do some self-examination to become aware of why, how, and to what extent it has been addicted to the WOD. Without this recognition, it will be impossible for the DEA to experience a substantial internal reform because any changes will be cosmetic and superficial given how dependent it is on the WOD. Therefore, as part of the recovery process, the DEA has to stop defending drug prohibition, acknowledge the damage the WOD has caused, and embrace a new drug policy model where drug use is defined as a public health concern not a crime.

Cutting Addiction to the WOD Will Be a Complex Process

Detoxification of chronic addiction is a complex and multifaceted problem that generates withdrawal effects and produces relapses as part of the rehabilitation process. The DEA will experience these symptoms from quitting the WOD such as loss of a meaningful bureaucratic life, loss of political status, a decreased budget, and deprivation of income as it gives up most, but not all, of its civil asset forfeiture operations. The effects of quitting the WOD will change the DEA's identity as the institution has been known today to become a smaller but more efficient and transparent agency with a new mandate to deal with drug trafficking and drug use. There will be immense resistance to these changes, it will take time and it will not be easy, but all of that is part of the recovering process.

Overcoming serious and long-term addictions, such as that of the DEA, is a hard challenge that requires help from experts and a detailed evaluation and stabilization process to select the most appropriate therapy. All of these measures could be done internally, but it is unlikely that the DEA will carry them out without support from outside and impartial actors. In other words, it would be extremely difficult for the DEA to detoxify from the WOD on its own. In fact, as the DEA stands today, I do not think the DEA wants to rehabilitate at all and end its addiction to the WOD because it does not believe there is anything wrong with such dependence. This attitude is not a surprise for those familiar with the nature of chronic addiction. More often than not, drug addicts are incapable of imagining life without their drugs of choice and may consider it is not worth the effort. Similarly, nearly five decades of addiction to the WOD is a great deal of dependence and the DEA is unable to realize the damage caused by the WOD to itself and the need to change course.

Consequently, the transformation of the DEA will not come from within, but when the millennial generation begins to fill out positions of power in it. As baby boomers and senior officials move to retirement, their old-fashioned mentality of drug prohibition will go away, too. There will be space then for new ideas and forward-thinking to address the needs of twenty-first-century problems using more efficient and effective tools. It is a matter of time and the tide of change regarding drug policy, drug legalization, and embracing harm reduction is inexorable. In the same way, a few years ago it seemed impossible that same-sex couples would ever have the opportunity to get married. Sooner rather than later, marijuana legalization and full drug decriminalization will be normalized and the DEA will be on board taking care of the regulatory process at the federal level while conducting operations against drug trafficking. Black market will still exist, but with a new mandate the DEA will have experts and scientists in charge of the decision-making process regarding regulation and the best law enforcement practices based on harm reduction. Empirical knowledge and evidence-based information will be crucial tools to decision-making processes and experts, not politicians, will be in charge of deciding the most important drug policies. Law enforcement will only be a last resort and minor component of the institution because drug trafficking and addiction will be defined as a multidimensional phenomenon.

FINAL THOUGHTS: DRUG TRAFFICKING AS A MULTIDIMENSIONAL PHENOMENON

A notion that has been emphasized throughout this book is the fact that drug trafficking is much more than just a criminal justice problem as most American politicians, DEA agents, and public officials assume it to be. Such idea is a narrow-minded perspective that reflects the mentality of drug prohibition but ignores the complex nature of the illicit drug trade. A negative effect of this position has been framing drug trafficking within an "us vs. them" narrative that oversimplifies the issue while demonizing anyone who is part of it. Perhaps the most harmful outcome is the inability of those in charge of executing drug laws (police, prosecutors, judges and so on) to see beyond this tunnel vision assumption and therefore it misses to recognize drug trafficking as a multidimensional phenomenon.

Yes indeed, drug trafficking is a crime issue, but it is also a political, economic, social, cultural, and ideological matter. This is the case because U.S. drug policy made by lawmakers (political dimension) has shaped drug trafficking (the WOD is an obvious example). Smuggling, selling drugs, money laundering and investing the proceeds of the drug trade in the legal market are profitable activities (economic dimension). Poverty, unemployment, and lack of opportunities are variables correlated with an increase of drug trafficking (social dimension) while narcoculture and its ramifications have created an identity for many drug traffickers (cultural dimension). Finally, religious beliefs and political dogmas have influenced how society defines and criminalizes drug use and addiction (ideological dimension). Altogether these phenomena explain why drug trafficking is a complicated and interconnected phenomenon that cannot be tackled if only one of its components (the criminal one) is addressed.

A new perspective to define drug trafficking from a criminal to a multifaceted issue is a difficult paradigm shift for believers of drug prohibition because it implies that the answer to the problem must be found beyond incarceration and punishment. Without this acknowledgement, the current situation of the WOD will continue indefinitely as it has been the case in the past fifty years. Understanding drug trafficking as a multidimensional phenomenon means that governments must prioritize strategies and policies to deal with the underlying social, economic, and political causes that contribute to and worsen this problem. Economic inequality, poverty, unemployment, political corruption, lack of social mobility, and poor governance are some of the most crucial societal problems correlated with the prevalence of drug trafficking activities.

In all countries where most illegal drugs are planted, harvested, processed, and exported to consumer markets there are similar economic, social, and political conditions. Whether it is cocaine in the Andes, heroin in Afghanistan and Mexico, or hashish (a potent marijuana resin) in Morocco, farmers and peasants in charge of producing these drugs are mostly poor, living in precarious conditions, with no access to education, and under corrupt or authoritarian political systems. Research and experts (McCoy 2003; Muehlmann 2014; Wainwright 2016, 9–27; United Nations Office on Drugs and Crime 2018) have shown that the majority of individuals who resort to drug production and drug trafficking are motivated by self-preservation to make ends meet, not to become rich or be the next kingpin villain. In fact, this trend is a prominent feature of all organized crime because this activity appears and thrives where the government is weak or nonexistent, where there is economic deprivation, ineffective social development, and high unemployment (Shaw and Reitano 2013; Wainwright 2016).

Yes, there will always be drug lords or kingpins who reap the benefits of the illegal drug trade to enrich themselves (even if drug legalization is fully introduced), but they are a tiny minority who normally pay a high price for their criminal activities with premature death or long-term imprisonment. Most individuals involved in the labor-intensive chain that is drug trafficking are there to earn a living and survive. Consequently, as long as the social and economic conditions that push people to resort to drug trafficking are not changed, this activity will never be realistically tackled. Thus, looking at the social and economic context where drugs are produced and exported in impoverished communities in the mountains of Mexico, Colombia, and Afghanistan, there is an evident pattern. These communities have long suffered from chronic underdevelopment, extreme poverty, lack of employment, and rampant dispossession.

U.S. drug policy has favored spending billions of dollars in law enforcement and military aid through foreign aid programs such as Plan Colombia and the Merida Initiative to combat drug trafficking organizations (Linthicum 2018). Such approach is unsustainable and ineffective, and there is evidence to prove it. Despite billions of dollars spent in anti-narcotics operations in Colombia, cocaine smuggling to the United States and demand has increased recently as noted earlier (United Nations Office on Drugs and Crime 2018). This adds on to the arguments put forward throughout this book that drug prohibition and the WOD have not addressed the American drug problem. They never will. Instead, anti-narcotics policies and programs must focus on the social, economic, and educational needs of people living in communities where drugs are produced. If poor farmers are able to make a living harvesting legal crops and have access to basic social services, education, and job opportunities, the likelihood that they will join the ranks of drug trafficking will decline considerably (Wainwright 2016).

The challenge is to realize that the illegal drug trade is multifaceted in essence, and if governments design strategies to address all the components of the problem, it will reduce it to a minimum and manageable scale. There are no "one-size-fits-all" strategies and every government and situation will have to be addressed on a case-by-case basis. However, there must be consensus between countries and solve this issue as a collective approach rather than single governments attempting to solve it on their own. They have not and they will not because drug trafficking is a transnational phenomenon that ignores borders and nationalisms. A common approach is necessary to decide a new drug policy but when applied at the local level it should be the community that decides who to deal with the practical issues. Thus, what works for the United States to deal with poverty, unemployment, and social dislocations in inner-city neighborhoods in Chicago or Baltimore, where drug dealing occurs, will not work for Mexico. What might work for Mexico providing jobs and crop subsidies to farmers in Guerrero and Sinaloa states to switch from poppy plant production to legal crops will probably not work for Afghanistan or Colombia. With some consensus, every country, city, and local government will have to develop and adapt their own processes to confront and set up official policies and strategies to deal with drug trafficking but also understand the problems as a multidimensional phenomenon and defining a unified progressive drug policy for the twenty-first century.

The American drug problem (and drug trafficking) can only be managed but never eradicated, given that drug use has been and will always be part of the human condition. Setting aside the politics, ideology, and moralistic arguments that people attach to drugs and their consumption, it is possible to get perspective and see drug trafficking more fairly and objectively. This fairness and objectivity are critical to deal with a problem that has become central for the nation-state in the twentieth and twenty-first centuries, not due to the problem itself but because how it has been defined and interpreted. As new global challenges (e.g., climate change, extreme inequality, forced migrations, cyclical economic crises, and epidemics) put unprecedented stress on governments at all levels, there is more interest to redefine priorities. Among them, there is growing consensus that the American drug problem demands a whole new interpretation using evidence-based data rather than the same and old formula of punishment and prison. The implication is that public officials must face the truth and engage in decision-making processes where ideologies, politics, and morality are not anymore the primary incentives to shape drug policies. This perhaps will allow politicians and pundits to comprehend the conclusion that Friedrich Nietzsche reached more than 130 years ago: "There is no such thing as moral phenomena, but only a moral interpretation of phenomena." I sincerely hope this is the case for the greater good in the United States and the rest of the world.

Glossary

Narco-*bloqueo*: a blockade by drug gangs on a major street or avenue using cars, trucks, or tractor-trailers that have been carjacked in order to disrupt law enforcement responses to crime activities.

Narco-cinema: films, documentaries, and TV series that depict narcoculture and drug trafficking stories where drug lords and their exploits are the main protagonists.

Narco-*dólares*: remittances or dollars that are the product of drug trafficking activities.

Narco-economy: an economic activity that creates wealth, usually at the local level from drug trafficking activities.

Narco-*elecciones*: when drug traffickers intervene in local or state elections through different means (e.g., corruption, violence, killing candidates, instilling fear, or suppressing voter turnout) to favor a candidate or political party that has been co-opted by organized crime.

Narco-*fiestas*: lavish parties thrown by drug traffickers featuring drug use, prostitutes, and famous narco-corrido bands or singers to celebrate special festivities.

Narco-*gobierno*: local or regional government where drug traffickers have become public officials or vice versa.

Narco-*insurgencia*: narco-insurgency, meaning the theoretical assumption that some drug trafficking organizations can overrun the democratic government locally, regionally, or nationally and become a parallel de facto power.

Narco-*inteligencia*: cartel's high-level espionage against rivals and targets.

Narco-literature: a new genre of fiction that details drug trafficking characters and exploits of the illicit drug trade.

Narco-*mensaje*: a hand-written drug message, usually with misspellings, left with dead bodies explaining why those people died and usually including a verbal threat to rivals.

Narco-saints: religious figures and images such as Jesus Malverde or the Grim Reaper (La Santa Muerte) allegedly worshipped by drug traffickers.

Narco-state: territory or government where official institutions have been infiltrated and compromised by drug trafficking organizations.

Narco-submarines: sophisticated custom-made submersible vessels built by drug traffickers and used to smuggle large quantities of cocaine.

Narco-telenovelas: television soap operas where the story and script are inspired by drug trafficking organizations or based on famous drug lords or fictional characters.

Narco-*tienda*: location in a neighborhood or area where drugs are sold to the public openly.

Narco-*tumbas*: expensive and elaborate tombs in cemeteries where dead drug lords are buried.

Narco-*túnel*: a drug smuggling tunnel along the Mexico-U.S. border.

Narco-videos: homemade videos using cellphone technology and posted on the internet featuring the torture, confession, and killing of rivals or announcing cartel's operations.

Narco-*violencia*: the use of violence by drug traffickers that can be characterized by the presence of high-caliber weapons, gruesome details, multiple victims (although not always), and employing public spaces to send a message. Another synonym for this type of violence is narco-killings.

Narco-wives: spouses or partners of famous drug lords.

Comando: a group of hitmen or assassins driving large pickup trucks or armored SUVs around a location or jurisdiction on the verge of conducting criminal activities on behalf of a drug trafficking organization or cell.

Descabezado: a decapitated dead body left on a public space, usually with a narco-message on the side meant to explain why that person died or left as a threat to rivals or public officials.

Descuartizado: a dismembered body left in a cooler, a bag, or just by itself exposed in a public space, usually with a narco-message on the side.

Encajuelado: from the word *cajuela* (car trunk) meaning body stuffed in a car trunk.

Encobijado: from the word *cobija* (blanket) in Spanish meaning body wrapped in a blanket.

Entambado: from the word *tambo* (metal oil barrel), meaning dead bodies squeezed into a 55-gallon metal drum.

Enteipado: from the word tape in English, meaning to wrap up a human body with packing tape before torturing and killing the person. Another synonym of this word is *encintados*, from the term *cinta* (tape in Spanish).

Halconear: from the word *halcón* (hawk) meaning an individual working for a criminal gang as a lookout.

La maña: another name to identify organized crime, a drug trafficker, or a drug cartel member.

La última letra: literally means the last letter of the alphabet, and it refers to the Los Zetas organization and subsequent fractions that developed a fearsome reputation for gruesome and savage violence against rivals and civilians.

Plaza: from the word *plaza* (public square or shopping center) meaning the drug corridor or territory controlled by a cartel in collusion with public officials.

Plomear: from the word *plomo* (lead) meaning to shoot bullets with a handgun or to kill someone with a bullet.

Poner el dedo: to rat someone out or to snitch on someone.

Rafaguear: to fire a burst with an automatic rifle like an AK 47 to one or more individuals in a public area such as a street intersection or sidewalk, meant to kill people.

Tabique: literally brick, but meaning marijuana compressed like a cinder block for trafficking large quantities for easier handling.

Selected Bibliography

Aaronson, Trevor. 2018. "Welcome to Law Enforcement's "Dark Side": Secret Evidence, Illegal Searches, and Dubious Traffic Stops." *The Intercept*, January 9, 2018. https://theintercept.com/2018/01/09/dark-side-fbi-dea-illegal-searches-secret-evidence/.

Aguilar, Andrea, Vicente Castellanos and Gabriel Pérez. 2013. "Formas de definición y presentación en el 'Corrido Alterado.'" In *La producción del conocimiento en las ciencias de la comunicación y su incidencia social*, edited by Andre Aguilar, Vicente Castellanos, and Gabriel Pérez, 326–349. México: Universidad Autónoma de Coahuila, Facultad de Ciencias de la Comunicación.

Aguilar Valenzuela, Rubén and Jorge G. Castañeda. 2012. *Los saldos del narco: el fracaso de una guerra*. México, DF: Editorial Punto de Lectura.

Ahmed, Azam and Nicole Perlroth. 2017. "Using Texts as Lures, Government Spyware Targets Mexican Journalists and Their Families." *The New York Times*, June 19, 2017. https://www.nytimes.com/2017/06/19/world/americas/mexico-spyware-anticrime.html.

Albarrán Torres, César. 2017. "Why Glamorising Narco Culture, On Screen and in Sydney's Pop-up Shop, is Wrong." *The Conversation*, April 10, 2017. https://theconversation.com/why-glamorising-narco-culture-on-screen-and-in-sydneys-pop-up-shop-is-wrong-75851.

Albertson, Dean. 1950. "Puritan Liquor in the Planting of New England." *The New England Quarterly* 23, No. 4 (December): 477–490.

Alexander, Bruce K. 2008. *The Globalization of Addiction: A Study in Poverty of the Spirit*. New York, NY: Oxford University Press.

Alexander, Michelle. 2012. *The New Jim Crow: Mass Incarceration in the Age of Colorblindness*. New York, NY: The New Press.

Allyn, Bobby. 2019. "Judge Rules Planned Supervised Injection Site Does Not Violate Federal Drug Laws." *National Public Radio*, October 2, 2019. https://www.npr.org/2019/10/02/766500743/judge-rules-plan-for-safehouse-drug-injection-site-in-philadelphia-can-go-forwar.

Andreas, Peter. 2013. *Smuggler Nation: How Illicit Trade Made America*. New York, NY: Oxford University Press.

Ángel, Arturo. 2019. "Nuevo récord de violencia en enero: 2 mil 928 homicidios y 164 víctimas de secuestro." *Animal Político*, February 20, 2019. https://www.animalpolitico.com/2019/02/violencia-enero-record-homicidios-secuestros/.

Anslinger, Harry J. 1937. "Marijuana, Assassin of Youth." *The American Magazine*, July, 1937, 124, No. 1: 18. https://www.redhousebooks.com/galleries/assassin.htm.

Arnaut Estrada, Alberto. 2018. *Hasta los dientes*. DVD. Directed by Alberto Arnaut Estrada. México, DF: Instituto Mexicano de Cinematografía.

Artículo 19. 2018. "389 agresiones de enero a julio de 2018: autoridades permiten impunidad y aumento de violencia." *Artículo 19*, November 2, 2018. https://articulo19.org/autoridades-permiten-impunidad-y-aumento-de-agresiones-contra-la-prensa/.

———. 2017. "Periodistas asesinados en México." *Articulo 19*, August 23, 2017. https://articulo19.org/periodistasasesinados/.

Asociación de Academias de la Lengua Española. 2015. *Diccionario de Americanismos*. Academia de la Lengua Española. Barcelona: Penguin Random House Grupo Editorial.

Associated Press. 2018. "No Coke, No Pepsi: Bottlers Leave Southern Mexican City Besieged By Crime." *Los Angeles Times*, June 14, 2018. https://www.latimes.com/world/la-fg-mexico-gang-violence-soda-20180614-story.html.

Astorga, Luis. 2016. *El siglo de las drogas: Del Porfirato al nuevo milenio*. México, DF: Debolsillo.

———. 2015. *Drogas sin fronteras*. México, DF: Debolsillo.

———. 1995. *Mitología del "narcotraficante" en México*. México, DF: Plaza y Valdéz.

Balderrama, Francisco E. and Raymond Rodríguez. 2006. *Decade of Betrayal: Mexican Repatriation in the 1930s*. Albuquerque: University of New Mexico Press.

Barabas. 2018. "Fantasy: Decorative Print Shirt." *Barabas*. Accessed May 23, 2018. https://barabasmen.com/products/fantasy-shirt-blue.

Bates, Daniel G. and Elliot M. Fratkin. 2003. *Cultural Anthropology*. 3rd edition. London, UK: Pearson.

Baum, Dan. 1996. *Smoke and Mirrors: The War on Drugs and the Politics of Failure*. New York, NY: Little, Brown and Company.

Belenko, Steven and Cassia Spohn. 2015. *Drugs, Crime, and Justice*. Thousand Oaks, CA: Sage Publications, Inc.

Benavie, Arthur. 2009. *Drugs: America's Holy War*. New York, NY: Routledge.

Bender, Steven W. 2012. *Run for the Border: Vice and Virtue in the U.S.-Mexico Border Crossings*. New York, NY: New York University Press.

Bergen-Cico, Dessa K. 2012. *War and Drugs: The Role of Military Conflict in the Development of Substance Abuse*. Boulder, CO: Paradigm Publishers.

Berke, Jeremy. 2016. "The DEA Made a Big Decision On Marijuana, but it Wasn't the One Everyone Was Hoping For." *Business Insider*, August 11, 2016. https://www.businessinsider.com/dea-refuses-to-reclassify-marijuana-2016-8.

Berke, Richard L. 1989. "Agents Accused: The Drug Fight's Dark Side: Corruption in Drug Agency Called Crippler of Inquiries and Morale." Special Report. *The New*

York Times, December 17, 1989. https://www.nytimes.com/1989/12/17/us/agents-accused-drug-fight-s-dark-side-special-report-corruption-drug-agency.html.

Bertram, Eva, Morris Blachman, Kenneth Sharpe, and Peter Andreas. 1996. *Drug War Politics: The Price of Denial*. Berkeley, CA: University of California Press.

Black's Law Dictionary. 2009. *Drug Trafficking*. Bryan A. Garner (ed.), Ninth edition. St. Paul, MN: West Publishing.

Blancornelas, Jesús. 2006. *El Cártel: Los Arellano Felix: La mafia más poderosa en la historia de América Latina*. México, DF: Random House Mondadori.

Blog del Narco. 2018. "Narco-language." *Blog the Narco*. Accessed June 20, 2018. https://elblogdelnarco.com/.

Boullosa, Carmen and Mike Wallace. 2016. *A Narco History: How the United States and Mexico Jointly Created the "Mexican Drug War."* New York, NY: OR Books.

Breaking the Taboo. 2011. Directed by Feilding Mellen, Cosmo and Andrade, Fernando. Espaco Filmes and TVF International.

Brecher, Edward M. 1970. *Licit & Illicit Drugs: The Consumers Union Report on Narcotics, Stimulants, Depressants, Inhalants, Hallucinogens, & Marijuana—Including Caffeine, Nicotine, and Alcohol*. Mount Vernon, NY: The Consumers Union Report.

Bump, Philip. 2019. "Want to Know Where Most Drugs Cross the Border? Look at the Border Patrol's News Releases." *The Washington Post*, February 1, 2019.

Bunker, Robert J. 2016. *Blood Sacrifices: Violent Non-State Actors and Dark Magico-Religious Activities*. Bloomington, IN: iUniverse Publications.

Campbell, Howard. 2009. *Drug War Zone: Frontline Dispatches from the Streets of El Paso and Juárez*. Austin, TX: University of Texas Press.

Canudas-Romo, Vladimir, José Manuel Aburto, Víctor M. García Guerrero, and Hiram Beltrán-Sánchez. 2017. "Mexico's Epidemic of Violence and its Public Health Significance on Average Length of Life." *Journal of Epidemiology & Community Health* 71, No. 2: 188–193.

Carey, Elaine. 2009. "'Selling is More of a Habit than Using'" Narcotraficante Lola la Chata and Her Threat to Civilization, 1930–1960." *Journal of Women's History* 21, No. 2: 62–89.

Carlsen, Laura. 2018. "Effects of Militarization in the Name of Counter-Narcotics Efforts and Consequences for Human Rights in Mexico." In *Beyond the Drug War in Mexico: Human Rights, the Public Sphere and Justice*, edited by Wil G. Pansters, Benjamin T. Smith, and Peter Watt, 76–94. New York, NY: Routledge.

Carpenter, David. 2018. "Legal Hemp in 2019 May Be a Boon For Stressed Out American Farmers." *Forbes*, December 20, 2018. https://www.forbes.com/sites/davidcarpenter/2018/12/20/legal-hemp-in-2019-may-be-a-boon-for-stressed-out-american-farmers/#625fb0be8f3b.

Carrazco Araigaza, Jorge. 2015. "En México Circulan 25 Millones de armas Ilegales." *Proceso*, June 2, 2015. https://www.proceso.com.mx/406115/en-mexico-circulan-25-millones-de-armas-ilegales.

Carrol, Rory. 2010. "Mexican Newspaper Asks Drug Cartels How To Prevent Its Staff Being Murdered." *The Guardian*, September 20, 2010. https://www.theguardian.com/world/2010/sep/20/mexican-newspaper-drugs-staff-murdered.

Casey, Edward S. and Mary Watkins. 2014. *Up Against the Wall: Re-Imagining the U.S.-Mexico Border*. Austin, TX: University of Texas Press.

Centers for Disease Control and Prevention. 2018. "U.S. Drug Overdose Deaths Continue to Rise; Increase Fueled by Synthetic Opioids." *Centers for Disease Control and Prevention*, March 29, 2018. https://www.cdc.gov/media/releases/2018/p0329-drug-overdose-deaths.html.

Central Intelligence Agency. 2017. "Illicit Drugs." The World Factbook. *Central Intelligence Agency*, May 15, 2017. https://www.cia.gov/library/publications/the-world-factbook/fields/2086.html.

Chasin, Alexandra. 2016. *Assassin of Youth: A Kaleidoscopic History of Harry J. Anslinger's War on Drugs*. Chicago: University of Chicago Press.

Chesnut, Andrew R. 2012. *Devoted to Death: Santa Muerte, The Skeleton Saint*. New York, NY: Oxford University Press.

Colorado Department of Public Safety. 2018. "Impacts on Marijuana Legalization in Colorado." *Colorado Division of Criminal Justice*, October 26, 2018. https://www.colorado.gov/pacific/publicsafety/news/colorado-division-criminal-justice-publishes-report-impacts-marijuana-legalization-colorado.

Correa-Cabrera, Guadalupe. 2017. *Los Zetas Inc.: Criminal Corporations, Energy, and Civil War in Mexico*. Austin, TX: University of Texas Press.

Coyne, Christopher J. and Abigail R. Hall. 2017. "Four Decades and Counting: The Continued Failure of the War on Drugs." *Cato Institute*, April 12, 2017. Policy Analysis No. 811.

Cronkite, Walter. 1971. *Eye on the World*. Colorado: Cowles Books Company.

Davidow, Jeffrey. 2004. *The U.S. and Mexico: The Bear and the Porcupine*. Princeton, NJ: Markus Wiener Publishers.

Debusmann, Bernd. 2009. "Among Top U.S. Fears: A Failed Mexican State." *The New York Times*, January 9, 2009. http://www.nytimes.com/2009/01/09/world/americas/09iht-letter.1.19217792.html.

Decker, Scott H. and Margaret Townsend Chapman. 2008. *Drug Smugglers on Drug Smuggling: Lessons from the Inside*. Philadelphia: Temple University Press.

Deibert, Michael. 2015. *In the Shadow of Saint Death: The Gulf Cartel and the Price of America's Drug War in Mexico*. Lanham, MD: Lyons Press.

De Mauleón, Hector. 2010. *Marca de sangre: Los años de la delincuencia organizada*. México, DF: Editorial Planeta Mexicana.

———. 2017a. "CJNG: el gran ganador de la Guerra contra el narco." *El Universal*, March 3, 2017. http://www.eluniversal.com.mx/entrada-de-opinion/columna/hector-de-mauleon/nacion/2017/03/6/cjng-el-gran-ganador-de-la-guerra.

———. 2017b. "Las zonas silenciadas en México." *El Universal*, August 29, 2017. http://www.eluniversal.com.mx/columna/hector-de-mauleon/nacion/las-zonas-silenciadas-de-mexico.

Department of Justice. 2019. "Drug Enforcement Administration Special Agent Convicted of Perjury, Obstruction of Justice and Falsification of Government Records." *Office of Public Affairs*, August 28, 2019. https://www.justice.gov/opa/pr/drug-enforcement-administration-special-agent-convicted-perjury-obstruction-justice-and.

Devereaux, Ryan. 2015. "Ghosts of Iguala. Mexico: How 43 Students Disappeared in the Night." *The Intercept*, May 4, 2015. https://theintercept.com/2015/05/04/how-43-students-disappeared-in-mexico-part-1/.

Dewan, Shaila. 2019. "A Growing Chorus of Big City Prosecutors Say No to Marijuana Convictions." *The New York Times*, January 29, 2019. https://www.nytimes.com/2019/01/29/us/baltimore-marijuana-possession.html.

Drake, David. 2012. "Real Trap Sh*t? The Commodification of Southern Rap's Drug-Fueled Subgenre." *Complex Music*, October 9, 2012. https://web.archive.org/web/20121013035755/http://www.complex.com/music/2012/10/real-trap-sht-the-commodification-of-southern-raps-drug-fueled-subgenre/page/1.

Drug Enforcement Administration. 2019. "DEA History." *U.S. Department of Justice*. Accessed January 16, 2019. https://www.dea.gov/history.

———. 2018. "2018 Drug National Threat Assessment." *U.S. Department of Justice*. Accessed January 28, 2019. https://www.dea.gov/sites/default/files/2018-11/DIR-032-18%202018%20NDTA%20final%20low%20resolution.pdf.

———. 2017. "2017 National Drug Threat Assessment Summary." *U.S. Department of Justice*. Accessed December 20, 2017. https://www.dea.gov/docs/DIR-040-17_2017-NDTA.pdf.

———. 2016. "DEA Announces Actions Related To Marijuana and Industrial Hemp." *U.S. Department of Justice*, August 11, 2016. https://www.dea.gov/press-releases/2016/08/11/dea-announces-actions-related-marijuana-and-industrial-hemp.

Drug Policy Alliance. 2019. "Issues." Accessed April 15, 2019. http://www.drugpolicy.org/issues.

———. 2014. "The DEA: Four Decades of Impeding And Rejecting Science." *Drug Policy Alliance*, June 8, 2014. http://www.drugpolicy.org/resource/dea-four-decades-impeding-and-rejecting-science.

Drugs, Inc. 2014. "Season 6." *National Geographic Channel*. Wall to Wall Media Ltd.

Edberg, Mark C. 2004. *El Narcotraficante: Narcocorridos & the Construction of a Cultural Persona on the U.S.-Mexico Border*. Austin, TX: University of Texas Press.

Ell, Kellie. 2018. "Ex-DEA Agent Turned Pot Venture Capitalist: Legalizing Marijuana is Good for the Economy." *CNBC*, January 11, 2018. https://www.cnbc.com/2018/01/11/ex-dea-agent-now-a-venture-capitalist-legal-marijuana-good-policy.html.

El Paso Intelligence Center. 2011. "Language of the Cartel: Narco Terminology, Identifiers, and Clothing Style." *Drug Enforcement Administration*, January 28, 2011. https://publicintelligence.net/ules-lulzsec-release-epic-language-of-the-cartels-narco-terminology-report/.

El Universal Data. 2015. "Desaparecidos." *El Universal*, 2015. Accessed August 27, 2017. http://interactivo.eluniversal.com.mx/desaparecidos/index.html.

———. 2019. "Liberan a 24 detenidos por caso Ayotzinapa, denuncia Alejandro Encinas." *El Universal*, September 15, 2019. https://www.eluniversal.com.mx/nacion/liberan-24-detenidos-por-caso-ayotzinapa-denuncia-alejandro-encinas.

Enciso, Froylán. 2015. *Nuestra historia narcótica: Pasajes para (re)legalizar las drogas en México*. México, DF Debate.

Epstein, David. 2016. "How DEA Agents Took Down Mexico's Most Vicious Drug Cartel." *The Atlantic*, January, 2016. https://www.theatlantic.com/magazine/archive/2016/01/drug-enforcement-agency-mexico-drug-cartel/419100/.

Escohotado, Antonio. 1999. *A Brief History of Drugs: From the Stone Age to the Stoned Aged*. Rochester, VT: Park Street Press.

Esquivel, J. Jesús. 2013. *La DEA en Mexico: Una Historia oculta del narcotráfico contada por los agentes*. México, DF: Grijalbo.

Equipo Argentino de Antropología Forense. 2015. "Documento inicial sobre investigaciones en el basurero de Cocula y Rio San Juan." *Press Released by Equipo Argentino de Antropología Forense,* February 7, 2015. http://www.eaaf.org/files/comunicado-eaaf_7feb2015.pdf.

Fagen, Richard R. 1977. "The Realities of U.S.-Mexican Relations." *Foreign Affairs*, July issue. The Council on Foreign Relations.

Federal Bureau of Investigations—FBI. 2019. "2018 Crime in the United States." *Uniform Crime Report*, September 30, 2019. https://ucr.fbi.gov/crime-in-the-u.s/2018/crime-in-the-u.s.-2018.

Fernández Menéndez, Jorge. 2018. *La noche de Iguala: secuestro, asesinato y narcotráfico en Guerrero*. Ciudad de México: Cal y Arena editores.

Fernández Menéndez, Jorge and Victor Ronquillo. 2006. *De los Maras a los Zetas: Los Secretos del Narcotráfico, de Colombia a Chicago*. México, DF: Grijalbo.

Ferreira, Susana. 2017. "Portugal's Radical Drugs Policy is Working. Why Hasn't the World Copied It?" *The Guardian*, December 5, 2017. https://www.theguardian.com/news/2017/dec/05/portugals-radical-drugs-policy-is-working-why-hasnt-the-world-copied-it.

Ferri Tortola, Pablo. 2014. "Testigo revela ejecuciones en el Estado de México." *Esquire*, September, 2014. http://www.esquirelat.com/reportajes/14/09/17/esxclusiva-esquire-Testigo-revela-ejecuciones-ejercito/.

Fieldstadt, Elisha. 2018. "Chicago DEA Agent Accused of Helping Dangerous Puerto Rico-based Drug Cartel." *NBC News*, December 20, 2018. https://www.nbcnews.com/news/us-news/chicago-dea-agent-accused-helping-dangerous-puerto-rico-based-drug-n950476.

Finnegan, William. 2010. "Letter from Mexico: Silver or Lead. A Drug Cartel's Reign of Terror." *The New Yorker*, May 31, 2010.

Former DEA Agent. 2019. "Conversations on the DEA and Written Feedback." *Personal Communication*. South Texas, USA.

Fox, Steve, Paul Armentano, and Mason Tvert. 2009. *Marijuana Is Safer: So Why Are We Driving People to Drink?* White River Junction, VT: Chelsea Green Publishing Co.

Frakt, Austin. 2016. "Politics Are Tricky but Science Is Clear: Needle Exchanges Work." *The New York Times*, September 5, 2018. https://www.nytimes.com/2016/09/05/upshot/politics-are-tricky-but-science-is-clear-needle-exchanges-work.html.

Gallegos, Zorayda. 2016. "El Cártel Jalisco Nueva Generación extiende su poder en territorio michoacano." *El Pais*, August 1, 2016. http://internacional.elpais.com/internacional/2016/08/02/mexico/1470089060_891176.html.

García Palafox, Galia. 2011. "Movimiento Alterado: Más allá del narcocorrido." *Vanguardia*, December 22, 2011. https://www.vanguardia.com.mx/movimiento alteradomasalladelnarcocorrido-1177464.html.

Gelder, Ken. 2007. *Subcultures: Cultural Theories and Social Practices*. New York, NY: Routledge.

Gibler, John. 2011. *To Die in Mexico: Dispatches from Inside the Drug War*. San Francisco: City Light Books.

———. 2015. "The Disappeared: The Story of September 26, 2014, the Day 43 Mexican Students Went Missing — And How it Might be a Turning Point for the Country." *The California Sunday Magazine*, January, 2015. https://stories.californi asunday.com/2015-01-04/mexico-the-disappeared-en/.

Gladwell, Malcolm. 2019. "Is Marijuana As Safe As We Think?" *The New Yorker*, January 14, 2019. https://www.newyorker.com/magazine/2019/01/14/is-mariju ana-as-safe-as-we-think.

Global Commission on Drug Policy. 2011. "The War on Drugs Report." *Global Commission on Drug Policy*, 2011. http://www.globalcommissionondrugs.org/reports/ the-war-on-drugs.

———. 2018. "Regulation: The Responsible Control of Drugs Report." *Global Commission on Drug Policy*, 2018. http://www.globalcommissionondrugs.org/reports/ regulation-the-responsible-control-of-drugs.

Global Financial Integrity. 2017. "Transnational Crime and the Developing World." *Global Financial Integrity*, March, 2017. https://www.gfintegrity.org/wp-content/ uploads/2017/03/Transnational_Crime-final.pdf.

Goldman, Francisco. 2016. "The Missing Forty-Three: The Mexican Government Sabotages Its Own Independent Investigation." *The New Yorker*, April 22, 2016. http://www.newyorker.com/news/news-desk/the-missing-forty-three-the-mexican -government-sabotages-its-own-independent-investigation.

González Flores, Luis A. 2013. "El Movimiento Alterado se cansa de la violencia." *Animal Político*, February 22, 2013. https://www.animalpolitico.com/2013/02/e l-movimiento-alterado-se-cansa-de-la-violencia/.

González Rodríguez, Sergio. 2015. *Los 43 de Iguala. México: verdad y reto de los estudiantes desaparecidos*. Ciudad de México: Anagrama.

Goodman, Joshua and Jim Mustian. 2019. "Feds Say 'Star' DEA Agent Abroad Stole Millions." *Associated Press*, January 15, 2019. https://www.apnews.com/7bbc491 56a7e47e6a1f6b3a37946ee12.

Grayson, George W. 2012. *La Familia Drug Cartel: Implications for U.S.-Mexican Security*. Carlisle, PA: Strategic Studies Institute.

Grillo, Ioan. 2019. "El Chapo's Conviction Isn't Enough." *The New York Times*, February 12, 2019. https://www.nytimes.com/2019/02/12/opinion/el-chapo-ver dict-conviction.html.

———. 2016. "In Mexico, Narco Films vs. Narco Reality." *The New York Times*, July 23, 2016. https://www.nytimes.com/2016/07/24/opinion/sunday/in-mexico-narco-films-vs-narco-reality.html.

———. 2011. *El Narco: Inside's Mexico Criminal Insurgency*. New York: Bloomsbury Press.

Guerra-Doce, Elisa. 2015. "Psychoactive Substances in Prehistoric Times: Examining the Archaeological Evidence." *The Journal of Archaeology, Consciousness and Culture* 8, No. 1: 91–112.

Guillen, Alejandra, Mago Torres, and Marcera Turati. 2018. "2,000 Clandestine Graves: How a Decade of the Drug War Turned Mexico Into a Burial Ground." *The Intercept*, December 13, 2018. https://theintercept.com/2018/12/13/mexico-drug-war-mass-graves/.

Gupta, Sanjay. 2015. "It's Time for a Medical Marijuana Revolution." *CNN*, April 20, 2015. https://www.cnn.com/2015/04/16/opinions/medical-marijuana-revolution-sanjay-gupta/index.html.

Hari, Johann. 2016. *Chasing the Scream: The First and Last Days of the War on Drugs*. New York, NY: Bloomsbury.

Harp, Seth. 2019. "Arming the Cartels: The Inside Story of a Texas Gun-Smuggling Ring." *Rolling Stone*, August 7, 2019. https://www.rollingstone.com/culture/culture-features/arming-mexican-cartels-inside-story-of-a-texas-gun-smuggling-ring-866836/.

Hartig, Hannah and Abigail Geiger. 2018. "About Six-in-Ten Americans Support Marijuana Legalization." *Pew Research Center*, October 8, 2018. http://www.pewresearch.org/fact-tank/2018/10/08/americans-support-marijuana-legalization/.

Hassan, Aisha. 2018. "All the Places in the World You Can (Legally) Smoke Weed." *Quartz*, October 17, 2018. https://qz.com/1427177/where-is-marijuana-legal-around-the-world/.

Heath, Brad and Meghan Hoyer. 2015. "DEA Agents Kept Jobs Despite Serious Misconduct." *USA Today*, September 15, 2015. https://www.usatoday.com/story/news/2015/09/27/few-dea-agents-fired-misconduct/72805622/.

Henman, Anthony and Pien Metaal. 2014. "Time for a Wake-Up Call: An Historical and Ethnographic Approach to the Regulation of Plant-Based Stimulants." *Transnational Institute*, December 2014.

Hollersen, Wiebke. 2013. "Portugal, 12 Years after Decriminalizing Drugs." *Der Spiegel*, March 27, 2013. http://www.spiegel.de/international/europe/evaluating-drug-decriminalization-in-portugal-12-years-later-a-891060.html.

Hope, Alejandro. 2018a. "Cinco predicciones para 2019." *El Universal*, December 24, 2018. https://www.eluniversal.com.mx/columna/alejandro-hope/nacion/cinco-predicciones-para-2019.

———. 2018b. "Sobre la geografía de la violencia." *El Universal*, May 14, 2018. https://www.eluniversal.com.mx/columna/alejandro-hope/nacion/sobre-la-geografia-de-la-violencia.

Horwitz, Sari and Carol D. Leonning. 2015. "DEA Agents Had 'Sex Parties' with Prostitutes Hired by Drug Cartels." *The Washington Post*, March 26, 2015. https://www.washingtonpost.com/world/national-security/report-dea-agents-had-sex-parties-with-prostitutes-hired-by-drug-cartels/2015/03/26/adb2d53e-d3bd-11e4-8fce-3941fc548f1c_story.html?utm_term=.e3b819cccb5c.

Human Rights Watch. 2018. "Dark Side: Secret Origins of Evidence in US Criminal Cases." *Human Rights Watch*, January 9, 2018. https://www.hrw.org/report/2018/01/09/dark-side/secret-origins-evidence-us-criminal-cases#.

———. 2017. "Mexico: Events of 2016." World Report 2017. *Human Rights Watch*, 2017. https://www.hrw.org/world-report/2017/country-chapters/mexico.

———. 2013. "Mexico's Disappeared: The Enduring Cost of a Crisis Ignored." *Human Rights Watch*, February 20, 2013. https://www.hrw.org/report/2013/02/20/mexicos-disappeared/enduring-cost-crisis-ignored.

Husak, Douglas and Peter de Marneffe. 2005. *The Legalization of Drugs: For & Against*. New York: Cambridge University Press.

Illades, Carlos and Teresa Santiago. 2014. *Estado de guerra: De la guerra sucia a la narcoguerra*. México: Ediciones Era.

Inciardi, James A. 2008. *The War on Drugs IV*. 4th edition. Boston: Pearson Education Inc.

——— (Ed.). 1999. *The Drug Legalization Debate*. 2nd edition. Thousand Oaks, CA: Sage Publications.

Inciardi, James A. and Karen Mcelrath. 2015. "The Evolution of Drug Taking and Drug Seeking in America." In *The American Drug Scene*, edited by James Inciardi and Karen Mcelerath, 3–23, 7th edition. Oxford: Oxford University Press.

Ingraham, Christopher. 2017. "Since 2007, the DEA Has Taken $3.2 Billion in Cash from People Not Charged with a Crime." *The Washington Post*, March 19, 2017. https://www.washingtonpost.com/news/wonk/wp/2017/03/29/since-2007-the-dea-has-taken-3-2-billion-in-cash-from-people-not-charged-with a crime/?utm_term=.67c79d7fd27b.

———. 2016. "Legal Marijuana is Finally Doing What the Drug War Couldn't." *The Washington Post*, March 3, 2016. https://www.washingtonpost.com/news/wonk/wp/2016/03/03/legal-marijuana-is-finally-doing-what-the-drug-war-couldnt/?utm_term=.72ddb99af037.

———. 2015. "Why Lawmakers are Increasingly Losing Faith in America's Top Drug Cop." *The Washington Post*, April 16, 2015. https://www.washingtonpost.com/news/wonk/wp/2015/04/16/why-lawmakers-are-increasingly-losing-faith-in-americas-top-drug-cop/?utm_term=.efc0fad9c94f.

InSight Crime. 2018. "The New Criminal Group Hitting Mexico's CJNG Where It Hurts." *InSight Crime*, July 24, 2018. https://www.insightcrime.org/news/analysis/new-criminal-group-hitting-mexicos-cjng-hurts/.

Instituto Nacional de Estadística y Geografía. 2018. "Datos Preliminares revelan que en 2017 se registraron 31 mil 174 homicidios." *National Institute of Statistics and Geography*, Press Release No. 310/18. July 30, 2018. http://www.beta.inegi.org.mx/contenidos/saladeprensa/boletines/2018/EstSegPub/homicidios2017_07.pdf.

Inter-Disciplinary Group of Independent Experts. 2015. "Informe Ayotzinapa." *Inter-American Commission of Human Rights*, September 6, 2015. http://prensagieiayotzi.wixsite.com/giei-ayotzinapa/informe-.

Inzunza, Alejandra S., José Luis Pardo, and Pablo Ferri. 2015. *Narco América: De los Andes a Manhattan, 55 mil kilómetros trae el rastro de la cocaína*. Mexico City: Tusquets editores.

Jasso, Carolina. 2018. "Las ejecuciones arbitrarias en México y su impunidad histórica." *El Universal*, February 21, 2018. https://www.eluniversal.com.mx/

observatorio-nacional-ciudadano/las-ejecuciones-arbitrarias-en-mexico-y-su-impu nidad-historica.

Jenkins, Phillips. 1999. *Synthetic Panics: The Symbolic Politics of Designer Drugs.* New York, NY: New York University Press.

Jouvenal, Justin. 2018. "From Defendant to Top Prosecutor, This Tattooed Texas DA Represents a New Wave in Criminal Justice Reform." *The Washington Post*, November 19, 2018. https://www.washingtonpost.com/local/public-safety/from-defendant-to-top-prosecutor-this-tattooed-texas-da-represents-a-new-wave-in-criminal-justice-reform/2018/11/19/e1dca7cc-d300-11e8-83d6-291fcead2ab1_story.html?utm_term=.6a594ac5c838.

Kahn, Carrie. 2019. "12 Journalists Have Been Killed In Mexico This Year, the World's Highest Toll." *National Public Radio*, September 12, 2019. https://www.npr.org/2019/09/12/759882660/12-journalists-have-been-killed-in-mexico-this-year-the-worlds-highest-toll.

Kail, Tony M. 2015. *Narco-Cults: Understanding the Use of Afro-Caribbean and Mexican Religious Cultures in the Drug Wars.* Boca Raton, FL: Taylor & Francis Group.

Karel, Richard B. 1991. "A Model Legalization Proposal." In *The Drug Legalization Debate*, edited by James A. Inciardi. 80–102. Thousand Oaks, CA: Sage.

Kiernan, John S. 2018. "Drug Use by State: 2018's Problem Areas." *WalletHub*, May 14, 2018. https://wallethub.com/edu/drug-use-by-state/35150/.

Kilmer, Beau and Greg Midgette. 2017. "Mixed Messages: Is Cocaine Consumption in the U.S. Going Up or Down?" *RAND Corporation*, April 28, 2017. https://www.rand.org/blog/2017/04/mixed-messages-is-cocaine-consumption-in-the-us-going.html.

Kilmer, Beau et al. 2014. "How Big Is the U.S. Market for Illegal Drugs?" *RAND Corporation.* Accessed November 18, 2018. https://www.rand.org/pubs/research_briefs/RB9770.html.

Kuhn, Cynthia, Scott Swartzwelder, and Wilkie Wilson. 2014. *Buzzed: The Straight Facts About the Most Used and Abused Drugs from Alcohol to Ecstasy.* 4th edition. New York, NY: W. W. Norton & Company.

Lakhani, Nina. 2017. "US Admits DEA Lied About Honduras 'Massacre' that Killed Four Villagers." *The Guardian*, May 25, 2017. https://www.theguardian.com/world/2017/may/25/us-honduras-drug-enforcement-administration-shooting.

Lancheros, Luz. 2016. "'Narco' Fashion is Big Business for Drug Dealers and Global Brands." *Metro*, January 19, 2016. https://www.metro.us/lifestyle/narco-fashion-is-big-business-for-drug-dealers-and-global-brands/zsJpas---zu42Y8DTEv9H.

Law Enforcement Action Partnership. 2019. "Drug Policy." *Law Enforcement Action Partnership.* Accessed January 30, 2019. https://lawenforcementactionpartnership.org/our-issues/drug-policy/.

Le Cour Grandmaison, Romain, Nathaniel Morris, and Benjamin Smith. 2019. "No More Opium for the Masses." *Noria Research and Mexican Institute at Wilson Center*, February 10, 2019. https://www.noria-research.com/no-more-opium-for-the-masses/.

Lembke, Anna. 2016. *Drug Dealer, MD: How Doctors Were Duped, Patients Got Hooked, and Why It's So Hard to Stop*. Baltimore, MD: John Hopkins University Press.

Levenson, Michael. 2020. "Former D.E.A. Agent Charged With Launderin Colombian Drug Money." *The New York Times*, February 23, 2020. https://www.nytimes.com/2020/02/23/us/dea-agent-arrested.html

Levine, Michael. 1990. *Deep Cover: The Inside Story of How DEA Infighting, Incompetence and Subterfuge Lost Us the Biggest Battle of the Drug War*. New York, NY: Dell Publishing.

Lilienfeld, Scott O. and Hal Arkowitz. 2014. "Why "Just Say No" Doesn't Work." *Scientific American*, January 1, 2014. https://www.scientificamerican.com/article/why-just-say-no-doesnt-work/.

Linthicum, Kate. 2019. "Meth and Murder: A New Kind of Drug War Has Made Tijuana One of the Deadliest Cities on Earth." *Los Angeles Times*, January 30, 2019. https://www.latimes.com/world/mexico-americas/la-fg-mexico-tijuana-drug-violence-20190130-htmlstory.html.

———. 2018. "Trump Says Mexico's Violence is a Threat to the U.S. Here Are 3 Ways the U.S. Helps Drive that Violence." *Los Angeles Times*, August 1, 2018. https://www.latimes.com/world/la-fg-mexico-violence-20180801-story.html.

Lomnitz, Claudio. 2008. *Death and the Idea of Mexico*. Brooklyn, NY: Zone Books.

López López, Andrés. 2008. *El cartel de los sapos*. México, DF: Planeta.

Lotto Persio, Sofia. 2017. "Crime in Mexico: Murder Rate Reaches Record High and Nobody is Talking About it." *Newsweek*, June 22, 2017. http://www.newsweek.com/crime-mexico-murder-rate-reaches-record-high-and-nobody-talking-about-it-628193.

Mallea, Paula. 2014. *The War on Drugs: A Failed Experiment*. Toronto, CA: DunDurn.

Marion, Nancy E. 2018. *Drug Policy and the Criminal Justice System*. Durham: Carolina Academic Press.

Martell, Carlos. 2019. "Las 50 ciudades más violentas del mundo." *Consejo Ciudadano para la Seguridad Pública y la Justicia Penal A.C.*, March 12, 2019. http://www.seguridadjusticiaypaz.org.mx/seguridad/1567-estudio-las-50-ciudades-mas-violentas-del-mundo-2018.

Martínez, Fabiola. 2016. "Servidores públicos, principales agresores de periodistas: SG." *La Jornada*, March 13, 2016. http://www.jornada.unam.mx/2016/03/13/politica/003n1pol.

Martyn, Amy. 2019. "Southwest Bust: DEA Agents Ambush Amtrak Passengers with Controversial Searchers and Seizures." *The Intercept*, August 31, 2019. https://theintercept.com/2019/08/31/dea-amtrak-passenger-search-albuquerque/.

May, Channing. 2017. "Transnational Crime and the Developing World." *Global Financial Integrity*, March 2017.

McCarthy, Justin. 2016. "One in Eight U.S. Adults Say They Smoke Marijuana." *Gallup News*, August 8, 2016. https://news.gallup.com/poll/194195/adults-say-smoke-marijuana.aspx.

McCoy, Alfred W. 2003. *The Politics of Heroin: CIA Complicity in the Global Drug Trade*. Chicago, IL: Chicago Review Press.

McDonald, James. 2005. "The Narcoeconomy and Small-town, Rural Mexico." *Human Organization* 64, No. 2: 115–125.

McDonnell, Patrick J. 2018. "Saga of Truck Filled with Bodies of Homicide Victims Sparks Scandal in Mexico." *Los Angeles Times*, September 18, 2018. https://www.latimes.com/world/la-fg-mexico-jalisco-bodies-20180918-story.html.

McDougal, Topher L. et al. 2015. "The Way of the Gun: Estimating Firearms Trafficking across the US–Mexico Border." *Journal of Economic Geography* 15: 297–327.

McKinley, James C., Jr. 2008. "Mexico is Magical to its Warlocks and Witches." *The New York Times*, March 28, 2008. https://www.nytimes.com/2008/03/28/world/americas/28iht-28mexico.11488341.html.

McWilliams, John C. 1990. *The Protectors: Harry J. Anslinger and the Federal Bureau of Narcotics, 1930–1962*. Cranbury, NJ: Associated University Presses.

Merica, Dan. 2017. "What Trump's Opioid Announcement Means — And Doesn't Mean." *CNN*, October 27, 2017. http://www.cnn.com/2017/10/26/politics/national-health-emergency-national-disaster/index.html.

Millán Valencia, Alejandro. 2017. "'Tacha', "buchón", "encobijado": cómo el mundo de los narcos se ha infiltrado en el español de México." *BBC Mundo*, September 7, 2017. http://www.bbc.com/mundo/noticias-41088115.

Miller, Richard L. 1991. *The Case for Legalizing Drugs*. New York: Praeger.

Miroff, Nick and Joshia Partlow. 2014. "Mexican Anti-cartel Militiamen Resisting Government Plan to Demobilize Them." *The Washington Post*, May 11, 2014. https://www.washingtonpost.com/world/the_americas/mexican-anti-cartel-militiamen-resisting-government-plan-to-demobilize-them/2014/05/11/afc5ae2c-e05f-4eb0-952c-a8c5c427f67f_story.html?utm_term=.138a785536a3.

Molloy, Molly. 2013. "The Mexican Undead: Toward a New History of the "Drug War" Killing Fields." *Small Wars Journal*, August 21, 2013. http://smallwarsjournal.com/jrnl/art/the-mexican-undead-toward-a-new-history-of-the-%E2%80%9Cdrug-war%E2%80%9D-killing-fields.

Monsiváis, Carlos; Jesús Blancornelas; Vicente Leñero; Sergio González Rodriguez; Marco Lara Klahr et al. 2004. "El narcotráfico y sus legiones." In *Viento Rojo: Diez historias del narco en México*, 9–44. México, DF: Plaza Janés.

Morín, Edgar. 2015. *La maña. Un recorrido antropológico por la cultura de las drogas*. México, DF: Penguin Random House.

Morris, Stephen. 1991. *Corruption and Politics in Contemporary Mexico*. Tuscaloosa: University of Alabama Press.

Mosso, Rubén. 2015. "En iguala, 131 cuerpos en 62 fosas clandestinas." *Milenio*, September 28, 2015. http://www.milenio.com/politica/Iguala-cuerpos-fosas-clandestinas_0_599940009.html.

Muehlmann, Shaylih. 2014. *When I Wear my Alligator Boots: Narco-Culture in the U.S.-Mexico Borderlands*. Berkeley, CA: University of California Press.

Museo del Enervante. 2018. "Personal Guided Visit to the Museum." *Secretaria de la Defensa Nacional*, July 3, 2018. Mexico City.

Mustian, Jim and Joshua Goodman. 2018. "DEA's Colombia Post Jarred By Misconduct Probes." *Associated Press*, October 3, 2018. https://www.apnews.com/2f1efb591fb54d519c706792f0629763.

Mustian, Jim and Faimon A. Roberts. 2017. "Veteran DEA Agent Chad Scott Charged with 10 Counts in Sweeping Federal Indictment." *The Advocate*, October 2, 2017. https://www.theadvocate.com/baton_rouge/news/courts/article_b7a3d084-a769-11e7-a164-2f4e0544948c.html.

Musto, David F. 1999. *The American Disease: Origins of Narcotic Control*. 3rd edition. New York, NY: Oxford University Press.

Nadelmann, Ethan. 2018. "The U.S. Needs to Decriminalize Drug Possession Now." *Rolling Stone*, November 26, 2018. https://www.rollingstone.com/politics/politics-features/united-states-decriminalize-drug-possession-nadelmann-760001/.

———. 1989. "Drug Prohibition in the United State: Costs, Consequences, and Alternatives." *Science* 245, No. 4941: 939–947.

Neumann, Ann. 2018. "The Narco Saint." *The Baffler*, March 2018. Issue No. 38. https://thebaffler.com/salvos/the-narco-saint-neumann.

Nogales International. 2018. "Former Nogales-based DEA Agent Pleads Guilty in Gun Case." *Nogales International*, August 14, 2018. https://www.nogalesinternational.com/news/former-nogales-based-dea-agent-pleads-guilty-in-gun-case/article_84431ec6-a000-11e8-bdf1-13e1f2e2af1d.html.

Nuñez González, Marco and Ramón Israel Alvarado. 2012. "Las buchonas: las mujeres de los narcos." In *Las Jefas del Narco*, edited by Arturo Santamaría Gómez, 101–123. México, DF: Grijalbo editors.

Office of the Inspectors General. 2017a. "A Special Joint Review of Post-Incident Responses by the Department of State and Drug Enforcement Administration to Three Deadly Force Incidents in Honduras." *U.S. Department of Justice*, May, 2017. https://oig.justice.gov/reports/2017/o1702.pdf#page=2.

Office of the Inspector General. 2017b. "Review of the Department's Oversight of Cash Seizure and Forfeiture Activities." *U.S. Department of Justice*, March, 2017. https://oig.justice.gov/reports/2017/e1702.pdf.

———. 2016. "Audit of the Drug Enforcement Administration's Management and Oversight of its Confidential Source Program." *U.S Department of Justice*, September 29, 2016. https://oig.justice.gov/reports/2016/a1633.pdf#page=1.

———. 2015a. "Review of the Drug Enforcement Administration's Use of Cold Consent Encounters at Mass Transportation Facilities." *U.S. Department of Justice*, January, 2015. https://oig.justice.gov/reports/2015/e153.pdf.

———. 2015b. "The Handling of Sexual Harassment and Misconduct Allegations by the Department's Law Enforcement Components." *U.S. Department of Justice*, March, 2015. https://oig.justice.gov/reports/2015/e1504.pdf#page=2.

Okrent, Daniel. 2011. *Last Call: The Rise and Fall of Prohibition*. Scribner Publishing.

Olmos, José Gil. 2013. "En el borde del paramilitarismo." *Proceso*, February 23, 2013. http://www.proceso.com.mx/334430/en-el-borde-del-paramilitarismo.

Olvera, Ramón G. 2014. "No toda la producción literaria de narcotráfico es "narcoliteratura."" *Sin Embargo*, September 13, 2014. http://www.sinembargo.mx/13-09-2014/1115521.

Osorno, Diego E. 2017. *La Guerra de los Zetas: Viaje por la Frontera de la Necropólitica*. 3rd edition. Ciudad de México: Penguin Random House.

———. 2009. *El cártel de Sinaloa: Una historia del uso político del narco*. México, DF: Penguin Random House.

Ovalle, Lilián Paola. 2005. "Las fronteras de la 'narcocultura'." In *La frontera Interpretada*, edited by CEC-Museo, 117–150. Universidad Autónoma de Baja California.

Paredes, Americo. 1958. *'With His Pistol in His Hand': A Border Ballad and Its Hero*. Austin, TX: University of Texas Press.

Partida, Juan Carlos G. 2015. "Brutal ataque del *narco* en Jalisco." *La Jornada*, May 2, 2015. http://www.jornada.unam.mx/2015/05/02/politica/002n1pol.

Payan, Tony, Kathleen Staudt, and Z. Anthony Kruszewski. 2013. *A War That Can't Be Won: Binational Perspectives on the War on Drugs*. Editors. Tucson, AZ: The University of Arizona Press.

Penn, Sean. 2016. "El Chapo Speaks." *Rolling Stone*, January 9, 2016. https://www.rollingstone.com/culture/features/el-chapo-speaks-20160109.

Pérez Salazar, Juan Carlos. 2014. "México: el cartel que protagonizó el peor enfrentamiento del gobierno de Peña Nieto." *BBC Mundo*, July 2, 2014. http://www.bbc.com/mundo/noticias/2014/07/140701_mexico_cartel_guerreros_unidos_jcps.

Peterson, Anne M. 1991. "DEA Agent Sentenced to Six Years Imprisonment for Drug Dealing." *The Associated Press,* March 1, 1991. https://www.apnews.com/84e47c4e39ac181f85be1f0c8006a12e.

Phelps, Timothy M. 2015. "Officials Criticize DEA's Light Punishment of Agents Who Forgot Man in Cell for 5 Days." *Los Angeles Times*, May 5, 2015. https://www.latimes.com/nation/la-na-dea-chong-20150505-story.html.

Phillips, Brian J. 2015. "How Does Leadership Decapitation Affect Violence? The Case of Drug Trafficking Organizations in Mexico." *The Journal of Politics* 77, No. 2: 324–336.

Philips, Tom. 2019. "Mexico Cartel Hangs Body from City Bridge in Grisly Show of Force" *The Guardian*, August 8, 2019. https://www.theguardian.com/world/2019/aug/08/mexico-bodies-police-uruapan-drug-cartels

Proceso. 2018. "México, tercer lugar en cirugías plásticas a nivel mundial: UNAM." *Proceso*, January 3, 2018. https://www.proceso.com.mx/517075/mexico-tercer-lugar-en-cirugias-plasticas-nivel-mundial-unam.

———. 2010. "Las buchonas de Jalisco, vidas al límite." *Proceso*, November 3, 2010. https://www.proceso.com.mx/99120/las-buchonas-de-jalisco-vidas-al-limite.

Quinones, Sam. 2016. *Dreamland: The True Tale of America's Opiate Epidemic*. New York, NY: Bloomsbury Press.

———. 2001. *True Tales from another Mexico: The Lynch Mob, the Popsicle Kings, Chalino, and the Bronx*. Alburquerque, NM: University of New Mexico Press.

Ravelo, Ricardo. 2012. *Narcomex: Historia e historias de una guerra*. New York, NY: Random House, Inc.

Recio, Gabriela. 2002. "Drugs and Alcohol: US Prohibition and the Origins of the Drug Trade in Mexico, 1910–1930." *Journal of Latin American Studies* 34: 21–42.

Registro Nacional de Datos de Personas Extraviadas o Desaparecidas—RNPRD. 2018. "Estadísticas y Notas Metodológicas." *Minister of the Interior* (Secretaria de Gobernacion). http://secretariadoejecutivo.gob.mx/rnped/consulta-publica.php.

Reichel, Philip L. 2018. *Comparative Criminal Justice Systems: A Topical Approach*. New York, NY: Pearson.

Reporters Without Borders. 2017. "2017 World Press Freedom Index." Reporters without Borders. https://rsf.org/en/ranking.

Reuters. 2019. "Mexican President Says State Was Main Violator of Human Rights." March 24, 2019. https://www.reuters.com/article/us-mexico-president/mexican-president-says-state-was-main-violator-of-human-rights-idUSKCN1R50WT.

Reymond, Nate. 2017. "Ex-DEA Agent Spared Prison Over Concealed Strip Club Ties." *Reuters*, February 8, 2017. https://www.reuters.com/article/us-usa-crime-dea/ex-dea-agent-spared-prison-over-concealed-strip-club-ties-idUSKBN15N2UE.

Richardson, James T. 1998. "Definitions of Cult: From Sociological-Technical to Popular-Negative." In *Cults in Context: Readings in the Study of New Religious Movements*, edited by Lorne L. Dawson, 29–38. New Brunswick, NJ: Transaction Publishers.

Riding, Alan. 1985. *Distance Neighbors: A Portrait of the Mexicans*. New York: Vintage Publisher.

Roberts, Tiffany. 2016. "Buchonas." *Univision*, May, 2016. https://www.youtube.com/watch?v=zAm1C85U_Ac.

Robinson, Melia. 2016. "This South American Country has Decriminalized All Drugs for 40 Years." *Business Insider*, June 10, 2016. https://www.businessinsider.com/uruguay-has-decriminalized-all-drugs-for-40-years-2016-6.

Romano, Andrew. 2017. "Weed Hits Home: In a New Yahoo News/Marist Poll, Parents and Children Are Surprisingly Open About Pot Use." *Yahoo News*, April 17, 2017. https://www.yahoo.com/news/weed-hits-home-new-yahoo-newsmarist-poll-parents-children-surprisingly-open-pot-use-091457209.html.

Salazar, Alonso J. and Ana Maria Jaramillo Arbelaez. 1992. *Medellín: las subculturas del narcotráfico*. Bogotá, Colombia: Cinep.

Saldívar Arreola, Rafael. 2012. "Análisis lexicológico del narcolenguaje en Baja California." PhD diss., Universidad Autónoma de Querétaro. http://ri.uaq.mx/xmlui/bitstream/handle/123456789/1123/RI000296.pdf?sequence=1&isAllowed=y.

Sallah, Michael, Robert O'Harrow Jr., Steven Rich, and Gabe Silverman. 2014. "Stop and Seize: Aggressive Police Take Hundreds of Millions of Dollars from Motorists Not Charged with Crimes." *The Washington Post*, September 6, 2014. https://www.washingtonpost.com/sf/investigative/2014/09/06/stop-and-seize/?utm_term=.a60e6b08ec58.

Sample, Ian. 2017. "Psychedelic Drugs Induce 'Heightened State of Consciousness', Brain Scans Show." *The Guardian*, April 19, 2017. https://www.theguardian.com/science/2017/apr/19/brain-scans-reveal-mind-opening-response-to-psychedelic-drug-trip-lsd-ketamine-psilocybin.

San Francisco Chronicle. 2019. "Feds Say Star DEA Agent Abroad Stole Millions." *San Francisco Chronicle*, January 15, 2019. https://www.sfchronicle.com/world/article/Feds-say-star-DEA-agent-abroad-stole-millions-13536064.php.

Santamaría Gómez, Arturo. 2012. *Las jefas del narco: El ascenso de las mujeres en el crimen organizado*. México, DF: Grijalbo.

Satter, Linda. 2018. "Little Rock-based DEA Agent Said To Take Cash to Shield Dealer." *Arkansas Democrat Gazette*, December 5, 2018. https://www.arkansasonline.com/news/2018/dec/05/lr-based-dea-agent-said-to-take-cash-to/.

Savage, Charlie. 2017. "D.E.A. Misled Overseers on Deadly Honduras Operations, Watchdogs Say." *The New York Times*, May 24, 2017. https://www.nytimes.com/2017/05/24/us/politics/dea-honduras-drugs.html.

Saviano, Roberto. 2006. *Gomorrah: A Personal Journey into the Violent International Empire of Naple's Organized Crime System*. New York City, NY: Mondadori.

Schedler, Andreas. 2015. *En la niebla de la guerra Los ciudadanos ante la violencia criminal organizada*. México, DF: Centro de Investigación y Docencia Económicas.

Scherer, Julio. 2008. *La reina del pacífico: es la hora de contar*. México, DF: Grijalbo Publishers.

Schlosser, Eric. 2004. *Reefer Madness: Sex, Drugs, and Cheap Labor in the American Black Market*. Boston: Houghton Mifflin Company.

Schuster, Kathleen. 2018. "5 Facts about Cannabis Laws in Germany." *Deutsche Welle*, March 10, 2018. https://www.dw.com/en/5-facts-about-cannabis-laws-in-germany/a-42709969.

Semple, Kirk and Paulina Villegas. 2019. "Mexico Approves 60,000-Strong National Guard. Critics Call It More of the Same." *The New York Times*, February 28, 2019. https://www.nytimes.com/2019/02/28/world/americas/mexico-amlo-national-guard.html.

Shaw, Mark and Tuesday Reitano. 2013. "The Evolution of Organised Crime in Africa Towards a New Response." *Institute for Security Studies*. Research Paper. April 12, 2013. https://issafrica.s3.amazonaws.com/site/uploads/Paper244.pdf.

Sheridan, Mary B. 2020. "More than 60,000 Mexicans have disappeared amid drug war, officials say." *The Washington Post*, January 6, 2020. https://www.washingtonpost.com/world/the_americas/more-than-60000-mexicans-have-been-disappeared-amid-drug-war-officials-say/2020/01/06/07a4ea56-24f8-11ea-9cc9-e19cfbc87e51_story.html

Shiffman, John and Kristina Cooke. 2013. "U.S. Directs Agents To Cover Up Program Used To Investigate Americans." *Reuters*, August 5, 2013. https://www.reuters.com/article/us-dea-sod/exclusive-u-s-directs-agents-to-cover-up-program-used-to-investigate-americans-idUSBRE97409R20130805.

Sierra Guzmán, Jorge Luis. 2012. "Armed Forces and Counterinsurgency: Origins of the Dirty War (1965–1982)." In *Challenging Authoritarianism in México*, edited by Fernando Herrera Calderón and Adela Cedillo, 182–197. New York, NY: Routledge.

Sin Embargo. 2013. "Movimiento Alterado: las polémicas "Canciones Enfermas" y la violencia como negocio." *Sin Embargo*, January 8, 2013. http://www.sinembargo.mx/08-01-2013/483513.

Singer, Merril and J. Bryan Page. 2014. *The Social Value of Drug Addicts: Uses of the Useless*. Walnut Creek, CA: Left Coast Press, Inc.

Skarpedas, Stergios. 2001. "The Political Economy of Organized Crime: Providing Protection When the State Does Not." *Economics of Governance*, Vol. 2(3): 173–202.

Sloman, Larry. 1998. *Reefer Madness: The History of Marijuana in America*. New York, NY: St. Martin's Griffin.

Smith, Benjamin. 2013. "Tragic Realism: The Rise of Mexican Narcoliterature." *The Conversation*, July 20, 2013. https://theconversation.com/tragic-realism-the-rise-of-mexican-narcoliterature-16375.

Sputnik. 2017. "The 'Dolls of Culiacan': New Plastic Surgery Craze Sweeps Mexican Cartel Land." *Sputnik*, October 4, 2017. https://sputniknews.com/latam/201704101052489833-mexico-dolls-plastic-surgery-drugs/.

Sullivan, John P. 2012. "Criminal Insurgency: Narcocultura, Social Banditry, and Information Operations." *Small War Journals*, December 3, 2012. http://smallwarsjournal.com/jrnl/art/criminal-insurgency-narcocultura-social-banditry-and-information-operations.

Stellin, Susan. 2019. "Is the 'War on Drugs' Over? Arrests Statistics Say No." *The New York Times*, November 5, 2019. https://www.nytimes.com/2019/11/05/upshot/is-the-war-on-drugs-over-arrest-statistics-say-no.html.

Stevenson, Mark. 2011. "Mexico's Hottest Fashion Craze: 'Narco Polo' Jerseys." *NBC News*, June 10, 2011. http://www.nbcnews.com/id/43357779/ns/world_news-americas/t/mexicos-hottest-fashion-craze-narco-polo-jerseys/#.WwSN-e4vyM9.

———. 2009. "Mexico Decriminalizes Small-scale Drug Possession." *The San Diego Union-Tribune*, August 20, 2009. https://www.sandiegouniontribune.com/sdut-lt-mexico-drug-decriminalization-082009-2009aug20-story.html.

Steward, Scott. 2019. "After a Year of Record Homicides, Here's What To Expect from Mexico's Cartels in 2019." *Business Insider*, February 6, 2019. https://www.businessinsider.com/mexicos-cartel-dynamics-and-drug-related-violence-in-2019-2019-2.

Tallet, Olivia P. 2018. "Changing Marijuana Laws in Canada and Mexico Create Pressure on Texas." *Houston Chronicle*, December 29, 2018. https://www.houstonchronicle.com/news/houston-texas/houston/article/Changing-marijuana-laws-in-Canada-and-Mexico-13496512.php.

Taylor, Willian B. 1979. *Drinking, Homicide, and Rebellion in Colonial Mexican Villages*. California: Stanford University Press.

The Brownsville Herald. 2019. "Mexico Investigates 8 Alleged Extrajudicial Killings." *The Brownsville Herald*, September 14, 2019. https://www.brownsvilleherald.com/news/local/mexico-investigates-alleged-extrajudicial-killings/article_e3f3b1c4-d66d-11e9-a494-b3235500d076.html.

The Economist. 2015. "Which Countries have the Death Penalty for Drug Smuggling?" *The Economist*, April 29, 2015. http://www.economist.com/blogs/economist-explains/2015/04/economist-explains-28.

———. 2009. "How to Stop the War on Drugs." March 5, 2009. 390, No. 8621. https://www.economist.com/leaders/2009/03/05/how-to-stop-the-drug-wars.

The International Institute for Strategic Studies—IISS. 2017. "Armed Conflict Survey Shows Conflict Moving into Cities Around the World." May 9, 2017. file:///C:/Users/Gabino/Downloads/ACS-2017-press-notice%20(1).pdf.

The Monitor. 2011. "Internal Struggle in the Gulf Cartel Could Weaken the Organization." *The Monitor*, October 29, 2011. http://www.themonitor.com/news/local/int

ernal-struggle-in-the-gulf-cartel-could-weaken-the-organization/article_076fda81-d46f-5900-86ce-c5478a9eee31.html.

The Sentencing Project. 2019. "Criminal Justice Facts." *The Sentencing Project*, 2019. https://www.sentencingproject.org/criminal-justice-facts/.

The U.S. Attorney's Office. 2019. "DEA Agent and International Narcotics Trafficker Each Plead Guilty In Connection With Decade-Long Narcotics Conspiracy." *Department of Justice*, August 9, 2019. https://www.justice.gov/usao-sdny/pr/dea-agent-and-international-narcotics-trafficker-each-plead-guilty-connection-decade.

Thompson-Hernández, Walter. 2019. "Where Mexican Folk Ballads Meet Trap Music." *The New York Times*, September 16, 2019. https://www.nytimes.com/2019/09/16/style/trapcorridos-chicano-los-angeles.html.

Tinker, Ben. 2019. "These States Have Been Hit the Hardest by America's Opioid Epidemic." *CNN*, February 22, 2019. https://www.cnn.com/2019/02/22/health/opioid-deaths-states-study/index.html.

Toro, María Celia. 1998. "The Political Repercussions of Drug Trafficking in Mexico." In *Latin American and the Multinational Drug Trade*, edited by Elizabeth Joyce and Carlos Malamud, 133–145. London, UK: University of London, Institute of Latin American Studies Series.

Transnational Institute. 2016. "Drugs and Democracy." *Transnational Institute*, 2016. https://www.tni.org/en/work-area/drugs-and-democracy.

Transparency International. 2007. *Global Corruption Report 2007*. New York, NY: Cambridge University Press.

Tuckman, Jo. 2019. "Mexico Uncovers 3,000 Secret Graves Hiding Bodies of Drug War Victims." *The Guardian*, August 30, 2019. https://www.theguardian.com/world/2019/aug/30/mexico-secret-graves-bodies-victims-drug-war.

———. 2014. "Mexican President Enrique Peña Nieto faces Outcry Over £4.4m Mansion." *The Guardian*, November 10, 2014. https://www.theguardian.com/world/2014/nov/10/mexico-president-enrique-pena-nieto-mansion-explain.

———. 2013. "Mexican Vigilantes Take On Drug Cartels— And Worry Authorities." *The Guardian*, October 28, 2013. https://www.theguardian.com/world/2013/oct/28/mexican-militias-vigilantes-drug-cartels.

United Nations Office on Drugs and Crime. 2019a. "Legal Framework for Drug Trafficking." *United Nations*, 2019. https://www.unodc.org/doc/wdr2018/WDR_2018_Press_ReleaseENG.PDF.

———. 2019b. "Drug Trafficking." *United Nations*. https://www.unodc.org/unodc/en/drug-trafficking/.

———. 2018. "World Drug Report 2018." *United Nations*. https://www.unodc.org/wdr2018/.

Universidad Iberoamericana. 2017. "Violencia y Terror. Hallazgos sobre fosas clandestinas en México." *Universidad Iberoamericana and Comisión Mexicana de Defensa y Promoción de Derechos Humanos, A.C.* Ciudad de México. http://www.cmdpdh.org/publicaciones-pdf/violencia-y-terror-hallazgos-sobre-fosas-clandestinas-en-mexico.pdf.

Ureste, Manu. 2019. "Durante sexenio de Peña, México se volvió el país más peligroso para ejercer el periodismo en AL: Artículo 19." *Animal Político*, April 2, 2019. https://www.animalpolitico.com/2019/04/periodistas-asesinados-mexico/.

USA Today. 2015. "DEA Agents Kept Jobs Despite Serious Misconduct." *USA Today*, September 22, 2015. https://www.usatoday.com/story/news/2015/09/27/few-dea-agents-fired-misconduct/72805622/.

U.S. Attorney's Office. 2018. "DEA Agent Arrested For Participating In Decade-Long Narcotics Conspiracy and Providing Firearms To Drug Trafficking Organization." *Department of Justice*, December 11, 2018. https://www.justice.gov/usao-sdny/pr/dea-agent-arrested-participating-decade-long-narcotics-conspiracy-and-providing.

U.S. Department of State. 2019. "Narcotics Rewards Program." *U.S. Department of State*, 2019. https://www.state.gov/j/inl/narc/rewards/275636.htm.

U.S. Food and Drug Administration. 2016. "Controlled Substances Act. Regulatory Information." *U.S Food and Drug Administration*. http://www.fda.gov/regulatoryinformation/legislation/ucm148726.htm.

Valdés Cárdenas, Javier. 2016. *Narcoperiodismo: La prensa en medio del crimen y la denuncia*. México City: Penguin Random House.

Valdés Cárdenas, Javier and Alfredo Méndez. 2008. "Detienen a El Mochomo, brazo derecho del Chapo Guzmán." *La Jornada*, January 21, 2008. http://www.jornada.unam.mx/2008/01/22/index.php?section=politica&article=003n1pol.

Valdés Castellanos, Guillermo. 2013. *Historia del narcotráfico en México*. México, DF: Editorial Aguilar.

Valenzuela Arce, J. M. 2002. *Jefe de Jefes: Corridos y narcocultura en México*. México, DF: Plaza & Janés.

Villalobos, Juan Pablo. 2012. "Against Narcoliterature." *English Pen*, April 19, 2012. https://www.englishpen.org/pen-atlas/against-narcoliterature/.

Villalpando, Rubén. 2010. ""Tregua", Pide *El Diario* al crimen en Ciudad Juárez." *La Jornada*, September 20, 2010. http://www.jornada.unam.mx/2010/09/20/politica/005n1pol.

Wainwright, Tom. 2016. *Narconomics: How to Run a Drug Cartel*. New York, NY: PublicAffairs.

Wald, Elijah. 2001. *Narcocorrido: A Journey into the Music of Drugs, Guns, and Guerrillas*. New York, NY: HarperCollings.

Walker, Samuel. 2015. *Sense and Nonsense about Crime, Drugs, and Communities*. 8th edition. Stamford, CT: Cengage Learning.

Walker, Samuel, Cassia Spohn, and Miriam DeLone. 2018. *The Color of Justice: Race, Ethnicity, and Crime in America*. 6th edition. Belmont, CA: Wadsworth, Cengage Learning.

Walters, Edgar and Jolie McCullough. 2018. "Texas police Made More Than $50 Million in 2017 from Seizing People's Property. Not Everyone Was Guilty of a Crime." *The Texas Tribune*, December 7, 2018. https://www.texastribune.org/2018/12/07/texas-civil-asset-forfeiture-legislature/.

Walton, Stuart. 2002. *Out of It: A Cultural History of Intoxication*. New York, NY: Harmony Books.

Wilkinson, Tracy. 2015. "Mexican Journalist Carmen Aristegui Fired from Radio Station." *Los Angeles Times*, March 16, 2015. http://www.latimes.com/world/mexico-americas/la-fg-mexico-journalist-fired-20150316-story.html.

Wing, Nick. 2014. "12 of the Sketchiest Things the DEA has Done While Waging the War on Drugs." *The Huffington Post*, October 23, 2014. https://www.huffingtonpost.com/2014/10/23/dea-controversies_n_5992324.html.

Winslow, Don. 2019. "The Dirty Secret of El Chapo's Downfall." *Vanity Fair*, March, 2019. https://www.vanityfair.com/news/2019/02/the-dirty-secret-of-el-chapo-downfall.

Woodman, Stephen. 2017. "Welcome to Mexico's Top Secret Drug War Museum." *Culture Trip*, September 8, 2017. https://theculturetrip.com/north-america/mexico/articles/welcome-to-mexicos-top-secret-drug-war-museum/.

Woody, Christopher. 2017. "Fake Vegetables, Frozen Sharks, and an Xbox—Here Are Some of Drugs Smugglers' Most Bizarre Methods." *Business Insider*, April 2, 2017. https://www.businessinsider.sg/drug-smugglers-methods-hiding-places-2017-4/.

World Health Organization. 2017. "Joint United Nations Statement on Ending Discrimination in Health Care Settings." *World Health Organization*, June 27, 2017. https://www.who.int/en/news-room/detail/27-06-2017-joint-united-nations-statement-on-ending-discrimination-in-health-care-settings.

Wright, Melissa W. 2017. "Epistemological Ignorances and Fighting for the Disappeared: Lessons from Mexico." *Antipode* 49, No. 1: 249–269.

Zavala, Oswaldo. 2018. *Los cárteles no existen: Narcotráfico y cultura en México*. Barcelona: Malpaso Ediciones, S.L.U.

Index

Note: Page numbers in italics denote figures.

About the Author

Gabriel Ferreyra, Ph.D.

Assistant Professor of Criminal Justice

Affiliation: California State University, Los Angeles

Dr. Ferreyra is an Assistant Professor of Criminal Justice at California State University, Los Angeles. He earned a J.D. from Universidad Michoacana in Mexico, an M.A. in Cultural Anthropology from the University of Texas at San Antonio, and a Ph.D. in Justice Studies from Arizona State University. He teaches Judicial Organization, Organized Crime, and Multiculturalism in the Criminal Justice System, among other criminal justice subjects. Dr. Ferreyra's research focuses on drug trafficking, transnational organized crime, drugs, courts, law, corruption, U.S. drug policy, and the U.S.-Mexico border. He has published several book chapters and peer-reviewed articles on his area of expertise and he is currently conducting ethnographic research from a multidisciplinary perspective on the U.S.-Mexico border to better understand trafficking patterns and other phenomena prevalent at the southwest border affecting both countries.